CONFUCIAN POLITICAL ETHICS

THE ETHIKON SERIES IN
COMPARATIVE ETHICS

The Ethikon Series publishes studies on ethical issues of current
importance. By bringing scholars representing a diversity of moral
viewpoints into structured dialogue, the series aims to broaden the
scope of ethical discourse and to identify commonalities and
differences between alternative views.

TITLES IN THE SERIES

Brian Barry and Robert E. Goodin, eds.
*Free Movement: Ethical Issues in the Transnational Migration
of People and Money*

Chris Brown, ed.
Political Restructuring in Europe: Ethical Perspectives

Terry Nardin, ed.
The Ethics of War and Peace: Religious and Secular Perspectives

David R. Mapel and Terry Nardin, eds.
International Society: Diverse Ethical Perspectives

David Miller and Sohail H. Hashmi, eds.
Boundaries and Justice: Diverse Ethical Perspectives

Simone Chambers and Will Kymlicka, eds.
Alternative Conceptions of Civil Society

Nancy L. Rosenblum and Robert Post, eds.
Civil Society and Government

Sohail Hashmi, ed., Foreword by Jack Miles
Islamic Political Ethics: Civil Society, Pluralism, and Conflict

Richard Madsen and Tracy B. Strong, eds.
The Many and the One: Ethical Pluralism in the Modern World

Margaret Moore and Allen Buchanan, eds.
States, Nations, and Borders: The Ethics of Making Boundaries

Sohail H. Hashmi and Steven P. Lee, eds.
Ethics and Weapons of Mass Destruction: Religious and Secular Perspectives

Michael Walzer, ed.
Law, Politics, and Morality in Judaism

William M. Sullivan and Will Kymlicka, eds.
The Globalization of Ethics: Religious and Secular Perspectives

Daniel A. Bell, ed.
Confucian Political Ethics

John Coleman, S.J., ed.
Christian Political Ethics

CONFUCIAN POLITICAL ETHICS

Edited by
DANIEL A. BELL

PRINCETON UNIVERSITY PRESS

PRINCETON AND OXFORD

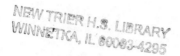
Copyright © 2008 by Princeton University Press

Published by Princeton University Press, 41 William Street, Princeton,
New Jersey 08540

In the United Kingdom: Princeton University Press, 3 Market Place, Woodstock,
Oxfordshire OX20 1SY

Library of Congress Cataloging-in-Publication Data

Confucian political ethics / edited by Daniel A. Bell.
    p. cm.—(The Ethikon series in comparative ethics)
    Includes index.
    ISBN 978-0-691-13004-0 ((hardcover) : alk. paper)—ISBN 978-0-691-13005-7
((pbk.) : alk. paper)   1. Confucianism and state.   2. Confucian ethics.
3. Philosophy, Confucian.   4. Political ethics.   I. Bell, Daniel (Daniel A.), 1964–
    BL1840.C65 2007
    172—dc22   2007021711

British Library Cataloging-in-Publication Data is available

This book has been composed in Sabon

Printed on acid-free paper. ∞

press.princeton.edu

Printed in the United States of America

10   9   8   7   6   5   4   3   2   1

PREFACE

DANIEL A. BELL

O ver the past several years, the Ethikon Institute has organized a number of high-level dialogue conferences in which authoritative spokespersons for diverse ethical traditions have presented the views of their respective traditions on particular topics and specific questions of great contemporary importance. The conferences are designed to identify and explore the commonalities and differences among different moral outlooks, both religious and secular. The results of these dialogue events are published in the Ethikon Series in Comparative Ethics. By thus encouraging a systematic exchange of ideas both within and across moral traditions, Ethikon seeks to advance the prospects for cross-tradition consensus and to facilitate the accommodation of abiding differences. Ethikon does not take a position on issues that divide its participants, serving not as an arbiter but as a forum for the cooperative exploration of diverse and sometimes opposing views.

The first three sections in this book consist of essays that were originally written for publication in earlier volumes of the Ethikon Series alongside a variety of other perspectives. They have been assembled here to provide ready and convenient access for readers with a particular interest in the relation of Confucian political ethics to contemporary social concerns. Henry Rosemont Jr.'s essay has been substantially expanded, and the others are published with minor revisions.

The book has two additional sections with essays on themes of contemporary political import. These essays address key Confucian concerns in a comparative framework. The first section consists of essays on Confucianism and contemporary feminism. Perhaps the main normative obstacle to the effort to revive Confucianism is the perception that Confucianism is an outdated patriarchal ideology that should be relegated to the dustbin of history. But the two essays in this section show that Confucianism can take on board feminist insights without altering its major values. Sin Yee Chan draws on the central values of Confucius and Mencius to argue that Confucianism need not pose any obstacles to gender equality in contemporary society. Chenyang Li shows that there is common ground between Confucian values and feminist care ethics. Whatever the extent of antagonism in previous history, Confucianism and feminism can learn from and support each other. Both essays have been revised for this book.

The final section, on war and peace, addresses issues of global concern. Ni Lexiong shows that early Confucian theorizing on war and peace was formed in a context that has similarities to the contemporary international system. Far from being an outdated philosophy, he argues that Confucianism can provide the philosophical resources for thinking about a more peaceful international order. Daniel Bell's essay spells out Mencius's theory of morally justified war and draws implications that may be helpful for dealing with the sorts of political concerns that China will face as it develops into a global power. Ni's essay was translated from the original Chinese and Bell's essay is published with minor revisions.

All the essays in the book argue for the abiding relevance of classical Confucian theory in the contemporary world. For much of the twentieth century, Confucianism was condemned by Westerners and East Asians alike as antithetical to modernity. But with the experience of rapid development in East Asia, it has been increasingly recognized that Confucian commitments to self-improvement, family ties, education, and the social good may actually have facilitated economic and political modernization in East Asian societies. The contributors to this book try to articulate the normative vision that may further promote the desirable aspects of such modernization, as well as provide resources to criticize the problematic aspects.

The political revival of Confucianism in mainland China may lend support to such efforts. China's president Hu Jintao has been actively promoting Confucian themes such as "harmony," "honesty," and "loyalty." The Chinese government has also been setting up "Confucian Institutes" in various countries with the aim of promoting Chinese language and culture around the world. It is not entirely fanciful to surmise that the Chinese Communist Party will be relabeled the "Chinese Confucian Party" in the next couple of decades. But the essays in this book show that Confucianism can often diverge from official interpretations. The Confucian idea of harmony means diversity in harmony, not blind conformity to official viewpoints. The Confucian foreign policy relies mainly on moral example, not threats of physical force.

If Confucianism shapes China's political future, it won't look like the political status quo, but neither will it look like Western-style liberal democracy. There may be some overlap with liberal goals like tolerance and respect for diversity, but the essays show that there should also be room for morally legitimate differences with liberal philosophy. The Confucian emphasis on relationality and affective ties may conflict with liberal autonomy in everyday ethical life. Given limited time and resources, governments often need to make hard choices and central Confucian values like filial piety may shape outcomes in ways that diverge from political practices in Western societies. Rather than condemn any deviations from liberal goals, anybody who wants to engage with East Asian societies in respectful ways must understand the Confucian ethical thinking that informs social and political practices in the region.

But which Confucian values should one appeal to? Religions such as Islam and Christianity have sacred texts, but Confucian texts express the voices of human beings, not God. The fact that Confucius says something does not necessarily mean it's true or that it's morally defensible today. So how does one select values from the complex and changing centuries-long Confucian tradition, interpreted differently at different times and places and complemented in sometimes conflicting ways with Legalism, Daoism, Buddhism, Christianity, and, more recently, Western liberalism? The contributors to this book generally hold the view that we should choose values that help us to think about issues and controversies of contemporary import. And they seek inspiration mainly from the classic works of Confucius and Mencius. In fact, what makes them classics is precisely that they provide resources for thinking about morally relevant concerns in different times and places. And they will be particularly useful for thinking about issues in East Asian societies that have been shaped by their Confucian heritage.

Can Confucian values also help us think about problems in non-East Asian societies? More grandly, perhaps, could Confucian values ever command international legitimacy? The actual history of Confucianism suggests that it can spread to other societies. Confucianism originated in the northern part of the territory we now call "China," and it spread slowly throughout China, Japan, Korea, and Vietnam. By the late nineteenth century, the East Asian region was thoroughly "Confucianized." Confucianism has fared less well in the twentieth century, but its recent revival, supported by the growing economic and political clout of the East Asian region, suggests that it will continue to spread. Another reason for being optimistic about the spread of Confucianism is that it doesn't come laden with heavy metaphysical baggage (to be more precise, the early forms of Confucianism, unlike the neo-Confucianism of Zhu Xi and others, tend to be vague about ultimate metaphysical commitments). Perhaps that's also why the contributors to this book derive inspiration mainly from classical Confucianism: one can draw on its ethical and political insights without completely abandoning religious commitments of various sorts. It is not uncommon today for people to identify with both Confucianism and Christianity, for example. From a normative standpoint, perhaps the main reason for being optimistic about the spread of Confucianism is that it provides resources for thinking about contemporary problems that affect most parts of the globe, such as worries about the corrosive effects of liberal individualism on family life and the impact of globalization on the international order. In fact, most of these essays are written with a Western audience in mind,[1] and the contributors argue that certain Confucian values can and should be taken seriously in Western societies.

On the other hand, we need to consider the reality that Confucianism may have psychological power mainly in East Asian societies that already identify with the tradition to an important extent. If similar values can be derived from other traditions such as Islam or Christianity, then adherents of those traditions are not likely to invoke Confucianism. Moreover, there may be areas of conflict with the central values of other traditions. For Confucianism, the first priority of the government is to provide for the material welfare of the people, whereas civil and political liberties are more central to the moral framework of Western political traditions. These differences of emphasis will manifest themselves in different foreign policies, and the tendency to dismiss either position as motivated entirely by crude realpolitik can only inflame international tensions. In such cases, it may be necessary to tolerate, if not respect, cultural difference.

The trustees of the Ethikon Institute join Philip Valera, president, and Carole Pateman, series editor, and the editor of this volume in thanking all who contributed to the development of this book. In addition to the authors and original volume editors, special thanks are due to the Ahmanson Foundation, the late Joan Palevsky, the Pew Charitable Trusts, the Doheny Foundation, and the Carnegie Council on Ethics and International Affairs for their generous support of the various Ethikon dialogue projects from which most of these essays and other books emerged. Finally, we wish to express our thanks to Ian Malcolm of Princeton University Press for his valuable guidance and support.

INFORMATION ON SOURCES

Chapter 1 was originally published in *Alternative Conceptions of Civil Society*, eds. Simone Chambers and Will Kymlicka (Princeton: Princeton University Press, 2002), 190–204.

Chapter 2 was originally published in *Civil Society and Government*, eds. Nancy L. Rosenblum and Robert Post (Princeton: Princeton University Press, 2002), 334–59.

Chapter 3 is an expanded and revised version of a chapter originally published in *Civil Society and Government*, eds. Nancy L. Rosenblum and Robert Post (Princeton: Princeton University Press, 2002), 360–69.

Chapter 4 was originally published in *Boundaries and Justice*, eds. David Miller and Sohail H. Hashmi (Princeton: Princeton University Press, 2001), 89–111.

Chapter 5 was originally published in *Boundaries and Justice*, eds. David Miller and Sohail H. Hashmi (Princeton: Princeton University Press, 2001), 112–35.

Chapter 6 was originally published in *The Many and the One*, eds. Richard Madsen and Tracy B. Strong (Princeton: Princeton University Press, 2003), 129–53.

Chapter 7 was originally published in *The Many and the One*, eds. Richard Madsen and Tracy B. Strong (Princeton: Princeton University Press, 2003), 154–58.

Chapter 8: An earlier version of this chapter was published in *Hypatia: A Journal of Feminist Philosophy*, vol. 9, no. 1 (Winter 1994): 70–89.

Chapter 9: An earlier version of this chapter was published in *Asian Philosophy* (http://www.tandf.co.uk), vol. 10, no. 2 (2000): 115–32.

Chapter 10: The Chinese version of this chapter was published in *Junshi lishi yanjiu* [Military Historical Research], vol. 2 (2001) (http://www. meet-greatwall.org/gwjs/wen/jswhgn.htm, visited 4 August 2006).

Chapter 11 was originally published in Daniel A. Bell, *Beyond Liberal Democracy: Political Thinking for an East Asian Context* (Princeton: Princeton University Press, 2006), 23–51.

EDITOR'S NOTE

In Chinese, names appear with family name preceding given name. But Chinese authors sometimes use the Western style of family name last if writing in English. In this volume, we followed the convention adopted by the authors themselves. For Chinese characters, we have adopted the Pinyin system of romanization.

NOTE

1. Essays written for a Chinese audience tend to be noticeably different than those written for an English audience. The editor of this book has been to several conferences on Confucianism in China, and he has rarely come across papers on the sorts of concerns that seem to animate English-language works on Confucianism, such as Confucianism's relationship with democracy, civil society, and feminism (partly, there may be political constraints, but different

cultural priorities also help to explain the differences). The methodology of Chinese-language essays is usually more historical and interpretative and less analytical and normative. The essays are often filled with idioms and historical references that won't make much sense to the uninformed Western reader. Ni Lexiong's essay has "Chinese" characteristics, but it also addresses an issue of global import that should be of interest to English readers.

PART ONE
STATE AND CIVIL SOCIETY

Chapter One

CONFUCIAN CONCEPTIONS OF CIVIL SOCIETY

Richard Madsen

Classical Chinese intellectual traditions (which were not confined to China proper, but had enormous influence throughout East Asia, particularly in Japan, Korea, and Vietnam) did not even have words for *civil society,* much less a theory of it. In Chinese, for instance, the word for *society* (*shehui*) is a neologism from the West, introduced into China via Japan in the late-nineteenth century.[1] Though based on classical Chinese characters, it was a new combination of characters, used in a new sense, to name a modern phenomenon—the development in Treaty Port cities of a separate societal sphere of life that could be at least analytically distinguished from separate economic and political spheres, which were also denoted by words new to the Chinese lexicon. The term *civil* is even newer, and less well established in modern Asian lexicons. In contemporary Chinese, for example, there are no fewer than four words that are used to translate the *civil* in *civil society.*[2] Alternatively, Chinese intellectuals today call civil society *shimin shehui,* which literally means "city-people's society"; or *gongmin shehui,* "citizens' society"; or *minjian shehui,* "people-based society"; or *wenming shehui,* "civilized society." These are all attempts to name phenomena and to articulate aspirations that have arisen in an urbanizing East Asia linked to a global market economy. In this confusing, transitional context, many intellectuals are feeling the need to develop new theories of civil society and new ways of developing such a society, even if they are not completely sure what to call it and how to link it—if it can be linked at all—with their cultural traditions.

Those traditions are complex, pluralistic, and full of conflicting and contradictory ideas about how to live a good life in a well-ordered world. Major strands include the Daoist celebration of natural, virtually anarchistic spontaneity, the Legalist pursuit of centralized political order through carefully controlled allocation of rewards and punishments—and the "thinking of the scholars," to which Western Sinologists in the nineteenth century gave the name "Confucianism." Systematized by great philosophers such as Zhu Xi into a comprehensive framework of ideas during the late Song Dynasty in the eleventh and twelfth centuries C.E., the "Neo-Confucian" tradition blended some metaphysical ideas from Buddhism with the moral teachings of Confucius (551–478 B.C.E.) and his disciples (particularly Mencius, 390–305 B.C.E.), which advocated a middle way between Daoist anarchism and Legalist authoritarianism.[3]

Unlike the Daoists, the Confucians searched for a stable political order. But unlike the Legalists, they insisted that such order had to be based on moral principles, not simply on power. Scholars in this tradition had vigorous disagreements about how people could know these principles and learn to apply them. On one side of these debates were what Wm. Theodore de Bary has called a relatively "liberal" interpretation, which would be consistent with many of the standards for human rights advocated by modern Western liberals—or at least "liberal communitarians."[4] But there were also authoritarian interpretations of the Neo-Confucian traditions. In East Asia today, apologists for authoritarian governments like that of Singapore invoke the Confucian tradition to suppress much of what would be considered part of civil society in the West. At the same time, prominent Asian intellectuals like Tu Wei-ming invoke more "liberal" strands of Confucianism to build a base for relative openness in East Asian societies.[5]

If there is to be a meaningful dialogue between modern proponents of Confucian thought, on the one hand, and theories of civil society that derive from the Western Enlightenment, on the other, it will, in my view, have to draw upon those relatively liberal strands of the Neo-Confucian tradition. These are the strands that I will emphasize in this chapter.

INGREDIENTS: WHO, AND WHAT, DOES CIVIL SOCIETY INCLUDE?

This question seems to envision a social framework that can gather together certain individual parts while excluding others. If this is so, the question fails to make sense in a Confucian context. Confucian thought does not conceive the world in terms of delimited parts.[6] The great social anthropologist Fei Xiaotong has given the following vivid account of the difference between Confucian and Western ways of thinking about the configuration of relationships that constitute a society.

> In some ways Western society bears a resemblance to the way we bundle kindling wood in the fields. A few rice stalks are bound together to make a handful, several handfuls are bound together to make a small bundle, several

small bundles are bound together to make a larger bundle, and several larger bundles are bound together to make a stack to carry on a pole. Every single stalk in the entire stack belongs to one specific large bundle, one specific small bundle, and one specific handful. Similar stalks are assembled together, clearly classified, and then bound together. In a society these units are groups. . . . The group has a definite demarcation line."[7]

The configuration of Chinese society, on the other hand, is "like the rings of successive ripples that are propelled outward on the surface when you throw a stone into water. Each individual is the center of the rings emanating from his social influence. Wherever the ripples reach, affiliations occur."[8]

The ripples can eventually reach everywhere. The Neo-Confucian vision was thus holistic. As Tu Wei-ming characterizes it, "[S]elf, community, nature, and Heaven are integrated in an anthropocosmic vision."[9] Insofar as discourse is driven by this holistic imagination, it is difficult to make the distinctions that are the staple of Western secular civil society discourse: between public and private, and voluntary and involuntary forms of association.

There are words in Chinese—*gong* and *si*—that translate as "public" and "private," but in the logic of Confucian discourse the distinction between them is completely relative. Once again, according to Fei Xiaotong:

Sacrificing one's family for oneself, sacrificing one's clan for one's family— this formula is an actual fact. Under such a formula what would someone say if you called him *si* [acting in his private interest]? He would not be able to see it that way, because when he sacrificed his clan, he might have done it for his family, and the way he looks at it, his family is *gong* [the public interest]. When he sacrificed the nation for the benefit of his small group in the struggle for power, he was also doing it for the public interest [*gong*], the public interest of his small group. . . . *Gong* and *si* are relative terms; anything within the circle in which one is standing can be called *gong*.[10]

Likewise, the distinction between voluntary and involuntary forms of association is blurry. In the West the family is the prototypical involuntary association; one does not choose one's parents. But in the Asian traditions there is a different way of thinking about the family. Fei Xiaotong again: If a friend in England or America writes a letter saying he is going to "bring his family" to visit, the recipient knows very well who will be coming. But "in China, although we frequently see the phrase, 'Your entire family is invited,' very few people could say exactly which persons should be included under 'family.' " A person can choose to include distant relatives or even friends as part of broadly conceived family. The involuntary relationships that make up the kinship group are expanded in indeterminate ways by voluntary affiliation.[11]

A traditional discourse centered on a holistic "anthropocosmic vision" and unable to make fixed distinctions between public and private, voluntary and involuntary forms of association—this would not seem a very promising basis for developing a coherent theory of civil society. Contemporary Chinese and other Asians are faced with social realities that cannot readily be encompassed by this vision. One of the words for civil society, it will be noted, is *shimin shehui,* "urban society." In modern metropolises like Hong Kong, Shanghai, Taipei, Tokyo, or Seoul, the Asian intellectual has to contend with extreme social fragmentation, industrial or postindustrial divisions of labor, populations influenced by global media and demanding opportunities for free, individualistic self-expression, and a powerful, globalized market economy—all of which put complex demands on the state.

There are those, of course, who think that the only way to confront these new challenges is through "all-out Westernization," rather than through any appropriation of the Confucian legacy. But others believe that it is neither possible nor desirable to discard that legacy.[12] When those who consider the reappropriation of the Confucian legacy consider the issue of civil society, they look to the intermediate associations between the nuclear family and the state. The logic of Confucianism makes it difficult to make sharp distinctions between the various elements in this intermediate realm. Instead of seeing different kinds of associations as independent entities, like so many separate sticks within a bundle of firewood, each with its own purposes and each at least potentially in competition with each other, they tend to think of the different elements as fluidly interpenetrating each other, like the ripples on a pond. When they use the word *minjian shuhui*—"people-based society"— to translate civil society, they do not usually connote popular groups acting independently of the state. They assume that people-based groups cannot properly exist without the general permission, guidance, and supervision of the government.

At one extreme, those envisioning such people-based groups from top to bottom might see them simply as a "transmission belt" between the state and the lowest realms of the society. (Ideologues in Mainland China and some apologists for the Singapore regime would fall into this category.) Public purposes infuse what we in the West would think of as private matters. At the other extreme, those envisioning people-based groups from bottom to the top are likely to blend what Westerners consider private matters with public affairs. They may think of groups like the family as legitimately being able to influence affairs of state. (Into this category might fall some of those who celebrate familistic, "guanxi capitalism," in which business deals are regulated by particularistic connections between relatives and friends rather than impersonally applied laws.) But most intellectuals working within the Confucian tradition fall between these extremes. For instance, they recognize the necessity for intermediate associations to maintain a large degree of autonomy from the state. Yet because of the difficulty that Confucian discourse has of offering a principled justification for such autonomy, they advocate it more on pragmatic grounds. An institutional embodiment of this stance is perhaps seen on contemporary Taiwan, which in many ways is witnessing a "springtime of civil society," with a tremendous proliferation of intermediate associations—religious, ethnic, commercial, environmentalist, feminist. To have a legitimate standing in Taiwanese society, all of these groups must be duly registered with an appropriate government ministry, and thus in principle accept government supervision. But there are now so many of these groups that the government could not regulate them, even it wanted to. For all intents and purposes these groups function as autonomous, voluntary associations. Members of such groups definitely seem to want this practical autonomy. But most seem reluctant to undertake the effort that would be necessary to establish a principled basis for it.[13]

SOCIETY: WHAT MAKES CIVIL SOCIETY A SOCIETY AND NOT A SIMPLE AGGREGATE?

The Confucian vision is radically social. As Herbert Fingarette puts it: "For Confucius, unless there are at least two human beings, there are no human beings."[14] The relationships that define the conditions for human flourishing were given a classic formulation by Mencius:

> Between parent and child there is to be affection
> Between ruler and minister, rightness
> Between husband and wife, [gender] distinctions
> Between older and younger [siblings], an order of precedence
> Between friends, trustworthiness[15]

This formulation assumes that human persons flourish through performing different, mutually complementary roles. Some roles should take priority over others—for instance, the role of parent is more important than the role of friend. But this formulation does not justify a top-down, authoritarian system in which it is the prerogative of superior people to give orders and the duty of inferiors blindly to obey.

There is another formulation of the basic Confucian relationships that does justify authoritarianism. That is the doctrine of the "three bonds," between ruler/minister, father/son, and husband/wife. Today, in common discourse, the core of Confucian teaching is indeed understood in terms of these authoritarian three bonds. According to Wm. Theodore de Bary, however, the three bonds "have no place in the Confucian classics, and were only codified later in [first century C.E.] Han texts."[16] They are of Legalist provenance, products of an age when Confucianism became the ideology of the imperial state. Apologists for Asian authoritarian regimes like to stress the importance of the three bonds. But Zhu Xi and most Neo-Confucians rarely mention them.[17] And when Tu Weiming and other modern Confucian intellectuals try to press Confucianism into the service of creating a democratic civil society, they claim that the Mencian vision of mutuality is the most authentic expression of Confucianism.[18]

Even if one tries to build a vision of civil society around the five relationships of Mencius, it would be difficult to avoid making moral distinctions between men and women and older and younger people that would be unacceptable to Western liberals. However, in theory at least, these distinctions would lead not to inferiority but to complementary reciprocity. The emphasis in the parent/child and husband/wife relationship would be on mutual affection and love, expressed energetically and creatively on all sides. The parent should instruct the child, but the child should also admonish the parent if the parent is doing something wrong. In the *Classic of Filial Piety,* the disciple of Confucius asks the Master, "[I]f a child follows all of his parents' commands, can this be called filiality? The Master replied, 'What kind of talk is this! . . . If a father even had one son to remonstrate with him, he still would not fall into evil ways. In the face of whatever is not right, the son cannot but remonstrate with his father.' "[19] In the *Classic of Filial Piety for Women,* "The women said, 'We dare to ask whether we follow all our husbands' commands we could be called virtuous?' Her Ladyship answered, 'What kind of talk is this! . . . If a husband has a remonstrating wife then he won't fall into evil ways. Therefore if a husband transgresses against the Way, you must correct him. How could it be that to obey your husband in everything would make you a virtuous person?' "[20]

A civil society grounded in such notions of creative reciprocity would discourage configurations of power that would prevent weaker members from acting as moral agents in the reciprocal exchanges that bind the society together. It would protect from retaliation members who exercised their duty to remonstrate with those in power. It would encourage everyone to receive the kind of education that would enable him or her properly to fulfill their responsibilities. It was in this spirit that the seventeenth-century Neo-Confucian scholar Huang Zongxi proposes, according to de Bary, "a constitutional program resembling, in some important respects, the constitutional system of the modern West."[21] There are two main elements in his proposal for institutional innovation. First is a Confucian justification for a rule of law that would place limitations on the ruler's power. Second is a proposal to strengthen schools and learned academies so that they could increase the numbers of civil servants and prepare them to perform an expanded range of functions in civil government—and could become strong centers for the expression of educated public opinion.[22] Huang's "scholarly forum was to be a well-defined, state-supported, fully accredited, and legal function of a duly constituted order, and yet as independent as possible in a society that lacked a middle class, popular press, church, legal profession or other supporting infrastructure independent of the state."[23]

Huang was recognized as one of the most learned men of his time, and his ideas resonated with other leading Confucian scholars during the early Qing dynasty. His ideas were not implemented during the Qing, but Chinese revolutionaries and reformers in the twentieth century have drawn upon them in the effort to create a Chinese version of Western constitutionalism. Although the actually existing structure of the imperial Chinese state and society was alien to Western notions of a civil society, the writing of scholars like Huang Zongxi demonstrates that there are intellectual resources within the Confucian tradition for imagining such a society—one based on a constitutionally limited state and on an array of mediating institutions, especially educational institutions.

VALUES: HOW IS CIVIL SOCIETY IMPORTANT? WHAT PARTICULAR VALUES DOES IT OFFER ITS MEMBERS THAT MIGHT BE UNOBTAINABLE IN ITS ABSENCE?

In the Confucian vision, as noted above, human flourishing can occur only if social relations have a proper moral basis. This means that people have to learn to discern what is the right way to behave and that for the most part they voluntarily act accordingly. A community based on force and fear cannot be a good community. But neither can a community based on an amoral clash of competing interest groups, even when this leads to a stable, peaceful balance of power and many opportunities for individuals to choose between rival versions of the good life. The Confucian project requires moral cultivation at all levels of the society.

This cultivation is to develop the mind-and-heart, an inextricable combination of mental and emotional faculties. The goal of this cultivation, as Tu Wei-ming puts it, "is not an idea of abstract universalism but a dynamic process of self-transcendence, not a departure from one's source but a broadening and deepening of one's sensitivity without losing sight of one's rootedness in the body, family, community, society, and the world."[24] This cultivation must begin within the family, and it is sustained at the most fundamental level by the rituals of family life. For most people in imperial China it stayed within the (extended) family. However, the more advanced levels of moral cultivation—the kind required to set oneself on the path to becoming a "gentleman," capable of responsible political leadership—required a plentitude of intermediary institutions: in the words of Tu Wei-ming, "community schools, community compacts, local temples, theater groups, clan associations, guilds, festivals, and a variety of ritual-centered activities."[25] Each of these institutions had its own integrity—its core practices were seen as ends in themselves, not just means to some larger, universal ends. But Confucian self-cultivation aimed to see these institutions in the widest possible context. With proper self-cultivation, a Confucian could see how a strong commitment to one's family would not be in conflict with commitment to one's community; and commitment to one's local community was not in conflict with commitment to the state. The more intimate commitments indeed should train one to engage properly in the broader commitments.

The challenges of creating stable societies with a common moral basis in the modern urban environments of contemporary Asia are far greater than the challenges facing Confucian thinkers in the predominantly agrarian societies of imperial China. The realization of the Confucian project under modern conditions would require more self-cultivation of more people, especially more of the cultivation that would enable people to place their family and local community commitments in the broadest possible context. This would require an even richer array of intermediary institutions than there were in imperial China. To fulfill the purposes of self-cultivation, these institutions would have to be seen as educational, in the broadest sense of the word. They would have to be based on humanistic principles, not just the pursuit of money and power for their own sakes. Their organizational structure would have to encourage the kind of give and take necessary for effective learning.

It is through such groups that Asian societies could become *wenming shehui,* "civilized societies," societies full of the values of civility. In the Confucian context, however, civility does not simply mean tolerance for rivals in a world of competitive coexistence—as in the context of the liberal-egalitarian vision of civil society. It means the eventual achievement of a kind of social consensus. The attitude of Huang Zongxi was characteristic of even the most "liberal" Confucian scholars. Huang advocated open discussion of public questions in the enhanced schools and academies that he proposed. "At the same time," as de Bary puts it, "it must be noted that by open discussion of public questions, Huang did not mean complete freedom of expression in all matters. As a Confucian he believed the upholding of strict moral standards was necessary to the social and political order; thus he was prepared to ban, on the local level, forms of moral impropriety and social corruption."[26]

Today, even citizens in relatively liberal East Asian regimes like Taiwan give general support to laws that ban breaches of filial piety. For instance, family law in Taiwan as well as in most East Asian countries mandates that children must take care of their aged parents—something that in Western liberal democracy is generally regarded as a private matter, no matter how desirable such a mandate might be. There is also a fair amount of social consensus in favor of laws formally banning the kind of pornography that would be protected by the First Amendment in the United States (even though in practice there are plenty of pornographic materials available in most East Asian countries). Finally, there is considerable support for government restriction of "irresponsible" (sensationalistic, scandalous) journalism, although intellectuals in the more open East Asian regimes are also concerned about how to protect legitimate criticism of people in power.

This concern for achieving social consensus is also reflected in the ordering of educational systems throughout contemporary East Asia. The assumption is that schools are supposed to develop not just technical skills but proper values and that the state should play an active role in ensuring that the proper values are indeed taught. There are ambiguities within traditional Confucian epistemology about how learning of proper values takes place. One school of thought stresses the need for the learner to absorb proper information. Another—with roots in the ideas of Mencius—sees learning as the unfolding of knowledge that is immanent in the learner. Depending on what side of the tradition one emphasizes, learning can involve greater degrees of indoctrination, on the one hand, and education, on the other. The Maoist government in China, obviously, emphasized indoctrination. From research academies and universities at the top to the "small groups" that honeycombed all levels of society and carried out "study sessions" throughout the grass roots, participants were expected to learn the proper political line and encourage one another, through criticism and self-criticism, to conform to it. In contemporary Taiwan, in sharp contrast, there is extremely lively and open intellectual discussion in universities and research institutes and in the media. (At the primary- and secondary-school levels, on the other hand, there is more of an emphasis on conformity than there would be in the United States.) Throughout all levels of society, a vast assortment of associations and community organizations try to develop and propagate their various visions about cultural, political, and economic issues.

Other East Asian societies, like Singapore, Japan, and South Korea, fall somewhere between these two extremes of emphasizing indoctrination versus education. And they differ similarly with respect to government and unofficial public opinion about how much social consensus is required and how it should be achieved. But even in Taiwan, which currently is probably the most open society in East Asia, there is less principled support for moral pluralism and more of a tendency to equate civility with social consensus than there would be in the classic liberal or the liberal egalitarian visions.

RISKS: WHAT RISKS AND LIABILITIES, IF ANY, DOES CIVIL SOCIETY POSE FOR ITS MEMBERS?

Perhaps the main risk to the Neo-Confucian project over the centuries has been its excessive idealism, its unrealistic assessment of the demands of ensuring social order in a large and complex society. As Tu Wei-ming notes,

> [B]y addressing, in a fundamentally humanist way, the meaning of politics, Neo-Confucian intellectuals not only developed their own distinctive style of political participation but also formulated the ritual of exercising power in East Asian politics. To be sure, it is easy to criticize the Neo-Confucian insistence on the inseparability of morality and politics as a failure to understand the political process as an independent arena of human activity. It was perhaps constitutive to their intention to moralize politics that they inevitably experience alienation from the center of power. The interjection of the category of "self-cultivation" into the discourse of *realpolitik* may seem naïve. Indeed, this has been widely interpreted by modern scholars as characteristic of the Confucian predicament: inner spiritual self-cultivation does not at all lead to positive social and political consequence.[27]

However, Tu argues that if seen from the proper perspective, the Neo-Confucian position does not have to be naïve. Indeed, Tu might argue that from a Confucian perspective it is Western liberalism that seems naïve, in its notion that political order can be maintained through technically expert management upon a citizenry divided by extreme ethical pluralism and predominantly focused on private pleasures rather than public duties. "The cliché that virtually all Confucian scholar-officials were actively involved in purifying the ethos and revitalizing the spirit of the community suggests that, as self-styled ministers of the moral order, their commitment to social transformation was, in their view, the calling of their political engagement."[28] Historically, Tu argues, the Confucians were extremely successful in their calling.

[I]t was in the shaping of the habits of the heart of the East Asian people that the Confucian persuasion exerted its enduring influence. The pervasiveness of the Confucian life-orientation was such that Confucian ethics manifested itself in morality books, peasant rebellions, entertainment, religious movements, and popular literature. . . . The learning of the heart and mind, with emphasis on human nature and feeling, became a grammar of action in East Asian social praxis not necessarily because of its impeccable logic in moral reasoning; its reasonableness in the practical living of ordinary people accounted for much of its persuasive power.[29]

Throughout the centuries, however, powerful Asian rulers themselves have thought that Neo-Confucianism was naïve about the dictates of power. When faced with the task of holding together a large and diverse empire, and especially when faced with the dangers of internal rebellion and external invasion, they often resorted to the hard-headed realpolitik of Legalism although usually without explicitly acknowledging this. In the twentieth century, the problems arising from increased population, increased fragmentation, civil war, and outside aggression have, of course, risen exponentially. It has often seemed to successful political leaders that they could not afford the humaneness of Confucianism. The last political campaign of Mao Zedong's regime, for example, was aimed at condemning Confucius (which was meant as a veiled criticism of Zhou Enlai) and praising the Legalists, whose vision inspired Mao's own form of dictatorship.[30] East Asian regimes that suppress dissent and engage in large-scale state-led mobilization are acting very much in the Legalist tradition, which is what remains if the Confucian vision proves itself to be insufficiently robust.

To succeed on their own terms in setting the political agenda in the contemporary world and thus in avoiding the slide into Legalist authoritarianism, Confucians need to find new ways of shaping the "habits of the heart" of the East Asian people. The greatest challenge to doing this, perhaps, is that posed by the development of mass society, atomized by widespread social mobility, distracted from public affairs by a globalized consumer culture, and vulnerable to manipulation by mass media. Confucian self-cultivation requires slow, hard work, difficult to sustain in a frenetic market economy. It requires the development of moral discipline, difficult to accomplish in the face of the self-gratifications promised by consumer culture. Classic Confucian education aimed to produce some "superior persons" whose authority would be respected and accepted by ordinary people—an elitist notion that goes against populist instincts encouraged by mass media and global popular culture, and against the notion of a *gongmin shehui,* a "citizens' society," in which each citizen has an equal right to participate in the polity.

Without creative adaptation, the Confucian vision may fail to be attractive to modern mass societies, and be unable to inspire a civil society possessed of enough civility to sustain orderly forms of democracy. If that happens, perhaps the only viable path toward political democracy would be an adaptation of Western liberal visions. Failing that, the probable outcome might be forms of authoritarianism arising out of indigenous East Asian traditions.

RESPONSIBILITY: HOW IS RESPONSIBILITY FOR HUMAN WELL-BEING PROPERLY SHARED BY, OR DISTRIBUTED AMONG, THE INDIVIDUAL, THE FAMILY, THE STATE, AND PRIVATE ASSOCIATIONS?

As noted above, in the Neo-Confucian vision social order is based on the proper performance of interdependent social roles. If everyone plays his or her roles properly—that is, if parents are good parents and children are good children, if rulers are good rulers and subjects good subjects, and so forth—then there will be peace all under Heaven. Sometimes it may appear that the roles one occupies in one sphere of life come into conflict with roles in other spheres. For instance one's role as a parent might seem to conflict with one's role as a loyal citizen or political subject. The Confucian position is that if one cultivates oneself fully enough and thus understands the responsibilities implicit in these roles deeply enough, one will find that there is ultimately no contradiction.

The roles and their attendant responsibilities are determined by cosmic Principle (*Li*). This Principle is an objective reality, and insofar as the moral life is to conform to such an objective reality, Confucian thought is like the Western natural law tradition. But there is an important difference. In the natural law tradition, people can know through reason the laws to which they should conform, and then it is the task of moral cultivation to achieve this conformity. But in the Confucian tradition, one cannot simply know the Principle through reason. This requires learning of the mind-and-heart, an embodied form of knowledge that is at least as affective as cognitive. It is the task of the Confucian to cultivate the moral sensibility that would enable him or her to apprehend this fundamental Principle. One becomes moral not by following external rules, but by struggling to develop the self.

The place for such self-cultivation is in the midst of the world. The Confucians, as Tu Wei-ming puts it, were "action intellectuals." It was their responsibility to be immersed in all the political and social conflicts of their time. But unlike the liberal who learns to live with conflict by tolerating it, the Confucian aspired to learn through conflict so as to overcome it by changing the rules of the game, so that the exercise of power would be subordinated to moral commitments, rather than vice versa.

In the midst of the world, Confucian self-cultivation involves some combination of academic study of classic literature, sincere participation in family, community, and political rituals, and meditative introspection. There is no pope of Confucianism to define correct interpretation of such things, only an ever-evolving consensus forged through discussion among whose who sincerely follow the Confucian Way. There is something almost existential about this, and it helps keep Confucianism from the dogmatism into which the natural law tradition can sometimes fall.

In general, though, the Confucian sense of social responsibility is biased toward the fulfillment of roles at the most fundamental levels of society. The opening statement of *The Great Learning*, the best known and most influential of all the Confucian classics, offers this summary of the Confucian moral and political program:

> The ancients who wished to illuminate "illuminating virtue" all under Heaven first governed their states. Wishing to govern their states, they first regulated their families. Wishing to regulate their families, they first cultivated their personal lives. Wishing to cultivate their personal lives, they first rectify their hearts and minds. Wishing to rectify their hearts and minds, they made their intentions sincere. Wishing to make their intentions sincere, they first extended their knowledge. The extension of knowledge lay in the investigation of things. For only when things are investigated is knowledge extended; only when knowledge is extended are intentions sincere; only when intentions are sincere are hearts and minds rectified; only when hearts and minds are rectified are personal lives cultivated; only when personal lives are cultivated are families regulated; only when families are regulated are states governed; only when states are governed is there peace all under Heaven. Therefore, from the Son of Heaven to the common people, all, without exception, must take self-cultivation as the root.[31]

This is a vision of rippling waves of interdependent, mutual responsibility extending through all the levels of the world. But the waves emanate from a center—the self. The cultivation of the self is an end in itself, not simply (as in the Western civic republican tradition, which otherwise has important affinities with Confucianism) a means to achieve a well-ordered polity. Self-cultivation cannot be done alone, however. It requires in the first instance a strong family, cultivation of which is also an end in itself. Eventually, it also requires a well-ordered state. One's most basic responsibilities, however, are to those closest to oneself—family and local community. Before there can be proper governance of the state, there must be proper self-cultivation leading to proper regulation of the family. A wise government, therefore, will support the individual, family, and local community in their work of mutual cultivation, but it will not attempt to preempt these functions.

FREEDOM: WHAT IS THE APPROPRIATE BALANCE BETWEEN INDIVIDUAL AUTONOMY AND CONSTRAINTS IMPOSED BY NONGOVERNMENTAL GROUPS?

For the Neo-Confucian, freedom is not the "freedom to choose." The fundamental building blocks of a civil society are nonoptional institutions. The foundation of the Confucian project was expanding family virtues beyond the confines of the home. The point of departure is the most nonvoluntary of human institutions, the family. For the Western liberal, even the family becomes like a voluntary association, whose members have easy exit and the ability to affiliate or not if they so please. For the Confucian, on the other hand, even voluntary associations, like learned societies or guilds, should be like families—their members should be bound by loyalties that make exit difficult. In the Neo-Confucian perspective, then, freedom does not consist in choosing which groups one will belong to. It consists in creatively contextualizing those commitments which fate has assigned. It involves more deeply understanding the meaning of one's roles as parent/child, ruler/minister, husband/wife, older sibling/younger sibling, and friend—so that one can flexibly, even playfully, reconcile these with each other and with all the other confusing roles that one must play in an evolving modern world. This task can provide wide latitude for action and immense challenges for personal creativity, and it can lead to a plethora of individualized responses to particular situations. Under the right circumstances, it can encourage vigorous entrepreneurial initiative. In practice, well-cultivated Confucians would have a great deal of freedom to choose. But in principle, their choices would be directed toward a larger goal, a dynamic, open process of spiritual development leading toward a truly *wenming shehui,* a civilized society of *gongmin,* or public citizens, rich in *minjian,* or people-based associations, within the conurbation of *shimin,* city people in the modern world.

FUTURE READING

Stephen C. Angle, *Human Rights and Chinese Thought: Cross-Cultural Inquiry.* New York: Cambridge University Press, 2002.

Daniel A. Bell and Hahm Chaibong, eds., *Confucianism for the Modern World.* New York: Cambridge University Press, 2003.

Wm. Theodore de Bary, *The Liberal Tradition in China.* New York: Columbia University Press, 1983; and Wm. Theodore de Bary. *Asian Values and Human Rights: A Confucian Communitarian Perspective.* Cambridge: Harvard University Press, 1998. Essays by one of America's leading Sinologists on the relevance of Confucian tradition to Western cultural and political concerns.

David Hall and Roger Ames. *Thinking through Confucius.* Albany: State University of New York Press, 1987. Introduction to Confucian ethics.

Donald Munro, ed. *Individualism and Holism: Studies in Confucian and Taoist Values.* Ann Arbor: Center for Chinese Studies, University of Michigan, 1985. Essays on connections between self and society in Chinese philosophical traditions.

Sor-Hoon Tan, *Confucian Democracy: A Deweyan Construction.* Albany: SUNY Press, 2003.

Shun Kwong-Loi and David Wong, eds. *Confucian Ethics: A Comparative Study of Self, Autonomy, and Community.* New York: Cambridge University Press, 2004.

Tu Wei-Ming. "Confucianism." In *Our Religions,* ed. Arvind Sharma. San Francisco: HarperCollins, 1993. Authoritative introduction to the Confucian tradition by a prominent proponent of Confucian humanism.

NOTES

1. Lydia H. Liu, *Translingual Practice: Literature, National Culture, and Translated Modernity—China, 1900–1937* (Stanford: Stanford University Press, 1995), 336.

2. William T. Rowe, "The Problem of 'Civil Society' in Late Imperial China," *Modern China* 19, no. 2 (April 1993): 142.

3. For a comprehensive summary of the tradition see Tu Wei-ming, "Confucianism," in *Our Religions,* ed. Arvind Sharma (San Francisco: HarperSanFrancisco, 1995), 141–227.

4. Wm. Theodore de Bary, *The Liberal Tradition in China* (Hong Kong: Chinese University Press of Hong Kong, 1983); and *Asian Values and Human Rights: A Confucian Communitarian Perspective* (Cambridge: Harvard University Press, 1998).

5. *Tu Wei-ming,* "Cultural China: The Periphery as the Center," *The Living Tree: The Changing Meaning of Being Chinese Today,* special issue of *Daedalus* 120, no. 2 (Spring 1991): 1–32.

6. See Donald J. Munro, introduction to *Individualism and Holism: Studies in Confucian and Taoist Values,* ed. Donald Munro (Ann Arbor: Center for Chinese Studies, University of Michigan, 1985), 1–30; see also the other essays in this volume, passim.

7. Fei Xiaotong, "Chinese Social Structure and Its Values," in *Changing China: Readings in the History of China from the Opium War to the Present,* ed. J. Mason Gentzler (New York: Praeger, 1977), 211. Originally published as *Xiangtu Zhongguo* (Shanghai, 1948).

8. Fei Xiaotong, "Chinese Social Structure and Its Values."

9. *Tu Wei-ming,* "Heart, Human Nature, and Feeling: Implications for the Neo-Confucian Idea of Civil Society," Reischauer Lecture, Harvard University; paper presented at the Ethikon Conference, Redondo Beach, Calif., July 10–12, 1998, 27.

10. Fei Xiaotong, "Chinese Social Structure and Its Values," 213.

11. Ibid., 211.

12. See the controversy over the 1988 Chinese television series *Heshang,* which was seen by many as advocating "all-out Westernization." Su Xiaokang and Wang Luxiang, *Deathsong of the River: A Reader's Guide to the Chinese TV Series "Heshang,"* trans. and eds. Richard W. Bodman and Pin P. Wan (Ithaca: Cornell East Asia Series, 1991).

13. Hsin-huang Michael Hsiao, "The Development and Organization of Foundations in Taiwan: An Expression of Cultural Vigor in a Newly Born Society," in *Quiet Revolutions on Taiwan, Republic of China,* ed. Jason C. Hu (Taipei: Kwang Hwa, 1994), 386–419; and Makito Noda, *Emerging Civil Society in the Asia Pacific Community: Nongovernmental Underpinnings of the Emerging Asia Pacific Regional Community,* ed. Tadashi Yamamoto (Singapore: Institute of Southeast Asian Studies; and Tokyo: Japan Centre for International Exchange, 1995).

14. Herbert Fingarette, *Confucius—The Secular as Sacred* (New York: Harper and Row, 1972), as quoted by Henry Rosemont, "Reply to Nosco," in paper presented at the Ethikon Conference, Santa Fe, N.M., January 15–17, 1999.

15. Mencius 3A:4, quoted in de Bary, *Asian Values and Human Rights,* 17.

16. de Bary, *Asian Values and Human Rights,* 124.

17. Ibid., 124–25.

18. Tu Wei-ming, "Confucianism," 186–94.

19. *Classic of Filial Piety,* as quoted in de Bary, *Asian Values and Human Rights,* 126.

20. Ibid., 128.

21. de Bary, *Asian Values and Human Rights,* 102.

22. Ibid., 100–9.

23. Ibid., 106.

24. Tu Wei-ming, "Heart, Human Nature, and Feeling," 22.

25. Ibid., 18.

26. de Bary, *Asian Values and Human Rights,* 107.

27. Tu Wei-ming, "Heart, Human Nature, and Feeling," 20.

28. Ibid., 23.

29. Ibid.

30. Jun Jing, *The Temple of Memories: History, Power, and Morality in a Chinese Village* (Stanford, Calif.: Stanford University Press, 1996), 53–54.

31. *The Great Learning,* in *Sources of the Chinese Tradition,* vol. 1, comp. Wm. Theodore de Bary, Wing-Tsit Chan, and Burton Watson (New York: Columbia University Press, 1963), 115.

Chapter Two

CONFUCIAN PERSPECTIVES ON CIVIL SOCIETY
AND GOVERNMENT

~

PETER NOSCO

Let me begin by explaining what I mean when I use the terms *civil society* and *Confucianism*, since both terms are used in widely varying ways. I regard civil society as inseparable from voluntary associations, but I view these voluntary associations somewhat more narrowly than do some students of the subject. That is to say, where some[1] would regard civil society as comprised of all voluntary and non-coercive social groups—excluding principally only the family and the state, participation in which cannot be regarded as, under ordinary circumstances, elective—I do not include public religious associations or affiliations, which for most people until relatively recent times have not had the same elective character, nor do I include participation in secret societies with a political character. That the most obvious involuntary (in the sense of nonelective) associations are those of the family or the state—both of which are fundamental and primary from a Confucian perspective—provides us with an immediate suggestion regarding what a Confucian perspective on civil society might resemble.

I shall also exclude the market from our understanding of civil society. Unquestionably, an increasing volume and complexity of transactions both within and without the marketplace characterize early modernity and strengthen the individual's sense of self as a competent and increasingly autonomous actor in an ever more complex social field. However, the historical coincidence of market culture, early modernity, and civil society in Europe and North America appears not to have been a comparable feature of East Asian societies, and so we look not to markets and their culture, except as they contribute to those qualities of competence and integrity that characterize human agency, and are suggestive of the emergence of a relatively autonomous self.

Civil society is often conflated with constitutionally structured society, but this is likewise not helpful in an East Asian context, where constitutions and their related institutions have most commonly been understood as conferred from above rather than generated from below.[2] And again, where civil society has often been associated with the public sphere, we are more interested here in the development of a private sphere of the sort that enables individuals to associate in ways potentially destabilizing to the organic society envisioned in Confucian societies.

As with many perspectives, the term *Confucianism* has likewise meant different things at different times—even different things, surely, at the same time—and this contributes to making this task particularly challenging. For decades, social scientists with a comparative bent have linked "Confucianism" with economic development—an ironic linkage in view of traditional Confucianism's hostility toward profit and disdain for merchants and commercial activity—and have designated such countries as Singapore and Taiwan as Confucian societies. The principal features of these "Confucian" societies—the "little tigers," as they are often styled— are on the one hand their social cohesion and order, and on the other hand their authoritarian governments, which embrace the mantle of benevolent paternalism. The now discredited economic linkage notwithstanding, any sense of "Confucianism" that privileges, say, Singapore over China would seem counterintuitive and deserving of reconsideration.

We understand that it is largely to the past where one must turn to find "Confucianism," but how far back does one go? The Confucianism of the Four Books—the *Analects*, *Mencius*, *Great Learning*, and *Mean*—certainly represents one "Confucianism" and is of course authoritative, but the authors of these works both lived in and posited times in which voluntary associations of virtually any kind simply were not a prominent feature. Further, from, say, the fall of the latter Han dynasty in 220 till the founding of the Song dynasty in 960, Confucian teachers in China largely relinquished the ontological battlefield to Buddhists. To be sure, so-called Confucian diviners offered insight into how to achieve good and avoid adverse fortune, but they had little to say on classical Confucianism's traditional concerns, such as how one might become a better ruler, "citizen," or family member.

After 960 Chinese Confucian scholars succeeded in refashioning and revitalizing their tradition so as to compete successfully with and eventually displace Buddhism as the intellectual and spiritual orthodoxy of the day. This revitalized Confucianism, commonly called Neo-Confucianism, represents a second "Confucianism," whose tradition was embraced in China, Korea, Japan, and Vietnam in so compelling a manner and to such a degree that it actually contributes to the definition of these lands as belonging to the cultural sphere of East Asia.[3] Neo-Confucianism posited the identity of both natural principles and moral principles, suggesting that analogues of the same principles that inform and govern the material world can be found within the human person in the guise of an originally good human nature or mind. Neo-Confucianism further asserted a two-fold praxis intended to recover and reassert these primordial seeds of goodness. On the one hand, orthodox Neo-Confucianism proposed studying the external world around one (the so-called investigation of things) in order to discern the role of principle within it and thereby to acquire objective knowledge concerning the seeds of one's original goodness. On the other hand, Neo-Confucianism also embraced the internal cultivation of one's originally good properties through such exercises as quiet sitting, and through the nurturing of seriousness and reverence, understood in East Asia as dimensions of the same word: *jing* in Chinese, *kei* in Japanese.

One might in comparable fashion identify yet a third "Confucianism" in the form of those institutions and ritual traditions which have played such prominent roles variously throughout the societies of East Asia. These would include an examination system that tested one's mastery of Confucian classical texts and commentaries as a prerequisite for participation in the civil service; institutionalized opportunities for individual remonstrance with the political order, which are examined toward the end of this essay; social regulations governing matters ranging from divorce to inheritance; rituals performed both within and without the home, intended to honor one's ancestors; and of central importance to us as a form of voluntary association, the role of private academies as well as official schools in training potential elites; and so on.

It is, however, the canon that ultimately defines who is or is not a "Confucian," and it is to this canon that we inevitably return for textual insight into the questions that concern us, questions such as: How is one to know if the Way is prevailing? What are the properties of true kingship? What is the role of learning in defining the individual? How does one's activity in individual relationships contribute to the larger goal of peace and order? How is one to cultivate and thereby transform oneself in the direction of pure goodness? Please note in this last regard that to the extent that the Confucian effort to achieve human perfection involves transformation in the direction of a moral absolute such as Heaven (Ch. *tian*, Jpn. *ten*), this activity has a manifestly religious character.[4]

The canon and the textual insight it offers are, however, ultimately insufficient for addressing all of the topics and questions that inform and structure this essay on civil society and government, and so we must also turn to history for answers to certain quite basic questions. Was there civil society in East Asia? If so, when and where did it develop? And if not—or at least not as the term has been generally understood in Europe and North America—are there perhaps ways in which we can modify the concept of civil society to provide an alternative working model applicable to East Asia?

This chapter attempts to address these questions. It surely goes without saying—but seems prudent to acknowledge nonetheless—that my answers to these questions will necessarily be open to argument by specialists in both civil society and East Asian social and political history. Further, the constraints of space necessarily limit the depth of our inquiry into the questions to be discussed, particularly since I at times try to historicize the issues. I thus fear that the specialist on East Asia will find my characterizations of the historical, social, and textual dimensions of this exercise frustratingly shallow, while the novice in East Asian matters will find them no less frustratingly complex and overly wrought. The specialist on civil societies will likewise surely find much of both a theoretical and practical nature with which to quarrel in my analysis. These reservations and disclaimers notwithstanding, it is evident that, if Confucianism can offer insights on and contribute to the clarification of issues that never developed in the "local cultures" that represent Confucianism's original setting—issues like ecology, human rights, and so on—then it can likewise offer its own perspective on civil society.[5]

BOUNDARIES

The discussion of Confucian perspectives on the boundary between civil society and the state—or, to rephrase the question, Where would Confucianism draw the line between the authority of government and that of other groups in the society?—is thoroughly speculative, for classical Confucianism never envisioned a society inclusive of secular, voluntary associations of the sort suggestive of my understanding of civil society. This kind of society requires not just a sense of the integrity of the individual as an actor capable of negotiating his/her interactions in a responsible and ultimately socially constructive manner—something Confucianism would affirm—but also an acknowledged sphere of privacy granted by the state and society to its individual and corporate members to enable unauthorized voluntary associations, and Confucianism has generally not distinguished between privacy and selfishness in these contexts.[6]

In ancient (Han) China, Confucianism accommodated the clan and village loyalties characteristic of the society of that age by accepting both the family and the community as laboratories in which one learns to progress and measure one's progress in the direction of goodness. And, in classical (Tang) Chinese and (Heian) Japanese societies, what was known as "Confucianism" of necessity accommodated the widespread individual religious and aesthetic affiliation with Buddhism and was of

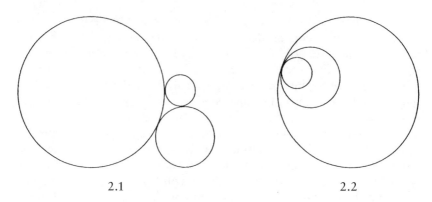

2.1   2.2

limited intellectual or spiritual appeal, even as its practical value to the public realm was generally acknowledged. Thus, when we ask where Confucianism would locate the boundary between the authority of government and that of other groups in society, our initial impulse is to visualize this in terms of circles that share a point of tangency, as in figure 2.1.

This perspective is mistaken, however, since classical Confucianism and its Neo-Confucian variants saw the relationship between the individual, the family group, and the state more as concentric circles, as represented in figure 2.2, and as articulated in the following famous passage from the *Great Learning*.

> The ancients who wished to manifest their clear character to the world would first bring order to their states. Those who wished to bring order to their states would first regulate their families. Those who wished to regulate their families would first cultivate their personal lives. Those who wished to cultivate their personal lives would first rectify their minds. Those who wished to rectify their minds would first make their wills sincere. Those who wished to make their wills sincere would first extend their knowledge. The extension of knowledge consists in the investigation of things. When things are investigated, knowledge is extended; when knowledge is extended, the will becomes sincere; when the will is sincere, the mind is rectified; when the mind is rectified, the personal life is cultivated; when the personal life is cultivated, the family will be regulated; when the family is regulated, the state will be in order; and when the state is in order, there will be peace throughout the world.[7]

One goal of Confucianism—and certainly the goal of greatest interest to those in positions of state authority—was to bring order to the state and thereby to spread peace throughout the world, but as this passage indicates the goal has its roots in the moral and spiritual ordering of the individual person and his/her family.

Further, Confucianism in many ways modeled its understanding of the state on its understanding of the family. In Confucianism, the ruler is unambiguously represented as the parent of the people, which reinforces an organic view of society as an enormous quasi family with the ruler as its paterfamilias. This being so, there is no more "space" or boundary between a Confucian ruler and Confucian citizen than between a Confucian father and Confucian son. And, just as the Confucian *Analects* insists that a filial son must never disobey (2:5), one fundamental responsibility of the Confucian "citizen" is to submit to that cosmically ordained authority which represents the incarnate mandate of Heaven to exercise terrestrial rule.

Historically, however, as societies in East Asia acquired the conditions of early modernity, a kind of "space" did indeed open between the state and the citizen, Confucian misgivings toward such space notwithstanding.[8] As elsewhere around the world, though perhaps not to the same degree as in Europe or North America, this sphere has the character of a public space, distinguished from both official and private spaces, and attendant to the emergence of this space is a boundary of sorts between the government and other groups or individuals in the society.

The factors responsible for this development are not unlike those identified with comparable developments in Europe: increased urbanization, with individuals uprooted from traditional village communities, and endeavoring to create new forms of association to combat the anomie and alienation that accompany such changes; an expansion of surplus wealth and the market, with an ever-increasing volume of transactions, including the commodification of a broad range of cultural products; a developed communication and transportation infrastructure, which contributes to the spread of literacy throughout the society, as well as increased opportunities for personal travel; and in religion, one observes the rise of "protestant" movements in East Asia, as in Europe, such as the Pure Land denominations of Buddhism, which privilege the individual's capacity to negotiate salvation on the basis of personal faith, and which at least conceptually diminish the role of the *ecclesia* as a mediating agency in this process. In a variety of ways, these developments reinforce a sense of the individual as competent on the one hand to negotiate the acquisition of an increasingly diverse range of material and cultural products, and on the other hand to enter into elective associations of an ever more variegated sort.

Confucianism cannot be credited with stimulating these changes, but it can be observed to respond to them in at least two noncongruent ways. First, one notes an increasing priority within Confucianism given to those forms of praxis that privilege interiority and self-cultivation, at the expense of the study of either the external world or the traditional classics. "Look inside yourself" becomes the message of much early-modern Confucian thought, for there you will find all that you need to know in order to become a perfected person. And second, one finds the reemergence and increasing prominence of forms of Confucianism that assert historicist as opposed to naturalist ontologies, arguing that the Confucian Way is not an unchanging set of universal principles, but rather is comprised of social and political practices that are conditioned by time and place.

The relevance of these changes for our understanding of boundaries between the state and civil society in East Asia rests in the rise of voluntary associations that pursued neither wealth nor power, salvation nor charity, but rather cultural identity and personal development. Accompanying the religious, social, and economic changes identified above was the rise of a secular and urban popular culture that for the first time made possible the successful marketing of cultural products—plays, novels and short stories, woodblock prints, and so on—that literally paid for themselves. That is to say, where in earlier times in East Asia the producers of such cultural products required either independent wealth or external patronage, hereafter it became possible for the producers of these cultural products to make an often lucrative living through their marketing. And one part of this cultural revolution was the rise of the private academy, in which forms of academic culture that had previously been restricted to those whose wealth or class entitled them to its acquisition were now made accessible to an altogether new class of enthusiastic cultural consumers.

This, I would argue, is the closest analogue one will find in East Asia prior to the twentieth century to the kinds of voluntary and noncoercive, nonfamilial associations characteristic of the rise of civil society in Europe, and it is here that I would situate the boundary of an admittedly limited public space between the state and individual in East Asia. Furthermore, and for the purposes of the discussion that follows, it is significant that the earliest and most successful private academies in East Asia were those that offered instruction in Confucianism. In China at least as early as the seventeenth century, one finds an intellectual like Huang Zongxi (1610–95) challenging the careerist orientation of much contemporary private and public instruction by arguing that in ancient times, "even the Son of Heaven did not dare to decide right and wrong for himself but shared with the schools the determination of right and wrong. Therefore, although the training of scholar-officials was one of the functions of schools, they were not established for this alone."[9] In a different vein, in Japan where there was no examination system, but where the expansion of private educational opportunities was at least as great as in China, one finds Huang's contemporary, Itō Jinsai (1627–1705), founding a private academy in Kyoto styled the Kogidō, or Hall of Ancient Meaning, where he offered instruction in Confucian textual studies to hundreds of tuition-paying students.[10] This is where I would locate a boundary between the state and one kind of quasi social group, and we shall continue our examination of the private academy and its significance for both popular culture and civil society in the next section.

NEEDS

The question of whether the state and civil society (as understood here, principally in terms of such voluntary associations as the private academy) need each other discloses the unbalanced and nonsymbiotic nature of their relationship in East Asia. Ultimately, voluntary associations are destabilizing to the Confucian ideal of the paternalistic state, just as voluntary associations are dependent in a Confucian society on the state's forbearance. Indeed, from the perspective of a ruler in a Confucian state, the "space" represented by any form of voluntary association—as we saw in the previous discussion of boundaries—is inevitably contingent and revocable, and to disclose this, let us reexamine the social and historical circumstances that fostered the emergence of the private academy in late-seventeenth-century Japan.[11]

In terms of urbanization, Japan at this time was certainly among the most urbanized societies in the world, with at least ten percent of its population living in settlements of ten thousand or more. Surplus wealth was more broadly distributed across an unprecedented range of social strata. Literacy rates were likely as high as anywhere else in the world, and there was a remarkably well developed communications and transportation infrastructure. The most important feature of this society, however, at least in terms of the emergence of the popular private academy, was the cultural liberality of the Japanese state.

It goes without saying that the term *cultural liberality* is problematic. Charles Frankel used it to refer to "an affirmative interest in the promotion of the diversity and qualities of mind which encourage empathetic understanding and critical appreciation of the diverse possibilities of human life."[12] This sense of cultural liberality was unarguably present in Japan during the last two decades of the seventeenth century and the first decade of the eighteenth, when Japan was ruled by the fifth Tokugawa shogun Tsunayoshi (r. 1680–1709), who styled himself in the guise of a Confucian monarch, sponsored debates among the various schools of Confucianism, and even lectured on the classics before assembled audiences of feudal lords (daimyō) and scholars. In 1690 Tsunayoshi even had a new home, the Shōheikō, or School of Prosperous Peace, built for the orthodox Hayashi school of Neo-Confucianism, locating it in nearby Yushima and awarding its chancellor, Hayashi Nobuatsu (1644–1732), with court rank. Not surprisingly, the shogun's interest in such matters encouraged others to follow suit, and as one early-modern Japanese scholar reflected on these years a century later, "literature and learning flourished widely. Every house read and every family recited [the classics]."[13]

Even more significant for the emergence of the private academy in Japan, however, was the fact that by the end of the seventeenth century, culture was no longer perceived to be the monopolized prerogative of any particular class or privileged group within the society, and that those who would once have been denied access to one or another form of cultural production could now purchase this culture from altogether willing purveyors. It is this sense of cultural liberality that made it possible in the late-seventeenth century for members of the newly ascendant merchant class to purchase, alongside their samurai classmates, instruction in such topics as Confucianism.

But there was still a third sense in which this era was culturally liberal, and it rests in the fact that the Tokugawa state was unconcerned with censoring or otherwise restricting modes of cultural production, so long as these modes were not perceived to be in any way destabilizing to the regime. The example of the government's attitude toward Kabuki drama is illustrative. When Kabuki performers were little more than theatrically skilled prostitutes, the government was indeed concerned over the street fighting that frequently erupted as samurai found themselves competing with one another for the sexual favors of different actresses and boy actors. But once the government mandated that Kabuki be a theater of adult males, the fighting diminished to the point where it was no longer perceived to be a problem, and the government in turn showed itself to be utterly unconcerned about either Kabuki staging or the content of its repertoire.[14]

The Confucian private academy in Japan benefited from these developments, enjoying the blessings of relative peace and prosperity, and flourishing as a result of the state's indifference toward matters of Confucian interpretation throughout most of the eighteenth century. But it cannot be said that Confucianism meaningfully contributed to these developments other than through its affirmative attitude toward a spirit of learning and inquiry. The irony, of course, is that as we have already observed, classical Confucianism would have regarded the rise of such voluntary associations as a private academy with skepticism at best, since Confucianism viewed society as an organic whole in which each person has his/her ordered role—a society that works harmoniously when each of these roles is fulfilled correctly in all circumstances, just as in a vast family. And, just as there is no room for a private sphere within the Confucian view of the family, the Confucian view of society remained one that found privacy ultimately indistinguishable from selfishness.

This is not to say that there was no room for, say, friendship and other similarly elective relationships within a Confucian worldview. Confucianism's five relationships—ruler/subject, parent/child, husband/wife, elder brother/younger brother, and friend/friend—explicitly acknowledge the importance and value of such voluntary and consensual relationships. But it is also abundantly clear that Confucianism gives priority to those relationships that are found within the household, and to those relationships in which there is a clear benefactor and beneficiary,[15] since these are the relationships that prepare one for citizenship and train one in goodness. For all these reasons, Confucianism would have been deeply skeptical, if not actively scornful, of the voluntary associations that comprise civil society, and it is in this context that from a Confucian perspective, all voluntary consensual associations benefited from the forbearance of the state. Consequently, from a Confucian perspective there is nothing that the state can be said to have needed from voluntary, consensual, or communal associations other than their obedient subservience, which in turn begs the question of liabilities.

Liabilities

The question of whether from a Confucian perspective civil society and the state pose liabilities for each other—or alternatively, what kinds of liabilities do rulers and ruled pose for one another?—and how these liabilities are to be averted or at least contained likewise represents a challenging speculative exercise. Inevitably we return to the creation of a private sphere—both at the level of the individual person and that of his/her voluntary associations—without which civil society (as I construe it) is unimaginable. Confucianism will necessarily view the presence of such a private sphere as a challenge to its organic, familylike view of the ideal society, and it will for this reason inevitably regard civil society as a potential liability to the paternalistic state.

To better understand the Confucian perspective, let us examine in some detail the fundamental Confucian tenet known as the rectification of names, which is actually an argument regarding the accuracy of terminology. Its locus classicus is in the *Analects*, where Duke Jing (r. 546–489 B.C.E.) of the state of Qi questions Confucius about government. Confucius is said to have replied, "Let the ruler be a ruler, the minister be a minister, the father be a father, and the son be a son." This much is well known to students of Confucianism, but less well known is the

Duke's response: "Excellent! Indeed when the ruler is not a ruler, the minister is not a minister, the father not a father, and the son not a son, although I may have all the grain, shall I ever get to eat it?"[16]

In the Confucian view of society, and as already observed, each person has an ordered place, and society may be assumed to go well when each individual correctly addresses his/her responsibilities in the context of each situation and relationship. It is the moral duty of the ruler to be the ruler—that is, to rule justly and benevolently and to give priority to the interests of his subjects over his personal profit. In a similar way, it is the moral duty of the father to be a father—that is, to preside over the affairs of his household in a manner that, like the ruler's, ensures not only that the physical requirements of his beneficiaries are met, but also that he fosters an environment in which their capacity to grow in the direction of moral goodness is addressed. Elsewhere in the *Analects* Confucius addresses this in terms suggestive of a modern perspective: "If names are not rectified, then language will not be in accord with truth. If language is not in accord with truth, then things cannot be accomplished."[17]

It would be tempting, though probably mistaken, in this context of a discussion of civil society to regard the doctrine of "rectification of names" as akin to the principle of subsidiarity. To be sure, the devolution to local entities of authority not claimed centrally was historically characteristic of the political orders of all East Asian countries. Nonetheless, from the perspective of Confucianism (as well as history), this is less a political principle than an example of the practical sharing of authority and responsibility in a manner perceived (in theory) to be conducive to advancement of the general good, and (in fact) to be consistent with the realities of power.

In a related vein, there is an element of reciprocity in the ruler-subject relationship (as in all benefactor-beneficiary relationships), and the responsibilities that thus attend it are decidedly mutual, but it is important to note that in the *Analects* these responsibilities begin with the ruler's example: "If a ruler sets himself right, he will be followed without his command. If he does not set himself right, even his commands will not be obeyed."[18] Early Confucianism emphasized the onus borne by the ruler to rule by the example of his own rectitude, and elsewhere in the *Analects* Confucius goes so far as to assert that for the survival of a state, the confidence of the people is ultimately more important than the quality of either the state's military capacities or the people's social welfare.[19] In this respect, it is noteworthy that in later imperial China, as Henry Rosemont has observed in his response to this chapter, the term for the government representative of the smallest (county) level was "father mother official" (*fu mu guan*).

Mencius (371–289 B.C.E.), whom the Chinese tradition has endorsed as Confucius's authentic interpreter, restated the perspective of the ruler's responsibility for the people's welfare in a doctrine that has come to be known as the "right of revolution." As it appears in the text that bears his name, King Xuan of Qi questions Mencius regarding whether there are any circumstances under which it is permissible for a minister to murder the king whom he serves. Mencius's answer is redolent of the earlier linguisticality of Confucius in the rectification of names: "He who injures humanity is a bandit. He who injures righteousness is a destructive person. Such a person is a mere fellow. I have heard of killing a mere fellow [like wicked King] Zhou, but I have not heard of murdering [him as] the ruler."[20] In other words, a wicked king who injures humanity or righteousness has failed to create the moral environment requisite to his people's growth in the direction of moral goodness and is for this very reason in default of the definition of a true king, making him eligible for replacement even through violence. It is also evidence of an emerging concept of "the people" in early Confucianism, though as Wm. Theodore de Bary has observed, Confucian government is government for the people rather than government by the people.[21]

Later Confucianism, however, tended to tilt the scales in favor of the state by conflating the ruler-subject relationship with that of the parent-child, in which the sense of mutuality is decidedly diminished. "Never disobey," is how Confucius summarized filial piety in the *Analects*,[22] even suggesting in one conversation that uprightness is to be found in a son's concealing the misconduct of his father,[23] and it is this understanding of filial piety that has largely animated Chinese social practice over the last thousand years and more. It is likewise this understanding of filial piety that came to serve as the basis for a Confucian redefinition of the relationship between the individual and the state.

Let us examine how an early-modern state like Tokugawa Japan used Confucian arguments to fashion an ideology in which the state's aspirations vis-à-vis its constituent members are clearly absolutist, at least during this state's first half-century of rule. As Herman Ooms has demonstrated, the Tokugawa state early on sought ideological support in a variety of places—Confucianism, Buddhism, folk religion, and so on—for the premise that its authority, which of course had its true origins in violence, was rooted in a benevolent paternalism. This ideological construction at once both effaced the contingent properties of the *bakufu*'s (central government) genesis, and articulated a rationale for an absolute authority akin to that of the father as head of household.[24] This again also represented an understanding of the state in which there was simply no room for the sorts of voluntary associations that are necessary for our understanding of civil society.

But as we have also seen, historical, social, and economic forces were already at work in seventeenth-century Japan, laying the foundation for the emergence of an individual private sphere that contended successfully with the Confucian perspective and its ideological expression. In the context of a discussion of the seventeenth-century Japanese state's policies toward religious bodies and their members, I have argued elsewhere that the Tokugawa state initially aspired toward absolute authority over the thoughts, words, and deeds of its individual members, and that the "underground" religious movements that arose at this time did so as a defensive practice. By the late 1660s, my argument continued, one also finds evidence of the state's realistic retreat from this absolutist aspiration, at least as far as the religious thoughts of its members were concerned, as it relaxed those policies which depended for their enforcement upon either the confessions of suspects or the fundamentally antisocial act of informing the authorities of the transgressions of one's neighbors. And it is in that retreat, I concluded, that one can locate the genesis of a heretofore unknown measure of individual privacy that was accorded—as privacy always is—by the state to its members for behavior the state eventually recognized as ultimately nonthreatening.[25] Furthermore, and again as I have tried to demonstrate, it was less than two decades later that the social, economic, and cultural forces of Tokugawa society contributed to the sharp increase in the volume and quality of individual transactions in the society, a change attended by the emergence of a richly diverse, commodified popular culture. These factors contributed to the individual person's integrity as a consumer and potential student of both ideology and culture, allowing in the process the formation of such volunteer associations as private not-for-profit study groups[26] and for profit academies.

Within those study groups and academies, there was an attendant change in the forms of Confucian interpretation that proved to be most popular. Where earlier "orthodox" teachings had emphasized a naturalist ontology in which the Confucian Way was perceived to be ineluctably linked to enduring first principles of both an immanent and transcendent character, by the midpoint of the eighteenth century, the historicist heterodox Confucian perspectives of Ogyū Sorai (1666–1728) win the day with their argument that the Way is simply a convenient comprehensive term for various political, legal, economic, ritual, and administrative practices that proved successful in the past and are inevitably conditioned by the circumstances of time and place.[27]

Again, Confucianism cannot be regarded as meaningfully responsible for the various transformations to Japan's seventeenth- and eighteenth-century polity discussed in this chapter, nor was the rise of the kinds of voluntary associations I have identified necessarily or inevitably destabilizing, but it is relevant to our discussion that Confucian heterodoxy was at least perceived to be part of the problem, and was addressed as such in a series of conservative "reforms" undertaken in the last years of the eighteenth century by the "Confucian" scholar-statesman Matsudaira Sadanobu (1758–1829). As the head of the Council of Elders (Rōjū) and shogunal adviser, Sadanobu addressed his "Prohibition of Heterodox Studies" to the head of the Shōheikō academy, whose commitment to orthodox Neo-Confucian interpretations was accurately perceived to have declined. Sadanobu's reforms, however, did not stop here and included such measures as: censorship of cultural productions deemed offensive to conservative Confucian morality; efforts to enlist the support of entrepreneurs and their guilds in regulating rice and precious-metal markets; the rebuilding and extension of coastal defenses to preserve Japan's isolation from European and North American representatives; a purge of the women assigned to service the shogun's pleasure, or at least those whose loyalties were suspect; sumptuary legislation that forbade the use of barbers and hairdressers and separated the sexes in heretofore mixed bathing facilities; and the sending of spies into bathhouses, brothels, and even barbershops to eavesdrop on potentially subversive discussions. Both the Confucian premises underlying these policies and their incompatibility with features of civil society are unmistakable, which, in turn, brings us to a discussion of how Confucianism would regard groups and individuals as the constituent components of a society at once both complex in its elements yet simple in its informing principles.

GROUPS AND INDIVIDUALS

From a Confucian paternalistic perspective, the state has a fundamental responsibility to interact in a socially constructive and nurturing manner with both individuals and families, but as we have already noted, the Confucian organic perspective on society left little room for the sorts of voluntary associations this chapter takes as characteristic of civil society. Let us begin by examining Confucian perspectives on the interactions between the state and the individual.

First, Confucian humanism places great responsibility on the shoulders of the individual person and regards it as the ruler's responsibility to teach individuals how to be essentially self-governing: "Lead the people with governmental measures and regulate them by law and punishment, and they will avoid wrongdoing but will have no sense of honor and shame. Lead them with virtue and regulate them by the rules of propriety (li), and they will have a sense of shame and, moreover, set themselves right."[28] At the same time, Confucianism would reject the notion of the human person as an *individual*, if by this term one means to suggest the presence of a free and autonomous self.

Confucianism fundamentally distrusts such axiomatic propositions in European and North American political culture as the "rule of law," instead preferring to foster a sense of self-worth that, it is assumed, will cause individual persons to regard any misconduct as demeaning and shameful.[29] Nonetheless, Confucianism does not suggest that, for this reason, individuals are in their solitary condition self-worthy, as others in the European classical liberal tradition have suggested. Where classical European liberalism might argue that individual integrity is akin to an inward capacity of the soul, and that persons thus enjoy an inherent measure of self-worth, Confucianism by contrast is uncompromising in its understanding of human worth as something manifested fundamentally in the context of relationship.[30]

Further, there is a clear tension between what we would nowadays regard as elitist and egalitarian principles in Confucianism. For example despite the obvious dignity accorded to individual persons in the previous quotation from the *Analects*, Confucius elsewhere in the same work asserts that commoners "may be made to follow [the Way] but may not be made to understand it," suggesting an unpromising view of the capacities of ordinary individuals.[31] Citizens not in government service "do not discuss its policies,"[32] according to Confucius, and ultimately, "[t]he character of a ruler is like the wind and that of the people is like grass. In whatever direction the wind blows, the grass always bends."[33] That there is also a cosmic dimension to the ruler's responsibilities with respect to benevolent and humane rule is unarguable, but the Confucian ruler nonetheless remains very much the paternalistic parent of the people.

This tension between egalitarian and elitist impulses is perhaps best expressed in the writings of Mencius, wherein we find Confucius's interpreter idealizing benevolent rule with remarkable imagery when he asserts that truly kingly government is found "when men of seventy [have] silk to wear and meat to eat, when the common people [are] neither hungry nor cold."[34] Mencius also clearly privileges the individual in such statements as, "All things are already complete in oneself," suggesting that the human person need not look beyond the self for the requisites of moral growth and even perfection.[35] At the same time, Mencius reinforces the vertical, inegalitarian, and organic Confucian view of the polity when he asserts: "There is the work of great men and there is the work of little men. . . . Some labor with their minds and some labor with their strength. Those who labor with their minds govern others; those who labor with their strength are governed by others. . . . This is a universal principle."[36] As disagreeable a perspective as this represents in the here-and-now, we perhaps need to remind ourselves that it is a perspective consistent with the realities of life in ancient China, as well as a perspective embraced by most enduring forms of premodern Chinese political thought.

Turning to the state's interactions with families, we have already observed the fundamental importance of the family from a Confucian perspective, but let us review the reasons for its importance from the perspective of the state. First, the family is the only social grouping discussed by Confucianism, for it is both the very laboratory in which individuals are to have their first experience with growth in the direction of goodness, and it is the site of those relationships which serve in barometer-like fashion to enable its constituent members to measure their progress (or retrogression) in this direction. We have already observed that of the five relationships on which Confucians focus, three (father/son, husband/wife, elder brother/younger brother) are to be found within the household. These relationships have a universal quality to them, and it is good to remind ourselves that unlike our current perspective on these relationships, classical Confucianism held that each of the three is a vertical and nonconsensual relationship. Second, Confucianism is remarkably specific regarding how each of the relationships is to be used in one's moral growth. Mencius credits the legendary sage Emperor Shun (third millennium B.C.E.) with appointing a minister of education to "teach people human relations, that between father and son, there should be affection; . . . between husband and wife, there should be attention to their separate functions; [and] between old and young, there should be a proper order."[37] Every relationship within the household thus provides one with daily opportunity to grow in specific moral directions. And third, the family is the most fundamental economic unit in society, and indeed from a Confucian perspective there is no context for imagining economic progress apart from that of individual households. In sum, the family emerges as the singular social unit with which the Confucian state proposes to interact.

CITIZENSHIP

Before one can address Confucian perspectives on the prerogatives and duties of citizenship, it is necessary to review the narrow understanding of citizenship in traditional—and, as will be argued, even in modern and contemporary—East Asia. If in European and North American political thought *citizenship* refers to the legal (constitutional) or quasi-legal (by common law or accepted precedent) rights and responsibilities of individuals within a state (understood as the collection of entities having a monopoly on the legitimate use of force), such was never the case with any of the premodern societies of East Asia, and even among East Asia's modern societies—all of which have constitutions of one sort or another—the matter of human, civil, and constitutional rights of citizens remains arguable, at least in practice if not in theory. Accordingly, and for the purposes of our discussion, *citizenship* is used here to refer narrowly to permanent residence in a country and membership in one of what Confucianism regarded as its traditional four classes: the ruling elite (be they intellectual, political-administrative, or military), agriculturalists, artisans, and merchants. When understood in this way, we can begin to identify both the responsibilities and the prerogatives of citizenship, so long as we recognize that the latter are to be understood more as reasonable expectations than as rights per se.

From a Confucian perspective, citizens may reasonably expect that their government will exercise constructive effort on their behalf in several fundamental areas: first, that the state will ensure that their most basic needs of food, shelter, and orderly society will be met, and that their physical well-being will be thereby assured; second, they are justified in expecting that their affairs will be administered justly and in a manner consistent with their interests and personal well-being—that is, those in authority over them will care for them as a father cares for his child; third, citizens are fundamentally entitled to an environment in which they are both encouraged by the ruler's personal example and enabled by the properties of their surroundings to grow in the direction of moral goodness; fourth, just as sons are entitled to remonstrate with their fathers, citizens are entitled to remonstrate with their state when they perceive the state to be defaulting on its responsibilities; and finally, in this early-modern context the Confucian citizen may even be entitled to a subjective measure of happiness.

The first three of these collectively constitute the essence of what Confucianism regards as humane or benevolent (Ch. *ren*) government. Though we have touched on its features variously in our discussions above, let us revisit this idealized expression of the relationship between the citizen and his state, which is perhaps most succinctly represented in Mencius's words to King Hui of Liang (r. 370–19 B.C.E.): "If Your Majesty can practice a humane government to the people, reduce punishments and fines, lower taxes and levies, make it possible for the fields to be plowed deep and the weeding well done, men of strong body, in their days of leisure may cultivate their filial piety, brotherly respect, loyalty and faithfulness, thereby serving their fathers and elder brothers at home and their elders and superiors at abroad."[38] The idealism is unmistakable, though we observe that it is tempered by the remarkable specificity of such measures as how the weeding and plowing are to proceed. We recall that it was likewise Mencius who defined the evidence of good government in terms of when "men of seventy [have] silk to wear and meat to eat, when the common people [are] neither hungry nor cold."

In a similar vein, Confucius maintained in the *Analects* (1:5) that no country can be regarded as well administered "unless the ruler attends strictly to business, punctually observes his promises, is economical in expenditure, shows affection towards his subjects in general, and uses the labor of the peasantry only at the proper times of year."[39] Here the emphasis on the ruler's effort is similarly unmistakable, indicating that Confucian governance is far more than simply a matter of harboring good intentions. And, as the seventeenth-century Confucian scholar and social critic Huang Zongxi argued, government did not emerge to bring order out of chaos, as Hobbes posited, but rather in order to overcome individual selfishness out of a concern for the common good, as in the following: "In the beginning of human life each man lived for himself and looked to his own interests. There was such a thing as the common benefit, yet no one seems to have promoted it. . . . Then someone came forth who did not think of benefit in terms of his own benefit but sought to benefit all-under-heaven."[40]

In contrast with classical Confucianism, which concentrated on these physical qualities of well-being, seventeenth- and eighteenth-century Confucianism also addressed such matters as remonstrance and happiness. Even though the *Analects* rejected the notion that individuals outside of government could "discuss its policies," later Confucians turned to what the *Analects* said about remonstrance within families to justify its application at the level of the citizen vis-à-vis the state. The locus classicus for this understanding of remonstrance appears in the context of Confucius's discussion of filial behavior: "In serving his parents, a son may gently remonstrate with them. When he sees that they are not inclined to listen to him, he should resume an attitude of reverence and not abandon his effort to please them. He may feel worried but does not complain."[41] Whether applied within the household or more broadly in the context of the citizen's relationship to the state, the message is unmistakable: when one discerns what one perceives to be wrongdoing on the part of one's superiors, one has the authority—if not actually the duty—to call this to their attention; if they agree and amend their ways, so much the better; but if they are disinclined to alter their course, then one may indeed experience disappointment, but one is not allowed to translate this disappointment into either resentment or opposition.

This principle has been variously expressed in East Asian history. For example, in China every citizen has for centuries enjoyed the right, at least in principle, to petition the government to seek redress, and from the Tang dynasty (618–907) onward the function of remonstrance was institutionalized within the bureaucracy in the Board of Censors (Yushi-tai), whose members were "officials of high prestige who had the primary duty of ferreting out cases of treason, misgovernment or maladministration and reporting them directly to the emperor."[42] This right of remonstrance continues, again at least in theory, to this day in China in its Petitions and Appeals Office on the south side of Beijing, though it is clear that for the contemporary petitioner the experience of remonstrance in China remains as frustrating and even dangerous as it was at times in the past.[43]

In Japan, one's experience with remonstrance was, if anything, variegated and inconsistent. During the early-modern period, there was an aggressive expansion of the use of remonstrance boxes at both the local (domainal) and capital levels, especially during the eighteenth century, providing important evidence for the expansion of "public spaces" within the society. Indeed, nearly two-thirds (thirty-five, or 64 percent) of Japan's fifty-five remonstrance boxes instituted prior to the Meiji Restoration of 1868 were established during the years 1721–91.[44] In Japan, just as in China, the boxes provided an opportunity for ordinary citizens in a broad range of matters to offer suggestions, to express complaints, and to present appeals, and they appear to have been used in Tokugawa Japan by members of all social classes. Nonetheless, it remained against Tokugawa law for anyone outside the government to suggest a change in national policy. One of the most extreme examples of this occurred in 1791 to the scholar Hayashi Shihei (1738–93), who proposed that Japan, being an island country, urgently needed to improve its coastal defenses. His punishment for this innocent and self-evident suggestion was a near-fatal six-month sentence in an Edo prison, a sentence meted out as part of the ideological retrenchment implemented in the Kansei "reforms" by the aforementioned culturally and socially illiberal "Confucian" statesman Matsudaira Sadanobu. In other words, "remonstrance" appears to have given one the opportunity to criticize public figures but not to propose public policy—that is, to complain but not to agitate.

Turning to the perhaps unexpected issue of whether happiness may be regarded from a Confucian perspective as one of the prerogatives of early-modern citizenship, let us turn to two examples. Writing in the early-eighteenth century, the Japanese Confucian naturalist Kaibara Ekken (1630–1714) regarded happiness (Jpn. *raku*) as part of the universal human endowment bestowed by heaven and akin to what we would call a sense of contentment.[45] This sense of happiness as a human endowment was strengthened even further by Ogyū Sorai into something akin to a human right. In the context of a discussion of the core Confucian virtue of goodness (Ch. *ren*, Jpn. *jin*), Sorai argued that it was the responsibility of the state to provide the conditions necessary for individual persons to experience "peace and contentment" (*annon*), and he maintained in near-Jeffersonian terms that such a conception of well-being included happiness: "This [*annon*, or peace and contentment] means that [the people] should be free from cold and famine and from molestation by robbers, that they should have feelings of trust in their neighbors, that they should be content to live in their country and their age, that they should find enjoyment in their various occupations, and [that they] should spend the whole of their lives in happiness (*raku*)."[46] Sorai's stance represents a remarkably comprehensive yet succinct statement of the conditions for human well-being from a Confucian perspective, and it is significant for our purposes here that happiness in this context appears to be no less fundamental than hearth, home, community, and vocation as elements that citizens are entitled to expect from their government.

In all of these ways, what we observe is that Confucianism endorses a broad range of expectations on the part of those who are governed. The physical properties of their well-being were the principal concern of classical Confucianism, but during the early-modern period, when public spaces were at the very least opened if not actually broadened, these expectations were expanded to include both the opportunity to express dissent and the prerogative of a fundamentally psychological sense of contentment. Having raised this issue of contentment, let us now turn to its inverse, or conflict.

CONFLICT

Confucianism has little to say about conflict, but this relative silence notwithstanding, it is not particularly difficult to imagine how Confucianism might seek to handle the conflicting demands of citizenship and voluntary membership or participation in associations outside the family or one's community of faith. Because of the benevolent paternalism Confucianism expects from a state, a Confucian perspective will inevitably favor the state in any adversarial proceeding with voluntary associations. We have already seen an example of this from Japanese history in Matsudaira Sadanobu's Prohibition of Heterodox Studies, in which the Japanese *bakufu* sought to exercise ideological censorship over academic enterprises (or at least those that enjoyed the state's patronage) branded as heterodox and hence as potentially destabilizing. It perhaps goes without saying that from a Confucian perspective, such conflict should not arise in the first place, and that the conflict itself constitutes prima facie evidence of the private entity's wrongdoing.

Less clear is how Confucianism would view a conflict between a family and the state. On the one hand, one can find evidence to support the view that a well-ordered family can never be in conflict with a well-ordered state, as when Confucius's student Youzi (538–457 B.C.E.) is quoted as having said, "Few of those who are filial sons and respectful brothers will show disrespect to superiors, and there has never been a man who is not disrespectful to superiors and yet creates disorder."[47] On the other hand, we have already observed the example of the upright Kung who is condemned by Confucius in the *Analects* (13:18) for having borne witness against his father, who stole a sheep. In this passage, it will be recalled, Confucius applauds the uprightness of fathers and sons who conceal each other's wrongdoing; historically, a major challenge for all states in East Asia has been overcoming the centripetal impulses of clans, villages, and other entities that posit their own interests in juxtaposition with those of the state. Confucianism unambiguously affirms the interests of households as well as the interests of the state, but entities between the two fare less well. Its approach to resolution of such conflict has traditionally been to articulate a commonality of interests expressed in transcendent principles, rather than to seek institutional means to balance conflicting interests.

Finally, like many traditions, classical Confucianism postulates the existence of an idealized realm in the remote past—a kind of ancient unconflicted terrestrial paradise characterized by universal harmony and peace from which humankind has fallen but that can nonetheless be resurrected in the here and now—and in such concepts as the rectification of names, one sees an implicit acknowledgment of the imperfect nature of society. It is the nature of this process of rectification that all individuals engage in an ongoing collective effort to improve society one person at a time, one household at a time, and eventually one state at a time. Thus from a Confucian perspective, all private and voluntary associations will necessarily be subordinate to the broader goal of creating a kind of heaven on earth.

Confucianism and Civil Society in Present-Day East Asia

By way of conclusion let us revisit the question asked at the outset, of whether one can discern even now in East Asia the kinds of voluntary associations that so prominently characterize civil society in its European and North American settings. As it happens, the question is by no means simple, and there is a vigorous and lively debate on this topic going on at this very moment.[48]

In a recent and important study of Japanese civilization, the sociologist S. N. Eisenstadt has suggested that more than other (post-)modern societies, Japanese society coheres as a result of the remarkably high levels of trust that exist horizontally at the level of the community, and vertically in terms of one's relationship with the state, with one's employer, and so on.[49] And like many other observers of contemporary Japan, Professor Eisenstadt locates the roots of this trust in the priority Confucianism attaches to maintaining correct relationships, both horizontally between persons and vertically between rulers and their subjects.

Nonetheless, events such as the Kōbe earthquake of January 1995, the sarin gas attack in the Tokyo subway system in March of that same year, and the Japanese government's inability during the 1990s to effect those economic reforms necessary to pull Japan out of the most prolonged recession in its modern history have combined to undermine the citizen's confidence in the state, and have made the citizen a far more discerning and discriminating consumer of state ideology than even just a decade ago. In the case of the earthquake, the state appeared to many Japanese citizens curiously inept in fulfilling its most basic responsibilities toward those who suffered loss, hardship, or injury.[50] Similarly with the sarin gas attacks of that same spring, the inability of Japan's civil and military forces of order to provide reasonable assurances of safety to commuters, shoppers, students, and the like suggested to many persons in Japan uncomfortably clear limits in a heretofore seemingly omnicompetent state. And in the economic realm Japan's prolonged economic slowdown of the 1990s as well as the government's apparent paucity of plausible ideas in the realm of either political economy or possible solutions to its micromanaged economy have undermined many citizens' confidence in the government's long-standing exhortation to sacrifice the needs of the present to the hopes of tomorrow. These factors have contributed to a crisis of confidence and breakdown of trust in Japan at the turn of the millennium that are all the more striking when we recall Ogyū Sorai's Confucian sense of *annon*, whereby the people "should be free from cold and famine and from molestation by robbers, . . . should have feelings of trust in their neighbors, . . . should be content to live in their country and their age, . . . should find enjoyment in their various occupations, and . . . should spend the whole of their lives in happiness."

Though sources of information for China are more limited than for Japan, it is evident that comparable phenomena are likewise contributing to a breakdown in whatever remains of the citizen's confidence in government to assure personal well-being. Probably the most dramatic examples of this at the level of the ordinary citizen are the widely reported instances of environmental degradation, which have apparently become common throughout rural China, and the breakdown in the Maoist social safety net as the modernization effort sacrifices the interests of individuals to the interests of the state.

At the same time, however, issues such as the environment are serving as catalysts for the formation of not-for-profit citizen movements, including philanthropic enterprises, watchdog groups, grass-roots organizations and so on, in both Japan and China, and are thereby further opening the space that I have argued in this chapter was initially opened by such entities as the private academy.[51] Whether this is further evidence of the end of history, as some would argue, it does suggest that as the integrity of the individual person is being buttressed on various fronts throughout the world, and as the private sphere of individual persons allows for their greater participation in public spaces, then the most basic features of civil society are likely to become increasingly common in formerly Confucian societies, just as they have elsewhere.

NOTES

I wish to thank Professors Marshall Cohen, Richard Madsen, Henry Rosemont, and Conrad Schirokauer, as well as the members of the Columbia University Seminar in Neo-Confucian Studies, for exceptionally helpful comments on earlier drafts of this essay.

1. For a more expansive perspective on civil society, see Michael Walzer's liberal-egalitarian perspective on civil society in *Alternative Conceptions of Civil Society*, eds. Simone Chambers and Will Kymlicka (Princeton: Princeton University Press, 2001). My differences with Professor Walzer notwithstanding, I have found his perspectives on civil society especially helpful in shaping my own.

2. See Sannosuke Matsumoto, "Nakae Chōmin and Confucianism," in *Confucianism and Tokugawa Culture*, ed. Peter Nosco (Honolulu: University of Hawai'i Press, 1997), 251–66. For a richly nuanced discussion of Confucian perspectives on Chinese law, especially dynastic law, and their implications for civil society in China, see Wm. Theodore de Bary, *Asian Values and Human Rights: A Confucian Communitarian Perspective* (Cambridge: Harvard University Press, 1998), esp. 90–117.

3. The other defining characteristics of East Asia as a cultural sphere are the use of Chinese characters, a tradition of Mahayana Buddhism, and an appreciation for China's centrality within the region.

4. See Rodney L. Taylor, "The Religious Character of the Confucian Tradition," *Philosophy East and West* 48, no. 1 (1998): 80–107.

5. See, for example, Wm. Theodore de Bary and Tu Weiming, eds., *Confucianism and Human Rights* (New York: Columbia University Press, 1997); and

Mary Evelyn Tucker and John Berthrong, eds., *Confucianism and Ecology: The Interrelation of Heaven, Earth, and Humans* (Cambridge: Harvard University Press, 1998).

6. Alida Brill argues that privacy is inevitably *"granted* to an individual only when others agree to honor [it], be it by compliance with the law or community custom" (emphasis added). *Nobody's Business: Paradoxes of Privacy* (Reading, Mass.: Addison-Wesley Publishing Co., 1990), xvi. For an interesting discussion of the distinction between selfishness and legitimate interests published after this essay originally went to press, see Stephen C. Angle, *Human Rights and Chinese Thought: A Cross-Cultural Perspective* (New York: Cambridge University Press, 2002).

7. Wing-tsit Chan, ed., *A Source Book in Chinese Philosophy* (Princeton: Princeton University Press, 1963), 86–87.

8. For a wide-ranging discussion of early modernity, see "Early Modernities," a special issue of *Daedalus* 127, no. 3 (Summer 1998). On Japan's early-modern transformation in the seventeenth and eighteenth centuries, see John Whitney Hall, introduction to *The Cambridge History of Japan*, vol. 4, *Early Modern Japan* (Cambridge: Cambridge University Press, 1991), esp. 1–6.

9. In Wm. Theodore de Bary, *Waiting for the Dawn: A Plan for the Prince—Huang Tsung-hsi's Ming-i tai-fang lu* (New York: Columbia University Press, 1993), 104.

10. On Ito Jinsai's Kogidō, see Richard Rubinger, *Private Academies of Tokugawa Japan* (Princeton: Princeton University Press, 1982), 49–56. Indeed, there was such a proliferation of private schools in Japan during the late seventeenth and eighteenth centuries that the humorist Ihara Saikaku (1642–93) inveighed against the ease with which untutored "crooks" could pass themselves off as experts and establish private schools where they duped the unwitting. See Ihara Saikaku, *Some Final Words of Advice*, trans. Peter Nosco (Rutland, Vt.: Charles E. Tuttle Publishing Co., 1980), 131.

11. The following argument is developed in greater detail in my *Remembering Paradise: Nativism and Nostalgia in Eighteenth-Century Japan* (Cambridge: Harvard University, Council on East Asian Studies, 1990), 15–40.

12. See the transcript of his lecture "The Foundations of Liberalism," in *Seminar Reports* 5, no. 1 (1976), Columbia University Program of General Education in the Humanities.

13. From the *Sentetsu Sōdan* of Hara Masaru (1760–1820), quoted in Masao Maruyama, *Studies in the Intellectual History of Tokugawa Japan*, trans. Mikiso Hane (Tokyo: Tokyo University Press, 1974), 115.

14. See two articles by Donald H. Shively, first his *"Bakufu* vs. *Kabuki"* in *Studies in the Institutional History of Early Modern Japan*, eds. John W. Hall and Marius B. Jansen (Princeton: Princeton University Press, 1968); and second, "Popular Culture" in Hall, *The Cambridge History of Japan* 4: 749–61.

15. I am indebted to Henry Rosemont for this perspective on Confucianism's five relationships, which have more commonly been expressed in terms of superiors and subordinates. See his "Classical Confucianism and Contemporary Feminist Thought: Some Parallels and their Implications," in *Culture and Self*, ed. Douglas Allen (Boulder, Colo.: Westview, 1997).

44 PETER NOSCO

16. Chan, *Source Book*, 39 (*Analects* 12:11).

17. Ibid., 40 (*Analects* 13:3).

18. Ibid., 41 (*Analects* 13:6).

19. Ibid., 39 (*Analects* 12:7).

20. Ibid., 62 (*Mencius* 1B:8).

21. Quoted with permission. For a related discussion, see also Wm. Theodore de Bary, *The Trouble with Confucianism* (Cambridge: Harvard University Press, 1991), 17–21, 37–38, 94–103.

22. Chan, *Source Book*, 23 (*Analects* 2:5).

23. Ibid., 41 (*Analects* 13:18). In this passage, Confucius is discussing with the Duke of She the merits of a man named Kung who bore witness against his father for stealing a sheep. Confucius is quoted as having said, "The upright men in my community are different from this. The father conceals the misconduct of the son and the son conceals the misconduct of the father. Uprightness is to be found in this."

24. See Herman Ooms, "Neo-Confucianism and the Formation of Early Tokugawa Ideology: Contours of a Problem," in Nosco, *Confucianism and Tokugawa Culture*, 27–61.

25. See my "Keeping the Faith: *Bakuhan* Policy towards Religions in Seventeenth-Century Japan," in *Religion in Japan: Arrows to Heaven and Earth*, eds. P. F. Kornicki and I. J. McMullen (Cambridge: Cambridge University Press, 1996), 135–55. For the distinction between privacy and secrecy, see Carol Warren and Barbara Laslett, "Privacy and Secrecy: A Conceptual Comparison," in *Secrecy: A Cross-Cultural Perspective*, ed. Stanton K. Tefft (New York: Human Sciences Press, 1980), 25–34.

26. Itō Jinsai's (1627–1705) Dōshikai (Society of the Like-Minded), which later grew into his Kogidō academy, would be just one example.

27. This, of course, is a much simplified version of the argument found in Maruyama's *Studies in the Intellectual History of Tokugawa Japan*. For a sophisticated and sensitive engagement of the Sorai school, see Tetsuo Najita, ed., *Tokugawa Political Writings* (Cambridge: Cambridge University Press, 1998).

28. Chan, *Source Book*, 22 (*Analects* 2:3).

29. Again, see de Bary, *Asian Values and Human Rights*, esp. 30–40.

30. I wish to thank Professor Steve Scalet for his help with this insight.

31. Chan, *Source Book*, 33 (*Analects* 8:9).

32. Ibid., 34 (*Analects* 8:14).

33. Ibid., 40 (*Analects* 12:19).

34. Ibid., 61 (*Mencius* 1A:7).

35. Ibid., 79 (*Mencius* 7A:4).

36. Ibid., 69 (*Mencius* 3A:4).

37. Ibid.

38. Ibid., 61 (*Mencius* 1A:5).

39. *The Analects of Confucius*, translated and annotated by Arthur Waley (New York: Vintage Books, 1989), 84.

40. de Bary, *Waiting for the Dawn*, 91.

41. Chan, *Source Book*, 28 (*Analects* 4:18).

42. Edwin O. Reischauer and John K. Fairbank, *East Asia: The Great Tradition* (Boston: Houghton Mifflin, 1960), 168. Charles O. Hucker has argued that the functions of remonstrance and surveillance were conflated during the Ming dynasty in China. See his "Confucianism and the Chinese Censorial System," in *Confucianism in Action*, ed. David Nivison (Stanford, Calif.: Stanford University Press, 1959), 182–208.

43. See Erik Eckholm, "Please, Mr. Bureaucrat, Hear My 20-Year-Old Plea," *New York Times* (national ed.), December 7, 1998, A-4.

44. On remonstrance boxes, see Luke S. Roberts, *Mercantilism in a Japanese Domain: The Merchant Origins of Economic Nationalism in Eighteenth-Century Tosa* (Cambridge: Cambridge University Press, 1998), 103–33.

45. On Ekken, see Mary Evelyn Tucker, *Moral and Spiritual Cultivation in Japanese Neo-Confucianism: The Life and Thought of Kaibara Ekken, 1630–1714* (Albany: State University of New York Press, 1989).

46. J. R. McEwan, *The Political Writings of Ogyū Sorai* (Cambridge: Cambridge University Press, 1962), 9; and Sakimoto Seiichi, *Nihon keizai taiten* (Tokyo: Meiji Bunken, 1969), 9:213.

47. Chan, *Source Book*, 19–20 (*Analects* 1:2).

48. See, for example, the website, http://www.us-japan.org/dc/cs, for papers presented in a series of workshops titled "Civil Society in Japan (and America): Coping with Change."

49. S. N. Eisenstadt, *Japanese Civilization: A Comparative View* (Chicago: University of Chicago Press, 1996). For the contrarian perspective, i.e., that the "general level of trust is higher among Americans than among Japanese" (130), see Toshio Yamagishi and Midori Yamagishi, "Trust and Commitment in the United States and Japan," *Motivation and Emotion* 18, no. 2 (June 1994): 129–66.

50. Bureaucratic paralysis "was blamed for needlessly inflating the death toll of 6,425." See the Associated Press report at cnn.com/world/asiapcf/9904/04/am-Lessons of Kobe.ap/index.html.

51. See, for example, the papers by Victoria Lynn Bestor, Katsuji Imata, and Masayuki Deguchi posted to the "Civil Society in Japan (and America)" website (above, n. 48).

Chapter Three

CIVIL SOCIETY, GOVERNMENT, AND CONFUCIANISM: A COMMENTARY[1]

~

HENRY ROSEMONT, JR.

In these remarks I should like to both compliment and complement Peter Nosco's "Confucian Perspectives on Civil Society and Government," adding a few perspectives of my own.

First, importantly, I believe Professor Nosco correctly reads the classical Confucian canon as describing the ultimate goal of human life as developing oneself most fully as a human being to become a *junzi* or, at the pinnacle of development, a *sheng ren*, or sage. And he is equally incisive in suggesting that treading the path (*dao*) of this human way (*ren dao*) must ultimately be understood as a *religious* quest, even though the canon speaks not of God, nor of creation, salvation, an immortal soul, or a transcendental realm of being. (And no prophecies will be found in its pages either.)

The importance of the ultimately *religious* nature of Confucianism must, I believe, be underscored, for several reasons. First, it has often been claimed that Confucianism is not a religion at all, but merely a code of deportment, and an elitist one at that. Kant is perhaps not atypical here: "Confucius teaches in his writings nothing outside a doctrine designed for the princes. . . . But a concept of virtue or morality never entered the heads of the Chinese."[2] More charitably, others have maintained that Confucianism can be seen as a "civil religion,"[3] but this, too, does not get at the core of what the classical writings are about.

A second reason for emphasizing the religious nature of Confucianism is that it brings together what the Master and his successors have to say about the aesthetic, sociopolitical, and moral dimensions of our all-too-human lives. Even a cursory reading of the classical texts shows clearly the necessity of our disciplining ourselves to lead *integrated* lives if and as we tread a path seeking meaning and satisfaction in our lives.[4]

To further appreciate Nosco's insight, I would add to it by suggesting that classical Confucianism is very probably the most socially oriented of all philosophical or religious traditions, East or West. Humans can develop their humanity and strive to achieve sagehood *only* through their interactions with other human beings. For Confucius I am not a free, autonomous, individual self; rather am I more foundationally a son, husband, father, friend, teacher, student, neighbor, colleague, and so forth. And I am *living*, not *playing*, these roles. When all of the human relationships in which I stand with others have been specified, and their interrelationships have been made clear, then I have been fully described as fundamentally a co-member of several overlapping communities. Such a person, clearly, will have little left over with which to piece together a free, autonomous, individual self.

Of course it would be absurd to claim that we are not social beings, but our sociality is at best peripheral in modern Western political and moral theory: From Hobbes to Rawls, the ultimate grounding for the major philosophical arguments is that we are free, rational, autonomous individuals. Our actual lives as deeply embedded social beings are equally ignored in the search for universal moral principles. In calculating the greatest happiness or ascertaining a generalizable maxim, I must *not*, as a moral agent, take into account the concrete particularity of the moral patient(s) toward whom I may have an obligation; they are one and all simply other free, rational, autonomous individuals.[5]

Now if it is free, autonomous individuals who come together in voluntary association—and thus form civil society—it follows that there will not be any voluntary associations of this kind in early Confucian thought (although there were some in practice, a point to which I will return).

Thus far my remarks pertain only to the classical Confucian tradition, not its Neo-Confucian successor, nor to the interpretations made of Neo-Confucian thinkers by their later Tokugawa counterparts in Japan. It is useful to essay a sweep of several of the historical dimensions of the entire Confucian tradition as Professor Nosco has done, but both the Song Neo-Confucians and Tokugawa scholars were very different from their classical predecessors, and it is the latter, I believe, who are most different from ourselves, and hence—to my mind at least—of greatest interest in contemplating alternatives to contemporary Western liberalism—and conservatism, too.

For example, Nosco both quotes and comments on Ogyū Sorai's reading of Confucianism as leading to happiness. Now this may well be a legitimate construal of the canon, but it is a stretch, because happiness is not described or discussed in the classical texts at any length. We seek contentment in our lives, but unlike the Greeks, happiness—either sensual or cognitive—is not a goal toward which the Master tells us to consciously strive, and it certainly was not a goal of any of the early Confucians to acquire property (although they could and often did so), which is what Jefferson was about when he replaced Locke's "Estates" with "the pursuit of happiness." (Sorai's predecessor, Kaibara Ekken, was closer to the classical tradition when he discussed the human ability to achieve a sense of contentment.)

Similarly for the Song Neo-Confucians, Nosco says of them that they "posited the equality of both natural principles and moral principles," and he is correct on this score. But Zhu Xi, the most famous and influential of the Neo-Confucians, lived a millennium and a half after Confucius, and his China was very different from the land of the Master. It had grown greatly in size and population, had developed economically and politically, had many urban centers, and had been deeply influenced for nine hundred years by the originally alien tradition of Buddhism. This later tradition does speak of deities, of creation, salvation, a transcendental realm of being, and a free, autonomous self (or, more strictly speaking ontologically, non-self).

Buddhism is replete with principles, and Zhu Xi formulated other principles to counter the Buddhist challenge. And he had interpretive license to do so, but he too had to stretch, because, in the sense of the term "principle," as used in contemporary political theory and moral philosophy, there are few, if any, principles to be found in the classical canon. The term *li*, usually translated as "principle," is central to Neo-Confucianism, but it rarely appears in any of the Classics, and when it does, it has more of its original meaning of "pattern," not "principle." In order to justify their interpretations, the Neo-Confucians equated *li* with *dao*, and while it may well be philosophically legitimate to do so, it was not done by the early Confucians. We will better appreciate and understand the latter philosophically if we see them as unprincipled amoralists; or so I have argued elsewhere.[6]

Thus, while Kant surely gave the Confucian writings a stalwartly chauvinistic reading, he was correct in saying the Master "knew nothing of morality," if morality is defined as requiring universal principles for action. The early Confucians did not do this, instead instructing us in how to learn how to do what was fitting, or appropriate, for the situation at hand; but contra Kant, this, too, might be considered as belonging to the ethical realm, perhaps all the more so as the instructions were also spiritual in nature. Again, then, it is the early Confucians who challenge most basically many common assumptions of modern Western liberalism; hence my focus on them. Against this too-hurried background sketch, let me turn briefly now to each of the six foci of Nosco's essay.

BOUNDARIES

Professor Nosco is right, I believe, in maintaining that the question of drawing boundaries between civil society and the state is not a meaningful one for classical Confucians. I would quarrel with his statement, however, that there were no voluntary associations in ancient China, and hence no civil society distinct from a government.

There were such voluntary associations, one of which is clearly reflected in the *Analects* itself: the association of Confucius and his disciples, who lived, studied, worked, and traveled together. After his death, at least three of the disciples formed associations of their own, as did several of their disciples in turn. And there were associations—schools—of Daoists, Legalists, and Mohists as well. Moreover, beginning at least as early as the Former Han, Daoist-inspired secret societies were forming, surely as voluntary associations (and according to legend if not historical fact, secret societies were often threats to the ruling dynasty).

But Nosco's point remains, because while there were indeed some voluntary associations in ancient China, the canon is absolutely silent about any philosophical or religious import they might have.

NEEDS

If the goal of human life is to develop one's humanity to the utmost, and this is to be done through enhancing and extending human relationships, then we have a clear criterion for measuring the worth of those groups to which each person belongs (family, clan, village, school, state, and human race): to what extent does each of these groups conduce to everyone's efforts to fully realize (make real) their potential? The several groups to which each of us belong need one another: the state cannot perform many of the functions conducive to human development that the family, clan, and village perform (most relationships are familial or collegial), but there are necessary ingredients—especially economic—of well-being that small groupings cannot realize on their own: repairing dikes, ditches, and roads, distributing grain from bumper harvest to famine areas, establishing academies, and the like. As a semi-aside, the idea that groups are to be evaluated by the criterion of enabling personal growth lets us see how Confucians might condemn the present Chinese government for incarcerating dissidents, and do so without recourse to the language of human rights principles. We rightly deplore the treatment of dissidents, but do so on the grounds that the government has violated the basic human rights of free, autonomous individuals. A Confucian, however—assuming that

the dissidents are indeed patriots and neither self-seeking nor traitorous—
would condemn the government on the grounds that remonstrance is
obligatory, and that preventing the dissidents from interacting with their
fellows denies them the opportunity of continuing to develop toward the
goal of becoming exemplary persons (*junzi*); universal human rights language would not be needed.

LIABILITIES

If the boundaries question is not one addressed within the Confucian
tradition, then neither is the liabilities question. Nosco is correct in this
section of his chapter when he says that Confucianism describes "an
organic, familylike view of the ideal society." Indeed, in later imperial
China, the term for the government representative at the smallest (county)
level was "father mother official" (*fu mu guan*).

I would soften, however, Nosco's claim that Confucians would necessarily see voluntary associations as a challenge to their views of the ideal
society. If such an association provided a means for interactively furthering one's humanity in ways that other groups did not, and helped us help
others in furthering their humanity, I believe they would strongly endorse such as association (my reading on this score is of course speculative, as is Nosco's; the classical texts are altogether silent on the matter).

I would also quarrel with respect to Nosco's translation of *Analects*
12:11 on the rectification of names. The use of the copula, and the italics with it, strongly suggests a stative orientation. But there are no copu-
las in classical Chinese, and hence a more accurate translation of the
passage would read: "The ruler [must] rule, the minister, minister, the
father, father, and the son, son." (This, too, is strictly speaking inaccurate, because there are no definite articles in classical Chinese either.)[7]

This is not a minor point. Some general philosophical views are not
made explicit in any tradition, but are rather sedimented in the grammar of the language used to articulate those views. Apart from context,
Chinese graphs cannot be put into standard grammatical categories of
noun, adjective, verb, adverb, and so on. It is more a language of relations and events than a language of things and states. In English we fully
understand "rulers must rule," and "ministers minister." There is a shift
of meaning for "fathers must father"—where the verb means "to sire"
rather than "to parent"—and "son, son" is positively ungrammatical.

For myself, "The son [must] son" gives us an insight into what Confucius was about, its grating character in English notwithstanding. A theme
that permeates the entire *Analects* is filial piety, and Confucius insists
that his disciples must always engage in the activity of "sonning"—even

after their parents have died, for the religious quality of their lives depends on it. In sum, Confucians are never being, they are always doing.

GROUPS AND INDIVIDUALS

Throughout his chapter, Nosco rightly emphasizes the centrality of the family in the Confucian tradition, as when he says, "[The family] is . . . the laboratory in which individuals are to have their first experience with growth in the direction of goodness." I would, however, replace his "individuals" with "persons," because it is more philosophically neutral; if we read "individuals" as free, autonomous selves, we will not find any such in the classical texts. If I am the sum of the roles I live, then I am not truly living except when I am active in the company of others. As Confucius himself said, "I cannot herd with the birds and beasts. If I do not live in the midst of other persons, how can I live?" (18.6).

While this view may seem strange to us, it is actually straightforward: in order to *be* a friend, neighbor, or lover, for example, I must *have* a friend, neighbor, or lover. Other persons are not merely accidental or incidental to my achieving personhood and struggling for goodness, they are essential therefore; indeed, they confer personhood on me, for to the extent that I define myself as a teacher, students are necessary to my life, not incidental to it. The most succinct statement of this view was given by Herbert Fingarette: "For Confucius, unless there are at least two human beings, there are no human beings."[8] (Note in this regard also that while Confucianism is, in my opinion, correctly characterized as religious, there are no monks, nuns, anchorites, or hermits to be found in the tradition.)

To summarize this woefully brief account of Confucian perspectives on groups and individuals: for Confucians, it is relationships with groupings "all the way down."[9]

CITIZENSHIP

With voluntary associations and civil society playing no role in Confucian thought, issues surrounding citizenship cannot arise; there is no term in classical Chinese that has anywhere near the range of meanings of the English *citizen*, nor its Latin root, *civis*. I believe Nosco agrees, for in this section on citizenship, he focuses on the concept of happiness, and on this theme I have little to say beyond what I said in adumbrated form earlier.[10]

We can, however, perhaps see citizenship somewhat differently if we attend to a passage in the *Analects* that Nosco cites earlier, a passage wherein Confucius says that uprightness in a son requires that he conceal the misconduct of his father from the authorities. He (Confucius) is thus unequivocal in answering the vexing question of whether one's highest loyalty is to the family or the state; the state loses every time. Similarly, we might also note that Socrates accepts straightforwardly that Euthyphro is going to prosecute a case at law but is astonished when he finds out the accused is Euthyphro's father.[11] But for Confucius, the question does not seem to be vexing at all; nor do we find anywhere else in the *Analects* or other early Confucian texts a discussion of a conflict situation, the final topic to be discussed herein.

CONFLICT

If, as I earlier claimed, there are no universal principles—especially moral or political principles—given in the classical texts, then obviously there cannot be any moral or political principles that conflict with one another (there is no term in classical Chinese that is even roughly analogous to *dilemma*). There is always an answer to the question, What should I do? But it will vary from situation to situation, and it will not invoke principles.

In order to make progress along the *ren dao*, human Way of the Confucians, we must fulfill the manifold obligations attendant on the roles we live. To be filial, I must son; to be a good friend I must friend; and to be a teacher, teach. It is by way of doing, and by following exemplars, and becoming one myself that I progress. Principles are not necessary for this progress, for the more I mature, the more able I will be to do what is fitting or appropriate in my interpersonal relationships based simply on experiences, and reflections thereon. As Nosco correctly observes in this connection, "Confucianism has little to say about conflict."

I am pleased that Nosco has abandoned the terms "superiors" and "subordinates" when describing the basic Confucian relationships, using "benefactors" and "beneficiaries" instead, which deepens our insight into the classical Confucian vision of human flourishing. I am largely beneficiary of my teachers, benefactor to my students (although these situations can work in reverse as well; I often benefit profoundly from my students). When young I was beneficiary of my parents; when old, my brother and I became benefactors. And although there is no time or space to elaborate here, this notion of benefactor/beneficiary can also be used to analyze relations between neighbors, siblings, colleagues, friends, and much more. I am benefactor of my friend when she needs my help, beneficiary when I need hers.[12] And of course there is a profound satisfaction that attends being a benefactor to one who has been a benefactor to you.

One untoward way of construing the Confucian vision on this score has been to allow persons, when they are in a benefactor position, to be not only authoritative in fulfilling their responsibilities, but authoritarian as well, and to use beneficiaries for their own ends. Chinese history is no less replete with despotic rulers, corrupt or incompetent officials or both, exploitative parents, dull pedants, and so forth, than the West. But these kinds of people are uniformly condemned in the classical texts, and just as we lose aesthetic, moral, and spiritual insight from the Bible if we focus solely on the Crusades, Inquisition, and Thirty Years' War, so too will we lose the aesthetic, moral, and spiritual insights and ideals of the early Confucian canon if we focus solely on its subversion by authoritarians.

Naïvely perhaps, the early Confucians do not seem to have worried overmuch about abuses of the benefactor relation, but they did have a theoretical reason for the lack of concern: I only make progress along the Way by fulfilling my roles, and a part of that fulfillment must be to assist the other in making progress along the Way, too. And because I am defined by my relationships, then, to whatever extent I help you flourish, I flourish as well; and hence, by exploiting you I diminish you, and hence I diminish myself. On this point if no other, Confucius would concur with Kant (although for *very* different reasons) that we are never to use another human being as a means only.

There is much more to say on behalf of studying the classical Confucius tradition in order to illuminate contemporary problems of morals, politics, and religion. I have said nothing in detail about spiritual progress or the importance of ritual, for example. And I have been altogether silent on the thoroughgoing sexism that characterized classical and imperial China, and the homophobia that characterizes the country right down to the present. But there is much that could be said on these matters if time (and space) permitted[13]; classical Confucianism is, to my mind, of great relevance today, especially as a viable alternative to the modern Western liberal tradition, so deeply grounded in individuals that communities are always suspect as confining, conformist, constraining, stifling the human spirit.

My claim that classical Confucianism is of great relevance today will surely and correctly be challenged by everyone who believes the modern nation-state, more or less as it exists in the capitalist industrial democracies, must be taken as a given in any realistic theorizing about politics or morality. Given the multiethnic nature of most nations today, and given the awesome power the governments of these states can exercise over their citizens, it is essential to have, for example, universal principles, human rights language, and more, to serve as conceptual checks on majority or governmental oppression.

I do not undervalue the importance of this orientation, or impugn the motives of most of its advocates, but one may also come from the other way: if there is much in Confucianism that speaks to the human condition; if it provides a way to lead an integrated life while contributing to the integration of the lives of others; if it cherishes what is good from the past yet is attentive to the needs of the present; if it shows us how the secular can become sacred; if it does these things *and* if it is true that such lives are becoming impossible to lead in contemporary individualistically oriented capitalist nation-states, then another conclusion suggests itself: we must begin to alter significantly the economic and political structures of contemporary nation-states, beginning with, and especially the United States.

Now it may seem that in order to make this argument I, too, must appeal to universal principles, or human rights language, or the concept of the free, rational, autonomous individual, or to all three, none of which can be found in the Chinese texts. Let me therefore conclude with one final example of the Confucian persuasion, one that poses (seeming) conflict, with respect to government.

One obligation of the Confucian *junzi*—exemplary person—is to assume an official position if called upon to do so, after which the ruler becomes second in importance only to one's parents; unswerving loyalty is demanded. Hence we can easily construct a seeming conflict situation: What is a moral minister to do when serving an evil ruler? If we are seeking principles—universal principles—to answer this question, then we are indeed in conflict.

But let us follow Confucius in his insistence that we look for moral exemplars from the past for guidance in our progress along the way. Two such culture heroes were King Wen and his son, King Wu. King Wen—his name means "polished," "cultured," "decorative," and now means "literature"—was a vassal of a thoroughly rotten Shang Dynasty emperor. He remained loyal, regularly remonstrating with the emperor (at some risk) to change his ways. He died unsuccessful in his efforts. King Wu—the name means "martial"—thereupon overthrew the Shang and established the most long-lived of all Chinese dynasties, the Zhou (1050–256 B.C.E.).

Thus the canon resolves the conflict.[14] If it does not seem to, we must keep in mind that again, there are no universal moral or political principles in classical Confucianism, and keep equally in mind that we are always acting, either as benefactors or beneficiaries, with specific others, then we can appreciate that for Confucians, the moral challenge question is never simply, What did you do? But rather is: What did you do, with whom, when? I am always to do what is appropriate with respect to the person(s) I am interacting with at a particular time. The unit of moral analysis in Confucianism is never the action, but the interaction between two or more human beings temporally situated.

Hence, I better live my roles as I better get to know the others with whom I interact, and the more interactions there are, the more I will get to know about myself.

Thus, as a moral minister, I must ask myself, just how bad is this ruler I am now serving? Is he beyond the pale? Might he be reformable? If so, do *I* have the requisite qualities necessary to reform him? Depending on which way the answers are given, my responsibility in my role as minister will be to continue to serve, with King Wen as my exemplar, or my responsibility as a follower of the Way will oblige me at the least to resign, or at the most to raise the flag of rebellion, following King Wu. Either way, there are neither moral principles nor moral conflicts; but in both cases there is both reasonable reflection, and consequent appropriate behavior, which we *could* consider political and moral (and as leading to the spiritual), if we extended the scope of the political and moral beyond what is generally circumscribed as the general boundaries of most contemporary Western political and moral theories.

Nosco concludes his essay with the observation that contemporary events, especially the internationalization of the market, will inevitably "buttress the integrity of the individual person" in Asia and elsewhere in the Third World. He may be right in this, but I hope not. The U.S. political, economic, and legal systems have been buttressing the autonomous self of American citizens to the point that it is becoming increasingly difficult even to think of ourselves as anything but consuming atoms, whose primary obligation is to do work we do not enjoy in order to buy things we do not need. And we must do all of this in a world of increasing economic inequality because of the depredations of transnational corporations whose relentless search for profits we are increasingly unable to check, because these corporations, too, are treated as autonomous individual selves in the legal system, and their political influence is so great we abandon political life. This sense of anomie is not altogether new; the poet A. E. Housman captured its essence with the lines, "And here am I / alone and afraid / in a world / I never made."[15] If we should lose the vision of human beings as relational selves, as essentially comembers of communities without which we cannot flourish, it will be a great loss indeed, which no civil society, voluntary association, or government, will ever be able to replace. And it is on this basis that I commend the texts of classical Confucianism to all people of goodwill concerned about the human condition in its present forms.

NOTES

1. This essay is an expanded version of one that originally appeared together with Peter Nosco's in *Civil Society and Government,* edited by Nancy

L. Rosenblum and Robert C. Post (Princeton: Princeton University Press, 2002). Then and now, the constraints of space and demands of a commentary have necessitated advancing some controversial claims in almost telegraphic form. Consequently I have made an embarrassingly large number of references to my own writings herein, where these claims have been put forward and argued in greater detail.

2. H. von Glasenapp, trans., *Kant und die Religionen des Osten* (Holgne-Verlag, 1954), cited in Julia Ching, "Chinese Ethics and Kant," *Philosophy East and West* 28, no. 2 (April, 1978): 169.

3. Beginning with Matteo Ricci, who initiated what came to be called the "accommodationist" position with respect to the issue of the Chinese—especially Confucian—reverence for ancestors and performing the rites and rituals attendant thereon. See Jonathan Spence, *The Memory Palace of Matteo Ricci* (New York: Viking Penguin, 1984). For a summary of the "Rites Controversy" that later focused on Ricci's position, see Daniel J. Cook and Henry Rosemont, Jr., *Leibniz: Writings on China* (Chicago: Open Court Pub. Co., 1994), 3–18.

4. I have developed this theme further in "Tracing a Path of Spiritual Progress in the *Analects*," in *Confucian Spirituality*, eds. Tu Weiming and Mary Evelyn Tucker (New York: Crossroad Publishing Company, 2003).

5. For more detailed arguments, see my "Which Rights? Whose Democracy? A Confucian Critique of Modern Western Liberalism," in *Confucian Ethics: a Comparative Study of Self, Autonomy, and Community*, eds. Kwongloi Shun and David Wong (Cambridge: Cambridge University Press, 2004).

6. On "amoralism," see my "Is there a Primordial Tradition in Ethics?," in *Fragments of Infinity*, ed. Arvind Sharma (Bridport, UK: Prism Press, 1991). For the "unprincipled" dimension, see my remarks below on Kings Wen and Wu.

7. References and translations from the *Analects* are all from Roger T. Ames and Henry Rosemont, Jr., *The Analects of Confucius: A Philosophical Translation* (New York: Random House/Ballantine Books, 1998), which also treats issues of translation and interpretation.

8. Herbert Fingarette, "The Music of Humanity in the Conversations of Confucius," *Journal of Chinese Philosophy* 10 (1983).

9. In the first publication of this chapter I cited Nancy Rosenblum's essay as the source for "all the way down." See her perceptive "Feminist Perspectives on Civil Society and Government" in *Civil Society and Government*, eds. Nancy Rosenblum and Robert Post (Princeton: Princeton University Press, 2002), the volume from which Professor Nosco's and my chapters have been taken.

10. Since first writing this essay I have profited greatly from Michael Nylan's "Mencius on Pleasure," and would now want to more cautiously comment on the lack of "happiness talk" in classical Confucianism, in light of her incisive analysis of the *Mencius* text. See *Polishing the Chinese Mirror*, edited by Marthe Chandler and Ronnie Littlejohn (Albany, NY: Global Scholarly Publications, 2007), which contains Nylan's essay and my response.

11. Plato, *Euthyphro* IV. 4. Translated by Lane Cooper in *The Collected Dialogues of Plato*, edited by Edith Hamilton and Huntington Cairns. New York: Pantheon Books, 1966.

12. See also my "On Confucian Civility" in *Civility*, ed. Leroy Rouner (Notre Dame, Ind.: University of Notre Dame Press, 2000).

13. On the former theme, see my "Is There a Universal Path of Spiritual Progress in the texts of Early Confucianism?" in *Confucian Spirituality*, vol. 1. On sexism and homophobia, my "Classical Confucianism and Contemporary Feminist Perspectives on the Self: Some Parallels, and Their Implications," in *Culture and Self,* ed. Douglas Allen (Nashville, Tenn.: Westview Pub. Co., 1997).

14. Although his arguments are different, Herbert Fingarette also maintains that there are no genuine moral dilemmas in the Confucian *Analects*. See his now classic *Confucius—The Secular as Sacred*, (New York: Harper & Row, 1972), esp. ch. 2: "The Way Without a Crossroads."

15. A. E. Houseman, *Last Poems*. New York: Henry Holt & Co., 1922, Poem XII.

PART TWO

BOUNDARIES AND JUSTICE

Chapter Four

TERRITORIAL BOUNDARIES AND CONFUCIANISM

⌒

JOSEPH CHAN

Territory is a political concept. It does not simply refer to a geographical space, but to "the land or district lying around a city or town and under its jurisdiction," as the *Oxford English Dictionary* defines it. The concept thus designates a relationship between a community of politically organized people and their space. In more exact terms, a territory is a geographical space that is under some kind of jurisdiction or control of certain people organized in the form of a political community. Similarly, the concept of territorial boundary does not simply refer to geographical boundaries; it denotes, rather, the limit of jurisdiction of a certain political community with regard to a certain geographical space. Territorial boundaries signify a separation of a political community from adjacent territories that are under different jurisdictions.

"Territory" in the Chinese language also carries this connotation of the jurisdiction of a political community. It is commonly translated as *jiang tu*: *jiang* means frontier or boundary, and *tu* means land. The two words together refer to the territory of a political unit. *Jiang* is itself a word about frontier or boundary. If emphasis is to be put on the concept of territorial *boundary*, *jiang yu* or *jiang jie* will be used. *Jiang* can be found in many ancient classical texts. It has, for example, appeared in *Mencius* six times.[1] Each time when the word appears in *Mencius*, it refers to the boundary of a state. For example, *chu jiang* means "out of a state,"[2] *ru jiang* means "enter into a state."[3] Like "territory," then, *jiang* and *jiang tu* are political concepts, and they refer to the territory or territorial boundaries of a political community.

It should be noted that the *concept* of territory or territorial boundary defined here is neutral with respect to the question of what form a political community takes. There are, of course, *conceptions* of territory and territorial boundary. Because of the close connection between territory and political community, different types of political community—and different theorizing of them—may generate different conceptions of the significance and functions of territory and territorial boundary. The territory and territorial boundaries of a modern, sovereign European nation-state, of the ancient Chinese empire, and of an ancient Greek *polis* may carry different significance and perform different functions. Questions about these conceptions, therefore, inevitably raise a series of questions about political communities—about their nature and purposes, their stage of development, the basis of political authority, their scope of jurisdiction, and their relations with other political communities.

Territorial boundary has become a significant issue primarily with the rise of the modern nation-state. The modern concept of nation-state comprises several elements: sovereignty, territory, and an equal status in the international system. The modern nation-state is at once both sovereign and territorial, in the sense that it has the impersonal, supreme legal authority to give and enforce the law within a demarcated territorial area. However, as Jean Gottmann notes, in ancient and medieval times, the authority of rulers rested primarily on the allegiance of individuals or organized bodies, rather than on the possession of land areas. From the late fifteenth century, the essence of political authority was gradually transferred to the control of well-defined territory. "The sixteenth century, however, was the decisive time in European affairs, when politics and legal doctrines began claiming territorial sovereignty as a prime attribute of kingdoms or states. By the end of the eighteenth century the notion of national sovereignty over well-delimited territory had come to the fore in political practice as well as in the theory of jurisprudence."[4]

Before the nation-state era, territorial boundaries were not clearly defined. They were dependent on the ability of the central government to control and administer the outer areas of the state rather than on the demarcation of territorial jurisdiction between states.[5] Border territories functioned primarily as buffer areas providing security for the state and facilitating trade with the outside world. Most of the time, however, emperors were more concerned with maintaining their administration in the inner areas than in the frontiers, unless the empire was engaged in self-defense or aggressive wars. Given this political reality, territorial boundaries did not seem to perform many functions other than being a buffer zone for security and trading, nor did they receive much theoretical reflection by political thinkers of ancient times. Thus it would not be a surprise to find that in Confucianism, as probably also in other premodern ethical traditions such as the ancient Greek, there was not much direct discussion on the question of territorial boundaries or on such related questions as ownership, distribution, diversity, or mobility. In fact, the latter set of questions have become significant only in the present world order, where globalization of technology, production and distribution of goods, and mass media have seriously constrained and challenged the sovereignty of modern territorial states. In a more or less globalized world order, the questions about the functions of territorial boundaries, the limits of state sovereignty, and the relations between political and territorial boundaries become significant practical issues.

Premodern ethical traditions may all lack systematic, direct discussions on issues of territory and territorial boundaries. But among them, different premodern traditions may also have different *internal* reasons for lacking those discussions. In this chapter, I shall try to explore some such internal reasons in Confucianism. I shall first briefly introduce the basic ideas in the Confucian ethical tradition, and then discuss the traditional Chinese conception of political community and the world. In order to bring out its uniqueness, I shall also compare it with the classical Greek conception. Then I shall try to show how Confucianism can be seen as having some bearing on the question of territory and territorial boundaries, despite the fact that these questions did not receive systematic theorizing in the tradition.

THE CONFUCIAN ETHICAL TRADITION

The Confucian tradition began before Confucius (551–479 B.C.E.), although it is difficult to date its birth.[6] If "Confucianism" means a tradition of thought wholly created by Confucius, then it is a misleading translation of the original Chinese *Ru jia*. Confucius regarded himself as a person who transmitted the old tradition rather than creating a new one. The Chinese term *Ru jia* means a school of *Ru*, "a type of man who is cultural, moral, and responsible for religious rites, and hence religious."[7] Nevertheless, it was Confucius who most creatively interpreted the rich tradition that he had inherited, gave it a new meaning, and expounded it so effectively that his views have influenced a great number of generations of *Ru* to come. *The Analects*, which is a record of the teachings of Confucius written by his students, is the most fundamental text in the Confucian tradition. The other two major exponents of Confucian thought in classical times were Mencius (c. 379–289 B.C.E.) and Xunzi (c. 340–245 B.C.E.). Their works, *Mencius* and *Xunzi*, are also important texts in the tradition.

Since the classical period, Confucianism has continued to evolve over more than two thousand years, and it has developed into a complex tradition with many different strands and variants. This makes any interpretation of Confucianism inevitably controversial, and any proposal to give an essentialist interpretation of the true nature of the tradition must be received with great caution and suspicion. What follows, therefore, is only one interpretation of Confucian ethics and political thought as developed primarily in the classical tradition. But this interpretation also takes account of the works of influential modern Chinese intellectuals, especially Confucian scholars. In this chapter, "the Confucian tradition" should be understood in this highly qualified sense.

The Confucian ethical tradition is a system of human relationships based on the virtue of *ren*. The moral ideal for each individual is the attainment of *ren*, the highest and most perfect virtue. *Ren* is a human quality, an expression of humanity. One way to understand *ren*, as Confucius himself does, is to say that *ren* is to "love your fellow men" (*ai ren*).[8] *Ren* is primarily expressed through human relationships, although later Confucians suggest that *ren* can be expressed also through a harmonious relationship between human beings and nature. For Confucians, the most natural and important site for the expression of *ren* is the family. Mencius says that young children naturally know to love their parents, and when they grow they will naturally respect their elders.[9] *Ren* manifested in the parent-child relationship is filial piety (*xiao*), and in the sibling relationship, brotherhood (*ti*). *The Analects* says that these two virtues form the root of *ren*.[10]

The familial virtues are not only the root of *ren* but also the basis of a stable social and political order. It is rare for a person who has the virtues of filial piety (*xiao*) and brotherhood (*ti*) to have the inclination to be rebellious against his or her superiors.[11] D. C. Lau, a translator of *The Analects*, comments that "if being a good son makes a good subject, being a good father will also make a good ruler. Love for people outside one's family is looked upon as an extension of the love for members of one's own family."[12] Confucianism gives a high priority to five basic relationships: father-son, husband-wife, elder brother-younger brother, ruler-ruled, and friend-friend. Among these five, the first three are familial relationships. Although the last two are nonfamilial, they are conceived analogously in familial terms. The ruler-ruled relationship is analogous to that of father-son, and friend-friend to elder brother-younger brother. The principles of conduct as required by benevolence for the two nonfamilial relationships, loyalty and friendship, have to be understood in light of their analogous familial principles, filial piety (*xiao*) and brotherhood (*ti*). Generally speaking, society is the family writ large. This is why some scholars have termed China a "familistic society, one in which the family, and the kinship system deriving from it, has an unusually strategic place in the society as a whole."[13]

While Confucianism takes the family to be the most fundamental social unit in Chinese society, it does not preach a petty-minded, close-knit society, for the Confucian family is also a highly elastic entity, and its spirit and care can be extended to places far away from home. Ambrose King has pointed out that the term "family" (*jia*) is conceptually unclear; and, theoretically, the family can be extended to cover the whole world (*tian xia*). "Sometimes it includes only members of a nuclear family, but it may also include all members of a lineage or a clan. Moreover, the common expression *ji jia ren* ("our family people") can refer to any person one wants to include; the concept of *ji jia ren* can be contracted or expanded depending upon the circumstances. It can theoretically be extended to an unlimited number of people and thereby becomes what is called *tian xia yi jia* ('all the world belongs to one family')."[14]

Part of the reason for the elasticity of the family is that the family is often used as a model to understand other social relationships, and hence its language and virtues are often stretched to cover nonfamilial spheres. But the more important reason lies in an important aspect of the Confucian conception of *ren*, an aspect that we have not discussed so far. While *ren* finds its most immediate and natural expression in the family, it never stops at the gateway of the home. Confucius says that when a young man is away from home, he should extend brotherhood (*ti*) to others and "love the multitude at large" (*fan ai zhong*).[15] *Ren* can transcend the natural bonds among family members because *ren* is also the ability of a person to "infer" another's needs and wants from one's own. "Now the man of [*ren*], wishing to be established himself, seeks also to establish others; wishing to be enlarged himself, he seeks also to enlarge others. To be able to judge *of others* by what is nigh *in ourselves*;—this may be called the [method of *ren*]."[16]

Confucius sometimes calls this method of *ren* the art of *shu*, which can be expressed positively or negatively. Positively, a man of *ren* seeks to establish and enlarge others insofar as he seeks also to establish and enlarge himself.[17] Negatively, *shu* tells us not to impose on others what we ourselves do not desire.[18] This art of *shu*, when applied to the familial virtues, becomes what Confucius and Mencius say respectively: "All within the Four Seas are one's brother."[19] "Treat the aged of your family in a manner befitting their venerable age and extend this treatment to the aged of other families; treat your own young in a manner befitting their tender age and extend this to the young of other families."[20]

Chinese historian Qian Mu (1895–1990) has suggested that the Chinese family can branch out vertically and horizontally to all mankind and integrate them into a whole. Filial piety (*xiao*) connects people vertically: it refers to a deep respect for the parents and all ancestors of a family, and by extension, to other people's parents and ancestors as well. Brotherhood (*ti*) connects people horizontally, which can be extended to anyone in the world, for as Confucius says, all within the Four Seas are one's brother. This elastic conception of the family has enabled the Chinese to slide easily from "familism" to "cosmopolitanism," back and forth.[21]

To summarize the points thus far: there are two features of the Confucian conception of human relationships and moral order that are particularly relevant to the present purpose of this chapter. The first is the *potentially unbounded* nature of human relationships and the scope of *ren*. Even though *ren* always begins in familial relationships, and one's attention and care should naturally be directly more to one's close partners such as family members than to strangers, Confucianism insists that the practice of *ren* has no outer limits, and its principles like *shu*, filial piety, and brotherhood have no outer limits as well. *Ren* implies the cultivation of oneself in relation to others, beginning with the family and friends, and ultimately, to the whole world. The second feature is the *elastic* nature of human relationship. It is not only that familial relationships (such as father-son) are often the basis for understanding the nature of other relationships (such as ruler-ruled); sometimes one's friends can be regarded as the very members of one's family. Familism in practice may mean closed-mindedness and exclusion, but in Confucian theory at least, it is elastic and has a strong degree of openness and inclusiveness.

This Confucian conception of the elastic and potentially unbounded nature of human relationships and moral order fits naturally with the traditional Chinese conception of the ideal political order. The highest political order for the Chinese is the order of *tian xia* (the world under Heaven), which has no territorial limit; and it provides the broadest site one could imagine for the practice of *ren* and for the actualization of one's self. I shall now articulate this traditional Chinese conception of political order.

THE CHINESE CONCEPTION OF *TIAN XIA*

In the classical Chinese ethical tradition, unlike in the modern conception, territory and territorial boundaries are relatively unimportant issues. This may be partly due to the fact, commonly acknowledged by all classical ethical and political theories alike, that these issues were not of any fundamental importance in premodern times. But there seems an internal, theoretical reason for the absence of discussion in the Chinese case. The Chinese conception of the ideal political order admits of no territorial boundaries. The Chinese notion of "the world under Heaven" (*tian xia*) represents the ultimate stage of the development of political order, whereas states are seen as an incomplete realization of the Chinese ideal. Liang Qichao (1873–1929) was probably the first modern

Chinese intellectual who stressed the importance of the notion of *tian xia* in understanding the traditional Chinese conception of the political order, and used such terms as "transnationalism" or "cosmopolitanism" to characterize it. His view influenced a few generations of modern Chinese scholars in interpreting the nature of Chinese politics and political culture. Liang writes, "Since civilization began, the Chinese people have never considered national government as the highest form of social organization. Their political thinking has always been in terms of all mankind, with world peace as the final goal, and family and nation as transitional stages in the perfecting of the World Order [*tian xia*]. China has contended, moreover, that government authority should never be the prerogative of any one group or section of mankind."[22]

In the following discussion, I shall basically follow this tradition of interpretation first developed by Liang. But I must first add two important qualifications about this tradition of interpretation. First, the traditional Chinese perspective of a world political order transcending states was developed before Confucius and Mencius. It was shared by different schools of thought, including Confucianism, and in itself this perspective is not uniquely Confucian. The Confucians simply inherited the basic political vocabulary of the day and accepted what was the generally shared vision of the world order. But, as we shall see later, Confucianism played an important role in shaping later understandings of what ought to be the proper nature and basis of the order of *tian xia*.

Second, it is important to note that the terminology used by Liang to describe the order of *tian xia* may be misleading. His terms "transnationalism" and "cosmopolitanism" seem to suggest that there is equality between nations and national cultures in the world order, and that the cosmopolitan political order should be neutral toward different nations and cultures. Understood in this way, these terms do not properly describe the traditional Chinese conception of world order. As will be explained later, the classical Chinese political tradition never held the view of equality between the cultures and ethical systems of different nations. On the contrary, the culture of the people in the central regions of China, the *zhu xia*, was, according to the traditional Chinese view, superior to those of the barbarians living on the four quarters of the continent and the rest of the world. It was thought that the superior culture should be transmitted to the world, and that the world should be under one rule, the rule of the most wise and ethical man. Looking from the outside, then, this view could perhaps be better termed as "imperialism" than "cosmopolitanism." But imperialism is not entirely accurate either, because it carries the connotation of a mighty nation using force to conquer or dominate other nations and cultures. The major scholars in the Confucian tradition, such as Mencius, opposed the use of force (although it was advocated by some other thinkers, and indeed it occurred). While Confucians adhered to the idea of *tian xia* being ruled by one culture and by one wise and ethical man, they typically favored peaceful persuasion and the setting of example by members of the culturally superior group. This point will be further developed below. Suffice it to say here that while Liang rightly pointed out that the notion of *tian xia* is useful to understand the traditional Chinese conception of political order, "transnationalism" and "cosmopolitanism" as coined by him to describe that conception can easily create misunderstandings.

The concept of *tian xia* is central to the Chinese conception of political order and territorial boundaries. From the West Zhou dynasty (1075–771 B.C.E.) through the Qin dynasty (221–6 B.C.E.), *tian xia* (literally translated, it means "all under Heaven") had appeared as a concept referring to a universal political order over and above the order of individual "states" (*guo*). But *tian xia* is a rich concept, and it can be used with varying degrees of abstractness. In its most concrete, institutional sense, it refers to universal kingship, or a kingdom or empire with universal jurisdiction. States (*guo*) are political units governed by feudal lords (*hou*), whereas the universal empire is founded and maintained by the Son of Heaven (*tian zi*), who possesses the mandate of Heaven. The distinction between the two kinds of political order emerged in the West Zhou dynasty, when the Zhou king was regarded not only as one feudal lord among others but as the Son of Heaven ruling over all states governed by feudal lords.

The disintegration of the Zhou dynasty led to the Spring Autumn and Warring States periods (770–221 B.C.E), which scholars call the "pre-Qin age." In this period, there were many states coexisting and fighting each other for a few hundred years. Although there was no corresponding political reality that matched the order of universal empire, *tian xia* was still frequently used in political and philosophical discourses, and the dominant political ideology was unificationism—the hope of merging all states into one giant empire with unlimited territorial boundary. Instead of being just a historical notion describing the political reality of the Zhou empire, the order of *tian xia* gradually became an ethical and political ideal guiding and judging the politics of the real world. The Confucian school of thought, as represented by Confucius, Mencius, and Xunzi, was particularly instrumental in idealizing the order of *tian xia*, and endowing it with much critical, ethical import. Mencius says that the great man practices the great way (*da dao*) of the world (*tian xia*).[23] Xunzi says that while individual states may be an object of seizure, *tian xia* is so grand and important that only a real sage is morally entitled to rule over it, and there are important moral principles governing the order of *tian xia*.[24] Even hereditary monarchy may not be legitimate if the monarch fails to conduct politics according to the moral principles grounding the order of *tian xia*. In this more abstract sense, then, the Confucian conception of *tian xia* refers to an ideal moral and political order admitting of no territorial boundary—the whole world to be governed by a sage according to principles of rites (*li*) and virtues (*de*). This ideal transcends the narrowness of states. As Benjamin Schwartz has observed, "Although the notion of universal kingship itself was pre-Confucian and was indeed taken for granted by most of the 'hundred schools' of thought during the late Zhou period, it does seem to become linked almost indissolubly over the course of time with an absolutization of the Confucian moral order."[25]

All these interrelated senses of *tian xia* can be found in classical Chinese historical and philosophical texts. And this makes translation of the concept into English difficult. Sometimes it means "the empire" or "the kingdom," sometimes it means, in a simple geographical sense, the whole world, and sometimes it points to a substantive conception of an ideal political and ethical order covering the entire world under the Heaven.[26]

Before proceeding to discuss in greater detail what a Confucian perspective would say on questions of territorial boundaries, I want to further emphasize the uniqueness of the Confucian perspective by comparing it to the classical Greek perspective. As I noted earlier in this chapter, unlike the modern conception of the state and territorial boundaries, both classical Greek and Chinese conceptions lack systematic discussions on territorial boundaries, because such boundaries play no important theoretical role in their political theories. But the two traditions may have different internal reasons for not giving an important role to territorial boundaries. Let me first briefly outline the classical Greek tradition, taking Aristotle and the Athenian tradition as representatives, and then compare it with the Chinese one. For Aristotle, although territory is one important *material* condition for a polis,[27] it is never an *essential* part of a polis. Territory is not part of the Aristotelian definition of the *polis*. For Aristotle, a *polis* is a community of citizens (*politai*) in a constitution (*politeia*).[28] Mogens H. Hansen, a historian of ancient Greece, argues that:

> Aristotle only picks up two of the three elements that comprise the modern juristic idea of a state—the people and the constitution: the territory is left out altogether, and that is not by chance. . . . We nowadays tend to equate a state with its territory—a state is a country; whereas the Greeks identified the state primarily with its people—a state is a people. Of course, the Greeks knew all about the territory of a state. But territory was not nearly as important for them as it is for us: in all the sources, from documents and historical accounts

to poetry and legend, it is the people who are stressed and not the territory, a habit of thought that can be traced back to the poet Alkaios round about 600 B.C.E. It was never Athens and Sparta that went to war but always "the Athenians and the Lakedaimonians."[29]

For Aristotle, the essence, or characteristic activity, of a *polis* is the deliberation and administration of public affairs by citizens sharing in a constitution, citizens who are capable of ruling and being ruled in turn.[30] A territory at most makes possible the activity of ruling and being ruled, since human activities need to take place somewhere. In itself, however, a territory is no part of the activity of ruling and being ruled as such. Here we can see why Aristotle insists that a *polis* must be strictly limited in terms of the size of its population and territory. A population and territory too large cannot be easily surveyed, and as a result citizens would find it difficult to "know each other and know what kind of people they are."[31] And this is detrimental to the activities of the *polis*, since such activities (electing officials, deliberating and making decisions on collective affairs, etc.) require knowledge of the people involved—their abilities, character, and political views.[32]

As in the classical Greek conception, territory and territorial boundaries are relatively unimportant issues in the classical Chinese tradition. However, unlike the Greek emphasis on the limited size of population and territory of a *polis*, the Chinese conception of the ideal political order admits of no territorial boundaries. Why did the Greeks and the Chinese have different views on the size of the territory of a political community? The answer lies, I think, in their different conceptions of political community and the essence of politics. As pointed out before, for the Athenians, politics is essentially public and collective, and the *polis* is the community of citizens as a whole taking part in the making of collective affairs. Citizens develop their virtues and obtain honor through collective activities in the face-to-face *polis*. It is this reason that explains why a political community must be limited in size. If the Greek conception of political community is *political* or *collective*, then the Chinese conception can be called *ethical*. In the Chinese conception, the importance of politics lies not in collective participation in collective decisions, but in its promotion of the highest moral good in individual lives (*ren*), and its accompanying moral order, a harmonious order of social relationships. As explained earlier, there are two features of the Confucian conception of human relationships and moral order that are important to the issue of a universal political order envisaged by the Chinese. The first is the potentially unbounded nature of human relationships and the scope of *ren*. The practice of *ren* begins from the individual self but can be enlarged through a series of concentric circles to include the family, the state, and ultimately the world (*tian xia*). Although the ideal of virtues and human relationships should first be cultivated in one's home, they can be practiced everywhere and are applicable to everyone irrespective of his or her place of residence or ethnicity. The second feature of the Confucian conception is the notion that the ideal social relationships are elastic enough to encompass many people. Because the Confucians see the moral order as having universal applicability and as being elastic enough to encompass many people, the political order, being an instrument to promote the moral order, is naturally seen as also universal, having no boundary of territory or of ethnicity.

I have described the traditional Chinese theory of *tian xia* and its relationship with the Confucian ethical theory. I have also briefly contrasted the Greek with the Chinese conceptions. In the next section, I shall try to relate this theory of *tian xia* to a number of issues concerning territorial boundaries. Classical Confucianism does not explicitly address these issues, and so I can only draw out implications both from the theory itself and from various major classical Confucian texts such as *The Analects*, *Mencius*, and *Xunzi*. The emphasis of the next three sections, on ownership, distribution, and diversity, is on describing how classical Confucianism would look at issues concerning territorial boundaries, given the nature of states and politics in the premodern period of Chinese history. In the last section of this chapter, I shall try to describe how the traditional picture was seriously challenged and rejected in modern times, how contemporary Confucian scholars have wrestled with the question of the nation-state within the constraints of Confucianism, and whether contemporary Confucianism could have anything further to say on the contemporary issues of territorial boundaries.

OWNERSHIP

According to the traditional Chinese perspective, the entire world, starting from the central regions of the continent and reaching beyond to the outer boundaries of the four seas, in principle belongs to the king, the Son of Heaven. According to the common saying: "There is no territory under Heaven which is not the king's; there is no man on the borders of the land who is not his subject."[33] This view is mentioned in *Mencius*[34] and *Xunzi*,[35] and the latter especially quotes it with approval. There are two features of the nature of this world empire that are worth mentioning. The first concerns the *unity* of the political order, the second concerns the *moral foundation* of this order.

The multistates system had persisted for more than five hundred years in the Spring Autumn and Warring States periods. It would not be inaccurate to compare this situation to that of the multistates/empires system in early-modern Europe. But instead of taking the European path of developing an international system of equal sovereign territorial states, the Chinese were always attracted to the ideal of universal kingship as first exemplified by the Zhou dynasty. The dominant ideology was grand unificationism (*tian xia da yi tong*). In this view, even when *tian xia* is disintegrated, sooner or later a ruler will rise as the Son of Heaven, unifying all states into one universal empire. Mencius was once asked how the Empire (*tian xia*) could be stabilized, and his reply was, "through unity" (*ding yu yi*).[36]

Given this ideological background, states and their territories were regarded as only transient entities. Ultimately they would have to be merged into the universal empire that reaches to the four seas. In fact, in the Spring Autumn period, scholars like Confucius and his disciples did not think that they owed allegiance to any one particular state. They rather traveled among the states to persuade and help the rulers to adopt and implement the principles of *ren* and *li* (or the Way). Confucius, Mencius, and Xunzi all regarded themselves as people whose ultimate goal was to help unify the world and develop a moral and political order according to the Way.[37]

The second point to make concerns the moral foundation of the universal political order. The Confucians have always stressed the importance of morality. They have never been willing to take politics as just a phenomenon of sheer power or a set of institutional arrangements. They believe that power and institutions can be effective only when they are set up, regulated, and used by benevolent leaders (leaders of *ren*). This can be seen from the following discussions relating to the ownership of territory and territorial boundaries.

The Confucians of Mencius's time had a consensus on the basis of the empire or the cosmopolitan order. They all believed that the possession and maintenance of the empire was based on practicing benevolent rule. For example, Mencius said, "The Three Dynasties won the Empire (*tian xia*) through benevolence (*ren*), and lost it through cruelty. . . . An Emperor (*tian zi*) cannot keep the Empire within the Four Seas unless he is benevolent; a feudal lord cannot preserve the altars to the gods of earth and grain unless he is benevolent."[38] "There are cases of a ruthless man gaining possession of a state, but it has never happened that such a man gained possession of the Empire."[39] *Xunzi* has a similar passage stressing the importance of benevolence as the basis of possessing the empire: "I say that a state, being a small thing, can be possessed by a petty man. . . . The empire is the greatest of all, and only a sage can possess it."[40] "[T]he worthiest of men could embrace all within the four seas."[41] It also follows from this theory that the mandate of the Son of Heaven is conditional upon his benevolent rule. If he fails to practice *ren*, he will lose his kingdom.[42]

Furthermore, Xunzi relates the proper way of acquiring the empire to the issue of territory. He holds the view that to gain the empire is above all to gain the hearts of the people, rather than to compel them to submit their lands and territories to the king. This view again indicates that in the Confucian conception of the political order, territory is only a derivative issue. The true basis of the political order lies in the voluntary submission of the people, and only a benevolent king could command such a voluntary submission. If a king, however small his state and territory may be, can win the hearts of the people of other lands, he can also naturally win their lands and territories. No doubt, territory can be an expression of the state's right or jurisdiction. But the right of the state depends not upon the sheer size or power of the state but upon whether it practices the Way. Here is an important passage from *Xunzi*:

> "Gaining the empire" does not mean that other men bring their own lands and territories and follow after him, but refers rather to no more than that his Way is sufficient to unify the people. If the people of other lands are indeed one with me, then why would their lands and territories abandon me and attach themselves to another? . . . "[A] territory of a hundred square *li* is sufficient to encompass every gradation of authority," and "the perfection of loyalty and trustworthiness and the evident manifestation of the principle of humanity and morality are ample enough to encompass all mankind." When these two principles are united, the empire can be gained and the feudal lords who are the last to make common cause are the first to be imperiled. An Ode says:
>
> > From the east, from the west,
> > From the north, from the south,
> > There were none who thought of not submitting.
>
> This refers to the unification of mankind.[43]

Mencius has a strikingly similar passage. In ancient times, the main purpose of territorial boundaries was for the security of a state. But Mencius insists that the advantageous terrain and solid walls of boundaries are much less important than the human factor in securing the safety of a state. Like Xunzi, Mencius believes that the key to success is the practice of the Way. "Heaven's favorable weather is less important than Earth's advantageous terrain, and Earth's advantageous terrain is less important that human unity. . . . It is not by boundaries that the people are confined, it is not by difficult terrain that a state is rendered secure, and it is not by superiority of arms that the Empire is kept in awe. One who has the Way will have many to support him; one who has not the Way will have few to support him."[44] In Confucianism, the effect of moralizing politics is indeed deep and pervasive.

DISTRIBUTION

Which goods (living space, natural resources, or products and services) do territorial boundaries properly reserve to some people and deny to others? Theoretically, territorial boundaries serve to distribute nothing, since strictly speaking there is no such thing as territorial boundary under the Confucian ideal theory of the cosmopolitan political order. But when that condition does not obtain, when there are states and political communities ruling over people in different territories, what would Confucianism say? It is difficult to be confident of an answer. Classical Confucianism has said virtually nothing on this subject. But one might perhaps argue that in Confucianism there seems no reason why one's moral duties to others must stop at the borders of one's political community. While it is true that *ren* is primarily relational and personal, there is practically no limit for extending *ren*: it can even be extended to strangers and people all over the world. Mencius's famous example of a child on the verge of falling into a well serves to illustrate this. For Mencius, a man with *ren* would be moved by compassion to save the child, not because he had personal acquaintance with the child's parents, nor because he wanted to win the praise of his fellow villagers or friends, but simply because of his concern for the suffering of a human person.[45] At the end of the same passage, Mencius says that if a man's heart is fully developed, "he can take under his protection the whole realm with the Four Seas, but if he fails to develop them [qualities of *ren*], he will not be able even to serve his parents." We have reason to believe that, for Confucianism, the practice of *ren*, whether it is by a state or an individual person, should transcend territorial boundaries. Mencius teaches his disciples: "Treat the aged of your family in a manner befitting their venerable age and extend this treatment to the aged of other families; treat your own young in a manner befitting their tender age and extend this to the young of other families."

The practice of *ren* does not stop at the gateway of one's home. Nor does it stop at the border of one's political community. This brings us to the Confucian ideal theory of social order, the ideal of the Grand Union. Confucius says:

When the grand course was pursued, a public and common spirit ruled all under the sky, they chose men of talents, virtue, and ability. . . . Thus men did not love their parents only, nor treat as children only their own sons. A competent provision was secured for the aged. . . . They showed kindness and compassion to widows, orphans, childless men, and those who were disabled by disease, so that they were all sufficiently maintained. . . . [They] accumulated] articles [of value], disliking that they should be thrown away upon the ground, but not wishing to keep them for their own gratification. . . . In this way [selfish] schemings were repressed and found no development. Robbers, filchers, and rebellious traitors did not show themselves, and hence the outer doors remained open, and were not shut. Thus was [the period of] when we call the Grand Union.[46]

DIVERSITY

According to the Chinese conception, the political order is based on neither ethnic nor territorial premises. The Chinese answer to the question of "Who should rule?" is this: the most virtuous sage. The sagely qualities have nothing to do with one's ethnic background. Mencius says that the early sage kings like Shun and Wen (prior to 2000 B.C.E.) were born in different times and in different "barbaric" regions hundreds of miles apart, yet both practiced the same way of the sage in the Central Kingdoms and became kings. "Shun was an Eastern barbarian; he was born in Chu Feng, moved to Fu Hsia, and died in Ming Tiao. King Wen was a Western barbarian; he was born in Chi Chou and died in Pi Ying. Their native places were over a thousand *li* apart, and there were a thousand years between them. Yet when they had their way in the Central Kingdoms, their actions matched like the two halves of a tally. The standards of the two sages, one earlier and one later, were identical."[47]

How would Confucians look at ethnic minorities? There are, I believe, four central elements in their attitudes toward ethnic minorities. First, Confucians in the classical period believed that people in the central regions of China, the *zhu xia*, were ethically and culturally superior to the barbarians living on the four quarters (*man, yi, rong, di*). Confucius says, "Barbarian tribes with their rulers are inferior to Chinese states (*zhu xia*) without them."[48] Mencius also held the view that the barbarians were inferior to, and hence susceptible to be influenced by the Chinese: "I have heard of the Chinese converting barbarians to their ways, but not of their being converted to barbarian ways."[49]

Second, Confucians held the view that these barbarians were also human beings capable of understanding, respecting, and developing human virtues (*de*) and practicing rites (*li*).[50] The Chinese should treat them with benevolence (*ren*), that is, in the same way as they treat their fellow Chinese. Fan Chih asked about benevolence. The Master said, "While at home hold yourself in a respectful attitude; when serving in an official capacity be reverent; when dealing with others do your best. These are qualities that cannot be put aside, even if you go and live among the barbarians."[51] "The Master said, 'If in word you are conscientious and trustworthy and in deed single-minded and reverent, then even in the lands of the barbarians you will go forward without obstruction.' "[52]

Third, and related to the second point, those who have successfully acquired virtues and practiced rituals would be regarded as people of *zhu xia* and members of the Central Kingdoms. In modern terms, they would become Chinese. The quality of being "Chinese" was thus defined more in ethical or cultural than in ethnic terms, and the Chinese empire was multiethnic. Han Yu (C.E. 768–824), a famous Confucian scholar of the Tang dynasty (C.E. 618–907), said that Confucius's *Spring and Autumn Annals* holds the following: For those feudal lords [in the Chinese regions] who adopt the rites (*li*) of the barbarians, we should regard them as barbarians; but for those barbarian states which are advanced enough to adopt the Chinese rites, we should regard them as Chinese states.[53]

Fourth, peaceful edification and persuasion rather than violent or military domination should be the strategy to deal with the barbarians. The Chinese should practice benevolent rule to attract people from the four quarters to reside in the Central Kingdoms. This view is consistent with the Confucian general emphasis on voluntary submission as the basis of political rule. "When distant subjects are unsubmissive, one cultivates one's moral quality in order to attract them, and once they have come one makes them content."[54]

To conclude, while Confucianism has a strong element of cultural elitism, it has no advocacy of brutal suppression or forceful domination of the "inferior" by the "superior" cultural group.

CONFUCIANISM, NATION-STATES, AND THE NEW WORLD ORDER

Thus far we have focused on the classical Chinese theory of world order and classical Confucian moral and political theory. One might ask, however, to what degree these theories correspond to what has actually happened in the history of Chinese politics before the modern age, and to what extent they still survive in contemporary Chinese politics. Benjamin Schwartz has argued that the Confucian ethical-political cosmopolitanism generally accords with what is found in pre-twentieth-century

Chinese history as the Chinese "perception" of the world order. The phrase "Chinese perception" is used advisedly by Schwartz, for he allows the possibility that the Sinocentric world order may not be an "objective" political fact accepted by all who became involved in it. Yet, as many historians (including Schwartz himself) have argued, many "barbarian" states, including those tributary states outside China and those foreign dynasties ruling over China, have in the end come to accept the Chinese perception of the world order.[55] This perception adopts "the concept of universal kingship and *tian xia* with concretely Confucian criteria of higher culture."[56] In this world order, China occupies the center and treats all foreign countries as alike and inferior to China.[57]

It should be noted, however, that the "Sinocentric" world order—the Chinese empire and its tributary system—was not like European imperialism by conquest and colonization. As some historians have argued, the tributary system had evolved primarily as a response to deal with foreigners who wished to have trading or diplomatic relations with China. The tributary system was also not exploitative in economic terms. Strictly speaking, there was no Chinese empire outside Chinese lands.[58] On the treatment of ethnic minorities, it was mentioned above that the classical Confucian attitudes toward ethnic minorities have two elements: superiority of the Chinese culture and peaceful transformation of the barbarian ones. While the superiority element was adopted by many Chinese (until the twentieth century), the peaceful strategy was not adhered to all the time. Generally speaking, throughout Chinese history the policy on ethnic minorities has oscillated from peaceful indifference or accommodation at one extreme to aggressive suppression and discrimination at the other.

A more "positive" and interesting case of toleration followed by syncretism was the gradual assimilation of the Jews who settled in China after the twelfth century. According to a recent study, the Jews were never discriminated against for being Jewish, and many of them successfully passed the civil service exams. Their success in these exams brought them government employment outside of their Jewish communities, resulting in a great number of intermarriages, and the "Confucianization" of Jewish intellectuals and sometimes entire communities.[59]

The Chinese perception of the world order was completely shaken up by Western invasions in the twentieth century. Prominent intellectuals such as Liang Qichao quickly accepted the Western multistate system, and came to the judgment that traditional Chinese "cosmopolitanism" led to the failure to develop a strong nation-state. Given the weak position of China in the world, both nationalist and communist governments in China have found that an order based on the notion of equal sovereignties would be advantageous to them. Cultural superiority has turned into a culture of despair; culturalism of the old days has now become nationalism.[60]

Since China has entered "the family of nations" in the modern era, territorial boundaries have become a more significant issue. Before this, as Wang Gungwu, a contemporary Chinese historian, notes, the Chinese borders in the northern and western regions had never been clearly defined. For many "kingdoms and tribal groups that accepted the Chinese tributary system, boundaries were either unclear or not contiguous with China, and their tributary missions arrived by sea."[61] But following her defeat in the Second World War, China eagerly reasserted control over territories lost to Western states and over her frontier areas with neighboring ones.[62] The model of a territorial sovereign state has often been used as a weapon to protect her territory, security, and internal affairs from Western interference. "Whatever happens in the Chinese territories is the internal affair of the sovereign state of China," the communist government regularly asserts.

One feature of the traditional Chinese conception of political order has, however, persisted stubbornly for more than two thousand years. Justifiably or not, the Chinese seem to have faithfully accepted the belief that political unity yields stability and strength in a country. Thus, despite the fact that China has been divided for lengthy periods in the past, "the driving force behind all governments has always been to reunify the empire."[63] The strong stand of the People's Republic of China on the question of unification with Taiwan, Hong Kong, and Macau has much to do with this long-lived ideology of unificationism. But even this traditional ideology is now couched in terms of the language of sovereignty and nation-state. The Chinese government claims that Taiwan, Hong Kong, and Macau belong to the same big Chinese family, and as such they are inseparable parts of the territory of China. Any movement for independence or separation in these regions would be seen as aggression against the sovereignty of China, which would never be tolerated.

So there are clear political and practical reasons that forced the Chinese to give up the traditional Chinese theory of world order, and to accept the modern world order of equal nation-states. But how did those Chinese who are still inclined toward Confucianism or who identify themselves as Confucians—many of them scholars and intellectuals—face these fundamental changes? Most of them embraced the new world order of equal nation-states and the language of state sovereignty, but how could they justify this change of attitude in terms of Confucian theory?

Answers to these questions may be found in the response of a Confucian philosopher, Mou Zongsan (or Mou Tsung-san) (1909–95), who was one of the most original and influential contemporary Confucian philosophers. Other contemporary philosophers include Tang Junyi (1909–78), who worked closely with Mou, and Xu Fuguan (1903–82). These philosophers' main contribution was twofold: they offered systematic and original expositions of Chinese philosophy, especially Confucianism, trying to show that it still offers a profound understanding of humanity and can give valuable spiritual insights to modern people; and they revised and further developed Confucianism to incorporate modern liberal political values such as freedom and democracy. Among these philosophers, Mou went a little further than others in trying to wrestle with the questions of the nation-state, sovereignty, and the world order within the constraints of Confucianism. Mou injected new meanings into the traditional Confucian distinction between the superior (Chinese) and inferior cultures (*yi xia zhi bian*) and the notion of *tian xia*, and he developed a view of culture and morality that suits the existence of different cultures having equal standing in the new world order.

Traditional Confucianism has a hierarchical conception of cultural and ethical systems, which themselves are closely interwoven. The people in the central regions of China, the people of *zhu xia*, were thought to be ethically and culturally superior to the barbarians living around those regions. Confucius himself helped to link culture and morality by arguing that rituals, music, poetry, and literature are all closely connected to the development of one's humanity and morality, and all these elements of a culture can be judged as more or less ethically superior or inferior. Because the Confucians thought they had grasped the nature of human virtues and vices better than others, and because their ethical views were developed within, and intermingled with, their own cultural and political contexts, it seems natural that they also came to believe that the culture of the central regions of China was superior to others. This belief, together with the view that the ethically and culturally superior people or individual person should rule the world, gave rise to the traditional Chinese theory of world order.

Thus, one way to reject this traditional picture is to reject the superiority of Chinese culture and to affirm a diversity of cultures that are worthy of equal respect. This is exactly what Mou does.[64] He argues that even if the Way of Heaven, or the *logos*, or humanity, is the same for all human beings in the world, it admits of different concrete expressions in different cultures. The four basic ethical instincts of human beings—the heart of compassion, of shame, of courtesy and modesty, and of right and wrong, as identified by Mencius[65]—are the same for everyone, but their concrete norms and modes of expression may vary from culture to culture. Similarly, the principle of benevolence, of righteousness, of rites, and of wisdom can be realized in different ways. Why is the diversity of expressions of the *logos* possible and inevitable?

Mou gives two reasons. First, the *logos* is abstract in itself and has to be fleshed out in human bodies and in human psyches, dispositions, and actions. But human psyches and temperaments (*qi zhi*) vary a great deal from individual to individual, and similarly a culture, which is a complex pattern of human values, attitudes, and norms of conduct developed over time, has its own "psyche and temperament" (*qi zhi*), which may be different from those of other cultures. There is no necessity for a particular culture to develop its psyche and temperament in a particular way; it is a result of all kinds of contingent factors. But just as different human psyches and temperaments may be complementary and make human life interesting, different cultural orientations and modes of expressions of the *logos* are something to be welcome rather than regretted. This is especially so if we also consider the second reason given by Mou. He argues that the *logos* or humanity is only known and grasped by human beings slowly in a piecemeal way. It will not be grasped in its entirety in one single act of human understanding. A culture begins life when it grasps partially the meaning of humanity. It grows by exposing itself to new experiences and adventures, and by learning from those of other cultures. So we ought to respect cultures, for they all make their own contributions to the development and expression of humanity.

But how does respect for cultures lead to an endorsement of the nation-state? Here Mou asserts, without much elaboration, that a culture evolves over time and develops into a tradition only with the support of social and political institutions. A nation-state, by giving priority to the culture of the national group in a political community, seems the best form of government that can help promote and further develop a national culture. I believe many standard arguments made in the West to support the idea of nation-state can fill the gaps left by Mou, but we have no space to rehearse them here.[66] My main concern here is to show how Mou tried to create room for a pluralistic view of cultures and hence a practical reason for the nation-state within Confucianism.

While rejecting the rigid hierarchical view of cultures in traditional Confucianism, Mou does not abandon the traditional notions of *tian xia* and *yi xia zhi bian* (the distinction of the superior and the barbarian); rather, he gives them a new meaning. For him, even though many different cultures are worthy of equal respect, there may be some ideologies or political powers that despise and destroy cultural traditions, and repress humanity. Mou sees communist states and ideologies as an example of this kind, and labels them as "barbaric." Any true Confucian must oppose the barbaric communist ideology and power because it demeans and represses humanity. Mou also retains the notion of *tian xia* and holds the traditional view that the greatest extension of human order must cover the entire world. The order of *tian xia* in modern times, however, can only mean harmonious peaceful coexistence of nation-states. This order does not replace smaller units such as families and states, but only supplements them and coordinates them in a way that facilitates the development of all states. Mou has in mind the role and nature of the United Nations as the coordinating body of the order of *tian xia*.

Mou expressed these thoughts in the 1950s, when the nation-state was regarded as the most appropriate form of government domestically and internationally, and when the United Nations was only recently established. Since the 1980s, however, we have seen important changes in the international economic and political order. Globalization of information technology and of the production and distribution of goods, the vast flow of immigration from developing countries to developed ones, and the emergence of supranational regimes such as the European Union—all these have markedly shaped the global order and the politics of nation-states. Scholars and writers of Confucianism have not yet responded to this new situation. In fact they are still grappling with basic issues like human rights and liberal democracy, trying to ascertain the extent to which Confucianism can embrace them without uprooting its central values.[67] Does Confucianism in its present state have anything useful to say on the issues of territorial boundaries in the present global order? In my view, it has something to say, but not much. Traditional Confucianism does say that the state has a responsibility to ensure a decent living for all, and that it is important to extend one's care to strangers as well as close friends and family members. So the Confucian emphasis on the unlimited scope of *ren* might be enough to reject "hard" territorial boundaries as defined by Loren Lomasky, which "confer substantial benefits or impose substantial costs on individuals in virtue of which side of the line they happen to find themselves."[68] But the Confucian view that it is natural and right for a person to show more concern for people close to him or her than to strangers would lead one to accept at least some kind of territorial boundary that distributes more resources to citizens of a community than to outsiders. Beyond this, however, Confucianism is not able to deal with complex questions about the distribution of entitlements and resources arising from territorial boundaries. In fact, it has not yet developed a theory of distributive justice within the context of a modern political community, let alone a theory of justice between states or a theory of entitlements of the citizens of a political community versus outsiders. Confucianism still has a long way to go before it can come to terms with these issues.

NOTES

The author wishes to thank Michael Nylan and Daniel A. Bell for their helpful comments on an early draft of this chapter.

1. References to Mencius and Xunzi are to the works of these two philosophers as preserved by later scholars. The authorship of *Mencius* is a controversial issue. Some argue that the main bulk of the work was written by Mencius himself. Others suggest it was compiled by an editor from notes taken by Mencius's disciples.

2. *Mencius*, bk. III, pt. B, 3; bk. IV, pt. B, 3. Unless otherwise stated, all translations of *Mencius* and *The Analects* are taken from *Mencius*, trans. D. C. Lau (London: Penguin Books, 1970) and *Confucius: The Analects*, trans. D. C. Lau (London: Penguin Books, 1979) respectively.

3. *Mencius*, bk. VI, pt. B, 7.

4. Jean Gottmann, *The Significance of Territory* (Charlottesville: University Press of Virginia, 1973), 17.

5. See Ishwer C. Ojha, *Chinese Foreign Policy in an Age of Transition: The Diplomacy of Cultural Despair* (Boston: Beacon Press, 1971), 146–47; and Wang Gung-Wu, *The Chinese Way: China's Position in International Relations* (Oslo: Scandinavian University Press, 1995), 53.

6. For more detailed discussion, see Liu Shu-Hsien, *Understanding Confucian Philosophy: Classical and Sung-Ming* (Westport, Conn.: Greenwood Press, 1998), chap. 1.

7. Tang Chun-I, *Essays on Chinese Philosophy and Culture* (Tapei: Students Book Co., Ltd., 1988), 362.

8. *The Analects*, bk. XII, 22.

9. *Mencius*, bk. VII, pt. A, 15.

10. *The Analects*, bk. I, 2.

11. Ibid., bk. I, 2.

12. Ibid., translator's introduction, 18.

13. This is Talcott Parsons's view, as cited in Ambrose Y. C. King, "The Status of the Individual in Chinese Ethics," in *Individualism and Holism: Studies in Confucian and Taoist Values*, ed. Donald J. Munro (Ann Arbor: Center of Chinese Studies, University of Michigan, 1985), 58.

14. Ibid., 61.

15. *The Analects*, bk. I, 6.

16. Ibid., bk. VI, 30. This translation is taken from "Confucian Analects," trans. James Legge, in his *The Chinese Classics*, vol. I (Hong Kong: Hong Kong University Press, 1960), 194.

17. *The Analects*, bk. VI, 30.

18. Ibid., bk. XII, 2; bk. XV, 24.

19. Ibid., bk. XII, 5.

20. *Mencius*, bk. I, pt. A, 7.

21. Qian Mu, *Zhongguo wen hua shi dao lun* (Taipei: Shang Wu, 1993), 50–53.

22. Liang Qichao, *History of Chinese Political Thought during the Early Tsin Period*, trans. L. T. Chan (Taipei: Cheng-Wen Publishing Company, 1968), 7.

23. *Mencius*, bk. III, pt. B, 2.

24. *Xunzi: A Translation and Study of the Complete Works*, vols. 1–3, ed. and trans. John Knoblock (Stanford: Stanford University Press, 1988), bk. 18. Hereafter cited as *Xunzi*.

25. Benjanmin I. Schwartz, "The Chinese Perception of World Order, Past and Present," in *The Chinese World Order: Traditional China's Foreign Relations*, ed. John King Fairbank (Cambridge: Harvard University Press, 1968), 278.

26. Mencius's usage of "All under Heaven" was standard: it starts from the continent but reaches to the Four Seas beyond the continent; it admits of no territorial boundary. Mencius was also explicit in following the established distinction between "All under Heaven" and states. Mencius says, "There is a common expression, 'The Empire (tian xia), the state (guo), and the family (jia).' The empire has its basis in the state, the state in the family, and the family in one's own self." See *Mencius*, bk. IV, pt. A, 5.

27. Aristotle, *The Politics*, trans. T. A. Sinclair (London: Penguin Books, 1981), 1325b33ff.

28. Ibid., 1276b1.

29. Mogens Herman Hansen, *The Athenian Democracy in the Age of Demosthenes* (Oxford: Blackwell Publishers, 1991), 58.

30. Aristotle, *The Politics*, 1326b11ff.

31. Ibid., 1326b11ff, 1326b39ff.

32. Ibid., 1326b11ff.

33. *Shi*, Lesser Odes, "Beishan."

34. *Mencius*, bk. V, pt. A, 4.

35. *Xunzi*, bk. 24. 1.

36. *Mencius*, bk. I, pt. A, 6.

37. Ibid., bk. III, pt. B, 3; see also Liang Qichao, *Xian Qin zheng zhi si xiang shi* (Shanghai: Zhong Hua Shu Ju, 1988[1936]), 194.

38. *Mencius*, bk. IV, pt. A, 3.

39. Ibid., bk. VII, pt. B, 13.

40. *Xunzi*, bk. 18. 2.

41. Ibid.

42. In *Mencius*, there are many passages carrying this message. See, for example, bk. IV, pt. A, 9.

43. *Xunzi*, bk. 11. 6.

44. *Mencius*, bk. II, pt. B, 1.

45. Ibid., bk. II, pt. A, 6.

46. "The Li Ji," trans. James Legge, in *The Sacred Books of the East*, ed. F. Max Muller (Oxford: Clarendon Press, 1885), vol. 27, bk. 7, 364–66.

47. *Mencius*, bk. IV, pt. B, 1.

48. *The Analects*, bk. III, 5.

49. *Mencius*, bk. III, pt. A, 4.

50. See *Xunzi*, bk. 1.

51. *The Analects*, bk. XIII, 19.

52. Ibid., bk. XV, 6.

53. Han Yu, "Yuan Dao," in *Han Yu san wen xuan*, eds. Gu Yisheng and Xu Cuiyu (Hong Kong: Joint Publishing [H. K.] Co., Ltd., 1992), 1–20.

54. *The Analects*, bk. XVI, 1. See also bk. XIII, 4, and *Mencius*, bk. XIV, 4.

55. Schwartz, "The Chinese Perception of World Order, Past and Present," 276–77. See also Wang Gung-Wu, "Early Ming Relations with Southeast Asia: A Background Essay," in *The Chinese World Order: Traditional China's Foreign Relations*, ed. John King Fairbank (Cambridge: Harvard University Press, 1968), 34–62; and Wang, *The Chinese Way*, 51–59.

56. Schwartz, "The Chinese Perception of World Order, Past and Present," 277.

57. Wang, "Early Ming Relations with Southeast Asia: A Background Essay," 61.

58. See Wang, *The Chinese Way*, 57–58; Ojha, *Chinese Foreign Policy in an Age of Transition*, 16.

59. See Wendy Robin Abraham, "The Role of Confucian and Jewish Educational Values in the Assimilation of the Chinese Jews of Kaifeng, Supplemented by Western Observer Accounts, 1605–1985" (Ed.D. diss., Columbia University Teachers College, 1989).

60. Ohja, *Chinese Foreign Policy in an Age of Transition*, chap. 2.

61. Wang, *The Chinese Way*, 53.

62. Ohja, *Chinese Foreign Policy in an Age of Transition*, 148.

63. Wang, *The Chinese Way*, 53.

64. The following discussion of Mou's ideas is based on Mou Zongsan, *Dao de de li xiang zhu yi*, 6th ed. (Taipei: Xue Sheng Shu Ju, 1985[1959]), esp. 39–67, 135–50, 245–62.

65. *Mencius*, bk. II, pt. A, 6.

66. See David Miller, *On Nationality* (Oxford: Clarendon Press, 1995).

67. For some recent efforts, see *Confucianism and Human Rights*, eds. Wm. Theodore de Bary and Tu Wei-Ming (New York: Columbia University Press, 1998). See also Joseph Chan, "A Confucian Perspective on Human Rights for Contemporary China," in *The East Asian Challenge for Human Rights*, eds. Joanne Bauer and Daniel A. Bell (New York: Cambridge University Press, 1999), 212–37.

68. See Loren Lomasky in *Boundaries and Justice* (Princeton: Princeton University Press, 2001), chap. 3.

Chapter Five

BOUNDARIES OF THE BODY AND BODY POLITIC
IN EARLY CONFUCIAN THOUGHT

∼

MICHAEL NYLAN

Neither the concept nor the term "Confucianism" existed until Jesuit missionaries in China felt the need to invent a Chinese counterpart for Christianity in Europe. Summaries of early "Confucian" teachings on a given issue, then, necessarily overlook one distinction important to early thinkers in China, while foisting on readers a second distinction anachronistic for the period: The term *Ru*, now employed to translate "Confucianism," originally referred simply to "classicists," and early thinkers were quite careful to distinguish between the set of professional "classicists" (*Ru*), many of whom employed the body of teachings they had mastered to further their own ambitions or those of their state, and the much smaller subset of self-identified ethical followers of Confucius (551–479 B.C.E.). In addition, the books that we now dub the Five "Confucian" Classics (the *Wu jing*) constituted a common store of knowledge for all literate Chinese in imperial China; as authoritative texts thought to encapsulate the Way of Antiquity, they were read on multiple levels besides the moral. This chapter, in order to focus on the complex issue of boundaries, inevitably downplays the still more complex conceptual problems that have arisen from the regular conflation of "Confucian," "classicist," and "Chinese."[1] For the purposes of this essay, I will adopt "Confucian" as a convenient category under which to group the materials found either in the Five Classics or in the writings of Confucius's most prominent early ethical followers.

Using this somewhat contrived definition, we can say that Confucian thought at its inception represented a series of loose teachings in support of moral action, rather than a unitary creed enjoining a discrete set of beliefs; in other words, it was an orthopraxy, not an orthodoxy.[2] To the degree that specific teachings were devised to guide the individual to the Confucian Way, they enjoined the would-be Confucian to weigh the relative claims of incommensurate goods in order to find the single most humane solution to problems posed by social interaction. This solution was then identified in Confucian literature as the "Middle Way." To take a single example, strict loyalty to one's superiors in the sociopolitical hierarchy was to be balanced by the subordinate's duty to reprimand his superior when necessary; likewise, the injustice inherent in any hereditary system of rank was to be offset by the social mobility inevitably fostered by the startling redefinition of "nobility" promoted by Confucius (wherein commitment to classical ideals replaced aristocraticbirth).[3] As Confucius distinguished himself from contemporary leaders on the basis of his consistent refusal to offer a set of rules about right and wrong,[4] sweeping generalizations about "Confucian" positions on any given topic can at best serve as vague "guideposts" to the Way, indicating proximate sites of ethical concern rather than the exact locations of ethical solutions.

If the model of the Sage-Master Confucius resists reductionist attempts, the subsequent history of Confucianism makes it even less amenable to easy characterizations. As an approach to rule and self-rule, a self-conscious "Confucian" movement emerged in the late Warring States period (475–222 B.C.E.), centuries after the death of the Master, Confucius, so that considerable controversy always existed as to the core content of the Supreme Sage's teachings. And though early Confucian classicism advocated certain archaic and archaizing practices in the hopes of curbing current social ills, it took *Ru* teachings in the long imperial period (221 B.C.E–C.E. 1911) some time to acquire some semblance of a coherent belief system; it did this in response to four main stimuli: (1) the concurrent articulation and widespread acceptance of Yin/yang and Five Phases cosmological conceptions; (2) the perceived need of the Chinese imperial state after unification in 221 B.C.E to have classicists on its payroll devise suitable criteria to evaluate candidates for public office; (3) the impact of Buddhism from the third century C.E. on; and (4) the introduction of Christianity more than a millennium later.[5] Still, because the Confucian Way was never an exclusive religion, but rather a series of precepts and practices designed to increase the adherent's capacity to feel and express sympathy for others, self-identified Confucians who came into contact with local cultures with their alternate structures were apt to readily absorb and accommodate other beliefs and practices. Some of these adaptations necessitated conscious reformulations of the basic Confucian teachings, of course, but many transformations seem to have occurred without attracting much notice, then or now. Meanwhile, to the utter consternation of late purists and the endless confusion of modern scholars, many of the most famous proponents of Confucian values down through the ages (e.g., Mencius and Han Yu) have sought to "prove" the value of Confucius's Middle Way by linking it with the preservation of a distinctive "Central States" identity, though entirely separate

"Chinese" ethnic and national identities were themselves relatively late and loose inventions, fleshed out in response to major "barbarian incursions," including those of the Western powers in the late nineteenth and early twentieth centuries.[6]

For the foregoing reasons, it is best to think of "Confucian" learning as a cluster of problems and themes evolving over time and place, as particular thinkers trained in classical texts chose to focus on a set of key concepts over others while integrating outside influences.[7] This chapter traces early Confucian notions of boundaries, where "early Confucian" refers to the Warring States and Han writings of self-identified Confucian thinkers. Such a focus fulfills two useful functions: First, the period under consideration was the formative stage in the development of Confucian teachings, a stage that is frequently ignored or misunderstood.[8] Second, my essay then complements Joseph Chan's submission to this volume, whose argument builds upon early twentieth-century readings of the early writers, not only in its easy conflation of the "Confucian" and Chinese traditions but also in its propensity to read into early texts what one historian calls "compensatory universalism."[9] Hence, the decision to have this essay draw most of its evidence from the rather small corpus of texts that early on—if erroneously—came to be most closely associated with the figure of Confucius: the Five "Confucian" Classics[10] and their attached traditions.

EIGHT TENETS

The authors of these texts seem relatively unconcerned about some of the questions that interest modern theorists on the topic of territorial boundaries. For example, Do differences in ethnicity-culture, language, religion, or moral practices constitute an appropriate basis for the division of living space between communities? Confucian teachers had good reasons for ignoring certain problems attending such divisions of living space. First of all, for most of the long history of Confucianism, Chinese and "barbarian" lived cheek-by-jowl in many areas, with "empire" as much a habit of mind as an actualized reality[11]; occasional enforced separations into different locales were most often mandated not by a "Confucianized" ruling elite, but by successive "barbarian" conquerors of China who feared that their own peoples would become overly sinicized. Given the admirable material culture, ritual elegance, and political stability that they associated with the Confucian way of life, early Confucians little feared that Chinese would be tempted to adopt barbarian ways wholesale.[12] Second, Confucius left his disciples in no doubt that "barbarians" and Chinese are "very much alike in nature, though they come to differ by custom"[13]; thus, the "barbarians," no less than the Central States inhabitants, could master the techniques of self-cultivation so as to realize their human potential. Since "all within the Four Seas are brothers," the early Confucians fervently hoped that the not-yet-civilized would eventually embrace their cultural patterns (*wen*), adopting their rites and their written language.[14] Third, as noted above, because the Confucian Way was a behavioral Way, not a religion, adherents in good conscience could profess equal devotion to the gods of the "native" Chinese religion, Taoism, and to the "foreign" gods of Buddhism, Manicheanism, or Christianity. "All roads lead to the Tao," as one Confucian classic put it.[15] Fourth, throughout China and all the East Asian countries that came under Confucian influence (Korea, Japan, and Vietnam), people spoke mutually incomprehensible languages though they shared a single writing system.[16] In short, a great diversity of languages, religions, moralities, and cultures coexisted as the norm within the Confucian cultural horizon, where neither cultural and linguistic boundaries nor ethical responsibilities ever neatly coincided with political borders.[17] Not surprisingly, then, Confucians made no strong practical or theoretical moves to erect fixed boundaries between communities or to restrict mobility across territorial boundaries—the popular myth of the Great Wall notwithstanding.[18] Perhaps the simplest way to categorize the disparate concerns expressed by self-identified followers of Confucius is to focus on the elaborate analogies framed between the physical body and the body politic. On the questions of ownership, autonomy, and the distribution of scarce resources, those analogies, then, underlie the following observations on the subject of "Confucian" boundaries.

In early Confucian theory, geographic boundaries are emphatically (a) permeable and (b) expandable, because the health of the body and body politic is thought to depend always on flow and change, rather than on fixedness. In addition, (c) neither the body nor the state is ever seen as the "possession of one man." Instead, both are conceived as entities held in trust, in effect "works in progress" extending over space and time.[19] To the Confucian, these obvious "facts" attesting to the blurry boundaries of the body and body politic by no means precluded order, for (d) order in the Confucian tradition emanates from a stable—precisely because it is not rigidly placed—center attuned to social and cosmic patterns. In the body, the center was defined as the heart/mind, locus of the proper motivations for social interaction; in the body politic, as the ruler or, in the absence of a good and wise ruler, the sage. (There was far less emphasis in early Confucian thought on an interior or distinctly "spiritual" life than we might expect, either from later Chinese traditions or from Western stereotypes of the "mysterious East.") However, (e) early Confucian writings insist on unambiguous territorial and social boundaries when boundaries are established for specific ritual purposes; such boundaries are to be promptly deconstructed once their ultimate ritual aims have been achieved. Thus (f) strictly physical demarcations, like contemporary social hierarchies, played a limited role as auxiliary "supports" to the twin centers of the heart/mind and ruler as the centers set about their all-important task of insuring proper relations, but the physical props for morality were thought to play a lesser role in moral cultivation than the suasive examples conveyed through family and scholastic affiliations, or sagely teachings. It was always the logic of moral situations and relational space, in other words—not the precise location of any thing, person, or event—that most attracted the "true" Confucians, those devoted to notions of ritual efficacy.[20] This was so in part because (g) the secure acquisition of true power depended upon the steady buildup of moral charisma, not upon the land, persons, or things at one's disposal. After all, a strain of Chinese folk wisdom preserved in the "Confucian" Classics and their associated traditions, most prominently in commentaries to the *Changes* (*Yi jing*), argued that (h) no possession—even land—is intrinsically good or lucky, since the relative benefits accruing from possession depend upon timing and location, as well as the owner's present rank and situation in life.[21]

Charismatic Power As a Function of Sharing Space

To support this series of eight hypotheses, some of which may strike readers as counterintuitive or just plain wrong, let me begin with a legend that many Confucians thought encapsulated much of the sacred Way of the Ancients. The story purports to relate events in the life of the pre-dynastic "founder" of the Zhou dynasty (c. 1050–256 B.C.E.), the very dynasty that set the pattern for all subsequent notions of cultivated society, according to Confucius.[22] Once upon a time a petty local ruler of the small state of Bin, named Danfu, found his fertile lands to be the envy of all his neighbors in the Central Plain of the area now known as China. Foreseeing the continual invasions to which his state would be subjected, Danfu reasoned, "The people enthrone a ruler in order to benefit from him. The people would fight back for my sake, but I cannot bear to kill fathers and sons in order to remain as their ruler!" In response to advisors who urged him to stay and fight to preserve the sacred ancestral temple, he replied that his duty to the ancestors was essentially a "private" obligation that must give way to his public duty to the people. So Danfu forsook his ancestral homelands, moving his home some sixty miles to the northwest, to a significantly less fertile district nestled in the foothills of Mount Qi. Then, to his astonishment, "the entire populace of Bin, bearing their old on their backs and carrying their children in their arms," followed him there on foot, at which demonstration of loyalty many neighboring states sought alliances with Danfu.[23]

This legend touches upon a number of the values that I have mentioned above: the (real) inconsequence of set boundaries; the potential for expansion (in this case, of authority and power) beyond the original boundaries; the state as shared possession; and the ruler as stable center of community life. And this legend is hardly an isolated one. Confucian compendia regularly associate the acquisition of charismatic power with similar acts of "yielding" space.[24]

To understand why this was so, we must put early Confucian beliefs within their proper historical context, taking into account the profoundly religious underpinnings of this humanistic world view, and then calculating the effects on its teachings of two contemporary debates on political ethics, along with early Chinese medical theories about the body. Regarding the religious background, as far back as the first written script in China (1300 B.C.E.), the entire area of the proto-Chinese polity was thought to enjoy the explicit protection of the ruler's ancestors who resided in heaven.[25] Back then, too, the very life of the ruler, let alone the possibility for his continuing physical health and good fortune, came as gift from these same ancestral spirits. In part because of the teachings of Confucius himself, eventually other persons of sufficient moral stature were thought to merit heaven's equal consideration, by virtue of their faithful conformity with what was widely perceived as the old aristocratic Way of the Ancients. In any case, because the earliest discourses in China could not envision a body or body politic surviving long without the active intervention of the beneficent gods, all the Confucian virtues in some sense boiled down to a willingness to express one's recognition of the heavy debts owed to others, both living and dead, for one's own life and property, a recognition that supposedly spurred the person to develop the imaginative and emotional capacities required to treat inferiors in rank, property, age, or understanding with genuine consideration (shu).

No doubt, the Confucians were even more aware of the moral obligation to requite ethical debts and exemplify personal generosity because their sense of group identity had been forged in the course of voicing their vehement opposition to two sorts of influential political theory in the late Warring States period: that of the Realpoliticians and that of Yang Zhu. The backers of Realpolitik argued that the state was in effect the possession of one man, the ruler, to do with as he chose. Then Yang Zhu—in the manner somewhat reminiscent of John Locke—stated that the physical body constituted the individual's most basic private possession, from which evolved rights to autonomy.

Thinking that both doctrines, in propounding absolutism and autonomy, undermined the will to seek the kind of delicate balance required for humane social orders, early Confucian teachers argued instead that the apparent owners of bodies and of states—the individual persons and the titled rulers—held these assets only temporarily in trust for all members of the community. Therefore, benefits associated with possession of the body or the state should be spread as widely as possible within the bounds of the respective communities (i.e., in the case of the family, shared with its members living and dead; in the case of the state, shared with all subjects in the state).[26] Apparent—even legal—possession of a body or a state, then, had little real standing in moral terms; blessings offered and requited through ritual were made to join communities across time and space.

Chinese medical theory underlined this Confucian emphasis on fluidity, since it posited the regular circulation of blood and *qi* (configured energy) as the primary definition of physical and moral health.[27] Accordingly, the health of the body politic was thought to depend upon the smooth flow of communication between ruler and people and the circulation of goods, on a strict analogy with the physical body: "When the ruler's virtue does not flow freely, and the wishes of his people do not reach him, there is stasis in the state. When stasis lasts for a long time, a hundred pathologies arise in concert, and a myriad catastrophes swarm in. . . . The reason that the sage-kings valued heroic retainers and faithful ministers is that they dared to speak directly, breaking through such stases."[28] Because, as one early classicist put it, "The Way of [true] humanity lies in making contact,"[29] the Confucians labored to devise suitable methods to optimize this flow of wealth and services: wealth would be regularly dispersed through ritual gift exchanges[30] and through the enforcement (under social pressure, under political and legal sanctions) of the ruling elite's duty to distribute grain and other basic necessities to the poor.[31] Moral learning would circulate throughout the realm from the true king and his ministers to commoners and then back from "those below" to the court, "exactly as vital *qi* circulates through the human body."[32] The state would facilitate this "appropriate" movement of persons and information within the realm.[33] Social mobility, for instance, would be encouraged through largely meritocratic educational and bureaucratic systems—a revolutionary idea attributed directly to Confucius.[34] And persons engaged in ritual would assume a variety of shifting roles, each identified with specific physical sites. Basically, "goods and grains [in company with people and ideas] shall be allowed to circulate freely, so that there is no hindrance or stagnation in distribution."[35]

Once these discrete strands of Confucian theorizing had been woven together, there resulted a remarkably coherent picture of the ideal state and the ideal person (the sage, who in the best of all possible worlds was also the king): these were robust circulatory systems producing a surplus of energy, which in turn boosted the moral and physical health of weaker things nearby, until "Moral influence irresistibly filled to over-flowing the whole of All-under-Heaven within the Four Seas."[36] In theory, this moral power knew no bounds, since it resonated with all things that were in sympathy with it, however distant in time and space, oper-ating like a tuning fork that magically sets to humming stringed instru-ments across the room.[37]

Consequently, the dividing lines between heaven and earth, between past and present, were to collapse, at least when the cosmos was lucky enough to be ruled by a sage-king: the Confucian exemplar "in contem-plating Heaven, becomes Heaven; in contemplating Earth, becomes Earth; in contemplating Time, becomes timely."[38] After all, "the sage is teacher to a hundred generations,"[39] because "all the ten thousand things were there within" him.[40] This was how "Confucian" classicists subtly reinterpreted the explicit claim of older elite traditions that "All land is the king's land / All humans within the borders are his subjects."[41] Hence, my preliminary characterization of territorial boundaries in Confucian discourse as eminently "permeable" and infinitely "expand-able." (Lands with fixed borders and kings without the requisite moral capacities to extend generosity to others through a process of "lik-ening to oneself"—like the sorriest of "skin-bound" persons—were considered woefully limited and so remarkably unappealing to the early Chinese.)[42]

To be realized, this ideal capacity to transcend ordinary boundaries (dubbed the "Great Peace" in the state and "sagehood" predicated on psychic equilibrium in the person)—a crossing-over not to be confused with a breakdown of order—depended fundamentally on the vibrant potency of the center (the ruler, in the case of the state). Confucian texts identify the ruler as "ultimate" locus or "center," even as "vibrating dipole"[43] of his state, not because rulers per se are an intrinsically more "valuable" breed of human beings than the rest of us; not even be-cause rulers have been anointed by Heaven.[44] No, the king is "center" because he, by virtue of his influential position, has the potential to gen-erate the greatest number of effective moral acts in all directions. Also, according to Confucian assumptions of "proximity" (a kind of geomo-rality), humans are more likely to attain moral enlightenment the closer their proximity to his suasive example. In consequence, the ruler func-tions as potential hub of all action.[45] Not surprisingly, then, the charac-ter for "king" (three parallel horizontal lines joined by a vertical) shows the king to be one who joins, symbolizes, and stabilizes the parallel moral realms of Heaven, Earth, and Man.[46]

"One starts with unity and proceeds to plurality," as one Confucian master wrote.[47] For him, as for all early Confucians, what mattered most was seeing that this vital center held firm. Then and only then would all the other things, people, and events lapse "naturally" into their correct places (*zheng*), with the result that each—human or nonhuman—would be free to develop spontaneously in its own distinctive pattern.[48] The moral center, the Confucians asserted, would hold so long as the heart/mind persists in choosing the right, so long as the emperor scrupulously "conforms to Heaven" (by watching the celestial patterns) and "orders things" on earth (by setting an exemplary pattern for morality, communicated through regular ritual performances).[49] One of the chief—if not the chief—way that the good ruler (or, in his absence, the sage) sets a compelling example of perfect virtue is by acknowledging the most elementary truth: that his most fortunate possession of a body, territory, and portable property represents the cumulative achievements of successive generations over time, and so the primary benefits of possession—economic wealth and moral insight—are to be shared with others in the community, particularly those who are noble-minded (out of admiration) or less fortunate (out of pity).[50]

Obviously, not a few rulers in real life were reluctant to exert the full measure of their charismatic influence, when such exertion would entail significant "sharing" of their persons, their goods, and their lands with others. Then the Confucians hastened to point out the practical advantages that would invariably accrue from acts of generosity: Sharing, they said, leaves the person secure from the threat that others will steal his things out of envy or need.[51] Sharing promises to yield aesthetic pleasures also, because "only the good and wise man is able to [i.e., fully knows how to] enjoy his possessions."[52] Sharing even binds the gods, ghosts, and men to the donor, thereby vastly increasing his power. "It was by sharing . . . that the [ideal] men of antiquity were able to enjoy," maintain, and pass on their physical patrimony (the body, the land, the possessions).[53] Supreme power, after all, rests in the person's ability to confidently call upon the aid of a unified community in a crisis: that "the people are prepared to die" for a person is what it means to be truly powerful.

Conversely, "One can never [truly] 'gain' the empire without the heart-felt admiration of the people in it."[54] Kings whose subjects are disloyal are rightly said to have "no men" in their service.[55] As a rule, to have insecure or disreputable possessions is tantamount to having no possessions at all, since such possessions bring no certain blessings. Those who do not acknowledge their obligations to others by sharing their blessings will doubtless find "their persons in danger and their territories reduced."[56] Nevertheless, the more cautious of the early Confucian masters were quick to remind followers that they had promised only that the steady accumulation of moral acts would yield unmistakable, if intangible influence; after all, *de* (charismatic virtue) operated on others just like the unseen wind. It was simply that intangible moral influence so often coincidentally brought tangible powers and possessions in its wake, as men came willingly to offer their goods and their persons to charismatic leaders.[57]

Organizing Space Appropriately

This early Confucian stress on the real if sometimes immaterial advantages of virtuous conduct coexisted with a strong and abiding interest in drawing lines and limits for material things in space. We see this in the many passages where the overwhelming moral influence of the Confucian exemplar is expressed in spatial terms, as when the ruler is compared to "the compass in motion describing a complete circle through the sites," or the carpenter's square, which "secures things [in their proper place]."[58] The unknown authors of the Confucian classics continually— some would say *ad nauseam*—listed among the paramount arts of ruling, reserved to sages and true kings, the art of organizing space appropriately. Certainly, the construction of temporary physical boundaries in space for ritual purposes—boundaries increasing in number and size in direct proportion to the importance of the ritual activities conducted within—was perceived as absolutely crucial, insofar as set boundaries helped focus the attention of less cultivated heart-minds upon that distillation of the truly holy (via communication and other reciprocal exchanges) that was the goal of ritual acts performed within the extra-sacred space. On the model of the "natural" or "spontaneous" Tao's ordering of large blocks of space and time in the universe, humans could partake of divinity whenever they managed to order, through ritual, their infinitely smaller spheres of human interaction.[59]

Hence, the strict spatial segregation by hierarchies of gender, rank, and age: "Men took the right side and women the left; men stayed behind another of a father's years."[60] The goal was not only to forestall overfamiliarity, lest that breed contempt between the groups, but also to grant each person his or her due allotment of private space. (The few rituals that worked to upset commonplace perceptions of the physical boundaries demarcating rank, gender, age, or social status, as when a young boy impersonating an ancestor took precedence over his father, somehow worked as exceptions that proved the rule; they merely served to underscore the profound moral utility of the normative space units that usually structured everyday life.) In any case, multiple references to ordering space pepper multiple chapters of the *Rites, Documents, Odes,* and *Mencius* classics, as well as the Han dynasty neoclassics. According to these accounts, the legendary sages of antiquity divided All-under-Heaven into five concentric regions; into four, nine, or twelve major provinces; and into innumerable well-field plots of nine hundred Chinese acres each. In each case, the sages had discerned an underlying order, which they sought to respond to and strengthen by further replication.[61] Spatial schemas, even spatial fantasies, were therefore one means by which early Confucian culture declared its faith in the inherently orderly processes of the cosmos, on the one hand, and in the vast human potential for constructed order on the other. Another was the Confucian—or was it merely Chinese?—preoccupation with place-naming, a skill by which unremarkable space was transformed symbolically into monumental "place" (i.e., space with a specific, memorable history).[62]

Confucians, too, were inclined to wax eloquent on the subject of halting "inappropriate" flows in physical space. That much flow was indeed appropriate and that this appropriate flow should be encouraged, all Confucian thinkers agreed upon. At the same time, flows must never be allowed to run on in a chaotic and uncontrolled fashion. (Once again, the analogy with the body worked, for the flow of blood and *qi* in the body must be contained within appropriate channels, lest there occur disastrous leakages of the vital substances.) In company with other thinkers of their time,[63] the Confucians firmly believed that the vast majority of people fared best—both in moral and in economic terms—when they stayed put in relatively small communities (in "natural" units of about "100 *li* [square]"), where shared histories and a uniform code of morality kept members alive to their obligations to care for one another humanely.[64] Most people who had left their ancestral graves far behind could be expected to feel a sense of what we today might call "alienation." Physically adrift, once they had lost their "rightful" place in the world, they were more likely to be beset with economic difficulties and psychic insecurities, which could then lead to the commission of serious crimes against properties and persons. (Of course, the Confucian theorists realized that most migrants had been driven from their lands by unjust wars, unwise policies, or natural disasters, in mass migrations that typically threatened the security of the state and its remaining inhabitants.) In further explanation of this, the Confucians were wont to explain that different types of location, each with its own characteristic climate, topography, and *qi* ("cold or hot, dry or moist"), were apt to engender varying aptitudes and habits in those born in different regions, making it all the more vital that a sage "at center" reveal to each separate group its own distinct Middle Path, which could then be harmonized with the others.[65]

Nonetheless, as the legend of good king Danfu suggests, the early Confucians thought the specific site of ritually demarcated space, let alone territorial possessions, to be comparatively unimportant, so long as the sage held forth "at center." (Could it be that the locations of land units mattered so little because they tended not to correspond exactly with the main units of organized society in China: the clan lineages and the professional affiliations?) For example, when the early Confucians discussed the Five Sacred Mountains, they glanced over questions about the precise location at which these Mountains were situated; they were intent upon seeing the right number of mountains grandly honored in ritual.[66] And once again, it was the ritual "center" among the Mountains, Mount Tai, that was deemed most important, though Mount Tai at no time corresponded to the actual geographical center of a Chinese or proto-Chinese state. Similarly, Chinese capitals were moved repeatedly over the course of Chinese history, sometimes several times within the course of a single dynasty, to suit the convenience of the emperor or to adapt to changing socioeconomic and political realities. The Confucians offered no vociferous protests; one chapter in the "Confucian" *Documents* instead celebrated the model king who moved his capital repeatedly.[67] For Confucians, what made a site holy over time was the quality and quantity of sacred acts enacted at the site (for example, the continuation of special sacrifices to the gods), where the sacred tended to include the mundane and the secular, as well as the overtly religious.[68] What made any city a king's capital, in particular, was the erection of ritual halls and educational institutions, where the classical Way of the Ancients—both the practice and theory of it—would be sponsored by the state and transmitted to successive generations.[69] The focus, in other words, remained on the accumulation of humane deeds fostering community, in the serene confidence that such accumulations ultimately would spawn signs of supramundane power in time or space.

Ultimately, this approach allowed Confucians remarkable play when imagining space in ethical terms. While no early Confucian ever exhibited a romantic love for wilderness terrain, as "the wastes" lay beyond the cycle of ritual obligations constructed by sages,[70] these same Confucians felt entirely comfortable adopting the shifting perspectives found in classic Chinese landscape art when faced with the need to formulate complex moral judgments. A famous passage from the *Gongyang* commentary to the *Spring and Autumn Annals* (a work ascribed to Confucius) will demonstrate my point. The commentary states: "When it [the sacred *Annals* text] takes the point of view of the capital, then the Central States' culture surrounding it [near the Yellow River] is considered 'outside' [and so meriting a different treatment]; and when it takes the point of view of the Central States, then the Yi and Di barbarians are considered 'outside.' "[71] Similarly, the Confucian thinker Mencius, in trying to persuade others that virtue is really the "natural" course for humans, weighed a series of possible implications of analogies constructed between "inside" vs. "outside" and "nature" vs. "nurture"; meanwhile, the *Rites* chapters tried to apportion mourning duties within the family circle, a most delicate ritual matter, through language that calculates degrees of kinship more or less "inside" or "outside."[72] Space had acquired this ethical character, for each and every aspect of the cosmos in its appropriate location revealed, to the enlightened heart-mind, the moral connections threading through the universe. Humans who yearned for true greatness had only to study and emulate the patterns of location to discern fundamental truths, as the *Book of Rites* attested in the following passage:

> The courses of the heavenly bodies supply the most perfect lessons, and the sages possessed the highest degree of virtue. Above, in the hall of the ancestral temple, there was a jar of wine, with clouds and hills represented on it on the east and with sacrificial victims represented on it in the west. Below the hall, the larger drums were suspended in the west, and the smaller drums that answer them on the east. The ruler appeared at the top of the steps on the east; his wife, in the apartment on the west. The sun makes its appearance in the east; the moon makes her appearance in the west. Such are the different ways in which the processes of dark and light are distributed in nature, and such are the arrangements for the [corresponding] positions of husband and wife.[73]

CONCLUSION

While the Confucian Way is all too often mischaracterized as a sort of slavish devotion to a monolithic tradition, it arose in reaction against prevailing conventions, out of successive attempts to selectively appropriate, reconfigure, and promote the most "nonregressive" (i.e., humanizing) tendencies within pre-Confucian traditions.[74] In the spirit of Confucian accommodation, we might consider borrowing certain messages drawn from Confucian history, the better to reconfigure our own moral priorities—all the more so as the Confucians have long been in the habit of contemplating a world in which a very many people are crowded into exceedingly tight spaces.[75] I myself applaud the clarity of the Confucian vision that requires vast empires to be balanced by sharp "turns toward the local," so that small communities, admittedly with the informed support of exemplary leaders at the pinnacle of power, are expected to define appropriate responsibilities and reasonable expectations for their own members.[76] Our society would surely profit as well from a consideration of the fundamental Confucian proposition that we "share" our bodies and our properties with others, for as long as we careen between belief in ourselves as fully autonomous, "self-made" beings and as pathetic creatures entrapped by our preconscious pasts while maintaining our nationalistic and global allegiances, we will tend to ignore the all-important roles of middle-level social groupings (the extended family, the immediate neighborhood) in fostering ethical action. The Confucian preference for "soft boundaries" for the body and body politic satisfies both moral and practical considerations.[77] Equally sound are related beliefs that Confucians have shared with thinkers of many other religious or philosophical traditions: first, that levels of self-cultivation, rather than quantities of material commodities, mark the fully mature adult; and second, that good states by definition find ways to single out moral adults for public recognition and rewards, so that their examples will be easily identified, closely studied, and widely emulated by society. According to the Confucian view, any society that celebrates mere freedom from intervention as its highest goal will inevitably pay a heavy price in terms of the physical, mental, and moral health of its members. Concomitantly, the just state, properly constituted, notwithstanding its extendable borders, owes to all its own people provisions for a secure economic livelihood (famine relief in times of natural disaster, the supervision of granaries and markets, and so on), no less than a fine education in moral thinking.

I end with an observation: We who tend—certainly in our more uncritical moments—to view ourselves as inheritors of a "Western tradition" must acknowledge that, thanks to our particular history, the knowledge of geography and indeed, the focus on boundaries, are intimately related to capitalism's expanding role in the nineteenth and early twentieth centuries. Hence, our propensity to see "space, as a social fact, as a social factor and as an instance of society, [as] . . . always political and strategic."[78] By contrast, early Chinese thinkers developed a distinct discipline of learning called *di li* ("Earth's patterns"; their closest counterpart to our "geography") which looked to ethnographic and historical knowledge, not iconic knowledge (the need for better maps and diagrams to aid expansion).[79] The Chinese interest in human history and human customs operated on three related assumptions: first, that the past was indeed relevant to the present and changing world; second, that space—like time—could be configured in such a way as to direct our attention productively to the very human need for frequent ethical interaction; and third, that this elusive yet desirable Way was itself reducible neither to objective knowledge nor to multiple acquisitions; rather, it was to be equated with the kind of learning that informs conscious, ethical action. Let us hope that our future endeavors more closely enter into the Chinese spirit of *di li* than that of the "Western" explorer-geographers, insofar as we take up the larger task of seeking ethical solutions to guide the cultivation of "All-under-Heaven."[80]

NOTES

1. For the confusion between "Confucianism" and "classicism" (both are *Ru*), see Michael Nylan, "Rethinking the Han Confucian Synthesis," *Imagining Boundaries: Changing Confucian Doctrines, Texts, and Hermeneutics*, ed. Kai-wing Chow, On-cho Ng, and John B. Henderson (Albany: State University of New York Press, 1999). Concerted efforts by responsible scholars to separate "Confucianism" from "Chinese" have repeatedly foundered. See, e.g., *A Confucian World Observed: A Contemporary Discussion of Confucian Humanism in East Asia*, eds. Tu Wei-ming, Milan Hejtmanek, and Alan Wachman (Honolulu: University of Hawaii Press, 1992).

2. For the very useful distinction between orthopraxy vs. orthodoxy, see William Watson, *Death Ritual in Late Imperial China*, eds. James L. Watson and Evelyn S. Rawski (Berkeley: University of California Press, 1988), chap. 1. For the Confucian concern with motivations and with practice, rather than with doctrines, see David Nivison, *The Ways of Confucianism* (Chicago: University of Chicago Press, 1996), 119. Probably, the Chinese conception of civilization (*wen*, literally "cultural patterns") became more "bookish" and more "historical" under later neo-Confucianism.

3. Confucius defined *zhong* ("loyalty") and *shu* ("consideration," "reciprocity," or "likening [others to oneself]") as the core of his teaching. See *Analects* 4/15.

4. *Analects* 18/8: "As for me, I am different from any of these. I have no 'thou shalt' or 'thou shalt not'." Cf. Arthur Waley, *The Analects of Confucius* (London: Vintage, 1938), 222.

5. Lionel Jensen, "The Invention of 'Confucius' and His Chinese Other, 'Kong Fuzi,'" *Positions* 1:2 (Fall 1993): 414–49; William W. Appleton, *The City of Cathay: The Chinese Vogue in England during the Seventeenth and Eighteenth Centuries* (New York: Columbia University Press, 1951). For "unified empire" as a late concept, probably postdating Confucius, see Gu Jiegang, "Qin Han tong yi de you lai he zhan guo ren dui yu shi jie de xiang xiang," *Gushi bian* 2 (1927): 1–10; Wang Yong, *Zhongguo di li xue shi* (Taipei: Student Bookstore rpt. of Shanghai, 1938 ed.), 12.

6. The term "Central States" was apparently coined in the Warring States period (475–222 B.C.E.) in the area that corresponds roughly to present-day northeast and central China, an area dominated by the Yellow River and long considered (erroneously) the single "wellspring" of civilization. As each of the ruling houses of the Central States traced its roots back to either Shang or early Zhou rule, elites in the Central States emphasized the great continuities among their cultures once they were confronted with the rise of two new superpowers

from outside the region: Qin far to the northwest, and Chu to the south. The Central States identity was based primarily on cultural identity.

"Chinese identity," by contrast, arose very gradually in response to a succession of "barbarian" conquests, e.g., that in C.E. 417, when the whole of northern China was conquered by the Toba nomads. It was not fully formed until after 1840, when the old culturalist arguments yielded to new arguments about race, which pitted Manchus against the Chinese, and the Chinese against the Euro-American imperialists.

7. See Nivison, *Ways of Confucianism*, 5.

8. Because later neo-Confucianism, influenced by Buddhism (itself influenced by the Greco-Roman world) shares more presumptions with Christianity, it requires less effort to appreciate it than the "stranger," pre-Buddhist classicism. Hence, the comment made by the scholar Jacques Gernet to a student specializing in Han classicism, "You have to admit that *your* Han people were a rather odd bunch, and that the Chinese of the 16th–19th centuries were quite different!" (reported in Anne Cheng, "Intellectual Self-Awareness in Han Times," paper given at the Association for Asian Studies annual conference, 1996).

9. The so-called "universalism" of *Ru* thought is undoubtedly the product of the Jesuit construction of "Confucianism" as "bearer of China's significance" in debates over truth, God, and representation. See Lionel M. Jensen, *Manufacturing Confucianism: Chinese Traditions and Universal Civilization* (Durham: Duke University Press, 1997), esp. 4, 260; Jensen, "Invention of Confucius," 415–49; D. R. Howland, *Borders of Chinese Civilization* (Durham, N.C.: Duke University Press, 1996), 7, 31, 199. Classical notions could easily be made to accommodate foreign notions of universal kingship, since the semantic fields of Chinese characters can be radically expanded to express new concepts. Magoshi Yasushi, for example, notes in a recent article one major shift in the meaning of fundamental vocabulary: that of *ren* (from "king's relatives" to "common people") in connection with the Mandate of Heaven theory. See "Kōkotsubun ni mieru hito" ("Men" in the Oracle Bone Script), *Tōhōgaku* 92:2: 17–29.

Early conceptions of kingship hardly correspond with the idea of "universal kingship," which presupposes a number of preexisting borders. Rather, the early Chinese are concerned with that portion of the known world under the direct protection of the ancestors (*tian xia*), a portion of territory that expanded over time, but had no precise theoretical limits until the late nineteenth century, when the modern notion of the nation-state imposed the necessity for precisely demarcated territorial boundaries. (Often *tian xia* now, by contrast, is translated not only as "the whole empire" but even as "the whole world.") Nonetheless, in early China, the legitimacy of political rule was quite closely tied to the possession of land. When, for example, the early Chinese were faced with the conundrum, "Why did the Supreme Sage not rule as Son of Heaven (i.e., emperor), given his obvious qualifications?" the classicists' answer was that Confucius lacked a territorial base from which to become ruler. See, e.g., Yang Xiong, *Fa yan*, in *[Xin bian] Zhuzi ji cheng* (Taipei: World Books, 1974), II, 10:30. Note finally that the early Ru school went on record opposing the notion that "moral good and the moral order are universal" (contra Chan, chap. 4 above, section on

"The Confucian Ethical Tradition"); that was the Mohist position, which Confucius, Mencius, and Xunzi vehemently opposed.

10. None of the Five Classics are reliably linked with Confucius before 100 B.C.E., nearly four hundred years after the Master's death in 479 B.C.E. To date, early traditions have only one of the "Confucian" Classics figuring largely in Confucius's teaching: the *Odes*, some version of which—oral or written—the Master reportedly urged his disciples to study. See Michael Nylan, *The Five "Confucian" Classics* (New Haven: Yale University Press, 2001), chap. 1; Steven Van Zoeren, *Poetry and Personality: Reading, Exegesis, and Hermeneutics in Traditional China* (Stanford: Stanford University Press, 1991). Note that the *Analects*, which purports to transcribe the conversations of Confucius with his disciples, was regarded as a secondary or supplemental "Classic" in Han times, since it did not record traditions handed down from high antiquity.

11. *Li ji*, "Wang zhi," 5/40 (Legge, I, 229–30) accepts this, for example. For more information, see Xing Yitian, "Tian xia yi jia: chuan tong Zhongguo tian xia guan de xing cheng" (The one family "under Heaven": the formulation of the traditional concepts of China and "All-under-Heaven"), *Qin Han shi lun kao* (Taipei: Dongda, 1987), 3–42, esp. 22ff. Cf. Zhao Diehan, "Chun qiu shi qi de Rong Di de li fen bu ji qi yuan liu," *Da lu za zhi* 11:2 (July 31, 1956): 6–13; 11:3 (Aug. 15, 1956): 21–25. The early ethical followers of Confucius were certainly aware of differences in ethnicity and language, but they regarded such distinctions as fundamentally less significant than a person's commitment to the Moral Way. See, e.g., *Analects* 3/5, which says, "The barbarians of the East and North who have retained their princes are not in such a state of decay as we inheritors of xia" (note Joseph Chan's completely different rendering of this passage, section on "Diversity"); and *Mencius* 3A/4, which refers to "the shrike-tongued barbarians of the South." Certainly, the *Gongyang Traditions* uses "barbarian" loosely to describe anyone of any ethnicity who fails to adopt the fine old Zhou system celebrated by Confucius. See Pu Weizhong, *Chun qiu san zhuan zong he yan jiu* (Taipei: Wenjin, 1995), 138–50.

12. *Mencius* 3A/4: "I have heard of the Chinese converting barbarians to their ways, but not of their being converted to barbarian ways." Note that the gap in the material standards of "barbarian" and "Central States" peoples was not so large under Eastern Zhou rule (771–256 B.C.E.) as it would become later.

13. *Analects* 17/2. The consensus in early China was that the Central States had adopted the models and institutions of the Odes, Documents, Rites, and Music for (their) government, while the Rong and Yi (barbarians) continued to lack these models. See, e.g., *Zuo zhuan*, Duke Ch'eng 2, *fu* 3. Such notions are the subject of Michael Loewe, "China's Sense of Unity as Seen in the Early Empires," *T'oung Pao* 80 (1994): 6–25, esp. 17ff.

14. *Analects* 9/13; 12/5; 17/2. Cf. *Analects* 3/5, trans. in note 11 above. This accounts for the popular legend, recorded in many places, including the "Tang wen" chap. of the *Liezi*, that Yu traversed the whole world, which he "mistook to be one state." The *Da Dai Li ji*, "Xiao xian," chap. states that all the distant lands submitted to the sage-ruler Shun. The importance of ritual practice lay in its capacity to "facilitate passages and/or to authorize encounters between

opposed orders." See Pierre Bourdieu, *Outline of a Theory of Practice*, trans. Richard Nice (Cambridge: Cambridge University Press, 1977), 120.

15. *Han shu* (Beijing: Zhonghua, 1970), 22:1027, where the "roads" belong to the Six Classics, later (e.g., in *Han shu* 30:1746) equated with all learning. Note that there have been no specifically religious persecutions in China, though state persecutions of religious groups have occurred when the groups threatened the hegemony of the Chinese state in economic and political matters (as when, for example, the tax-free lands attached to major monasteries threatened the economic health of the imperial budget). This chapter does not specifically address the question of slavery, which played a small role in early China, with most slaves being either war captives or criminals. See Clarence Martin Wilbur, *Slavery in China during the Former Han Dynasty* (Chicago: University of Chicago, 1943).

16. Linguists, such as Dr. Mary Erbaugh (City University, Hong Kong), are wont to say that the only difference between a "dialect" and a "language" is that a language has a standing army behind it. On the sage-king's provisions for linguistic incomprehensibility, see *Li ji*, "Wang zhi" 5/40 (Legge, I, 229–30). Of course, one question that immediately arises in connection with language is, why the persistence of the Chinese worldview in Japan, Korea, Vietnam, and other of China's neighbors into the midnineteenth century? A good start has been made in Howland, *Borders*, which notes that countries sharing the use of the special Chinese literary language (*wen yan wen*) were often dubbed "countries sharing Civilization" (*wen ming*), a term that obviated reference to political borders (p. 7).

17. Here I am reminded of the remark recorded of the Emperor Sui Yangdi when he crossed the Yangtze river during a campaign: "I am father and mother of the people. How can I be constrained by this mere belt of water, and so fail to assist those in trouble?" See *Nan shi, zhuan* 10, "Chen benji" (Basic annals of Chen) (Beijing: Zhonghua, 1975), 1:307.

18. *Mencius* 1B/5 explicitly states that under the true kings, there was to be "inspection but not levies at border stations." *Mencius* 2A/5 tells the ruler to make conditions such that "travellers . . . [from other states] will be only too pleased to go by way of your roads." For the myth of the Great Wall as territorial boundary, see Arthur Waldron, *The Great Wall of China* (Cambridge: Cambridge University Press, 1990).

19. Even in the case of the dead ancestor, ritual-time and shrine-space continued to define the person, as is clear from the early stelae accounts and the performative formulas of the liturgies for the deceased. See Kenneth E. Brashier, "Evoking the Ancestor: The Stele Hymn of the Eastern Han Dynasty (25–220 C.E.)" (Ph.D. thesis, Cambridge University, 1997).

20. This probably explains the well-known propensity of Chinese to regard as truly "ancient" a pagoda entirely rebuilt in 1912 on a Tang dynasty site. It is not so much the bricks or even the site that matters, but the moral acts that occurred there over time.

21. Cf. the famous Chinese proverb about "the old frontiersman's horse." For the *Changes*, see Kikuchi Kiyokatsu, "Chūgoku ni okeru chūō no kenkyū:

Ekikyō o chūshin to shite" (Research on the "center" in China: with the *Changes* as center), *Risshō Daigaku kyōyōbu Kiyō* 24 (1991): 25–40; Willard J. Peterson, "Making Connections: 'Commentary on the Attached Verbalizations' of the *Book of Change*," *Harvard Journal of Asiatic Studies* 42:1 (1982): 67–116; and Michael Nylan, ed. and trans., *T'ai hsüan ching, or The Canon of Supreme Mystery by Yang Hsiung* (Albany: State University of New York Press, 1993; hereafter *THC*). A useful overview of some of these issues is provided by Robin D. S. Yates, "Body, Space, Time, and Bureaucracy: Boundary Creation and Control Mechanisms in Early China," *Boundaries in China*, ed. John Hay (London: Reaktion Books, 1994), 62. By sites (i.e., Space), the early Chinese meant "locations favorable or unfavorable for a given action."

22. *Analects* 3/14, wherein Confucius says, "I follow Chou."

23. *Shi ji* (Beijing: Zhonghua, 1959), 4:113–14. Cf. *Shang shu da zhuan*, attributed to Fu Sheng, ICS Ancient Chinese Text Concordance Series No. 5 (Hong Kong: Commercial Press, 1994), 27.

24. For example, Mencius insists that the virtuous founders of the Shang and Zhou dynasties were willing to submit to smaller powers. *Mencius* 1B/3 repeats legends of virtuous heirs who yielded territory and rank, including Taibo, Bo Yi, and Shu Qi. See Nylan, "Confucian Piety and Individualism," *Journal of the American Oriental Society* 116 (Jan.–March, 1996): 1–27.

25. One later manifestation of this tight connection between the ancestors or Heaven and their people below can be found in the presumed correlations between Earthly markings (the works of man) and Heavenly doings (the works of the gods: the demarcation of time zones, calendrical practices, the production of climate and distinctive things); these are formulated in the *fen ye* theory, which enjoyed great popularity in China from at least Han times. Still, one must note that neither the word *Zhongguo* (originally "Central States," rather than the "Middle Kingdom" of the Orientalists) nor the word *tian xia* ("All-under-Heaven") is found on the bronze and bone inscriptions. It is also hard to accept the "Shang" dynasty as fully "Chinese," despite accounts of the later systematizing texts in the Han. See Robert W. Bagley, "Shang: China's First Historical Dynasty," in *The Cambridge History of Ancient China: From the Origins of Civilization to 221 B.C.*, eds. Michael Loewe and Edward L. Shaughnessy (Cambridge: Cambridge University Press, 1999). William G. Boltz, "Inscriptions, Monumentality and Literacy in Ancient China: The Role of Writing in the Shang and Early Western Zhou" (unpublished ms.), makes the useful distinction between "early civilization in China" (where China is only a geographic designation) and "early Chinese civilization."

26. *Mencius* 1A. Cf. Yang Xiong, "The Plume Hunt": "[The emperor] shares with the common folk, and by this means he has attained his present success," trans. after David Knechtges, trans., *Wenxuan, or Selections of Refined Literature*, vol. 2 (Princeton: Princeton University Press, 1987), 135.

27. For the relation of moral health to the flow of *qi*, see *Mencius* 2A/2. Nathan Sivin, "State, Cosmos, and Body in the Last Three Centuries B.C.," *Harvard Journal of Asiatic Studies* 55:1 (1995): 5, states: "In China, ideas of Nature, state, and the body were so interdependent that they are best considered a single

complex." Cf. G.E.R. Lloyd, *Adversaries and Authorities* (Cambridge: Cambridge University Press, 1996), chap. 9.

28. *Lü shi chun qiu* 12/10a-b, trans. modified from Lloyd, *Adversaries*, 191. A number of classical and Confucian texts, such as Lu Jia's *Xinyu*, make similar arguments, though the point is more concisely stated here.

29. Yang Xiong, *Fa yan* 3:7. Cf. *Han shu* 56:2507, where the bad state is described as one in which the *qi* is completely blocked.

30. See Nylan, "Confucian Piety"; Mayfair Mei-hui Yang, *Gifts, Favors, and Banquets: The Art of Social Relationships in China* (Ithaca: Cornell University Press, 1994).

31. See, e.g., *Mencius* 1A/3. The ruler's duty to redistribute wealth is also the subject of the "Great Plan" chap. of the *Documents*. *Mencius* 1B/4 makes it the ruling elites' business to distribute aid to the needy. *Mencius* 2A/8 justifies the states' taxation by its periodic redistribution to the poor. For the practical ramifications of the failure to redistribute wealth, see *Mencius* 1B/6, 8 on the Mencian right to rebel, an expanded version of the Mandate of Heaven theory.

32. Sivin, "State, Cosmos," 22.

33. *Li ji*, "Wang zhi" 5/22 (Legge, I, 216), where audiences and sacrifices are conducted by the king in each and every outlying domain, bringing the royal presence there; meanwhile, lists of local market prices, descriptions of local peoples, and such are compiled, in the hopes that local conditions will "come alive" to the throne at the center. With state expenditures also, provisions were to be made for adjusting the "outgoing by the incoming."

34. The slogan "Employ the Worthy" began with the Mohists, a group that aimed to "reform" the *Ru*. However, the germ of the idea may be traced to Confucius's insistence on teaching the aristocratic Way of the Ancients to persons of low rank, so long as they were sufficiently motivated; also to Confucius's insistence that he, along with other followers of the Way, was fit to advise kings, despite his low rank. Mencius (late fourth century B.C.E.) urged rulers to found schools at the village, prefectural, and county levels, so as to maximize the contributions to the state of local talents. In practice, the educational institutions of imperial China (including the examination systems) were not as meritocratic as usually assumed, since wealth, social position, and official rank gave distinct advantages to certain candidates hoping for advancement.

35. *Xunzi*, chap. 9; trans. follows Burton Watson, *Basic Writings* (New York: Columbia University Press, 1963), 43.

36. *Mencius* 4A/6; trans. follows D. C. Lau, *Mencius* (New York: Penguin, 1970), 120. For claims that a man of virtue can start with a small state, and within 5–7 years come to rule the empire, see ibid., 4A/7; for "moving towards goodness" as related to "expansiveness," see *Mencius* 7A/13.

37. Kenneth J. DeWoskin, *A Song for One or Two: Music and the Concept of Art in Early China* (Ann Arbor: University of Michigan Press, 1982), 73ff.

38. *THC*, "Xuan wen," 453. In some sense, Confucians put potentially dangerous exchanges between Heaven and Earth (as in the legend of Zhongli) on a new footing.

39. *Mencius* 7B/15.

40. *Mencius* 7A/4. Wang Yangming (1472–1529) took this to mean that for the perfected person, "all things are one body" (so that he feels as deeply for all things as for himself).

41. Ode 205. For the idea that "there is nothing 'outside' [or 'foreign'] to the [true] king," see *Gongyang Traditions* (hereafter *Gongyang*), Duke Cheng 15. For the claim that "A son does not consider that he has his own self, nor does an official," see *Shi ji* 47:1909.

42. The phrase "skin-bound" person comes from John Emerson, "Yang Chu's Discovery of the Body," *Philosophy East and West* 46:4 (1996): 536, which cites, among others, Marriot, Takeo Doi's *The Anatomy of Dependence* (1973), and Louis Dumont's *Essays on Individualism* (1986). Notions of "individual autonomy" and states' rights would have mystified most early Chinese and disgusted the Confucians. Thus, some have described the "traditional self" in China as "plural," "diffuse," "empty," and "divided." I dispute the last two characterizations, since the ideal person in such societies is full (of potential interactions with others) and strongly centered, in a word, "integrated" and "integrating" (*cheng*). Hence, the early *Ru* emphasis on the *rong* ("capacity to encompass") of the sage or sage-king: see the "Hong fan" chap. of the *Documents*; also Liu Xiang, *Shuo yuan*, chap. 1. Moral men like Confucius are to be *bo* ("wideranging"); by legend, some sages even sport four eyes and four ears, signifying their concern for all things in all directions.

43. The phrase is that of Ezra Pound's, used in his translation of the Confucian classic, the "Zhong yong."

44. The oldest beliefs in China presumed that the king was "center" by virtue of genealogy; as the direct descendant of the Supreme Ancestor in heaven, the Lord on High, the king had the capacity to apply for favors from the ancestors, though he acted on behalf of his family members. Late in the Warring States period, theorists argued that any man who was a sage had the right to achieve political power. Such beliefs seemed to be confirmed when a commoner, Liu Bang, ascended to the throne in 206 B.C.E. For the king as center, see, e.g., *Shi ji* 99:2716.

45. This would explain why Confucius, the "uncrowned king," never ascended the throne nor transformed the world: he had no throne from which to affect ever-expanding circles of subjects. Enthroned kings, when good, have the people "acknowledge their virtue" and "return to their virtuous example" (both *gui de*), as explained in *Hou Han shu* (Beijing: Zhonghua, 1965), 79A:2561. Note that while theorists associated with other "schools" were intent upon establishing a physical place (Kunlun) as *axis mundi*, the Confucians worked to establish the human ruler as *axis mundi*. See Gu Jiegang, "Yu gong zhong de Kunlun," *Li shi di li* 1 (1981): 3–8. The Legalists also acknowledged the ruler as center, but on a very different ethical basis: that the ruler had "fixed" (i.e., pacified) and therefore owned all the land in all directions. See the inscription on the Qin stele at Langya, as recorded in *Shi ji* 6:244–45. For the term "proximity," see Howland, *Borders*, 14, 40.

46. Dong Zhongshu: "Occupying the center of Heaven, Earth, and Man, passing through and joining all three—if it not be the king, who can do this?" See *Chun qiu fan lu*, sec. 43 (11:5a–5b).

47. *Xunzi*, chap. 9. Xunzi in chap. 32 promises that the final result of "holding fast to unity" and "behaving like Heaven and Earth, . . . sun and moon" will be that "the empire is but a single corner" of the area under the ruler's influence.

48. A favorite Confucian phrase was *ge de qi suo* ("May each attain its proper place"). See, e.g., *Xunzi*, chap. 9; Dong Zhongshu, cited in *Han shu* 56:2503. That the particular form of each and every creature was devised for the common good is the assumption of Dong, cited in *Han shu* 56:2520. Cf. the discussion in Yang Xiong's THC, Tetragram 2, Appraisal 2. Note finally that "center-ultimate," as elaborated in the *Changes*, *Rites*, and *Documents* canons, nonetheless is associated invariably with flexibility and responsiveness to changes over time and place.

49. *Han shu* 56:3509.

50. For the Confucian insistence that there are no self-made men, but only sageking inheritors of accumulated achievements, see Pan Piao, "On the Destiny of Kings," as translated in *Sources of Chinese Tradition*, vol. 1, eds. Wm. Theodore de Bary, Wing-Tsit Chan, and Burton Watson (New York: Columbia University Press, 1960), 176–80. For the king's duty to share blessings with others, see *Mencius* 1A/1–4.

51. Therefore, even in the relatively modernized "south" China of the early twentieth century, collective possession, rather than private possession, was the norm, as noted by Fei Hsiao-t'ung, *Peasant Life in China* (New York: Oxford University Press, 1946), chap. 4 ("Property and Inheritance") and chap. 11 ("Land Tenure"). Items of clothing, esp. undergarments and hair ornaments, were the sole exceptions to the general rule of collective possession; they alone were considered "personal" or "private"—rather than family, village, or state—property.

52. *Mencius* 1A/1. Secure enjoyment of pleasures in the company of others is said to be always greater than any enjoyment of secret or personal pleasures (*Mencius* 2A/1). "Sharing enjoyment with the people" is, in fact, Mencius's definition of "true kingship" (*ibid.*, 1B/1). Cf. Xunzi's famous dictum (chap. 4): "The man of Yue feels at home in Yue, the man of Chu feels at home in Chu. However, a [true] gentleman feels at home in elegant culture [wherever it is found]."

53. *Mencius* 1A/1. The "Ru xing" chapter of the *Li ji* states that the good *Ru* will consider the territory he has acquired to be the "accomplishment of just deeds." Xunzi's chapter, "On Ritual," offers two related arguments: (1) that sacrificial offerings are important because they habituate the person to sharing with the unseen, thereby refining her powers of imagination; (2) that the true king ensures that selfish acts by officials are severely punished. Both these Confucian thinkers may have derived their emphasis on sharing from the "Hong fan" chap. of the *Documents*, whose argumentation begins with the paradoxical premise that to give away power is to gain it. See Michael Nylan, *The Shifting Center: The Original "Great Plan" and Later Readings*, Monumenta Serica Monograph Series, no. 24 (May 1992).

54. *Mencius* 4B/16. As *Mencius* 1A/7 argues: "Now if you would practice benevolence in the government of your state, then all those in the Empire who seek office would wish to find a place at your court, then all farmers would wish

to till the land in your outlying regions, and all merchants to enjoy the refuge of your market-places."

55. See *Mencius* 1A/2; *Mencius* 1B/12: "Practice benevolent government and the people will be sure to love their superiors and die for them." For the expression, "no men," see, e.g., Ode 258.

56. *Mencius* 4A/2. Mencius writes, to seek to "to extend one's territory by such means [that are typically employed] is like looking for a fish by climbing a tree" (*Mencius* 1A/7). The analogy is made to hitting the target in archery; it requires a kind of focus, not strength (*Mencius* 5B/1; cf. 4A/3; 5A/1). Xunzi puts the case succinctly: It is the dictator, not the true king, who is intent upon "opening up lands" and waging war against his neighbors (chap. 9).

57. See for example *Analects* 2/18. One translation of this passage evokes this idea well, that by Waley, *Analects of Confucius*, 92.

58. THC, "Xuan tu." Cf. Tetragram 2/App. 2: "A pivot set directly center/ Sweeps full circle, not in angles." Similarly, the heart-mind, so long as it is "unbiased" and "upright," seeking only the common good, is said to be like the balance and plumb line.

59. The Confucians believed that each aspect of Heaven and Earth, as well as time, reveals the innate capacity within all living beings for order and harmony. Accordingly, they "divided space up into distinct units, each with its own peculiar concrete characteristics and each coordinated with time: the east was spring, the south summer and so on." See Robin Yates, "Body, Space," 61ff. Cf. Sekiguchi Jun, "Keishokan keisei katei no ichi kōsatsu" (An investigation into the process of canon formation), *Saitama Daigaku kiyō* 28 (1993), on Yi Feng. For ritual "wrapping" of space to enhance certain human relations, see Joy Hendry, *Wrapping Culture* (Oxford: Oxford University Press, 1993), 98–137.

60. *Li ji*, "Wang zhi" 5/46 (Legge, I, 245).

61. It is therefore the sage-king who "correctly positions the month [or moon]" (i.e., even controls time and space), since he emulates Heaven's brilliant order and thereby brings it to perfection. This is the explicit premise of the entire *Gongyang Traditions*, which purport to elucidate the *Chun qiu* ascribed to Confucius himself.

62. Early Confucians certainly knew the Mohist canon, which argued: "Spatial positions are names for that which is already past."

63. Thinkers we would now, on the basis of anachronistic criteria, call the Realpoliticians (or Legalists), the Agriculturalists, and the proto-Taoists, among others (e.g., Shang Yang, Zhuangzi, Laozi).

64. Ikeda Yuichi, "Chūgoku kodai no seikatsuken to hō hyakuri: toshi no nōson o megutte" (The sphere of life and its ambience in ancient China: towns and villages), *Chūgoku no toshi to nōson* (Tokyo: Kyūkoshoin, 1992), 29–59. This article shows that the 100 *li* territorial unit was considered the largest, stable moral unit outside the family. Sages, of course, were notable exceptions to this general rule. Yu, the primeval flood-queller, supposedly traversed the entire length and breadth of "All-under-Heaven," without ever stopping at his home to take rest and comfort.

65. Confucians were agreed that the location of one's birth affects one's "natural" predispositions (good and bad). The *Li ji*, "Jing jie" chapter, gives

this as the reason for having more than one "Confucian" classic, as the different classics together provide a range of tools to use in ruling peoples with different dispositions. Confucians debated whether these "natural" dispositions were to be fostered or restrained. Confucians, in any case, were not surprised to find that laws and customs varied over time, as the *qi* that informs human nature varies over time and place.

66. See James Robson, "Moving Mountains and Competing Yüeh: The History and Historiography of the Southern Marchmount" (unpublished ms.). Following Miyazaki Ichisada's work, Robson shows that the identity of the Five Sacred Mountains changes over time, though Mount Tai, considered the ritual "center" for the group (but not the geographic center), is always included. Cf. Tong Shuye, *Zhongguo gu dai di li kao lun wen ji* (Hong Kong, n.p., 1987), 7ff., 18–19.

67. *Documents*, "Pan geng." Regarding the early imperial moves of the capital, the dynastic histories (e.g., the *Shi ji* biography of Lou Jing) clearly show that there was no perceived need to place the capital at the geographic center of the land; see *Xi Han hui yao*, chap. 64. For the earliest notions of the "King's City" in China, see Nancy Shatzman Steinhardt, *Chinese Imperial City Planning* (Honolulu: University of Hawaii Press, 1990), chap. 1; and Li Min, *Shang shu yu gu dai shi yan jiu* (Henan: Zhongzhou shuhuashe, 1983), chap. 13.

68. Paul Wheatley, *Pivot of the Four Quarters: A Preliminary Enquiry into the Origins and Character of the Ancient Chinese City* (Edinburgh: Edinburgh University Press, 1971), chap. 5, suggests that the central point could be moved or duplicated in a new site, as geometrical space was less important than existential space. "The sacred space delimited in this manner within the continuum of profane space provided the framework within which could be conducted the rituals necessary to ensure that intimate harmony between the macrocosm and microcosm without which there could be no prosperity in the world of men" (p. 418). By contrast, in communities that accept monotheistic religions based on revelation, only certain geometrical locations can become sacred because that is where God has chosen to reveal his message. For the secular as the sacred, see Herbert Fingarette, *Confucius: The Secular as Sacred* (New York: Harper & Row, 1972).

69. For example, during the Han dynasty (206 B.C.E.–C.E. 220), four institutions defined the capital: the Biyong (Circular Moat); Mingtang (Sacred Hall); Lingtai (Numinous Terrace); and Taixue (Imperial Academy). Palaces could be built anywhere, so many "traveling palaces" were built far from the capital.

70. Hence, my jaundiced view of the many scholars who have tried to claim that the Chinese, including the Confucians, have a finer appreciation for the merits of preserving the natural environment than people from "the West." Probably, a certain reverence for the land is to be found more often among farmers than among the urban population, especially farmers whose ancestral shrines are situated near their farmlands, and 80 percent of the Chinese population until quite recently were farmers. Still, the Chinese have been no less loathe to destroy their natural environment than we. On this, see He Bochuan, *China on the Edge* (San Francisco: China Books and Periodicals, 1991), chaps. 2, 4, and Vaclav Smil's many publications.

71. See *Gongyang*, Duke Ch'eng 15. Cf. the story that is told of Confucius: "When Confucius ascended an eastern hill, he thought [his home state of] Lu small; when he ascended Mount Tai [the sacred peak in the east], he thought the empire small" (cited in Tong Shuye, "Han dai yi qian Zhongguo ren de shi jie quan nian yu yu wai jiao tong de qu shi," *Zhongguo gu dai di li kao zheng lun wen ji* (Shanghai: Zhonghua, 1962), 3. Note that Confucian definitions of community do not generate a fixed distinction between "inside" and "outside" persons. In the nineteenth century, this question would reoccur in a new form: Are countries sharing the Chinese written literary language to be considered "insiders" or "outsiders" in the new era of nationalism?

72. A late example of this tendency to examine complex questions from shifting perspectives can be found in Wang Fuzhi's (early seventeenth century) *Shangshu yin yi* (Eliciting the meaning of the documents), which bases its analysis on the difference between the "heaven seen from the point of view of men" and the "heaven seen from the point of view of the myriad things." See Yamaguchi Hisakazu, "Sonzai kara ronri," *Tōhōgaku* 57 (1979): 48–61.

73. *Li ji* 10/29 ("Li yun" chap.), trans. modified from Legge, *Li ki*, I, 410–11.

74. The phrase "nonregressive" comes from Heiner Roetz, *Confucian Ethics of the Axial Age* (Albany: State University of New York Press, 1993), 5.

75. E. N. Anderson, Jr., "Some Chinese Methods of Dealing with Crowding," *Urban Anthropology* 1:2 (1972): 141–50.

76. *The Case Against the Global Economy, and for a Turn toward the Local*, ed. Jerry Mander and Edward Goldsmith (San Francisco: Sierra Club, 1996), esp. Part II. See Fox Butterfield, "Study Links Violence Rate to Cohesion in Community," *New York Times*, Aug. 17, 1997, p. 27.

77. Adopting the terminology of Loren Lomasky.

78. James Hevia, "Guest Ritual and Interdomainal Relations in the Late Qing" (Ph.D. thesis, University of Chicago, 1986), 246. Those who did not participate in the classical cultural patterns were not so much "uncivilized" or "barbarian" as undifferentiated—without a place in the hierarchy of the moral universe understood as Civilization.

79. To possess a map of a certain territory implied the right to rule that area, so maps were generally given at the ceremonies of investiture for local princes. Otherwise, the production of maps was tied to a desire for military conquest. Thus, the production of maps lagged far behind many other forms of cultural production in imperial China. There were, for example, no maps of Japan readily available before the sixteenth century, when Japanese pirates began to raid the southeast China coast in large numbers.

See Cordell D. K. Yee, "Chinese Maps in Political Culture," in *The History of Cartography*, vol. 2, bk. 2, eds. J. B. Harley and David Woodward (Chicago: University of Chicago, 1994), 71–95; Joseph Needham, "Geography and Cartography," *Science and Civilisation in China*, vol. 3 (Cambridge: Cambridge University Press, 1959), 543–56.

80. Final note, April 1, 2006: I am pleased to participate in this volume. The editor, Daniel Bell, has asked me to clarify my original note 9 for the sake of the general reader. I am a historian of the classical era. There is no doubt in my mind that the Warring States thinkers, in speaking of "Tianxia," were preoccupied

with the political world best known to them, the Central States (Zhongguo). These thinkers were not particularly interested in "universals," for at least two reasons: first, they believed the Central States civilization defined by marriage and mourning rituals to be manifestly superior to anything else they knew; and second, they were "persuaders" (*shuizhe*) who needed to craft their arguments to particular audiences (typically, at any given time, to rulers and their ministers at a single court).

However, to persuade those in power to adopt a particular policy, they often posited, for the sake of argument, a typical person having certain basic needs (physical, social, and psychological). So while it would be historically inaccurate, in my view, to argue that Mozi or Mencius, to name but two examples, advocated "universal views" or conceived of a general audience (not to mention a wide readership!), both thinkers urged their followers to look for "friends in history" (to imagine conversations taking place between the exemplary dead and the living). In that spirit, we may look to the works of the Warring States and Han thinkers for inspiration and guidance about modern dilemmas. On the subject of transmission from master-persuader to disciple, see Michael Nylan, "Textual Authority in pre-Han and Ham," *Early China* 25 (2001), 1–54.

PART THREE

ETHICAL PLURALISM

Chapter Six

CONFUCIAN ATTITUDES TOWARD ETHICAL PLURALISM

~

Joseph Chan

The Confucian Tradition

As a tradition of thought, Confucianism began life in China more than 2,500 years ago. Although its core ideas can be traced back to the teachings of Confucius (551–479 B.C.E.), this tradition was never thought to be wholly created by Confucius himself. In fact, the original Chinese term of Confucianism, *Rujia*, makes no reference at all to Confucius. Confucius himself stressed that he was not an inventor of any radically new vision of ethics or ideal society, but only a transmitter of the old tradition—the rites and social values developed in the early Zhou dynasty (traditionally, mid-eleventh century to 256 B.C.E.). Nevertheless, it was Confucius who most creatively interpreted the tradition he had inherited, gave it a new meaning at a time when it became stifling, and expounded it so effectively that his views have influenced a great number of generations of *ru* to come. *The Analects*, a record of his ideas and teaching compiled primarily by his disciples and later scholars, is the most fundamental text in the Confucian tradition. However, Confucius handed down no systematic philosophy, nor is *The Analects* a treatise on ethics. *The Analects* left a number of basic questions undeveloped, such as those about human nature, the metaphysical grounds of ethics, and the proper organization of the state. It was Mencius (approx. 379–28 B.C.E.) and Xunzi (approx. 340–245 B.C.E.) who filled in the details more systematically and developed the tradition into new, and different, directions. The thoughts of these three thinkers together constitute the classical tradition of Confucianism.

Confucianism has continued to evolve ever since its inception, in part as a response to the political needs of the time (as in Han Confucianism), and in part to the challenges of other schools of thought (as in Song-Ming Confucianism). Han Confucianism had made Confucian ethics and politics rigid and hierarchical, placing the father and ruler at the center of absolute power in the family and polity respectively. Song-Ming Confucianism, on the contrary, turned its inquiry inward into the human mind in order to meet the challenges of Buddhism, and constructed robust theories of the inner life of human individuals. No matter what innovations were made in these later developments, however, classical Confucianism, especially the Mencius strand, has been recognized as the canon of the tradition, something that later thinkers claimed only to appreciate, vindicate, and enrich, and this was exactly the kind of moderate claim made by Confucius himself regarding his attitude toward the tradition before him. In this sense, a deep respect for tradition—thinking that it was the sages in the past who had got things right—has always been a salient mark of Confucianism.

But what are the core ideas in Confucianism? And how much influence has it had? Most simply put, Confucianism holds that people should cultivate their minds and virtues through lifelong learning and participation in rituals; they should treat their family members according to the norms of filial piety and fatherly love, respect the superiors and rulers, and show a graded concern and care for all; learned intellectuals above all others should devote themselves in politics and education to promote the Way and help build the good society. Even this brief characterization enables us to see that the Confucian vision of human life has fundamentally shaped the Chinese culture and the basic structure of society in the past 2,000 years or so. Its vision, however, has extended far beyond the Chinese borders and has penetrated deeply into its neighboring countries. Today, those East Asian societies that have been influenced by Confucian culture, namely, Korea, Japan, Singapore, Taiwan, Hong Kong, and mainland China, have undergone modernization and are exposed to the powerful forces of global capitalism, which have eroded their Confucian cultural traditions to a considerable extent. But Confucian values such as the importance of the family, the respect for learning and education, and the emphasis on order and harmony remain significant in these societies.

CONFUCIAN ETHICS: STRUCTURE AND SUBSTANCE

The Perfectionist Structure of Confucianism

Like such other major ancient traditions as the thoughts of Plato and Aristotle, Confucianism contains profound reflections on ethics, society, and politics. These ancient traditions of thought developed conceptions of the good life, the good society, and ideal politics. Although these conceptions differ importantly in their substantive content, their structural features are strikingly similar. They are what I would call perfectionist theories of ethics, society, and politics. On ethics, these traditions of thought base ethical judgments about values, virtues, and norms—or, in short, conceptions of the good life—on their understandings of human nature or principles of nature (I call this ethical perfectionism). On society, these theories regard social groups as important sites where people develop ethical capacities and skills necessary for the good life (social perfectionism). On politics, these theories hold the view that one of the major aims of the state is to help people pursue the good life by means of law, education, provision of resources, and coordination of social groups and their activities (political perfectionism).

The issues that this essay addresses concern the proper role of society and the state in dealing with disagreements over ethical judgments. The views of Confucianism on this set of issues are determined in part by its substantive content and in part by its structure as a perfectionist theory. The substantive content of Confucianism will be discussed in detail shortly. Here we can briefly lay out the typical responses of perfectionist theories, of which Confucianism is an instance, to this set of issues. As a theory of ethical perfectionism, Confucianism is inclined to view ethical disagreements as something regrettable, or something that is a result of human errors that can be overcome through proper ethical or rational training. As a theory of social and political perfectionism, Confucianism is inclined to suggest that disagreements should be removed as much as possible, and that the state should be led by the wise and the ethically better informed so as to resolve those conflicts and equip people with appropriate mental and ethical capacities.

This perfectionist perspective has a certain attractiveness but it also faces serious challenges posed by the conditions of modern society, which John Rawls calls "reasonable pluralism." There are at least two challenges to perfectionist theories. First, the legitimacy of a perfectionist state would seem to be undermined if it promotes a conception of the good life that can be reasonably disputed by people who do not hold that conception. Second, even if the conception of the good life is correct and beyond reasonable doubt, there is a danger for a perfectionist state to paternalistically or moralistically impose its favored conception on people who fail to see its correctness. What ideas within perfectionism can prevent a perfectionist state from sliding into authoritarian rule? These two challenges are hard questions for Confucianism, because, first, it does not have the modern notion of personal autonomy to counter state paternalism or moralism,[1] and, second, its conceptions of the good life and ideal society have become increasingly problematic in modern society. These difficult questions cannot be adequately dealt with here. Rather the main aim of this chapter is primarily descriptive and reconstructive. I describe traditional Confucian conceptions of the good society and the good life, and see what attitudes Confucians may hold toward ethical disagreements and social regulation.[2] Through this analysis we can begin to understand the difficulties confronting contemporary scholars who try to develop a new Confucian perspective relevant to the needs and aspirations of people in modern society.

The Substantive Content of Confucian Ethics

We need first to describe the substantive content of Confucian ethics before examining the question of ethical uniformity or pluralism in society. In doing this, it is important to bear in mind the historical character of Confucianism.[3] As said in the previous section, Confucius basically inherited the order of rites and social values developed in the early Zhou dynasty. What, then, are the core aspects of Zhou's system of rites that Confucius had inherited? The central core of the system of rites in Zhou was a system of relationships of differentiated roles and duties. The central principle as summarized in the *Book of Rituals* is: respect and obey those who are in a superior social position (the emperor and the noble lords); show filial piety to one's parents; show respect to the elderly in one's family; and maintain the distinction between men and women. The *Book of Rituals* says that, whereas many social conventions and norms can and should change, these basic principles of human relationship should never change.

These principles were endorsed by Confucius, as well as by Mencius, Xunzi, and the later generations of Confucians. The *Book of Rituals* recorded a conversation between Confucius and the duke of Lu. The duke asked, Why do gentlemen give high regard to rites? Confucius replied that rites are the basis of human life. Without rites, we have no directives to guide us in religious ceremony; without rites we would not be able to differentiate between the ruler and the minister, the superior and inferior, old and young, man and women, father and son, and elder brother and younger brother; and without rites we would not be able to determine the intimate and the distant in social interaction.[4] Confucius thus accepted the basic social order developed in Zhou. For him, there was nothing wrong with this system of rites. Equally, the political institutions and laws developed on the basis of this system of rites were basically sound. Yet, the once prosperous and stable Zhou dynasty could not escape the fate of decline and was disintegrating into several states that were under constant threats of internal power struggles and external aggression. Confucius's reflection on the problems of social and political disorder led him to conclude that the root of the problems was the weakening of rites and ethical norms because powerful feudal lords were generally unwilling to be bounded by rites—people, especially those in power, became self-centered, arrogant, undisciplined, and corrupted.[5] His solution is therefore to revitalize Zhou's system of rites, by giving it a new ethical foundation, by showing its attractiveness to common people and the elite alike, and by arguing that a return to this system was the key to order and harmony in society. In his attempt to solve the problem, Confucius advocated an ingenious conception of rites, which treats rites as not merely external rules constraining people's behavior and distributing powers and duties, but essentially as a necessary part of a conception of an ideal moral person—the man of *ren*, an inner requirement of morality founded in humanity. Rites are based on and required by a deeper ethical foundation, *ren*.

The moral ideal for each individual is the attainment of *ren*—the highest and most perfect virtue. *Ren* is a human quality, an expression of humanity. It can be manifested in different virtues, from personal reflection and critical examination of one's life to respect, concern, and care for others. On the personal dimension of *ren*, Confucius says, "to return to the observance of the rites through overcoming the self constitutes *ren*."[6] On the interpersonal dimension, he says that *ren* is to "love your fellow men [*ai ren*]."[7] In dealing with others, the ideal of *ren* requires us to practice the art of *shu*, an ethics of sympathy and reciprocity, which can be expressed positively or negatively. Positively, it tells us to seek to establish and enlarge others insofar as we seek also to establish and enlarge ourselves.[8] Negatively, it tells us not to impose on others what we ourselves do not desire.[9] In another place, Confucius says that the method of *ren* is the ability to understand sympathetically the needs of others in light of the needs of oneself as a human being. "Now the man of [*ren*], wishing to be established himself, seeks also to establish others; wishing to be enlarged himself, he seeks also to enlarge others. To be able to judge *of others* by what is nigh *in ourselves*;—this may be called the [method of *ren*]."[10]

These attitudes and qualities of self-examination, sympathetic understanding, and caring for others are essential to the spirit and vitality of rites. Confucius says, "What can a man do with the rites who is not benevolent? What can a man do with music who is not benevolent?"[11] Rites in Confucius's time stressed the hierarchy of social relationships and the differentiation of roles and duties according to one's status in those relationships. Without the spirit of *ren*, these aspects may easily lead to, at best, mechanical observance of rules without a humanistic concern for others or, at worst, selfish domination of the stronger party over the weaker one. *Ren* thus serves to instill a strong humanistic spirit into rites, providing an ethics of sympathy, reciprocity, and care into an otherwise essentially hierarchical system of social relationships. In more concrete terms, the superior party in a hierarchical relationship should always show concern to the inferior. For example, the ruler should show benevolence to the people, the father should show fatherly love to the son, and the husband should show respect to the wife.[12] Harmony is easier to achieve in a relationship in which *ren* is the guiding spirit.

On the other hand, it is important to note that to Confucius *ren* is still expressed through the system of rites, which differentiates human relationships into varying degrees of intimacy and varying degrees of inequality of status. The ideal of love expressed by *ren* is constituted by reference to rites, and this makes love a graded concern for others rather than a pure impartial concern for all. While one's love can be extended to anyone in the world, one's parents and other family members should always have a priority in one's love for others. In the same vein, the ideal of harmony is meant to coexist side by side with hierarchy. The son is expected to show filial piety to his parents, and the people are to respect and be loyal to the emperor. *Ren* not only harmonizes the rites but makes them more pervasive and stable. In short, they complement and restrain each other at the same time. The marriage of *ren* and rites helps contain an unequal relationship in harmony; it also helps people practice the ethics of benevolence to everyone without failing to give special respect and concern to those in special relationships.

The Confucian Conception of Ideal Society: Strong Emphasis on Uniformity

The Importance of Uniformity

Confucian ethics was a response to the disintegration of the Zhou's polity and the decline of its rites. The solution of Confucius, as discussed earlier, was to revive the rites by founding them on a deeper ethical ideal of *ren*. Confucius and Mencius believe in the powerful effect of rites based on *ren*. If men learn to cultivate *ren* and follow rites, there will be social and political stability and harmony. "It is rare for a man who has the virtues of filial piety [*xiao*] and brotherhood [*ti*] to have the inclination to be rebellious against his superior."[13] "Mencius said, 'If only everyone loved his parents and treated his elders with deference, the world would be at peace.' "[14] Adherence to *ren* and rites by members of a community is essential to the stability and harmony of that community. For Confucius, however (and on this matter for Mencius and Xunzi as well), it is those in the political establishment who have a specially strong duty to practice *ren* and rituals. If they can behave according to *ren*, these classical masters believe, they will practice a kind of benevolent politics that puts people's well-being in first priority, attract voluntary submission of the ruled, motivate people to follow the way and practice *ren*, and achieve a well-ordered society with harmonious social relationships.

In order to help people to cultivate *ren* and to understand clearly and to follow the norms in accordance with their roles in social relationships, Confucius proposes that people should adhere to a commonly shared set of names and vocabularies that have significant social functions. This is the famous doctrine of "rectification of names." Uniformity in naming and in understanding the ethical meaning of names is indispensable to the harmony of society.

> "Duke Jing of Qu: asked Confucius about government. Confucius answered, 'Let the ruler be a ruler, the subject a subject, the father a father, the son a son.' "[15]

> Zilu said, "If the Lord of Wei left the administration of his state to you, what would you put first?" The Master said, "If something has to be put first, it is, perhaps, the rectification of names. . . . When names are not correct, what is said will not sound reasonable; when what is said does not sound reasonable, affairs will not culminate in success; when affairs do not culminate in success, rites and music will not flourish; when rites and music do not flourish, punishments will not fit the crimes; when punishments do not fit the crimes, the common people will not know where to put hand and foot."[16]

These passages suggest that essential to an ideal society is a high degree of uniformity, or shared social consensus, in the naming of social roles and positions, the specification of the responsibilities that fall upon the people occupying these roles and positions, and the identification of the appropriate norms according to which others should treat the people in those roles and positions. In this sense, the Confucian social ideal aims for ethical uniformity. Failing to rectify names, and failing to set up clearly a set of ethical standards about roles and responsibilities for people to follow, would result in mistaken judgments and wrongful actions, leading ultimately to nothing but moral and social disorder.

How rigid and exhaustive is this ideal of ethical uniformity? To what extent does it allow different or conflicting ethical judgments? The answer depends on how rigid or flexible are the contents of *ren* and rites that define the basic structure of society. This is an important issue, for it determines directly the Confucian position on the further question of what kinds of ethical disagreement are acceptable and what are not. The central core of rites that define the appropriate duties and norms of conduct are stated in very similar ways by the classical Confucian thinkers.

Confucius: Let the ruler be a ruler, the subject a subject, the father a father, the son a son.[17]

Mencius: Love between father and son, duty between ruler and subject, distinction between husband and wife, precedence of the old over the young, and faith between friends.[18]

Xunzi: The relationships between lord and minister, father and son, older and younger brothers, husband and wife, begin as they end and end as they begin, share with Heaven and Earth the same organizing principle, and endure in the same form through all eternity.[19]

These relationships, and the accompanying principles governing them, then, constitute the core substance of rites. They are supposed to be unchanging, for the Way or the Principle of Heaven and Earth, upon which these relationships are based, never changes. They are not only moral principles but also social and political. The spirit of these principles is to make distinctions between different social roles and positions and, with the guidance of *ren*, to maintain a hierarchical system of human relationships in the spirit of reciprocity and harmony. Unlike the liberal conception of society and politics, Confucianism sees no separation between public and private morality. The rites at once govern political, social, familial relationships, with the latter being the most basic foundation of all others. Society and politics are closely knitted together under a single ideal.

Any view that rejects these basic principles of human relationship, or any action that violates them, would be regarded by Confucians as fundamentally wrong. This can be seen by Confucians' rejection of Mohism, which preaches an impartial, universal love of all human beings. Mencius heavily criticized this doctrine as not respecting the special relationship between father and son. It denies filial piety. Mohist doctrine therefore was regarded by Mencius as entirely unacceptable and unreasonable. I shall come back to this debate between Mencius and Mohism. The main aim here, however, is to show that the core substance of *ren* and rites set the moral limits to people's conduct.

Room for Plurality of Judgments and Ethical Disagreements

Insofar as the framework of *ren* and rites remains unchallenged, Confucians are often ready to accept a plurality of diverse or contradicting ethical judgments. Many occasions and circumstances allow for individual moral discretion and choice, and for revision of social norms. Here legitimate differences in ethical judgments or courses of action may arise. In what follows, I mention two types of situation of this kind. The first concerns the application of rites and the importance of moral discretion. Rites as norms of conduct and virtues sometimes cannot give precise guidance to people when they make concrete moral decisions. There may be novel situations, borderline cases, and hard cases (where some rites are in conflict with each other) that call for interpretive judgment and moral discretion. As a result, Confucians often emphasize the importance of discretion (quan),[20] flexibility (wu gu),[21] and timeliness (shi)[22] in making moral decisions in particular circumstances.[23] These are important qualities that a gentleman ought to develop, and Confucius was praised for being timely in action, instead of stubborn and inflexible: "There are four things the Master refused to have anything to do with: he refused to entertain conjectures or insist on certainty; he refused to be inflexible or to be egotistical."[24] "Confucius was the sage whose actions were timely."[25] If after careful and conscientious deliberation, two persons equipped with ren come up with two different or contradictory judgments and courses of action, Confucians would tell us to respect both of the judgments. "The Master said, 'How straight Shi Yu is! When the Way prevails in the state he is as straight as an arrow, yet when the Way falls into disuse in the state he is still as straight as an arrow. How gentlemanly Qu Boyu is! When the Way prevails in the state he takes office, but when the Way falls into disuse in the state he allows himself to be furled and put away safely.' "[26] This is an example in which two men find themselves in similar circumstances (living in an unjust state) but take contradictory courses of action (one chooses to pursue the Way in politics and the other withdraws from it), yet Confucius respects and praises both of them and their chosen course of actions.[27]

The second type of situation concerns revision and selective use of rites. While endorsing the basic system of Zhou's rites, Confucius did not dogmatically believe that all rites as norms of proper conduct cannot change. Although the essence of filial piety or respect for the superior are constant, ways of expressing these norms may change. For instance, the essence of filial piety consists in caring for and supporting one's parents and respecting them, but the concrete ways of expressing caring and respect may change (Confucius protested against the extravagant burial practices of the age). Second, some rites may seem inappropriate when judged with a deeper ethical perspective or lose their attractiveness in a new circumstance.

The Master said, "A ceremonial cap of linen is what is prescribed by the rites. Today black silk is used instead. This is more frugal and I follow the majority. To prostrate oneself before ascending the steps is what is prescribed by the rites. Today one does so after having ascended them. This is casual and, though going against the majority, I follow the practice of doing so before ascending."[28]

The Master said, "Follow the calendar of the Xia, ride in the carriage of the Yin, and wear the ceremonial cap of the Zhou, but, as for music, adopt the *shao* and the *wu*."[29]

These passages suggest two things about the Confucian attitudes toward rites. First, one should not blindly follow the rites as endorsed by society or the majority. Rather, one should adopt a reflective moral attitude to examine the ethical reason behind a rite and to determine whether that rite is appropriate. Second, a rite can and should change if the circumstance changes. Confucius himself stresses that we should critically learn and select appropriate rites developed in different periods and places.

To conclude, the ideal society in Confucianism is one of a high degree of ethical uniformity. The uniformity is based on the ethical ideal of *ren* and rites, which sets the bounds for morally permissible behavior. However, the application of the ideal of *ren* and rites often requires individual moral judgment and discretion. Also, some rites may change, and should change, if social circumstances change. Confucians would allow a plurality of judgments on concrete interpretation and application of the ideal in situations where the ideal does not have clear, determinate implications.

POLITICAL REGULATION

We should distinguish between ethical disagreements within the bounds of Confucian conceptions of *ren* and rites and those which violate those bounds. The first are family disputes, in which case Confucians would respect a person who exercises his ethical capacities and deliberates carefully but reaches a decision different from that of others. However, for those views which present an ethical perspective seriously at odds with the very core contents of *ren* and rites, Confucians would be inclined to reject them as unreasonable. In the face of fundamental ethical disagreements, it is unlikely that Confucians would say, "while I believe my views are correct, your views are not unreasonable either." For Confucians, when a debate comes down to ethical fundamentals, there is little room for reasonable disagreements. There is no substantial middle ground between, to use Thomas Nagel's words, "what it is unreasonable to believe and what it is unreasonable not to believe."[30]

How would Confucians deal with serious disagreements? Would they invoke the state to ban what they regard as unreasonable views or actions? Here Confucians have two different sets of reasons leading to opposite recommendations. The first set of reasons pushes for governmental banning and is derived from the kind of ethical, social, and political perfectionism that Confucianism endorses. The second set of reasons favors a noncoercive approach, which is derived from the Confucian faith in morality and dislike of the use of coercion. Let me now turn to the first set of reasons.

We have seen that Confucians based their ethical theory on the Way, the Heaven, or human nature. They also seem to be confident that their basic ethical beliefs correctly capture the Way and the principles of the Heaven. The Confucian ethical ideal is to be achieved through transformation of individual moral life and through implementing the basic social relationships in society and politics. The emperor and ministers are expected to behave according to the ethical requirements and to act benevolently and righteously so as to promote the material and ethical well-being of the common people. There is no fundamental separation between the familial, the social, and the political spheres. All parts should be ordered in mutually supportive ways to achieve the ethical ideal. This ideal, if achieved, can at once solve problems of individual morality, social harmony, and political stability.

As a theory of ethical perfectionism, Confucianism would likely treat with great suspicion ethical perspectives that are at odds with the core substance of the Confucian ideal. It tends to see these perspectives as "heresies." As a theory of social perfectionism, Confucianism would be worried about the harmful effects of heresies on social harmony and stability, which are important values in the Confucian scheme. Finally, as a theory of political perfectionism, Confucianism would expect the political rulers to help maintain or restore the Way in the face of heretical challenges.

One telling example of this tendency is Mencius's attitude toward two schools of thought in his time. The egocentric philosophy of Yang Zhu (fourth century B.C.E.) is regarded by Mencius as "denial of one's prince" and the philosophy of Mozi (fourth century B.C.E.), which preaches universal love, is "a denial of one's father." "If the way of Yang and Mo does not subside and the Way of Confucius is not proclaimed, the people will be deceived by heresies and the path of morality will be blocked."[31]

However, from a logical point of view, all this does not necessarily lead to the use of coercion by the state to maintain uniformity and combat heresies. If Confucians believe, as J. S. Mill does, that the best way to combat false doctrines and opinions is by better arguments, then they would not necessarily endorse governmental suppression of speech. In addition, if Confucians believe that the best way to correct ethically wrong actions and promote virtues is by education and socialization, then no coercive punishment would necessarily follow. Do Confucians hold these two views? I believe they do explicitly hold the second but not so clearly the first. This leads to the second set of reasons mentioned earlier.

A Noncoercive Approach

It is well known that Confucians do not favor the use of legal coercion to foster virtues or prevent people from indulging in the bad or debased. The reason for this has to do with the nature of moral life. Confucians reckon that legal punishment cannot change one's heart or soul; only moral education and rites can. As Confucius says, "Guide them by edicts, keep them in line with punishments, and the common people will stay out of trouble but will have no sense of shame. Guide them by virtue, keep them in line with the rites, and they will, besides having a sense of shame, reform themselves."[32] One cannot be compelled by force to be virtuous. To live a genuinely virtuous life, the agent must see the point of that life—he or she must endorse the virtues, be motivated to live by virtues, and enjoy that life. "One who is not benevolent cannot remain long in strained circumstances, nor can he remain long in easy circumstances. *The benevolent man is attracted to benevolence because he feels at home in it.*"[33] The cultivation of virtues is done through education and practice in rites—it is rites, not physical force, that make people feel at home with virtues. This point has significant bearing on personal freedom as absence of coercion. To act virtuously, we must act for the right reason. Avoidance of punishment is not a right reason for virtuous action. The law is thus not a good instrument of moral edification. Anyone recognizing this point would want to limit the scope of criminal law. Neither should punishment be used to prevent the bad from influencing the good, for Confucius thinks that the best method is still moral edification by example, and he urges the rulers to set a good example. "Lord Ji Kang asked Confucius about government, saying, 'Suppose I were to kill the bad to help the good: how about that?' Confucius replied: 'You are here to govern; what need is there to kill? If you desire what is good, the people will be good. The moral power of the gentlemen is wind, the moral power of the common man is grass. Under the wind, the grass must bend.' "[34] Confucius puts demanding standards of moral behavior on the rulers and gentlemen, not the common people. This is consistent with the general spirit of tolerance in Confucianism—"to set strict standards for oneself, and make allowances for others."[35] Confucian tolerance is not grounded on liberal values like personal independence or sovereignty or any notion of a moral right to wrongdoing. It is grounded on sympathy, on the view that coercion is ineffective in promoting *ren*, and on a particular approach to moral edification.[36]

However, it is important to note the limits of this argument. The argument focuses on the person who is ethically wrong. The idea is that coercion offers little help to his moral life. But if our concern is for people who would be adversely affected by his ethical wrongdoing rather than the wrongdoer himself, then the argument has nothing to reject any suggestion to prevent coercively the wrongdoer from affecting others. For instance, consider a certain type of unethical deed so influential that it subverts the basic structure of a Confucian society. If the use of force is proved to be the best among all options or the least of all evils in preventing this from happening, there seems no fundamental tenet in Confucianism that would prevent it from using coercion.

Having discussed unethical deeds, we now turn to the issue of unethical or heretical thoughts. The Confucian argument against the use of force in suppressing unethical or wrong beliefs is even less explicit than the argument against deeds. Perhaps we can go back to the example of Mencius's criticism of Yang Zhu and Mohism. While Mencius uses very strong words to condemn the two schools of thought, he does not advocate the use of political weapons to ban them. Instead, he says whoever can combat them "with words" is a true disciple of the sages. "I wish to follow in the footsteps of the three sages in rectifying the hearts of men, laying heresies to rest, opposing extreme action, and banishing excessive views. I am not fond of disputation. I have no alternative. Whoever can, *with words*, combat Yang and Mo is a true disciple of the sages."[37] Mencius does not explain why he asks people to combat heresies with words. One possible reason for this is perhaps the view that only through thorough exposition and criticism of those doctrines can doubts and mistaken thinking be completely dispelled; and only by this means can people have a stronger confidence in the Way. Confucians would not object to this Millian reasoning, although we are not sure how far they can go along this line of argument. Confucians do put much stress on the need of moral learning, understanding, and deliberation in the cultivation of virtues. Confucius's education emphasizes not only learning, but also thinking and examining.[38] Similarly, Mencius also underscores the importance of understanding and inquiry in one's moral life.[39] Human life-situations are varied and complex. Confucius asks us to find out the mean and make the best decision in the midst of many half-truths and extreme views. If a person does not have any opportunity to be exposed to contrary views and falsehood, he will not be able to develop the ethical and mental capacities to make the best judgment or hit at the mean in many practical situations of human life. In short, an oppressive environment does not help people to develop the reflective understanding and deliberative capacities essential to a successful moral life.[40]

Nonetheless, this argument shares the same limitation of the argument against using coercion to prevent or punish unethical deeds. The argument is an instrumental one, and both the harmful effects of wrong ethical beliefs and one's critical and ethical capacities admit of degree. If there is a situation where coercion or suppression can prevent a heresy from spreading its harmful effect on people's minds and at the same time only constitutes a slight impediment to the chance for people to develop their mental and ethical capacities, then Confucians would find no principled reason against doing so.

To conclude, we have seen two tendencies of thought in Confucianism. The first tendency is to favor governmental regulation and control of ethical beliefs or deeds that violate the basic bounds of *ren* and rites. This tendency is based on the special nature of Confucian perfectionism that stresses moral uniformity, social harmony, and political stability. Confucianism does not accept a liberal separation of morality into the public and private spheres—the first sphere of morality is enforceable by the state while the second belongs to the business of civil society only. Unlike the antimoralistic and neutralist strands in liberalism, Confucianism regards the ethical content, or the morality or immorality, of an action always as *one* relevant reason for the state to promote or prohibit it. But this reason has to compete with other reasons, which may or may not outweigh the first. These competing reasons come from what I call the second tendency of thought regarding political regulation. The second tendency favors noncoercive means (education and rites) to deal with this problem. It is based on the Confucian beliefs on the proper way to moral cultivation, on the importance of moral thinking and deliberation, and on the ineffective nature of coercion in promoting virtues. It is also based on an approach of moral socialization that puts a much greater moral demand on rulers rather than the common people. While the second tendency always serves to restrain the use of coercion, it does not constitute an absolute restraint. In each particular case, a Confucian would have to weigh the possible consequences and consider all relevant reasons in that case before he makes up his mind on the need for governmental coercion. Xunzi has exactly this advice: "When one sees something desirable, he must consider whether or not it will lead to detestable consequences. When he sees something beneficial, he must carefully consider whether or not it will lead to harmful consequences. All these consequences must be weighed together in any mature plan before one determines which desire or aversion, choice or rejection, is to be preferred."[41] In this spirit the following issues of ethical disagreement will be examined.

CITIZENSHIP

In Confucianism, there are no citizens, only subjects and rulers. Yet subjects do have legitimate *opportunities* that they can reasonably expect from society and *duties* that they are legitimately expected to perform in turn. In this sense we can talk about the status—legitimate opportunities and duties—of women as subjects in society. The status of women in Confucianism is largely discussed in connection with the relationship between husband and wife, which is one of the most important human relationships to be governed by *ren* and rites. Thus the issue of women is part of the core of the Confucian ideal of human relationships. Confucianism would take a clear position on this question and would allow little room for permissible disagreements. Confucianism would require the state to regulate the basic duties and opportunities that women ought to have according to whatever conception of gender relationship it believes to be the ethically correct one.

Like most other parts of the world in ancient times, women in traditional China occupied an inferior status to men. Women were excluded from serving in the government. Female children could not receive education in schools. Women's main roles and responsibilities were domestic. Not only did Confucianism not challenge gender inequality, it implicitly or explicitly endorsed it. Today, we can still see a significant degree of gender inequality in countries like South Korea and Japan over which Confucianism still has a relatively strong hold. However, is there any deep Confucian reason to support its endorsement of the subordination of women? Let me first describe some Confucian positions on the role of women in society, and then examine whether these positions can find strong support from within Confucian ethics.

The Mencius characterizes basic human relationships in the following way: "love between father and son, duty between ruler and subject, *distinction between husband and wife*, order between the elder and the young, faith between friends."[42] "Distinction" (*bie*) is used to describe the husband-and-wife relationship. While the word itself does not say what is to be distinguished, it is generally believed that it refers to the functional distinction between the roles of men and women inside and outside of a family. The common traditional saying that "males are primary in the external, females are primary in the internal" confirms this understanding. Men in the family are expected to take care of external affairs, and women domestic affairs. This, however, does not imply that men have no final control of family affairs. The distinction refers to duties, not authority. The husband is expected to make final decisions on important family matters and to set a good moral example to his wife and children. "The *Book of Odes* says, 'He set an example for his consort, and also for his brother, and so ruled over the family and the state.' "[43] The distinction between internal and external duties is thus primarily meant to limit the involvement of women's activities in the household.

In a recent essay, Sin Yee Chan argues that some implications seem to follow from this division of labor. "First it would imply excluding a woman from serving in the government if her role is merely domestic and she should never speak about the external affairs. This exclusion is an important deprivation for it would lead to the exclusion of women from the ideal of a morally cultivated person, *junzi*."[44] That these implications do follow seems to be confirmed by both history and textual evidence. As a matter of history in classical China, women were indeed excluded in politics, although there were a few exceptions, particularly the female family members and relatives of emperors. One passage in *The Analects* interestingly shows how Confucius reacted to the case of a woman's participation in government. "Shun had five officials and the Empire was well governed, King Wu said, 'I have ten capable officials.' Confucius commented, 'How true it is that talent is difficult to find! The period of Tang and Yu was rich in talent. With a woman amongst them, there were, in fact, only nine.' "[45] That Confucius casually discounted the woman from the list of talented officials shows his stance that women ought not to take part in government.

It follows from the exclusion of women from serving in the government that they are also excluded from having the opportunity to receive formal school education that prepares people to become gentlemen, *junzi*, whose typical duty is to participate in and contribute to politics. Women had to stay at home and receive whatever education their families could afford or would be willing to provide. Typically, women received a narrower range of knowledge than men, and they were taught the proper rituals and duties for females in the household.[46]

However, the Confucian attitude on the role of women does not fit comfortably with other major elements in Confucian ethics. The first Confucian element that may challenge gender inequality is that females and males are regarded in early Confucianism as being equal in terms of their inborn moral instincts and capacities. Unlike Aristotle, who thinks that women are biologically inferior to men in rational capacities, Mencius is of the view that the most important feature that defines a human being, namely, *ren* as an inborn moral instinct and potentiality to be fully realized, is equally distributed among males and females. The second element is Confucius's famous principle that education should be open to all.[47] He was proud of the fact that, as a teacher, he has never "denied instruction to anyone who, of his own accord, has given [him] so much as a bundle of dried meat as a present."[48] Confucius never had a female student. Perhaps he was never approached by any woman for education, given the prevailing norm in his time was that women should receive their special type of education at home. But if there were one woman approaching Confucius for education, it would be difficult for him to refuse her, given the nondiscriminatory ideal of education he advocates.

These two elements combined together will produce some significant implications. Because women have the same moral potentiality as men, if they are given the same education as men, they could equally develop and cultivate the moral capacities as men do that are necessary to political participation. In other words, women can become gentlemen, *junzi*. This leads to the final element that may challenge the subordination of women. Confucians hold a meritocratic view of distribution of political offices. Offices ought to be held by people who have appropriate ethical and rational capacities, irrespective of their class background or ethnic origin. The famous competitive examination system for recruiting officials in traditional China was conducted on this meritocratic basis. Now, if women could perform just as well as men in ethical and rational capacities, there seems no Confucian reason to bar them from taking part in the examination except the earlier doctrine of the functional division of labor between men and women. But it is precisely this doctrine that lacks deep Confucian justification. It does not cohere well with the Confucian view of the equal moral nature of human beings, the Confucian ideal of education, and its meritocratic criterion for distribution of political offices.

We may ask, then, why Confucians held strongly to gender inequality? I suspect the real reason is sociological rather than ethical. In a primitive, labor-intensive agricultural economy, the most efficient division of labor in the family is that men work outside to make a living and women stay at home to nourish babies and take care of children and the elderly. A stable set of patriarchal norms and principles is important for the maintenance of this division of labor and power, which in turn is essential to the survival of the family which is the most important economic unit in an agricultural society. Now we live in a modern industrial society where there is no strong sociological ground for the necessity of this division of labor. In fact, contemporary Confucians today typically favor the modern view that women should enjoy the same basic civil and political opportunities as men. I think such a change of attitude can be justified by appealing to the three elements in Confucianism identified here.

LIFE-AND-DEATH DECISIONS

Legalization of assisted suicide is a contemporary issue, which has received no discussion in the traditional Confucian discourse. At the risk of overspeculation, we may try to draw some relevant implications from within the tradition. I believe this issue is one for which we can expect a plurality of views even within the bounds of Confucian ethics.

Confucians value human life, but they put moral life higher than biological life. Suicide is sometimes morally justifiable. In a recent paper, Pingcheung Lo argues that for Confucians there are two general circumstances in which people can, and sometime should, choose death in order to preserve a higher moral life.[49] First, sometimes one can, or should, sacrifice one's life in order to uphold *ren* and *yi* (righteousness), which are supreme values in the Confucian ethical thought. We have the Confucian teaching of "to die to achieve *ren*" (*sha shen cheng ren*) and of "to lay down one's life for a cause of *yi*" (*she sheng qu yi*). Confucius said, "For Gentlemen of purpose and men of benevolence while it is inconceivable that they should seek to stay alive at the expense of benevolence, it may happen that they have to accept death in order to have benevolence accomplished."[50] One can choose to die for the sake of the country, or to save the lives of one's family members or other people. This is what we may call altruistic suicide. In addition, one can also choose to die for one's self, for the sake of preserving one's honor and dignity. To choose suicide in face of humiliation by one's enemy, or to choose suicide in order to avoid the indignity of being unfairly tried in court, would be met with approval.

However, these two morally justifiable circumstances of suicide do not lend immediate help to the morality of assisted suicide. Let us discuss the case of altruistic assisted suicide first. An aged mother with terminal illness might want to hasten her death in order not to become a heavy burden on her family members. This motivation certainly expresses an attitude of benevolence, and in itself it would not be disapproved by Confucian ethics. However, such a move would be strongly dissented by her family members, especially her children who have a strong and clear moral duty to look after their parents. Any person with a sense of filial piety would not want to endorse a law that allows parents to undergo assisted suicide just for the sake relieving the burden of family members.

How about self-regarding assisted suicide? Again, the proceeding discussion does not lend immediate help. For one thing, Confucianism approves suicide primarily when it serves strong moral causes. In this case, it is the possibility of losing one's *moral* honor or dignity in face of humiliation that justifies suicide. It does not entail the approval of the act of killing oneself when one's life is threatened by terminal illness and intense pain. In addition, Confucianism does not recognize the liberal value of personal autonomy or individual sovereignty, which is often claimed to imply a moral right to terminate one's own life as and when one sees fit. Confucianism would not appeal to any notion of a general moral right to suicide concerning the issue of assisted suicide.

While the above Confucian views on suicide do not give direct support to assisted suicide, there is no clear and strong ground in Confucianism to reject it either. Confucianism values human life, but it is not clear that it entails a negative attitude toward assisted suicide in the case of terminal illness. Some might argue that according to Confucianism a human life has a great value even if it is immobile and full of pain, and even if the dying person does not want to bear with this pain any more. However, some others might argue that for Confucianism, the value of life lies primarily in human activity, in the cultivation of virtues and excellence, and in interacting with others and contributing to the well-being of them. Thus it is not clear that Confucianism would accept the idea of "sanctity of life" even in a situation where a person can only spend the rest of his life on his deathbed suffering from immense pain. So there seem to be disagreements over the exact meaning and implication of the Confucian view of the value of life regarding the terminally ill. But whatever the interpretations, assisted suicide for the terminally ill does not violate the more basic moral content of *ren* and rites. It does not seem to constitute a violation of *ren* if one chooses to terminate one's life is this situation. Here we seem to have reached the zone of permissible differences. The act of terminating one's own life in the case of terminal illness with great pain is neither required by *ren* nor opposed by it. It lies in the area where different people should be allowed to make different choices.

Moreover, as far as people other than the one suffering from terminal illness are concerned, there is one reason, though not a conclusive one, for them not to oppose assisted suicide. Confucianism emphasizes the importance of compassion and benevolence. If a dying relative or friend of a person requests death in order to avoid the tormenting pain that no palliative treatment can help to relieve, that person, if moved by compassion, would be inclined to agree to assisted suicide. I would even argue that from a Confucian perspective, the person's own controversial interpretation of the Confucian view on the value of life is less important than his duty to show compassion to the suffering of others.

However, one Confucian concern has not been addressed thus far. While Confucians may agree that assisted suicide is morally permissible, they would be concerned about the role of the patient's family in making the ultimate decision concerning assisted suicide. For Confucians, familial relationships are the most important personal or social relationships an individual has and are central to his or her well-being. Members of a family are supposed to care for each other, and to take each other's well-being as part of one's own. This is of course not to suggest that the family should have absolute authority over its members—even the father has no such absolute authority over the son if what the father does violates the bounds of morality. Rather, the point is that in a closely nested Confucian family, one would not think one is the sole sovereign over one's own life or the sole caretaker of one's well-being. How one should live, and die, should be a matter of the entire family's concern. What this means in the case of assisted suicide is that the patient who requests assisted suicide should consult with his or her family members, be sensitive to their feelings and concerns, and try to reach a decision that the family as a whole thinks is the best. Of course, other members of the patient's family are expected to show care and compassion to their dying member, and put the well-being of the latter in first priority. But it would be wrong, from a Confucian point of view, if the other members are left out in the consultation process between the patient and the doctor or in the process in which the medical decision is made.

It seems that this emphasis of family involvement in medical decisions is still very common today in East Asian countries that have a Confucian heritage. One such observation is made by the Japanese medical ethicist Kazumasa Hoshino, who writes:

> Japanese people are not accustomed to making medical decisions regarding their own diseases by themselves without consulting the family. This is because of their deep regard and respect for the opinions and feelings of the family. When one member of the family becomes sick, it is the responsibility of the entire family to look after him. . . . The family knows that the care of the sick member is a family matter. In these circumstances, it seems rather natural for the family to first decide on the best medical procedures and to care for him. . . . Eventually, decision-making for medical procedures and care for the patient may be done with the mutual consent of both himself and the remaining members of the family.[51]

Ruiping Fan, a Chinese medical ethicist, concurs with this observation and further argues that the practice of family involvement in East Asian societies "has been shaped by the Confucian understanding of the nature of the family and individuals. . . . It is a Confucian moral requirement that one should take one's family as an autonomous unit from the rest of society, flourishing or suffering as a whole. Hence the injury, disease or disability of one family member must be taken as a problem of the entire family, and thereby the medical decision should be made by the family as a whole."[52]

To conclude, from a Confucian point of view, the request of a terminally ill person for assisted suicide violates no principles of *ren*, and it belongs to the legitimate sphere of personal choice. Also, compassion and benevolence supply people a reason not to refuse such a request. But Confucians would stress that the family of the patient should be involved in the decision making as to whether the option of assisted suicide ought to be taken up by the patient. Thus far we have only discussed the moral dimension of assisted suicide. There are many consequentialist reasons for and against the legalization of the practice that we should consider but cannot here. Also, the principle of family involvement can create problems in its implementation. What should be done if the family cannot reach a consensus? Should all members of a patient's family, or only some representatives, be involved in the medical consultation and decision? These are taxing questions that require careful consideration, and inevitably there would be reasonable disagreements on what the best policy, all things considered, would be. Confucians would have no firm commitment to the legislation of assisted suicide if these difficult issues are not settled.

HUMAN SEXUALITY

Early Confucian masters had a positive attitude toward sex. *The Mencius* in particular affirms that human desire for sex is part of human nature. It is not something that we need to despise or repress.[53] The *Book of Rituals* (book 9) also says that appetite and sex are the major desires of human beings. However, "sexual desire" in the traditional Confucian discourse refers to heterosexual desire or sexual attraction between the male and female. There was no explicit discussion on homosexual preferences, and there was no affirmation or condemnation of homosexuality. Homosexuality was not uncommon in traditional China, however. There are historical records of emperors having homosexual relationships with young ministers and mates, and ministers and the upper class having affairs with young men and male prostitutes. The descriptions of these homosexual behaviors were not cast in a negative light. On the other hand, as far as I know, there was no socially approved homosexual marriage or union of any kind in China.

Given the lack of discussion of homosexuality in the Confucian texts, any attempt to find out a "Confucian" attitude on homosexuality is highly speculative. I myself would speculate that while Confucians might regard homosexuality as a kind of deviance, it may not be immoral as such—especially if some people are *born* a with homosexual tendency. Moreover, as explained earlier in this chapter, Confucians generally do not favor the use of coercion in trying to change people's conduct. Hence Confucians would tend not to support criminalization of homosexual behavior. However, if the focus of discussion is on homosexual marriage, I believe Confucians would find it harder to accept, for the following reasons. Confucians regard heterosexual union as natural, reflecting the order of nature. Classical Confucian texts all share the belief that the sexual union of man and woman gives life to all things, just as the constant intermingling of the Heaven and Earth gives shape to all things. The *Yi-Jing* regards the male (*Yang*) and female (*Yin*) as complimentary parts of a natural whole. Mencius says that "a man and woman living together is the most important of human relationships."[54] The union of man and woman is not only natural but has the socially important function of procreation. It makes possible other human relationships. The *Book of Rituals* says that without marriage there will be no father and son, nor emperor and minister.[55] This leads to the next point about the social importance of (heterosexual) marriage.

Confucians in the classical time understood marriage not simply as a private business between a man and woman, but between two families. A man marries a woman not for his own sake alone but for his family's sake. In the words of the *Book of Rituals*, marriage has to do with serving one's family and ancestors and continuing the family line by procreation.[56] Marriage is not the creation of a new family but an expansion and continuation of the husband's. (Family is also understood to be made up of heterosexual union with a view to procreation.) Marriage is thus intimately linked to filial duties. One of the main duties of filial piety is to produce children so as to continue the family tree. Having no heir is regarded as the worst way of being a "bad son."[57] A filial son is expected to get married and produce children. The two acts go together in filial piety.

This traditional Confucian understanding of marriage and family still to a certain extent shapes the values of the Chinese in Hong Kong and mainland China, to give just two examples. According to the findings of a recent research that interviewed gays in Hong Kong, many gays told the same story that when they disclosed their sexual orientation to their parents, what their parents worried and were upset about the most was that their gay sons would not get married and produce children. This was especially true when the son was the only offspring in the family.[58] Similarly, in mainland China the problem with homosexuality is not mainly in the sexual activity itself but with its inconsistency with the family relationships that are at the heart of social structure in China. There are now a fair number of people in China who have gay and lesbian relationships; but most of them feel an overwhelming pressure to enter into a heterosexual marriage that produces children. Sometimes they continue their homosexual relationships while being married; but usually they have to give them up (with much pain and sorrow) at the point of being married.[59]

If we use this traditional understanding of marriage and family as a criterion to assess homosexual marriage, then it is clear that Confucians would not recognize it as a legitimate form of marriage, for it violates the very basic meaning and function of marriage as understood by Confucians. However, some might argue that such a traditional Confucian perspective of marriage faces serious challenges from the changing norms and expectations of marriage in modern society. Wouldn't this traditional perspective lead us to reject not only homosexual union but those heterosexual couples who get married on the basis of mutual affection and romantic love, who do not want to procreate, and who intend to form a nuclear family independent of the parents' families? As the number of heterosexual couples holding these attitudes is steadily increasing in China and other East Asian societies, wouldn't Confucians today condemn these heterosexual couples and take away their right to marry as well?

These questions raise a serious problem about the contemporary relevance of the traditional Confucian conception of marriage and family. This conception would alienate a great number of people, heterosexual and homosexual alike. If a contemporary version of Confucianism is prepared to revise its conception of marriage so as to accept the decision of married couples not to procreate, then why can't it also allow homosexual marriage? However, if its new conception of marriage allows homosexual marriage, what is so specifically Confucian about this conception? I raise these questions not in order to answer them, but only to show the difficulty of searching for a social and political perspective that is attractive to modern men and women and yet sufficiently connected with traditional Confucianism to be worthy of the name "Confucian."

NOTES

I would like to thank Daniel A. Bell, Richard Madsen, Peter Nosco, Tracy Strong, and Lee Yearley for helpful comments.

1. However, as I argued elsewhere, there is a conception of moral autonomy that supports to a certain extent civil and personal liberties understood as absence of coercion. But beyond a certain point it lends no further support to them. Confucianism requires the modern notion of personal autonomy to give a stronger justification for liberties. For detailed arguments for this view, see my "Moral Autonomy, Civil Liberties, and Confucianism," *Philosophy East and West*, vol. 52, no. 3 (July 2002): 281–310. I thank Lee Yearley for drawing my attention to the notion of moral autonomy in Confucianism.

2. This process requires, as Lee Yearley suggested to me, both elaboration and emendation of the Confucian tradition. Needless to say, the interpretation, elaboration, and even emendation given in this chapter are controversial.

3. My description of Confucianism is based on classical Confucian texts, as they form the most important basis of the Confucian tradition. The texts that I use are mainly *Confucius: The Analects*, trans. D. C. Lau (London: Penguin Books, 1979), and *Mencius*, trans. D. C. Lau (London: Penguin 1970), although I also occasionally refer to *Xunzi: A Translation and Study of the Complete Works*, Vol. 2: *The Book of Rituals*, trans. J. Knoblock (Stanford: Stanford University Press, 1990)—reference to this is from the original Chinese text; an English translation can be found in *Li Ching: Book of Rites*, trans. James Legge (New York: University Books, 1967).

4. *The Book of Rituals*, 27: 1.

5. Ibid.

6. *The Analects*, XII: 1

7. Ibid., XII: 22.

8. Ibid., VI: 30.

9. Ibid., XII: 2, XV: 24.

10. Ibid., VI: 30. This translation is taken from "Confucian Analects," trans. James Legge, in his *The Chinese Classics, vol. 1.* (Hong Kong: Hong Kong University Press, 1960), 194.

11. *The Analects*, III: 3.

12. On the notion that the husband should respect the wife, see *The Book of Rituals*, 27.

13. *The Analects*, I: 2. See also, 2: 21.

14. *Mencius*, IV: 12.

15. *The Analects*, XII: 11.

16. Ibid., XIII: 3.

17. Ibid., XII: 11.

18. *Mencius*, III A: 4.

19. *Xunzi*, IX: 15.

20. *The Analects*, IX: 30.

21. Ibid., IX: 4.

22. *Mencius*, V, B: 1.

23. For a good discussion on this point, see A. S. Cua, *Moral Vision and Tradition: Essays in Chinese Ethics* (Washington, D.C.: Catholic University of America Press, 1998), 257.

24. *The Analects*, IX:4, see also XVIII: 8

25. *Mencius*, V, B: 1.

26. *The Analects*, XV: 7.

27. For a similar view, see *Mencius*, II, A: 2.

28. *The Analects*, IX: 3.

29. Ibid., XV: 11.

30. Thomas Nagel, *Equality and Partiality* (New York: Oxford University Press, 1991), 161.

31. *Mencius*, III B: 9; see also II A: 2.

32. *The Analects*, II: 3.

33. Ibid., IV: 2 (italics added).

34. Ibid., XII: 19, trans. from S. Leys, *The Analects of Confucius* (New York: W.W. Norton, 1997).

35. Ibid., XV: 15.

36. The above discussion draws on my "A Confucian Perspective on Human Rights for Contemporary China," in *The East Asian Challenge for Human Rights*, eds., Joanne R. Bauer and Daniel A. Bell (Cambridge: Cambridge University Press, 1999), 232–33.

37. *Mencius*, III B: 9 (italics added).

38. See *The Analects*, II: 15, XIX: 6, VII: 8, and IX: 8.

39. *Mencius*, VII A: 5.

40. For a more detailed discussion of this point, see my "Moral Autonomy, Civil Liberties, and Confucianism."

41. *Xunzi* book III; translation is taken from Cua, *Moral Vision and Tradition: Essays in Chinese Ethics*, 260.

42. *Mencius*, III, A: 4 (emphasis added).

43. *Mencius*, I A: 7.

44. See Sin Yee Chan, "Gender and Relationship Roles in Confucius and Mencius," (unpublished manuscript, 1998), 8–9.The analysis of the early Confucian views on gender inequality here is heavily indebted to this essay. See chap. 8 of this book for a revised version of Sin Yee Chan's essay.

45. *The Analects*, VIII: 20.

46. See Wm. Theodore de Bary, *Asian Values and Human Rights: A Confucian Communitarian Perspective* (Cambridge, Mass.: Harvard University Press, 1998), chap 7.

47. *The Analects*, XV: 39.

48. Ibid., VII: 7

49. Ping-cheung Lo, "Confucian Views on Suicide," Occasional Paper Series, (Centre for Applied Ethics, Hong Kong Baptist University, 1997). At the end the paper draws out some implications of the Confucian views on suicide regarding the issue of assisted suicide. The following discussion on suicide is indebted to this paper, although I draw a different conclusion on assisted suicide.

50. *The Analects*, XV: 9; see also *Mencius*, VI, A: 10.

51. Kazumasa Hoshino, "Bioethics in the Light of Japanese Sentiments," in Kazumasa Hoshino, ed., *Japanese and Western Bioethics* (Dordrecht: Kluwer Academic Publishers, 1996), 16–17. This quote is taken from Ruiping Fan, "Self-determination vs. Family-Determination: Two Incommensurable Principles of Autonomy," *Bioethics* 11 (1997): 316. The point of view developed in this and the last paragraph is indebted to Fan's article.

52. Fan, "Self-Determination vs. Family-Determination," 317.

53. *Mencius*, VI, A: 4 and V, A: 1.

54. Ibid., V, A: 2.

55. Bk. 44: Rites of marriage: 3.

56. Bk. 44: 1.

57. *Mencius*, IV, A: 26.

58. S. Y. Ho, "Politicising Identity: Decriminalisation of Homosexuality and the Emergence of Gay Identity in Hong Kong" (Ph.D. thesis, University of Essex, United Kingdom, 1997).

59. See Robert B.Geyer, "In Love and Gay," in Perry Link, Richard P.Madsen, Paul G. Pickowicz, eds., *Popular China: Unofficial Culture in a Globalizing Society* (Boulder, Colo.: Rowman and Littlefield, 2002). I thank Richard Madsen for drawing my attention to this essay.

Chapter Seven

TWO STRANDS OF CONFUCIANISM

~

LEE H. YEARLEY

P rofessor Chan's essay is rich, clear, appropriately critical, and (when warranted) appropriately appreciative. I aim in what follows only to sketch out a few separable but related comments that may aid our understanding of his essay and the important issues he treats. My comments are made, then, in what I take to be the spirit of a comment from *The Analects* of Confucius on the subject of who can be taught: "If I give out one corner and they don't come back with the other three corners, then I don't go on."

Let me begin with a methodological consideration—or, put in a less stuffy way, a consideration about approaches to topics like the ones Chan considers. Those who are wary about methodological inquiries may be relieved to know that I believe this one is relevant not only to the essay but also to the larger enterprise of the book of which it is a part. We need to distinguish between two kinds of development that can occur when we ask new or different questions of a tradition: elaboration and emendation. Both draw on the results of modern scholarship and reflection, and therefore they can relate closely but delinating them illuminates much.

Elaboration utilizes modern historical and textual scholarship to understand the language and context of texts. It is especially important with ideas that appear in forms that either make them easily misunderstood or allow their challenge to be easily overlooked. Emendation utilizes modern theoretical analyses and formulations to clarify, test, and reformulate the ideas the texts present. It involves complex decisions about what is and is not fundamental to the tradition. The examples Chan treats obviously exemplify this process. But much of his essay necessarily is also involved in it (which he graciously acknowledges), as when he quite properly asks at various places both what has been characteristic of the tradition and what resources it may have to meet new challenges.

A word more on these two processes. Elaboration can either be a benign scholarly activity close to philology or be so close to emendation as to be almost indistinguishable from it. Simple elaboration is, however, often needed to penetrate the density of traditions as alien from most of us as is Confucianism and thereby to bridge, if not always diminish, their distance from us. An example is the Confucian version of the basic Chinese conception of *wu wei*, often translated as "inaction" and said to refer either to an action unguided by thought or to a kind of passive withdrawal. In fact, however, the conception refers to a complex picture of what human agency can be, one that is as far from passivity as it is from feckless spontaneity.

The actual process of emendation is a complicated and, at times, dangerous, activity. Emendation, that is, might so change the original that a disinterested observer could well wonder what role the traditional text played. The text can seem only a device to jog the interpreter's reflections or, far worse, to give him or her an authority he or she otherwise would not have. The dangers here are serious and involve substantial decisions. For example, is the apparent denial of many powers to woman in classical Confucianism a distortion of the fundamental position or a basic implication of it? Throughout the process, then, we need to remain alert to the possibility that in some cases no genuine emendation is possible. When this occurs, we face ideas that have their attractions but are finally unacceptable.

The processes operating here lead us to deal constantly with two demands that initially may appear to be incompatible or even only to generate conflict—what I call the demands of being both credible and appropriate. To meet the demand of being credible is to formulate Confucian ideas about ethical pluralism in a way that is credible to, accords with the conditions of plausibility found in, our common contemporary experience, informed as that experience is by modern scientific explanations, historical consciousness, and ideas about the rights of all humans. To meet the demands of appropriateness is to formulate those Confucian ideas in a way that is appropriate to, shows appreciative fidelity toward, their meaning as judged by the most basic norms found in the tradition. Meeting both demands a kind of balancing act, and it may in some cases—such as ethical pluralism—not be possible.

The distinctions noted here and the dangers of the warnings about emendation inform my second point, which I will frankly describe as an exaggeration in the direction of truth. I would argue there are two major strands in the Confucian tradition, even if elements of each strand appear in many Confucian thinkers, and the distinctions between them are important for us because they can lead to very different postures on issues about ethical pluralism. The most influential and sophisticated proponents of the respective strands are Xunzi and Mencius, and I use the names of those two thinkers as labels for each strand.

The differences between the two strands can be stated in terms of the cosmogonies that underlie them, the role past sages play in them, and the distinctive moral emphases they produce. In the Mencius strand, Heaven gives each person a nature, and therefore anyone can become a sage, a fully flourishing, benevolent person. In the Xunzi strand, past sages best understood Heaven's plans and provided highly differentiated social forms that need to be followed if humans are to be perfected. In the former the sages are grammarians of human nature; in the latter they are legislators to human beings. In the former virtues like benevolence and righteousness are highlighted. In the latter virtues like ritual (*li*) and loyalty are highlighted.

It is fair to say, I think, that in much of the Confucian tradition, and Chan's essay reflects this, the Xunzi strand has been more prominent, and therefore notions of, for example, hierarchical rules and ritual have been dominant. (In one of those complex ironies that traditions exhibit, the intellectual and governmental elite often expressed a commitment to Mencius—as they understood him—even though their practice more closely followed the strand represented by Xunzi.) The Mencius strand has also been present, however, and when it is in ascendancy, notions of discretion, such as those Chan notes, are highlighted and tensions between righteousness or benevolence and ritual are pronounced.

With both strands, if especially with what became the dominant form of the Mencius strand, metaphysical commitments underlie their respective positions. It may be that any perfectionist picture (and Chan rightly characterizes Confucianism as perfectionist) has such commitments, but these two strands surely do. The commitments are, however, quite different in form, importance, and possible contemporary viability. Each strand, of course, can be emended in order to fit into a pluralist frame. Nevertheless, both the emendations needed and the difficulties involved in making the emendations, take very different forms depending on the strand that is treated.

Put telegraphically, the Xunzi strand has a development model, and the later form of the Mencius strand, which I call a Neo-Confucian model, has a discovery model. (These distinctions also have a temporal dimension—that is, between Confucianism before and after it encountered Buddhist metaphysics.) In a developmental model, a common model in many traditions, human nature has an innate constitution that manifests itself in processes of growth and culminates in specifiable forms. That fulfillment occurs, however, only if the organism is both uninjured and properly nurtured. The basic conceptual model is, then, relatively simple and it draws on a biological framework. A basic set of capacities exist and their unhindered, nurtured development generates qualities that lead to specifiable actions or characteristic forms. Those, in turn, provide the standard that allows observers to determine a being's nature and to judge whether any specific action represents its nature in normal, exemplary, or defective fashion. In such a model, processes of cultivation, social and individual, are absolutely crucial.

In a discovery model, in contrast, human nature exists as a permanent set of dispositions that are obscured but that can be contacted or discovered. People do not cultivate inchoate capacities through appropriate social forms. Rather they discover a hidden ontological reality that defines them, whatever may be the reigning social forms. The two models differ, then, both in the character of the ontological ideas they rely on and also in the ways in which their notions of human perfection depend on those ideas.

The ideas of perfection in a discovery model are much more deeply embedded in specific ontological ideas than are the ideas of perfection in a developmental model; Neo-Confucian ideas fundamentally rely on, that is, a distinctive metaphysical picture. The level of embedding is important because I think it is very difficult to defend, to make plausible, a Neo-Confucian ontology and the discovery model it manifests. Most directly relevant here, I also think it is considerably more difficult to imagine a discovery model generating a lively notion of pluralism. Difficult but not impossible I should add: the issue is structurally similar to what is involved in generating notions of pluralism from certain kinds of theistic or Platonic pictures.

Allow me to end by briefly commenting on two other points in Chan's essay. First, a prominent motif at several points is the role of "good argument" in the Confucian tradition, and I think one feature of this subject is important not simply for the Confucian tradition, but for the more general issue of ethical pluralism. I would distinguish the persuasively presented from the "well argued" when ethical inquiry is the subject, and suggest that the Confucian tradition has usually emphasized the former— and had very good reasons to do so. Indeed, many Confucian texts are excellent instances of reasoned attempts to doubt the value, when the subject is ethics, of many kinds of reasoned arguments.

"Persuasively presented" is, of course, a considerably wider category than is "well argued," and any full examination necessarily involves complex issues about the character of rhetoric and all those subjects that follow in its wake. Confucians recognize, for instance, just how dangerous rhetoric can be and yet they also attempt, both in their interpretive theory and in their practice, to display how rhetorical language presents realities that can be made evident or compelling in no other way. Most important to us, however, is the issue of the fit of a focus on persuasive presentation with pluralistic ideals, an issue that spawns various questions, most of which receive detailed if controversial Confucian responses.

A practical one, for example, concerns the control of those institutions that teach rhetoric and disseminate persuasively presented ideas. A theoretical one concerns what exactly is implied by the central Confucian claim that most forms of ethical presentation are not the shadowgraphs of ideas: that is, that the language we use is not the mere adornment of an idea but is constitutive of the idea, is not just a device to persuade the recalcitrant or intellectually inept but is what makes possible any appropriation of an ethical position.

My second, final point concerns the issue of the place of autonomy inside the Confucian tradition, an issue Chan quite rightly focuses on at points and also has treated in other work. Our disagreement may be slight, given different possible meanings for the notion of "autonomy" and our agreement that a modern Western sense of autonomy is not present in traditional Confucianism. I do think, however, that a distinctive sense of autonomy is present (especially in the Mencius strand of Confucianism) and briefly discussing how it can fit into a pluralistic view is productive.

Crucial to much of the Confucian tradition is the distinction between semblances of virtue and virtue. Semblances of virtue generate activities that resemble the activities of real virtue but lack important elements in it, and the notion appears in a central Confucian notion, the idea of the village honest person (*xiangyuan*). Such people are called the thief, not the epitome of virtue because their apparently virtuous actions arise from an imperfectly virtuous character. Such people do a virtuous act not for itself but for consequences that a nonvirtuous people would desire. Or they choose it not for their own reasons but because of some secondhand support such as custom, unexamined authority, or the inertia provided by accepted, routine reactions.

My suggestion, then, is that we may find in Confucianism a sense of autonomy that, although different from many modern Western ones, is both full-blooded and worth considering for its pluralistic implications. It may, for example, rest on the notion that truly fine human behavior has not only acquisitive but also expressive motives. That is, especially laudable people choose a virtuous action not only because it contributes to goods they want to acquire but also because it expresses their conception of the good.

PART FOUR

CONTEMPORARY FEMINISM

∼

Chapter Eight

GENDER AND RELATIONSHIP ROLES IN THE *ANALECTS* AND THE *MENCIUS*

~

SIN YEE CHAN

It is indisputable that traditional Confucianism endorsed patriarchy. However, the explicit subordination of women in Confucianism only started with the Han Confucian Dong Zhongshu (179?–104? C.E.). Dong aligned the female with the cosmic force of *yin* and the male with *yang*. More importantly, he converted the complementary and equal relationship of *yin* and *yang* as portrayed in the *Book of Changes* to a hierarchical relationship of *yang* presiding over *yin*.[1] The Neo-Confucians exacerbated this trend. Zhu Xi (1130–1200 C.E.) commented, "Good and evil can be applied to describe yin and yang. It can also be applied to describe the male and the female."[2] But what is the early Confucian conception of gender like before the inclusion of the elements of *yin* and *yang*? Does it also imply the subordination of women?

In this essay I aim to explicate this early Confucian conception of gender and examine its relationship to the subordination of women as portrayed in the *Analects* and the *Mencius*. In doing this, I do not assume that Confucius (551–479 B.C.E.) or Mencius (372–289 B.C.E.) held an explicit conception of gender, or that they appealed to such a conception to justify the subordination of women. Instead my project is to provide a philosophical reconstruction of the relationship between the conception of gender implicit in the two texts[3] and the various forms of subordination of women the two texts endorsed. In particular, I shall argue that this conception of gender is primarily a functional distinction assigning women to inner/domestic duties, and men to outer/public duties. I shall then show how this conception of gender plays out in the context of the Confucian relationship role system. Finally I shall argue that this conception of gender can neither justify those forms of subordination of women, nor itself be justified on Confucian grounds. One can discard this early Confucian conception of gender, without relinquishing one's commitment to the core doctrines of early Confucianism.

Before looking at the texts themselves, I would like to explain briefly my decision to focus on the *Analects* and the *Mencius* for analysis. Most works on the early Confucian conception of gender (such as those of Ames and Hall, Black, Guisso, Li, Raphals, and Rosemont)[4] rely extensively on other Confucian texts such as the Five Classics,[5] as well as historical texts such as the *Zuo Chuan* and the *Guo Yu*.[6] While these discussions have benefitted us with great insights, a focused and detailed analysis of the *Analects* and the *Mencius* on the question of gender is still much called for. For such a study can highlight a conception of gender that is devoid of the influence of the *yin yang* correlation, especially when it is seen as implying a natural or cosmic hierarchy. Moreover, whereas the other Confucian texts focus more on the description of historical practices and events, the *Analects* and the *Mencius* are the indisputable philosophical articulations of the ideologies of early Confucianism. Analysis of these two texts therefore should allow us to attend to the more theoretically sophisticated layers of the early Confucian conception of gender. And this, in turn, will enable us to position, interpret, and evaluate the conception within the context of the early Confucian moral, social, and political ideologies which, after all, are on the same textual terrain as the conception itself.[7]

THE CONFUCIAN CONCEPTION OF GENDER

In asking what the early Confucian conception of gender is like, we are asking how maleness and femaleness are understood in early Confucianism. We should note that gender differences are distinct from sex differences. Sex differences pertain to physiological features related to procreation and biological reproduction. Gender differences, on the other hand, are social constructs in the sense that they represent an *interpretation* of sex differences.[8] For example, while the ability to bear children is a feature of the female sex, being nurturing and motherly are gender traits society attributes to females.

Most studies of the early Confucian conception of gender concur that it is *complementarity*, rather than subordination, that is emphasized in women's gender role. And they often refer to two different bases for drawing the gender distinction: 1) the *yin yang* correlation and 2) the *nei wai* (inner-outer 內 外) distinction.[9]

With regard to the first basis, the *yin yang* cosmic forces are seen as complementary to each other as well as hierarchically related. The male and female genders, which presumably are derived from these two forces, are believed to inherit these traits as well.[10] Guisso's comment is typical of such a view: "That male and female were different, as different as heaven and earth, yang and yin. . . . In an organically holistic universe, male and female were inextricably connected, each assigned a dignified and respectable role and each expected to interact in co-operation and harmony. The fact remains, however, that the relationship is not an equal one."[11]

The second basis, the *nei wai* (inner-outer) distinction, refers to the distinction between the private/domestic sphere and the public/social sphere. Constructing the gender distinction on this basis means that females are assigned to the inner, and males to the outer sphere. This gender distinction actually denotes two kinds of separation. The first is a physical separation between the sexes: a guard between males and females (*nan nu zhi fang* 男女之防). This does not mean only that males and females are physically separated in that women's activities are confined to the domestic sphere. It also means that within the domestic sphere, interaction between males and females, including husbands and wives, follows rules of strict physical separation, such as "males and females did not use the same stand or rack for their clothes. The wife did not presume to hang up anything on the pegs/stand of her husband; nor to put anything in his boxes or satchels; nor to share his bathing house" (*Book of Rites*, chap. 12).[12]

The second kind of separation denoted by the gender distinction is a functional distinction—as a division of labor. It is the idea that "males are primary in the outer, females are primary in the inner (*nan zhu wai, nu zhu nei* 男主內女主外)." Women are assigned to handle the domestic affairs, such as nurturing the children, cooking, weaving, and other household work. Men, on the other hand, handle public and social affairs, such as farming, commerce and, for some men, holding government office.[13]

Do these observations about the early Confucian conception of gender apply to the *Analects* and the *Mencius*? We find that the terms "inner" and "outer" are predicated on unmarried women and unmarried men respectively (*Mencius* 1B:5). The two separations based on the inner-outer distinctions described earlier are also mentioned. Reference to the physical separation is explicit:

#1. "When giving and receiving, man and woman should not touch each other." (*Mencius* 4A:17).

The functional distinction is implicit: When thinking of taking over Shun's two wives, Xiang said, "his two wives should be made to look over my quarters" (*Mencius* 5A:8). Likewise, the duties of the common men are related to husbandry, while those of the common women center on the care of the aged in the family (*Mencius* 7A:22).[14]

Since the texts do not refer to the yin-yang correlation, or contain any other way to mark the gender distinction, we can conclude that the inner-outer distinction forms the sole basis for the conception of gender in the texts.

With regard to the two separations, we find that the texts emphasize the functional separation over the physical one.[15] Five references are made to the former (*Mencius* 3B:3,4; 5A:8; 5B:5; 7A:22), while only one is made to the latter (*Mencius* 4A:17). Moreover, even though the physical separation is said to apply to the husband-wife relationship according to the *Book of Rites*, when the separation is discussed in the texts, it is in the context of a case about brothers- and sisters-in-law. This suggests that, at least as far as husbands and wives are concerned, the main distinction males and females should observe is the functional distinction. So we can conclude that the conception of gender portrayed in the texts is primarily the functional one noted above.

We have to be cautious in interpreting the functional separation, however. Note that the basis of the separation, the inner-outer distinction, does not imply a *dichotomy* between the domestic and the public domains. In Confucianism, family is seen neither as completely separate from nor as secondary to the public domain.[16] Not only is family the training ground for moral cultivation, the continuous practice of familial virtues such as filial piety anchors success in the public domain:

#2. "When the ruler feels profound affection for his parents (*qin*), the common people will be stirred to benevolence" (*Analects* 8:2).

This is so because, according to the Confucian philosophy, a ruler is to be a role model who does not interfere with political administration. His political power rests on his possession of moral virtues. His task is to set the standard of order and virtues for his people with his own exemplary behavior:

#3. "If there was a ruler who achieved order without taking any action, it was, perhaps, Shun. There was nothing for him to do but to hold himself in a respectful posture and to face South" (*Analects* 15:5).

Given these two assumptions (of continuity between the family and the public domain, and of ruling by example) we should not be surprised to find that males are still assigned the role of ruler of the family, despite their belonging to the outer realm:

#4. The *Book of Odes* says, "He set an example (刑) for his consort, and also for his brother, an also ruled over the family and the state" (*Mencius* 1A:7).

Consequently, to say that women are assigned to the inner realm merely means that their primary duties lie in managing household affairs, not that they are in charge of the family.[17] And to say that men are assigned to the outer means that their primary duties lie in managing external affairs, even though they still rule over the family.

So what role does this gender conception play in the Confucian social world? The answer can be seen in the following passage:

#5. "And so he appointed Hsieh as the Minister of Education whose duty was to teach the people human relationships: love between father and son (child), rightness between ruler and minister, distinction (*bie* 別) between husband and wife, order between the elder and the younger, and faith between friends" (*Mencius* 3A:4).

There is little doubt that the distinction (*bie*) referred to in the passage is the gender distinction.[18] For whenever the different roles of husbands and wives are described in the texts, the gender distinction in the sense of the functional distinction is always assumed. For example:

#6. It is said in the *Book of Rites*, "A prince ploughs himself, and is assisted (by the people) to supply the millet for sacrifice. His wife keeps silkworms and unwinds their cocoons, to make the garments for sacrifice." (*Mencius* 3B:3)

That men are doing the farming and women are doing the weaving is a paradigmatic instance of the gender distinction. And it is these tasks that the prince and his wife, the role models for the husband-wife relationship, undertake in the important rite of making sacrifice.

With this understanding, we can see that the significance of the gender distinction is clearly demonstrated in passage 5. Note that the Five Relationships mentioned in the passage are the quintessence of the Confucian social order. The fulfillment of the role duties related to these Five Relationships is in turn the paramount moral duty of a Confucian agent. And for each of these relationships, there is a governing principle. For example, love is the governing principle of the father-son (child) relationship. The gender distinction is taken as the governing principle of one of the Five Relationships, namely the husband-wife relationship, and is placed on a par with the other important Confucian values such as love, rightness, order, and faith. In other words, the gender distinction is one of the pillars structuring the Confucian social world.

IMPLICATIONS

At first glance this conception of gender as basically a functional role seems to imply the element of *mutuality* that is already embodied in the husband-wife relationship in the following ways: The husband-wife relationship is based on humans' natural appetites for sex (*Mencius* 1B:5), which is mutually shared by males and females (*Mencius* 6A:4). Moreover, since having no heir is seen as being unfilial in the worst way (*Mencius* 4A:26), and since all parents wish their children to have families

(*Mencius* 3B:3), filial piety requires both genders to establish the husband-wife relationship. In brief, having a family is the mutual goal of both sexes.

Emphasizing the functional distinction between husband and wife brings into relief the very nature of cooperation between the two within the context of raising a family. The roles of husband and wife are as partners and teammates. Each makes a distinctive and complementary contribution to the attainment of the common goal. In this way, each deserves recognition of his or her worth, and each maintains his or her identity as someone with distinct interests, not a mere instrument. It is no accident that musical harmony, exemplified by performance on the Chinese lute and zither, is the paradigmatic metaphor for the husband-wife relationship. This may also help to explain why another word for wife, (qi 妻), connotes equals (qi 齊).[19]

A closer examination, however, make us doubt whether this conception of gender constitutes a positive influence on the status of women in early Confucianism. Alison Black suggests that the gender distinction in early Confucianism might support a subordination of women because men with their free access to public life were in a better position to acquire wisdom. And wisdom is relevant to superiority in Confucianism.[20]

While this observation is interesting, I believe it does not go far enough. To say that an access to public life means a privileged access to wisdom is to assume that only a specific kind of wisdom has value. For one may argue that domestic confinement nurtures the sort of wisdom involved in handling close personal relationships, as well as intellectual knowledge about children's psychology and physical well-being.

Of course Black can reply by pointing to the Confucian conception of wisdom, which is more about *moral* wisdom than just intellectual knowledge, as the objection suggests. But the question remains: Why is moral wisdom linked to public life?

I think Black's observation is close to the mark, but still does not hit it. Moral wisdom is important in Confucianism, but it is not as important as the ideal of a *junzi*. A *junzi* is a person who possesses the ideal virtue of *ren* (benevolence), which is an all-encompassing virtue, including others like wisdom, respect, faith, . . . etc. And the essence of this ideal virtue is benevolence or love for fellow humans. The functional distinction leads to women's subordination in early Confucianism because it poses a hurdle to women's achieving this ideal of *junzi*.[21] This is so because women cannot *take up political positions* or serve in the government.

Serving in the government can be seen as required for the attainment of the ideal of *junzi*.[22] Bringing benefit to the world is an integral part of the Confucian ideal: "In obscurity a man makes perfect his own person, but in prominence he makes perfect the whole empire as well" (*Mencius* 1A:9). Hence, the duty to serve in the government is prescribed by Confucius:

#7. "Show yourself when the Way prevails in the Empire, but hide yourself when it does not. It is a shameful matter to be poor and humble when the Way prevails in the state. Equally it is a shameful matter to be rich and noble when the Way falls into disuse in the state" (*Analects* 8:13).

However, given their domestic role, there seems no way for women to perfect the empire through serving in the government.

I think there is another, though perhaps less obvious, reason for the need to transcend the household. One has to be open to challenges and trials if one is to have unwavering commitment to the Way: One of the manifestations of having supreme courage is that "if one finds oneself in the right, one goes forward even against men in the thousands" (*Mencius* 2A:2). To be a *junzi*, "he has to be able to stay firm and not be deflected from his purpose even in moments of crisis" (*Analects* 8:6). A great man "cannot be led into excesses when wealthy and honored or deflected from his purpose when poor and obscure, nor can he be made to bow before superior force" (*Mencius* 3B:2).

All these opportunities for trials and challenges are closed off to women. A man can demonstrate his commitment to the Way by the choices he makes in various trying situations. Given her domestic role, a woman, on the other hand, is a mere dependent on males, either her father or, if she is married, her husband. She has no power to make any important decisions, even those regarding her own affairs, like the choice of her husband or whether to divorce.[23] Since her future is not in her own hands, she cannot demonstrate her commitment to the Way as a man can, nor does she face the same level of temptation or risk. For example, she cannot refuse an important office, because she will never be offered one.

Consequently, it is not surprising that Confucian virtues are often defined in the context of serving in the government:

#8. Confucius said, "There are five things and whoever is capable of putting them into practice in the empire is certainly benevolent. . . . If a man is respectful he will not be treated with insolence. If he is tolerant, he will win the multitude. If he is trustworthy in word his fellow men will entrust him with responsibility. If he is quick he will achieve results. If he is generous he will be good enough to be put in a position over his fellow men" (*Analects* 17:6).

In short, the Confucian conception of gender seems to have the effect of excluding women from the ideal of *junzi*. This might in turn lead to another exclusion: the *exclusion of women from receiving the Confucian education*. Since the purpose of Confucian education is to help people acquire the virtue of *ren* and become a *junzi*, education and office-holding are seen as closely connected[24].

"When a man in office finds that he can more than cope with his duties, then he studies; when a student finds that he can more than cope with his studies, then he takes office" (*Analects* 19:13).

Thus it can be argued that if women can never become *junzi*, it is pointless to give them a Confucian education, even though the texts never seem to suggest that they are incapable of learning. Since the acquisition of a Confucian education is perceived to be an indispensable part of moral cultivation, women would never be considered the moral equals of men.

GENDER AND THE FORMS OF SUBORDINATION OF WOMEN

The Confucian conception of gender therefore implies the three-fold exclusion of women from political participation, and thus from the ideal of *junzi* and, consequently, from a Confucian education. What remains to be shown is whether these exclusions, which are forms of subordination of women, were actually endorsed by Confucianism.

Let us first consider the issue of education. Confucius did advocate educating everyone without discrimination (*Analects* 15:39), and Mencius claimed that one of the three delights of a *junzi* is to educate the most talented people in the empire (*Mencius* 7A:20). Yet among the thousands of students of Confucius and Mencius, none was a female. We learn how Confucius educated his own son (*Analects* 16:13), but there is no hint that he also educated his daughter. These facts point to an acceptance, if not also endorsement, of the prevailing practice of excluding women from receiving a Confucian education.[25]

The texts also seems to be in conformity with the prevailing distrust of women's political participation,[26] as expressed in sayings like, "If the hen crows in the morning, the household will be in ruin"[27], "A wise man builds a city, a wise woman ruins a city" (Book of Odes, #264).[28] Despite the fact that the *Analects* and the *Mencius* contain many references to historical and contemporary political figures, there is not a single reference to any female political figure. But there were women who played an active role in politics. For example, the mother of King Wu (the founder of the Zhou dynasty) actively assisted her son in overthrowing the Shang dynasty. Even so, when commenting on King Wu's remark that he had ten capable officials, Confucius only said, "How true it is that talent is difficult to find! . . . With a woman amongst them, there were, in fact, only nine" (*Analects* 8:20). Confucius just excluded the woman from the list of those with talent. All of this makes clear his position on the issue of women's participation in government.

Furthermore, despite the Confucians' strong belief in the importance of emulating role models and their practice of constantly referring to sages, none of the Confucian sages or role models is female. Indeed, not one woman is praised in the texts. But this is not due to a lack of praise-worthy women before or during the time of Confucius and Mencius, as evidenced in the historical texts and the *Biographies of Virtuous Women*.[29]

GENDER AND THE CONTEXT OF THE CONFUCIAN ROLE SYSTEM

Black remarks that gender is not a basic polarity in early Confucian cosmology.[30] Perhaps a similar comment can be made about gender in the Confucian social ideology. Gender distinction is placed within the Confucian role system (passage #5). This means that it has to be governed by the fundamental assumptions of the system. When analyzing the ruler-minister and the father-son relationships, the two most elaborated relationships of the role system in the texts, we find that these assumptions include merit, reciprocity, and respect. To fully understand how the Confucian conception of gender plays out, we have to see how it interacts with these assumptions.

1. Merit

Hierarchy is a common feature of the Confucian role system. For example, both the ruler-minister and the father-son relationship are hierarchical. What is interesting about the Confucian hierarchy is its alleged basis in merit. The merit that is relevant is moral virtue. Those who occupy the superior position are supposed to be more virtuous than, and should serve as inspiring models for, those who are in the subordinate position. Ideally, a ruler should attract his subjects with his virtues and preserve heaven's mandate by constantly renewing and developing his virtues (*Analects* 20:1). Similarly, a father should nurture the virtues of his son (*Mencius* 4B:7) so that his son would inherit his ambition (*Analects* 1:11).

For reasons mentioned previously, women might be seen as less virtuous than men. Given the alleged merit basis of the Confucian role system, women as wives would then be subordinated to men as husbands. A husband is to set an example for his wife (passage #4). In turn, the advice a bride receives from her mother is to be obedient: "to be docile (shun 順) is the Way of a wife or concubine" (*Mencius* 3B:2).

While the merit basis of the Confucian role system can explain why women as wives are subordinated to men as husbands, it alone cannot fully explain why the Way of wives and concubines is docility. For docility is not the *predominant* virtue required of the other subordinate counterparts such as ministers or sons, as it is of wives.

Why is there such a discrepancy? To find the answer, we have to look at the different governing principles of the various relationships—love between father and son, rightness between ruler and subject, and distinction between husband and wife. Now when rightness, or concern for the Way, is the principle governing the ruler-minister relationship, the predominant duty of a minister is to see that the Way prevails in the empire. This implies a consequent duty to remonstrate with his ruler when the latter deviates from the Way. He may even need to relinquish his office if his remonstration is constantly ignored. While remonstration and resignation can be done in a deferential manner, they are still inconsistent with docility, at least in the sense of strict obedience to the judgment of the superior.[31] Hence docility cannot be the cardinal virtue of a minister.

However, for the father-son relationship, love is the predominant principle and rightness is only secondary: fathers and sons should not take each other to task for immoral behavior, for this would undermine the affection between them (*Mencius* 4B:30). It is even appropriate for a father to cover up for his son when the latter steals a sheep and vice versa for the son (*Analects* 13:8). When rightness is only secondary, docility can be expected of a son in order to enhance the harmony of the father-son relationship: "When one is not docile to one's parents, one cannot be a son" (*Mencius* 4A:28).[32] Yet since the principle of love requires a son to perform a variety of duties including, for example, support for his parents, the Way of the son cannot be confined to mere submission but must consist in a more encompassing virtue like filial piety. This again gives room for justified insubordination on the part of the son when submission conflicts with other more important requirements of filial duty. Thus even the sage Shun defies his parents in order to get married. For getting married and having an heir is considered to be the most important filial duty (*Mencius* 4A:26).

The husband-wife relationship is governed by the principle of distinction. Since rightness is not the primary virtue, docility may once again be a relevant virtue. But in this case, it is made paramount. Perhaps the reason has to do with the principle of distinction as a functional distinction. A clear chain of command might better ensure the efficiency of the functional team of husband and wife. Moreover, since women are excluded completely from the ideal of *junzi* and a Confucian education as a consequence of the functional division, the moral superiority of a husband with regard to his wife is even more pronounced than that of a father to a son. Docility therefore can be further justified on the ground of the moral superiority of a husband in addition to the functional consideration of streamlining authority.[33]

2. Reciprocity

Father and son are urged to reciprocate with love to each other (*Mencius* 7B:24 and *Analects* 17:21). Similarly rulers and ministers should reciprocate with respect (*jing* 敬) to each other (*Mencius* 2B:2, 4A:1, 4B:3). Yet reciprocity does not necessarily eliminate the hierarchical nature of a relationship. For reciprocity only ensures that good is returned for good, not that the same kind of good must be returned. For example in a hierarchical relationship such as that between a protector and a protege, affection and respect can be reciprocated for protection and guidance.

Similarly the ruler-minister and the father-son relationship both remain hierarchical despite reciprocity because the parties involved often do not reciprocate with goods of the same kind. For example, children's reciprocal duty is to serve and please their parents (*Analects* 1:7), and a minister should reciprocate with his best efforts to serve his ruler (*Analects* 3:19).

As applied to the husband-wife relationship, husbands have a duty to support wives: "A clear-sighted ruler in determining the property system ensures that people should have enough to care for the parents and to support (*chu* 畜) the wife and children" (*Mencius* 1A:7). The support is reciprocated with submission.

While reciprocity cannot entirely eliminate hierarchy, it still ensures that the reciprocating parties have moral duties to each other and enjoy equal status as bearers of moral claims. Thus, a child can complain about negligent and affectionless parents (*Mencius* 5A:1); a minister can relinquish the office when the ruler does not treat him with respect (*Mencius* 4B:14); and a wife can complain about her husband who brings shame to her when he begs for the leftovers of sacrificial food (*Mencius* 4B:33). More importantly, reciprocity gives women as mothers leverage over males as sons.[34] Since a mother, like a father, has contributed to the care and love of the child, the child should reciprocate with filial piety to both parents (e.g., *Analects* 1:7, 2:6, 4:19). Thus even when a mother does wrong and ignores the child's advice, the child should remain obedient and reverent (*Analects* 4:18).[35] Despite this, a mother still enjoys less authority than a father, since the father is the ruler of the family (passage #4).

In brief, even though reciprocity in the role system does not change the fact that the female gender as a whole is subordinate to the male gender, it does help to ameliorate the subordination of women substantially.

3. Respect

Above all, all the role relationships follow rituals (*li* 禮) whose spirit is respect (*Mencius* 6A:6). The very basic form of respect is to respect the dignity of the other person, without which one would choose death rather than life (*Mencius* 6A:10). Certainly this ideological bulwark cannot fully guarantee that the Confucians would not, in practice, severely repress women. The Song Confucians provided a prime example of such severe repression.[36] However, when this happens, the repression deviates from the role system as depicted in the texts.

In sum, when the Confucian conception of gender plays out in the role system, it implies the subordination of women as wives to men as husbands in that wives have to be docile to husbands. On the other hand, the subordination of women is to some degree held in check by the assumptions of reciprocity and respect.

CRITIQUE

Does the domestic role really imply the exclusion of women from the ideal of junzi? Perhaps not.

#9. Simply by being a good son and friend to his brothers, a man can exert an influence on government. In so doing a man is, in fact, taking part in government. How can there be any question of his having actively to "take part in the government" (*Analects* 2:21)?

#10. "To stand in the center of the Empire and bring peace to the people within the Four Seas is what a *junzi* delights in, but that which he follows as his nature lies elsewhere" (*Mencius* 7A:21).

If practicing virtues at home is equivalent to taking part in the government, then some virtuous women can be said to take part in the government. Alternatively, if cultivating one's nature rather than serving in the government is the most important duty of a *junzi*, and if women have the capacity to cultivate their natures, then there is no reason to exclude them from the ideal of *junzi*.

The crux of the problem turns on whether women have the ability to cultivate their natures and become morally virtuous. The texts fail to provide any evidence for thinking that women are innately less virtuous than men. The four innate minds—the minds of commiseration, shame, deference, and judgment—are universally shared (*Mencius* 2A:6). Without this assumption of universality, Mencius cannot make his claim that humans, and not just men, are innately morally good.[37]

Certainly the moral potential needs to be developed by one's undertaking moral cultivation. But there is no reason to think that women cannot engage in moral cultivation. The two root virtues of the Way, filial piety and deference to the elder brother (*Analects* 1:2), are familial virtues that can still be acquired by women in their domestic role; so are the other Confucian virtues like faith (*xin*), generosity (*hui*), respect (*jing*), loyalty (*zhong*), and wisdom (*zhi*).

Indeed women are portrayed in the texts as capable of moral judgments. Like common men, common women are attracted by the virtues of the sage rulers. They select their rulers by voting with their feet (*Mencius* 3B:5), that is, by running toward the good rulers and away from those they deem to be bad. And either common men or common women can make the moral error of being inflexible (*liang*) (*Analects* 14:17). Women are portrayed as capable of feeling shame, one of the innate moral sentiments (*Mencius* 4B:33); and their weeping during mourning can arouse the moral sentiments of people and bring about changes in social customs (*Mencius* 6B:6). In brief, if women can engage in moral cultivation as men do, then according to passage #10, women's domestic role should not hinder them from attaining the ideal of *junzi*.

Perhaps the defender of the exclusion thesis can still make the following replies. She may agree that passage #9 is about the interconnectedness between the family and the state. But she may insist that it should be read as addressed to people who are *potential* office holders only. By potential office holders, she may mean people who would actually become office holders *if certain circumstantial conditions were to obtain*—for example, if they were recognized by the ruler, if the ruling government followed the Way, or if they were not bound by the mourning rule to stay away from public office. Passage #7 does support the idea that actually serving in the government is not a necessary precondition for being a *junzi*. When the Way does not prevail, it is one's duty not to serve. But given their domestic role, women cannot even be potential office holders. No change in the circumstantial conditions can enable them to serve as officials. In this way, it could be argued, women are still excluded from the ideal of *junzi*.

Similarly, the defender may agree that passage #10 shows that the cultivation of one's nature is more important than serving in the government. But, she may argue, this does not show that serving in the government is not a *necessary condition* for attaining the ideal of *junzi*.

This defense is weak, as it relies on interpretations that are mere conjectures. Though one cannot absolutely rule out such readings, there is little evidence to support them, at least from the immediate context of the passages.

More importantly, a requirement to serve (or be available to serve) is, I believe, *inconsistent with the Confucian political philosophy*. In saying this, I do not deny that the ideal of *junzi* involves the goal of perfecting the empire, or that the goal should be accomplished through political means. What I challenge is whether serving in the government is the *only political means* to accomplish the goal.

The crux of the issue lies in the Confucian insight of the continuum between the family and the state.[38] The distinction between the social and the political is simply a matter of degree. The political is not an autonomous sphere, but is just the social sphere writ large. Hence, the family is the basis of a good social-political order, and the foundation of a good government consists in extending the familial virtues to the world. If this is true, then serving in the government cannot be the only means of exercising one's political influence. Familial virtues could be translated into political influence in many other ways. For example, women who excel in familial virtues could train the next generation, and hence profoundly affect the future of the state.[39]

Most importantly, as seen in passage #3, the best way to exert one's political influence is to serve as a role model. This is the way of a *junzi*: "The virtue of the *junzi* is like wind; the virtue of the small men is like grass. Let the wind blow over the grass and it is sure to bend" (*Analects* 12:19). The domestic role of women should not exclude them from serving as role models for others. Recall the wives of Hua Zhou and Ji Liang. Being good at mourning for their husbands, they transformed the practice of the whole state (*Mencius* 6B:6). Perhaps a daughter who has an exemplary virtue of filial piety can also stir the whole state to benevolence, just as a ruler who has filial piety does (passage #2).

We noted earlier that another obstacle to including women in the ideal of *junzi* is their lack of exposure to the risks and challenges that are required to establish a *junzi*. With regard to this, there is no reason why certain Confucian practices could not be revised in order to allow women to have access to those risks and challenges. For example, if women are given the autonomy to choose and divorce their husbands,[40] they can have the opportunity to demonstrate their commitment to the Way and be subject to the same kind of risks and temptations that face men, even while remaining in their domestic role. For wives can then be seen as analogous to ministers. Just as virtuous males attract good rulers, women can determine their own destiny and attain honor by attracting with their virtues good males of influence for marriage. Similarly they could assert their moral integrity by divorcing vicious husbands, even though this may mean poverty and hardship.[41]

If my arguments are correct, then women can have access to political influence, and trials and challenges despite their domestic role. The obstacles to including them in the ideal of *junzi* and consequently in a

Confucian education are thus removed. An important consequence then is to call into question the subordination of wives to husbands on the basis of merit. For now there is no obvious reason why wives must be morally inferior to their husbands in all cases.

A defense of the subordination of wives might be made by claiming that there is another basis for the Confucian role system: the *naturalistic basis*. That is, the idea that the hierarchical relationships are based on heaven (*tian*) and nature. In the texts heaven and nature are closely connected: "A man who knows his own nature will know heaven. By retaining his heart and nurturing his nature, he is serving heaven" (*Mencius* 7A:1). Given the naturalistic basis, even virtuous people like Confucius cannot become rulers despite their superiority in virtues. For rulers are supposed to have heaven's mandate (*Mencius* 5A:5).

However, as we have seen, the naturalistic basis of the husband-wife relationship is humans' natural appetite for sex. Yet this appetite at best points to the setting up of a family, if Mencius is right that sexual relationships require legitimization by marriage (*Mencius* 3B:3). But why assume that a family must be hierarchically structured?

One might still try to defend the hierarchical nature of the husband-wife relationship by claiming that, to the Confucians, hierarchy is a given in human relationships. The two root virtues of the Way, filial piety and deference to the elder brother, both involve hierarchical relationships of father-son and elder-younger. Thus, it could be said, the important Confucian relationships must all be hierarchical.

Is this true? Consider the friend-friend relationship, which is also one of the Five Relationships. This is a relationship *between equals* that is based on the virtue of faithfulness: "In making friends with others, do not rely on the advantage of age, position or powerful relations. In making friends with someone you do so because of his virtue" (*Mencius* 5B:3). Thus when Duke Ping of Chin befriends a commoner Hai Tang, the Duke "entered when Hai T'ang said 'enter,' sat down when Hai Tang said sit down" (*Mencius* 5B:3). Friends reciprocate with advice and guidance to each other, but they do not defer. Given the mutuality and complementary elements in the husband-wife relationship, which we have previously seen, there is no reason why it should not be more akin to the friend-friend relationship. After all, it is Xun Zi who conceives of hierarchy as a cosmic principle. Such thinking, one can argue, is absent in the *Analects* or the *Mencius*.

So far, I have argued that the Confucian conception of gender understood as a functional division does not really support the various forms of subordination of women we have noted earlier. It is now time to look at the justifiability of the Confucian conception of gender itself.

First I want to argue that, contrary to Guisso and Black, this conception of gender is not based on any appeal to different innate psychological traits or abilities inherent in males and females. Guisso argues that the exclusion of females from education reflects the belief that women have limited intellectual capacity.[42] Analogously, Black thinks that the following passage suggests the comparative irrationality of women:

#11. "It is hard to take care (*yang* 養) of the women and the small men. If you get them get too close, they become insolent. If you keep them at a distance, they complain" (*Analects* 17:25).

But their claims are disputable. Guisso's argument is a non sequitur. There are many possible reasons why women are denied education besides a belief that they have innate intellectual limitations. Our earlier analysis provides one such reason. In reply to Black, we can point to the interpretation by Cai Renhou 蔡仁厚. Cai powerfully argues that passage #11 does not express misogyny, because the word "*Nuzi*" (women) does not refer to women in general; rather it refers to females who are counterparts of the male household underlings, small men (*xiao ren* 小人), of whom a *junzi* takes care.[43]

After all, we must remember that Mencius's theory of human nature emphasizes universality: the sage and common humans are of *the same kind*, and every human has the same preferences in taste, sound, beauty, and the same inherent moral goodness (*Mencius* 6A:7). Hence there is no clear textual evidence that women are thought to be inferior in their innate intellectual or rational capacities. Nor is there any evidence in the texts to support the view that because women are thought to be innately more patient, gentle, and loving, they are considered as more apt for domestic tasks.[44]

So is the Confucian conception of gender justified? One attempt to defend it is to point to the consideration of efficiency. That is, the conception aims at achieving efficiency through a division of labor. Moreover, given the Confucian appreciation of the importance of family and the familial virtues, there is perhaps a need to highlight and separate family from other social institutions. Consequently, to the Confucians, the inner-outer or domestic-public distinction is a natural kind that the division of labor should map onto.

Yet these reasons fail to fully justify the Confucian gender roles. For the question remains: Why are women assigned the internal role and men the external role and not the reverse? One possible reply is to point to the biological function of women. Hence Black suggests that, "as child bearer and child nourisher, the woman is inevitably more confined than the man to hearth and home."[45]

But this statement is indisputable only if we assume the existence of family. In Plato's *Republic*, for example, women's biological role does not imply domestic confinement. And even if we assume the existence of family, as the Confucians would certainly insist we do, there is still a big gap between being *more* confined and being *completely* confined to home and hearth. And complete confinement is what distinguishes the Confucian gender role.[46]

More basically, even if we assume that some sort of division of labor is necessary, there is still no convincing reason, Confucian or otherwise, *why the division must be mapped onto the sex distinction.* After all, if the point is about efficiency, shouldn't the division of labor be based on principles like tracking the different aptitudes or interests or preferences of workers, rather than their sexes, unless there is reason to believe that these other differences are gender based? And as I have argued, the texts do not suggest any belief in innate gender differences in aptitudes or preferences.

Furthermore while the inner-outer distinction may have special significance in Confucianism and may have important implications on how we should deal with people within the family, we still have to ask why all other distinctions, including the gender distinction as such, should be mapped onto it.[47] For example, the texts also refer to other distinctions like that between the aged and the young (*Mencius* 6A:4), and between those who use their minds and those who use their muscles (*Mencius* 3A:4), but there is no prescription that the aged should stay at home and the young should work outside, or vice versa.

In consequence, we should note that the conception of gender is not an integral part of the core of the Confucian philosophy. For its removal can still leave both the inner-outer distinction and the Five Relationships largely intact. The family can still be prized above all the other social institutions. And husbands and wives can still be unified on the basis of functional cooperation, though no longer according to the division of domestic and outer duty.[48] Discarding this problematic conception of gender should leave the core of the early Confucian philosophy unscathed.

GENDER AND THE FORMS OF SUBORDINATION OF WOMEN REVISITED

So far I have argued that the Confucian conception of gender cannot really support the exclusion of women from the important opportunities of pursuing the ideal of *junzi*, serving in the government, and getting a

Confucian education. Therefore it cannot support the subordination of wives to husbands either. However, the texts also seem to endorse the following forms of subordination of women:

1. Asymmetry in sexual access

Since sexual access requires legitimization by marriage (*Mencius* 3B:3), women's sexual access would be more restricted than males if polygamy is the exclusive prerogative of males. And the texts do indeed endorse the institution of concubinage. In an approving way, the sage Shun is said to enjoy the attendance of his wives (*Mencius* 7B:6).[49]

2. Objectification of women

Women are sometimes portrayed as objects that can be transferred and enjoyed for sexual pleasure:

#12. "The men of Qi made a present of singing and dancing girls. Ji Huan Zi accepted them and stayed away from court for three days" (*Analects* 18:4).

Sometimes, women can even be appropriated as possessions:

#13. Xiang said, "The credit for plotting against the life of Shun goes to me. The cattle and sheep go to you, father and mother, and the granaries as well. But the spears go to me. . . . His two wives should also be made to look after my quarters" (*Mencius* 5A:2).

3. Neglect

Women are almost invisible in the texts. In contrast to the huge population of male characters depicted in the texts, women are seldom mentioned either as individuals or even as members of female categories such as mothers and wives. In the few cases where individual women are mentioned, they are usually not given independent identity, but are referred to as someone's wife or mother (*Mencius* 5A:1,8, 6B:6).[50] Only once in the *Mencius*, and never in the *Analects*, is there an expression of a woman's opinion—that of the wife of a man from Qi, who ironically is a fictional character (*Mencius* 4B:33).

Finally, we should note that two of the Five Relationships, the father-son and ruler-minister relationship, are formulated in a gender-biased way. Given women's domestic role, they are automatically excluded from the ruler-minister relationship. For the *fuzi* (father and son) relationship, one can argue that the word "*zi*" means child, which can refer to either a son or a daughter. Yet mother (*mu*) is still excluded from that formulation.[51] In fact a gender-neutral formulation can be achieved by replacing the word "*fu*" (father) with the word "*qin*" (親 parent/intimate), which has often been used to refer to one's parents (as in passage #2).

It is not obvious how the Confucian conception of gender can account for all these other forms of subordination. For example, how does it explain why women are treated as sexual objects? Indeed, given Mencius's recognition of women as sexual subjects who have sexual needs of their own, it is hard to see what Confucian reason exists for subordinating women in these ways. This result, however, should not be surprising. Why should we suppose that patriarchical practice would be based on theoretical reasons instead of prejudices or the particular conditions of individual societies?

CONCLUSION

I have argued that the conception of gender as illustrated in the *Analects* and the *Mencius* is basically a functional one that assigns women a domestic role. I have shown how this conception might imply the exclusion of women from various important opportunities, which would result in the further subordination of women as wives to men as husbands when the conception is placed in the context of the Confucian role system. On the other hand, I have shown how the Confucian role system can at the same time be seen as a positive influence on the status of women through its elements of reciprocity and respect. Finally, I have argued that the Confucian conception of gender does not really justify the exclusion of women from important opportunities, and that the conception itself is not justified either.

In closing, is there any special lesson we can learn from examining the early Confucian conception of gender? At least two things come to mind. First, even though the assignment of females to the domestic sphere has, for ages, been an almost universal practice in the world, the criticism of this assignment fares differently in the Confucian context than in the others. For example, to many contemporary feminists, this gender assignment accounts for the subordination of women because it deprives women of economic independence and, hence, also political power.[52] In contrast, the Confucian case emphasizes the moral rather than the economic implications of the gender assignment: excluding women from an important moral ideal.

Second, it is not a difficult task to redeem the subordinate status of women in early Confucianism, as their inferiority, at least as shown in the texts, is seen as contingent and functional rather than innate and biological. Perhaps we can see this more clearly by comparing briefly the Confucian view with those of Plato and Aristotle.

Early Confucians and Aristotle both exclude women from the possibility of attaining the ultimate moral ideal. However, for Aristotle, the exclusion is biologically and innately determined; women are biologically inferior.[53] Their inadequacy in the reasoning faculty makes them incapable of attaining the ideal of a contemplative life. Such biological determinism is absent in the Confucian conception of gender. Similarly, even though Plato advocates in the *Republic* that the female guardians are to share all the tasks of their male counterparts, he thinks they fare worse in every pursuit. The best performers of these tasks are all males, even though some women perform better than some males (*Republic* 455d3–5). Consequently, he talks about producing men and women of the best possible kind instead of the best human beings as such (456e), and suggests that women should be given a lighter share of the guardian duties than men because they are the weaker sex (457b).

In contrast, the Confucians make no denigrating remarks with respect to the innate ability or nature of women. If women turn out to be morally inferior, it is perhaps only because of their functional gender role, which after all is contingent.

IMPLICATIONS FOR CONTEMPORARY SOCIETY

The above analysis also has a number of interesting implications on how gender equality and women's roles are to play out in modern society. First, it shows that the traditional conception of gender has even less plausibility in the context of our contemporary society. Recall that the Confucian conception of gender is based on the inner-outer (domestic-public) distinction that restricts women entirely to the domestic sphere. I have shown the various problems of this conception. Now, some of these problems become more acute in modern society. For example, one presumable justification for the conception is its functional contribution to the maintenance of a family—women managing the family household and men working in the public domain are efficient divisions of labor for the best interests of the family. Even assuming that this justification was plausible in ancient China, our contemporary society is another story. With the advancement of technology, women need not be tied to the career of reproduction, and household work need not require a full-time effort. Institutional changes such as the introduction of day care, schools with hours of operation synchronizing with adults' work hours, flexiwork time, home office, part-time jobs, domestic helpers, etcetera, all help to enable women and men to make their contributions in the workplace while raising children and maintaining a family. For families that prefer to have a full-time homemaker, a stay-at-home dad is a viable alternative to a stay-at-home mom. That families can still flourish with women participating in workplace is a fact in contemporary society. Asian societies with Confucian heritage are no exception. For example, the 2002 female labor force participation rate was 46.6 percent in Taiwan, 52 percent in Hong Kong, 49.7 percent in South Korea, and 53.4 percent in Singapore. Yet families still thrive in those countries.[54]

The second implication our above analysis has on contemporary society concerns gender equality within the family. Our analysis shows that women have the same moral potential as men do to become *junzi*. Consequently, it means that either the husband or the wife can be the head of family if that role belongs to the more morally cultivated person— who can make better decisions, and become the better role model for the whole family. However, this claim is made based on the assumption that Confucianism advocates hierarchism rather than equality between spouses. Whether this assumption is true or not in theory, one can argue that, in practice, making either the husband or the wife the head of family may be harmful, especially in modern society. The determination of moral superiority between two adults is in itself a very difficult matter. It may be even more so in the case of modern marriage, where married couples voluntarily choose to share their lives together often because they share, to a great extent, common values, interests, mutual respect, and appreciation. To determine moral superiority between two very similar persons is very arbitrary. To do so therefore would create unnecessary discontent and rivalry. Moreover, since moral cultivation is a lifelong, continuous process, it would be more beneficial to set up a system in which both the husband and the wife would give utmost respect and encouragement to each other, and be partners rather than competitors in the process of moral cultivation. Hence, both should assume the shared responsibility of being the role model and the head of family, as well as the housework chores. Gender equality in the Confucian account therefore would support partnership and equality in the family.[55]

The third implication pertains to the ways in which women could attain the moral ideal of *junzi* in our contemporary society. It is obvious that to strive to be a *junzi*, women need to avail themselves to the opportunity of education, moral challenges, and political offices as early Confucianism prescribes. However, in the context of modern society, this does not just mean that women should aspire to become scholars and political leaders who are society's moral role models, and who help to shape and implement benevolent social and political policies. For with modernization and its corollary development of civic society and the market economy, people's lives are interwoven to an unprecedented degree.

Therefore, political positions are not the only roles that can have massive impacts on society and people's lives. Professionals—whether CEOs, lawyers, medical practitioners, journalists, engineers, or artists—also contribute to the protection and improvement of the various pillars of the modern society; they are responsible for the upholding of specific standards and values pertaining to their professions, and for initiating innovations and expanding new frontiers for their field of specialization.

It is true that Confucius warns against people becoming specialists (*Analects* 2:12) as he believes that specialists have only restricted abilities and perspectives, and therefore should be ruled by generalists who have broad visions and talents. This belief however is no longer applicable to the modern society where the specialist/generalist distinction has new meaning. The development of social sciences and the emphasis on expertise enable/require leaders to have specialized training in management, administration, and leadership skills, so that they are no longer mere generalists as in ancient China. Also, with the intensive division of labor in the modern economy, everyone has to be a specialist. On the other hand, the interconnectedness of modern society requires competent specialists/professionals to have adequate general knowledge of the various aspects of society. Hence being a professional no longer carries the negative connotation that it previously did. Given this new meaning of a specialist, modern women should have no hesitation in acquiring training as professional, and should make use of the wide variety of options available to them in exercising their aptitudes and talents, and should dedicate their commitment to become a *junzi* and bring benefits to the world through their professions.[56]

Finally, it is interesting to note that perhaps the very basis of the Confucian conception of gender, that is, the inner-outer distinction, is important for contemporary society not because of its role in genderization, but because it highlights the following Confucian insight: the domestic and the public realms are not dichotomous, instead they are in a continuum.[57] The continuity between these two realms means that the family is the training ground for the future generation of citizens. As pointed out by liberal philosophers such as John Rawls and Susan Okin, family is where justice, mutual respect, and other values pertaining to modern citizenship are inculcated.[58] Moreover, it also means that the same principle of concern, benevolent regard, and respect that govern relationships among family members should also govern those among citizens, as well as those between citizens and the government. How to spell out the full implications of this principle in modern society is the challenge that Confucianism has to meet.

All these implications for modern society seem to suggest that the Confucian position on gender shares many similarities with that of liberal feminism. I do believe that this is true, and that the differences be-tween the two positions do not lie so much in the practical implications as in the reasons they use to justify the practice. Equality, free choice, and individuality are the ultimate intrinsic values in liberal feminism. Gender equality therefore is a theoretical derivation from these values. The Confucian position, however, does not subscribe to either of these values. Rather the flourishing of family and the ideal of *junzi* provide the justification of how gender is played out. For example, if a certain kind of hierarchical treatment among people is proved to be more effec-tive in bringing about moral development, then the Confucians would endorse it, no matter whether it is a hierarchy of gender, age, or learn-ing. The Confucian position also means that the flourishing of family is a priority—seeking other personal goals such as the development of one's talents and interests at the expense of family harmony and flour-ishing is not endorsed by Confucianism. If the inner-outer distinction were the only way to achieve family flourishing, the Confucians would endorse the distinction even if it would result in the subservience of one gender. Consequently, it is not incorrect to say that gender equality is a necessary component in liberal feminism, but only a contingent one in Confucianism.[59] Nevertheless, contingency or not, Confucianism's com-patibility with gender equality would definitely help it attain a more smooth integration into modern societies.

NOTES

1. Dong Zhongshu 董仲書, Chunqiu fanlu 春秋繁露 (Taipei: Commercial Press, 1984). For discussion of the complementary relationships of yin/yang in the Book of Changes, see Xu Fuguan, 徐復觀, "*Yin yang wuxing guannian zi yanbian ji ruogan youguan wen xian de chengli shidai yu jieshi de wenti*" 陰陽五行觀念之演變及若干有關文獻的成立時代與解釋的問題, Wenzhu pinglun 民主評論 v. 12, no. 19–20 (1961).

2. See *Zhou Lianxi ji* 周濂溪集 (Taipei: Commercial Press, 1973). Here Zhu Xi associates males with *yang* and goodness, and female with *yin* and evil. Due to the practice of the Chinese language which generally puts *yin* before *yang*, male before female and good before evil, a literal reading of the quotation causes confusion.

3. Hereafter whenever I use the phrases, "the two texts" or "the texts", I am referring to the *Analects* and the *Mencius*, unless I specify otherwise.

4. See Roger Ames and David Hall, "Chinese Sexism," in *Thinking From the Han* (Albany: SUNY), 1988; Alison Black, "Gender and Cosmology in Chinese Correlative Thinking," in *Gender and Religion*, eds. Caroline Bynum, Stevan Har-rell, and Paula Richman (Boston: Beacon Press, 1986); Richard Guisso, "Thunder Over the Lake: The Five Classics and the Perception of Woman in Early China," in

Women in China, eds. Richard Guisso and Stanley Johannesen (New York: Philo Press, 1981); Lisa Raphals, *Sharing the Light* (Albany: SUNY, 1998); Chenyang Li, "The Confucian Concept of *Jen* and the Feminist Ethics of Care: A Comparative Study," *Hypatia*, Winter 94, 9(1): 70–89, and Henry Rosemont, "Classical Confucian and Contemporary Feminist Perspectives on the Self," in *Culture and Self*, ed. Allen Douglass (Boulder: Westview Press, 1997).

5. The *Five Classics* are early Confucian works which include the *Book of Odes*, the *Book of History*, the *Book of Music*, the *Book of Changes* and *the Book of Rites*. The *Five Classics* however contain many materials dated after the Warring States period, i.e. after 222 B.C.E.

6. For a detailed descriptions of women's condition in the Chou dynasty, see Liu Dehan 劉德漢, *Dongzhou funu wenti yanjiu* 东周婦女問題研究 (Taipei: Taiwan xuesheng shuju), 1990.

7. In making this claim, I am sharing the traditional assumption that the *Analects* basically represents the ideas of Confucius himself. This assumption however is currently challenged by Bruce and Taeko Brooks in their ground-breaking book, *The Original Analects* (New York: Columbia University Press, 1998). They argue that the *Analects* is largely an accretion of the works of Confucius' later followers spanning between 500 B.C.E. and 249 B.C.E. I have no ambition to address their challenge in this essay. I shall just point out that since they attribute only chapter four of the *Analects* to Confucius himself, almost all the *Analects* passages I quote in the essay are interpolations according to them. Note also that I shall still occasionally refer to other Confucian texts besides the *Analects* and the *Mencius* for clarification and elaboration.

8. For a discussion of the concept of gender, see Ann Oakley, *Sex, Gender and Society* (New York: Harper and Row, 1972).

9. See n. 4 above. See also Bao Jialin 鮑家麟, *Readings in Chinese Women History* (Taiwan: Cowboy Publishing Ltd., 1979).

10. As noted earlier, *yin yang* as hierarchically related, instead of merely complementary, is a later conception starting from the Han time.

11. Guisso, op. cit., 59.

12. James Legge, trans., C. C. Chai and W. Chai eds., *Li Chi: Book of Rites* (New York: University Books, 1967).

13. Some interpreters believe that these two separations, especially the first one, were not strictly observed. See Raphals, op. cit., chapters 8 and 9 for the argument as well as a fuller elaboration of the two distinctions. Xu Zhuoyun 許倬雲makes a similar observation. Xu, "Cong zhou li tuice yuangu funu gong-zuo" 從周禮測遠古婦女工作 in Bao Jialin, ed., *Readings in Chinese Women History*, op. cit.

14. See also Mencius 3B:3, 4; and 5B:5.

15. Based on the analysis of other Confucian texts, Susan Mann and Lisa Raphals also conclude that the functional distinction is the more important one in the early Confucian conception of gender. See Susan Mann, "Grooming a Daughter for Marriage" in *Marriage and Inequality in Chinese Society*, eds. Rubie Watson and Patricia Ebrey (Berkeley: University of California Press, 1991); and Raphals, op. cit., 212–13.

16. Ames and Hall make a similar observation in pp. 98–99 of their book.

17. Aristotle makes a similar point about the gender role in the family. See J.A Smith and W. D Ross, eds., *The Works of Aristotle* (Oxford: Oxford University Press, 1952), 716–30.

18. This interpretation is found in Zhu Xi, *Si shu jizhu* 四書集注 (Peking: Zhonghua shuju, 1983); Liang Zhengting 梁正廷, *Mengzi jingu* 孟子今詁 (Hong Kong: Shanghai Publishing Co., 1973); and Yang Bojun 楊伯峻, *Mengzi shizhu* 孟子釋注 (Hong Kong: Zhonghua shuju, 1989).

19. Xu Shen 許慎, *Shuo wen jiezi* 說文解字 (Taipei: Bolin shuju, 1973), 638.

20. Black, op. cit., 170.

21. Lisa Raphals argues convincingly that some women did in fact manage to overcome the imposition of the inner-outer distinction and went beyond the domestic realm to acquire significant intellectual and moral virtues prized by early Confucianism (Raphals, op. cit).

22. D. C. Lau also observes that the holding of office and study are the twin activities inseparable from the concept of a *junzi*. D. C. Lau, *Confucius, The Analects* (New York: Penguin, 1979), 31. In addition, the conception of the close connection between the ideal of *junzi* and political involvement is well articulated in the early Confucian classic *The Great Learning*.

23. For example, Confucius decides to whom his daughter and his niece should be married (*Analects* 5:1,2). I shall discuss the issue of divorce more in a later section.

24. In depicting the women of seventeenth-century China, Dorothy Ko comments, "Since literacy and knowledge of the Classics constituted the gateway to bureaucratic appointments and hence political power, reading and writing were deemed, at least in theory, an exclusive male privilege." Ko, *Teachers of the Inner Chambers* (Stanford: Stanford University Press, 1994), 53.

25. This does not mean that women received no education at all. They did learn about subject matters like domestic duties, appearance refinement and female crafts. In particular, they were educated about the four female virtues: women virtues (*fu de* 婦德), women words (*fu yan* 婦言), women looks (*fu rong* 婦容) and women works (*fu gong* 婦工). See *Book of Rites*, op. cit., chapters 4 and 6.

26. There was a conference at Gui Qiu in 651 B.C.E. at which the feudal lords agreed that women should be excluded from state affairs. For a discussion of women's political role in the Zhou dynasty, see Liu Yongcong 劉詠聰, *Nuxing yu lishi* 女性與歷史 (Hong Kong: Hong Kong Educational Publishing Co., 1993).

27. *Shangshu zhengyi* 尚書正義, in *Shi san jing zhushu* 十三經注疏 (Peking: Zhonghua shuju, 1980), chapter 11, 183.

28. James Legge, ed., *The She King* (Hong Kong: Hong Kong University Press, 1960), 559.

29. For a more detailed discussion of the positive portrayal of women in ancient Chinese texts, see Lisa Raphals, *Sharing the Light*, op. cit.

30. Black, op. cit., 184.

31. Chen Ta-chi 陳大齊 makes an interesting discussion on the connection between rightness and submission. Chen Ta-chi, *Mengzi dai jielu* 孟子待解錄 (Taipei: Commercial Press 1980).

32. Confucius does accept a son's remonstration against his parents. But he maintains that a son should still obey his parents when his remonstration is ignored (*Analects* 4:18).

33. This does not mean that defiance is never permissible for a wife. But it would be very exceptional.

34. Instead of appealing to reciprocity, Guisso explains the superiority of mothers over sons by referring to the correlation of age and youth. Guisso, op. cit., p.60.

35. Sometimes a mother even has the authority to expel her son for serious misconduct. See Li Zhongdong 李宗侗, *Chunqiu zuoquan jinzhu jinyi* 春秋左傳 今注今譯 (Taipei: . Commercial Press, 1972), chapter 2. The *Book of Rites* however contains contrasting advice. It prescribes for a woman to follow her son if her husband has died. *Book of Rites*, op. cit., chapter 11.

36. For example Cheng-i believed that for women, to die from starvation is a trivial matter in comparison to loosing their chastity, which is a serious matter. Chan Wing-tsi, ed., *Reflections of Things at hand* (New York: Columbia, 1967), chapter 6.

37. Roger Ames disputes this claim of human universality in *Mencius*. See Roger Ames, "The Mencian Conception of Ren Xing: Does it mean 'Human Nature?'" in *Chinese Texts and Philosophical Contexts*, Henry Rosemont, Jr., ed., (La Salle, Illinois: Open Court, 1991).

38. Interestingly contemporary feminist political philosophers also challenge the strict dichotomy between the domestic and the political domains. Indeed one reason Susan Okin gives in arguing for the connection between these two domains is akin to that of Confucianism. She claims that family has important political implications because it is the place where we cultivate the capacity of empathy. And empathy is an essential component of the cardinal "public" virtue of justice. Susan Okin, *Justice, Gender and the Family* (Basic Books, 1989), 9–15.

39. The educational influence of women as mothers is well recognized by the early Confucians. For example, in the *Biographies of Virtuous Women*, the first chapter is devoted to portraying exemplary mothers.

40. Note that Confucianism already allows the right to divorce, though exclusively to males. According to *Shi Ji*, even Confucius himself divorced his wife. See Liu De-han, op. cit., 91.

41. As pointed out by Lisa Raphals, the ruler-minister and the husband-wife relationships have often been seen as analogous in early Confucian commentaries. (op. cit., 12).

42. Guisso also concludes that the practice of physical separation between the sexes implies a fear of the danger of female sexuality. This conclusion, however, is different from the rationale given in the *Book of Rites* (chapter 31) that the separation is merely to prevent licentiousness, which could as easily be caused by males (Guisso, op. cit., 57–58).

43. Cai Renhou 蔡仁厚, *Kongzi sixiang yinan sanze shijie* 孔子思想疑難三則 試釋, *Legein Monthly* 128, no. 2 (1986).

44. Women are indeed portrayed as having different psychological attributes than males in the *Book of Rites*. They are seen as more affective and partial: "Now the affection of a father for his sons is such that he loves the worthy and places in a lower rank those who are not able. The affection of a mother for her sons is such that she loves the worthy, but also pities those who are not able. A mother loves (*qin* 親) but does not honor (*zun* 尊), a father honors but does not love" (chap. 31). But the passage does not say that the attributes are innate.

45. Black, op. cit., p.169.

46. This biological argument becomes especially lame in our modern society where technology can minimize the necessity of home confinement due to pregnancy and child nourishment.

47. I am grateful to Arthur Kuflik for urging me to elaborate on this point.

48. And even if its removal does imply undermining the functional distinction as the principle governing the husband-wife relationship, finding a substituting principle should not be a serious problem. Candidates like respect or harmony are virtues congenial to the spirit of Confucianism as well as to the husband-wife relationship.

49. The texts only contain references to husbands' divorcing wives (Mencius 4B:30) but not the other way round. I will not judge whether this implies the acceptance of the prevailing practice of restricting the prerogative to divorce to husband only. For the practice of divorce, see Liu, 87.

50. The only exception is Nan Zi (*Analects* 6:28)

51. In *Chun Qiu* there is another version of the Five Relationships which does include mother—the relationships between father, mother, elder, younger and child. See Jiao xun 焦循, *Mengzi Zhengyi* 孟子正義 (Shanghai: Commercial Press, 1935), 227.

52. See Carol Pateman, *The Sexual Contract* (Stanford: Stanford University Press, 1988); and Susan Okin, op. cit.

53. J. A. Smith and W. D. Ross, eds., *The Works of Aristotle* (Oxford: Oxford University Press, 1952), 716–30. For discussion of Aristotle's view on gender and biology, see Lynda Lange, "Woman is not a rational animal: On Aristotle's biology of reproduction" in *Discovering Reality* Sandra Harding and Merrill Hintikka, eds. (Reidel Publishing Company, 1983).

54. G2003 Statistics on International Labor Force by Council of Labor Affairs, Executive Yuan http://dbs1.cla.gov.tw/stat/h04921ch1.doc

55. The above analysis about the gender relationships in a family is based on the assumption of heterosexual family household. What would Confucius say about homosexuality and homosexual family is a complex issue that cannot be dealt with here.

56. I am grateful to Daniel Bell for raising the question of the Confucian position on specialists.

57. See my paper, "The Personal is Political: Confucianism and Liberal Feminism," in *The Politics of Affective Relations: East Asia and Beyond* eds. Hahm Chaihark and Daniel Bell (Lanham: Lexington Book), 2004.

58. John Rawls, *A Theory of Justice* (Cambridge: Belknap Press of Harvard University Press, 1971); and Susan Okin, *Justice, Gender and the Family* (New York: Basic Books, 1989).

59. I am grateful to Daniel Bell, Joseph Chan, Jiwei Ci, Chad Hansen, and my colleagues David Christensen, Arthur Kuflik, Don Loeb, and Derk Peerboom for their stimulating discussion and their careful and critical reading of earlier drafts of this essay. I also thank the Department of Philosophy, University of Hong Kong for supporting my research on this essay.

Chapter Nine

THE CONFUCIAN CONCEPT OF *REN* AND THE FEMINIST ETHICS OF CARE: A COMPARATIVE STUDY[1]

〜

CHENYANG LI

The purpose of this essay is to compare two philosophies that have seldom been brought together, Confucianism and feminism. Specifically, I will compare the concept of *Ren*, the central concept of Confucian ethics, and the concept of care, the central concept of feminist care ethics.[2] Originated from a feudal society, Confucianism has been typically patriarchal. It has a long history, and in some areas of the world it is so deeply involved in people's lives that it may properly be called a religion. Like most religions, Confucianism has given little recognition to women. Feminist care ethics is relatively new. As a philosophy, it is growing quickly and has become a force not to be ignored. One striking feature of this care ethics is that it is antipatriarchal. This means that it is against not only male dominance in society but also against "male/masculine" ways of thinking in general. So one might suppose that Confucian ethics and feminist ethics are diametrically opposed to each other. This essay does not aim to show the differences between the two, which are many, but the similarities, which are customarily ignored.[3] Do Confucian ethics and feminist care ethics have anything in common? If so, what are these common aspects? How important are they? While refraining from directly evaluating the validity of the two ethics, which goes beyond the domain of the present study, I will show that they share common grounds far more important than have been realized and that these shared qualities would make it possible for Confucianism and feminism to learn from and support each other. Toward the end of this essay, I will discuss political implications drawn on this comparison.

REN AND CARE: AS THE HIGHEST MORAL IDEALS

Morality concerns the code of acceptable behavior in a society. One's understanding of the nature of morality has much to do with one's understanding of the nature of society. In investigating Confucian ethics and feminist care ethics, we should first note that both the Confucian society and the society advocated by the care perspective philosophers are noncontractual societies.

Western social contract theorists typically regard individuals as rational beings with self-interests and certain rights. Individuals enter society as if they had signed a social contract with each other for the purpose of mutual gain, and by this contract their individual rights are guaranteed. Thus the relation between members of a society is like a contractual relation. In contrast, the Confucian views the society as a large family in which the ruler's relation to the subjects is like that of a father to his children. For Confucius, just as there is no contract within the family, there is no contract in the society either. The philosophy of managing a good family and that of managing a good society are essentially the same. The modern Western division of "public sphere" and "private sphere" simply does not exist in Confucianism. Some feminists hold a similar analogy between a family and a society. Virginia Held, for instance, attacks the assumption that human beings are independent, self-interested, or mutually disinterested, individuals. She believes that "relations between mothers and children should be thought of as primary, and the sort of human relation all other human relations should resemble or reflect."[4] The relation between mothers and children is to a large extent nonvoluntary and hence noncontractual.

This way of understanding the nature of human societies is crucial for the unfolding of Confucian ethics as well as the feminist care ethics discussed here. For if the society is a contractual society, justice is served only if each participant's rights are guaranteed; as long as these rights are not violated, morality is satisfied. Neither Confucian nor feminist care ethics bases its morality primarily on individual rights. As Carol Gilligan observes, a woman's "construction of moral understanding is not based on the primacy and universality of individual rights, but rather on a 'very strong sense of being responsible to the world.' "[5] Within this construction, the moral dilemma is not "how to exercise one's rights without interfering with the rights of others," but how "to lead a moral life which includes obligations to myself and my family and people in general."[6] For Confucius, the concept of individual rights has no place in morality. Morality is primarily a matter of fulfilling one's proper role in the society, as a son, a brother, a father, and, further, as a ruler or a subject under the ruler. In this noncontractual society, for the

Confucian, the key concept to guide human relations is *Ren*, and for the feminist of this perspective, care.

Confucianism is also called "the philosophy of *Ren*" (仁學 "*Ren xue*"). The concept of *Ren* occupies a central place in the Confucian philosophy. In the *Analects*, Confucius mentioned *Ren* over one hundred times, but he never formally defined it. In the English world, scholars have translated *Ren* by many terms—benevolence, love, altruism, kindness, charity, compassion, magnanimity, human-heartedness, humaneness, humanity, perfect virtue, goodness, and so on.[7] These translations reflect the two senses in which Confucius used the word "*Ren*," that is, "*Ren* of affection," and "*Ren* of virtue."[8] In the sense of "*Ren* of affection," *Ren* stands for the tender aspect of human feelings and an altruistic concern for others.[9] Confucius said, "*Ren* is to love others" (*Analects* 12.22).[10] One can readily experience the sense of *Ren* if willing to do so. Confucius said, "Is *Ren* indeed so far away? If we really want *Ren*, we should find that it is at our very side" (7.29). In *Mencius*, *Ren* is treated almost exclusively in the sense of affection. Mencius made *Ren* as affection the foundation of his ethics. He said, "No one is devoid of a heart sensitive to the suffering of others. . . . The heart of compassion is the beginning of *Ren*" (2A.6), and "for every person there are things one cannot bear. To extend this to what one can bear is *Ren*" (7B.31). Sympathy naturally arises in one's heart when one sees other people suffer. One would not want to bear seeing sufferings. To extend this feeling to other things in the world and thus make it a general disposition is called *Ren*. In this sense, *Ren* is benevolence, love, altruism, tenderness, charity, compassion, human-heartedness, humaneness, and so on.

In the other sense, the sense of "*Ren* of virtue," *Ren* is a general virtue that has to be realized among other virtues. For example, Confucius said, "You achieve *Ren* if everywhere under Heaven you can practice the five: courtesy, breadth, good faith, diligence and clemency" (17.6). In this sense, a person of *Ren* is a morally perfect person, and *Ren* may be translated as "perfect virtue," "goodness," and "human excellence."

Although the relation between "*Ren* of affection" and "*Ren* of virtue" is subject to different interpretations, one thing is certain: a person cannot have the latter without the former. A person who has *Ren* as a general virtue cannot lack *Ren* as affection. In order to understand Confucian ethics we must first of all understand the concept of *Ren* as affection.

The word "*Ren* (仁)" in Chinese consists of a simple ideogram of a human figure and two horizontal strokes.[11] It can be seen as a person reaching out to others. The two horizontal strokes suggest human relations. What is the nature of human relations? What is the core of the concept of *Ren* as affection? If benevolence, love, altruism, kindness, charity, compassion, human-heartedness, and humaneness all define the concept of *Ren*, what do all these terms have in common? I would suggest that, taken as a virtue of human relations, "caring" is the essence of every one of these terms. If a person does not care for others, he or she cannot be described in any of these terms. For example, benevolence is the kindly disposition to do good and promote the welfare of others. If one does not care for others, he or she cannot be benevolent. Confucius came close to a definition of *Ren* when he said "*Ren* is to *ai* 愛 others" (17.22). Although "love" is the common translation of "*ai*," the English word expresses an emotion stronger than "*ai*." The *Shou Wen Jie Zi*, a major lexicon of ancient Chinese, interprets "*ai*" as "*hui* 惠" that is, clemency or kindness. In Chinese, "*ai*" is often used in phrases such as "*ai hu* 愛護" ("take good care of") or "*ai xi* 愛惜" ("cherish"). In the phrases "*ai mo neng zhu* 愛莫能助" and "*ai wu ji wu* 愛屋及烏," "*ai*" is best understood as "caring for tenderly." They respectively mean "I care about it but cannot help" and "caring for the house along with the bird on its roof." "Caring" is more appropriate in expressing this tender feeling one has toward people and things.

In *Mencius*, *Ren* as "caring" is more evident. If a child were to fall into a well, why should one care? Mencius believed that a person cares because he or she has compassion. A person has a natural disposition to be *Ren*, to care, and therefore to act to save the child. One does not have to love the child to save her. In situations like this, a person who holds a "who cares?" attitude is one without a human heart. Although the heart of *Ren* is natural, Mencius also said that a moral person needs to develop one's heart of *Ren*, along with the heart of shame, of courtesy and modesty, and of right and wrong. "If one is able to develop all these beginnings that one possesses, it will be like a fire starting up or a spring coming through" (2A.6). Moral cultivation and development will make the natural instinctual heart of *Ren* a mature moral virtue. Like Confucius, Mencius's ideal form of government is one of *Ren*. He saw that princes of some states took people away from their work during the busy farming seasons, making it impossible for them to till the land and minister to the needs of their parents. Thus parents suffered cold and hunger while brothers, wives, and children were separated and scattered. These princes did not care for their people. Mencius believed that in order to become a true king, one must care and practice the government of *Ren* toward the people (1A.5). In other words, caring, or *Ren*, is the way to become a good ruler. Both Confucius and Mencius believed that if a government is really one of *Ren*, one which takes good care of its people, there would be no crime or poverty. If the ruler cares for his people, he will make sure that people do not miss their farming seasons, and thus they will have good harvests in good years and be prepared for bad years. When people have enough food, they behave themselves well and do not steal or rob. It is not that we do not have enough punishment; nor is it that we do not have enough taxation. It is that we do not have enough care, and this sometimes makes life unbearable. What we really need is care.

Whether Confucius and Mencius are right in their opinions is open to discussion. What we can conclude from their teachings is that, in Confucian philosophy, to be a person of *Ren* one must care for others. So, even if the entire concept of *Ren* cannot be reduced to "caring," at least we can say that "caring" occupies a central place in this concept. As Lik Kuen Tong has properly concluded, Confucianism is a care-oriented humanism and the Confucian love ("*ai*") is a caring, responsible love.[12] To understand the care orientation of Confucian ethics is the key for us to understand the concept of *Ren* as Confucius's highest moral ideal.

In the feminist care perspective, the highest ideal of morality is caring. In her book, *In a Different Voice*, Carol Gilligan found that "morality, for these women, centers on care."[13] A moral person is one who cares for others, or as Nel Noddings puts it, "one-caring." Noddings writes, "It is this ethical ideal (caring), this realistic picture of ourselves as one-caring, that guides us as we strive to meet the other morally."[14] While Confucius believed that a person of *Ren* is one who "wishing to sustain himself, sustains others; wishing to develop himself, cares for the development of others" (6:28), a female interviewee in Gilligan's study equates morality with caring for others and considers responsibility to mean "that you care about that other person, that you are sensitive to that other person's needs and you consider them as a part of your needs."[15] Another interviewee believes that "if everyone on earth behaved in a way that showed care for others and courage, the world would be a much better place, you wouldn't have crime and you might not have poverty."[16] She would agree with Confucius and Mencius that a good government as well as a good person is one that cares, and promotes care, for the people. Gilligan writes, "The ideal of care is . . . an activity of relationship, of seeing and responding to need, taking care of the world by sustaining the web of connection so that no one is left alone."[17]

As the highest moral ideal, care serves as the guidance of one's moral behavior. In our world, things are often complicated. People may get into moral dilemmas that have no easy solutions. In such cases, all we can ask people to do is to care for those who will be affected by their decisions. A really caring person is not one who merely sits there and says to oneself, "I care." One must make an effort to look into the situation and the effects of possible decisions. Afterwards, we may praise one for having been caring or accuse one for having not been caring enough (therefore people may have been hurt). But it is unreasonable to demand more than that. Things are not perfect. We cannot demand anyone to make things perfect. As long as one cares reasonably enough, morality is satisfied.

Then why should I care? For the care ethics, I am obliged to care because I place the utmost value on the relatedness of caring. As Noddings puts it, "This value itself arises as a product of actual caring and being cared-for and my reflection on the goodness of these concrete caring situations."[18] In Confucian philosophy, we find a similar line of argument. Confucius never addressed what the purpose of *Ren* is. *Ren* is the destiny of humankind and is good in itself. Asking "why should I be *Ren*?" would be like asking "why should I be good?," which has no proper answer except that we value it. Confucius seemed to have taken it for granted that humans want to be good. When his disciple asked him whether a person of *Ren* would ever complain about what might seem an undesirable situation because of being *Ren*, Confucius said, "If you seek *Ren* and get it, why should you complain?" (7.14; my translation). Similarly as Confucius values *Ren* as a virtue with value in and of itself, Noddings believes that "caring is important in itself."[19] Only with care can a person be a moral person. Only in the practice of caring, can a person become a moral person. It is caring, not the consequences of it, which establishes moral values. At this point both Confucianism and the feminist care ethics differ widely from utilitarianism and consequentialism. *Ren* and care are not to be justified in terms of the consequences they bring about, though the consequences are generally desirable. As the highest moral ideals, *Ren* and care are good in themselves.[20]

REN AND CARE: ETHICS WITHOUT GENERAL PRINCIPLES

In the *Analects*, Confucius talked many times about how to become a person of *Ren*. But each time he came up with something different. He never gave a general principle. This is by no means negligence. *Ren* cannot be achieved merely by following general principles.

In the last two thousand years a vast number of rules have been developed in the Confucian tradition. For instance, there were rules that girls and boys older than seven should not sit at the same dining table; and a man would have to accept the bride picked by his parents, whether he liked her or not. But we must note the differences between Confucian rules and rules in rule-based ethics, for example, Kantian or utilitarian ethics. First, these rules are not an essential feature of Confucian morality. At the same time, different places often have different rules, even though they all are "Confucian." And over the years these rules have changed; many have even disappeared. Yet Confucian ethics remains.

Second, these rules are specific rules, not general principles. They are not like the utilitarian principle that one should always maximize total net utility, or the Kantian principle that one should always treat people as ends. In Confucianism, these specific rules are guidelines for young people to learn *Li* 禮, that is, proper social behavior or civility. Rules of *Li* are important, but learning *Ren* is more important. Confucius indicated that without *Ren*, *Li* is of no use (3.3). For him, being ethical is being *Ren*; it is not merely a matter of following specific rules.[21]

Where Confucius talked about reciprocity (*shu* 恕), he talked about things mostly like general rules. Confucius told his disciple Shen that his philosophy had one thread that ran through it. When others asked Shen about it, Shen said "loyalty and reciprocity" (4.15). "Loyalty" (*zhong* 忠) here means loyalty to one's cause. If one is loyal to one's cause, one should exert all one's strength to the cause. "Reciprocity" means being considerate of others. But Confucius's notion of reciprocity goes beyond that of the rights and justice perspective. Proponents of the rights/justice perspective also believe in reciprocity. Their notion of reciprocity is the basis for the social contract: if you do not infringe upon my rights, I will not infringe upon yours. Confucius believed in the Golden Rule: "Never do unto others what you do not want others to do to you" (12.2). He also believed that a person of *Ren* should sustain others if he wishes to sustain himself, and care for the development of others if he wishes to develop himself (6.28). That is, instead of leaving people alone, he should understand others' situations and care for them. Clearly, Confucius extended the notion of reciprocity beyond the limit of the "rights perspective" to the "care perspective." For Noddings, caring has the distinctive feature of motivational displacement. She writes, in caring, "when we see the other's reality as a possibility for me, we must act to eliminate the intolerable, to reduce the pain, to fill the need to actualize the dream," and in caring, there is "a total conveyance of the self to the other."[22] When one wants to do something, one should ask, "How would my action affect others?"; "Would I want a person to do this if I were in their situation?" This way of thinking requires more than noninterference. This kind of reciprocity is different from rules in Kantian or utilitarian ethics. It demands that one should care for others.

To say "always care for others" is very different from saying "always follow such and such a general rule." Traditional Western ethical theories have principles or general rules for people to follow. Utilitarianism, for example, follows the rule to maximize total net or average utility. In addition to general rules, there is also the thesis of universalizability. This is the idea that if one person is obliged to do x under certain conditions, then everyone under sufficiently similar conditions is obliged to do x, with no exceptions. While the care perspective does not entirely deny that we can receive some guidance from principles, there seem to be no general rules to determine whether a situation is sufficiently similar to another. More often than not general principles do not solve problems for us. We need to inquire into individual cases. Noddings said that her feminist care ethics "does not attempt to reduce the need for human judgment with a series of 'Thou Shalts' and 'Thou Shalt nots.' Rather, it recognizes and calls forth human judgment across a wide range of fact and feeling, and it allows for situations and conditions in which judgment may properly be put aside in favor of faith and commitments."[23] For example, there can be no general principles that will give a mother a definitive answer to whether she should send the money to charity or spend it on her child's favorite meal. It really depends on individual situations, and individual situations vary from time to time and from place to place.

What makes Confucian ethics more like feminist care ethics than justice ethics is not that they both have or do not have rules but that they both remain flexible with rules. When a rule fails to work, instead of trying to make up another rule, as justice ethics would do, they will readily accept flexibility with rules. Noddings writes: "The one-caring is wary of rules and principles. She formulates and holds loosely, tentatively, as economies of a sort, but she insists upon holding closely to the concrete."[24] In caring, a person may get into conflicts. Noddings gives us an example in which a professor receives a research proposal from graduate student B. In the proposal B proposes to do research that requires deceiving the subjects involved in the research.[25] On the one hand, the professor does not want to hurt B by turning the proposal down. On the other hand, the professor is not sure whether the subjects would be hurt by the experiment. If they would not be hurt and B succeeds in the research, then everything would be fine. But what if they are hurt? In cases like this, there would be no general infallible rules or principles to follow. It is not to say there cannot be any rules. There are rules. But rules cannot give us infallible solutions in conflicting situations of caring.

Moreover, even though we can follow rules, rules do not have the overriding power in deciding our actions. Noddings thinks that although general principles call for support to the socially oppressed people, a caring person would fight along with her father and brother against the oppressed if they are on the opposite side of the oppressed.[26] While this may sound extreme, it does make the point clear: general rules are not absolute. This is so because, as Joan C. Tronto put it, "The perspective of care requires that conflict be worked out without damage to the continuing relationships. Moral problems can be expressed in terms of accommodating the needs of the self and of others, of balancing competition and cooperation, and of maintaining the social web of relations in which one finds oneself."[27] Under certain circumstances, a caring person needs to break the rules in order to preserve social relations.

Confucius again would share the view of these feminists. He believed that, even though we normally consider theft to be wrong, a son should not expose it if his own father stole a sheep from his neighbor (13.18). He said, "In serving his father and mother a man may gently remonstrate with them. But if he sees that he has failed to change their opinion, he should resume an attitude of deference and not thwart them" (4.18). At first glance, this may sound immoral. But if *Ren* and care are the highest moral ideals, it is only reasonable to follow Noddings's and Confucius's way, especially given the gradation of caring (which will be discussed later).

Often Confucianism leaves the impression that filial piety to one's parents is absolute. This is not so. In Confucianism, a person has many duties. Besides filial piety to parents, one also has the duty of loyalty to the ruler. The two duties may come into conflict. For instance, when the country is being invaded, a man has the duty to answer the ruler's call to fight at the front line. But what if his aging parents also need his daily assistance? Under situations like this one, Confucianism offers no general rules to solve the problem. It depends on individual circumstances and, as long as one cares, he can be *Ren* even though failing to perform his duty.

Focusing on *Ren* of affection, Mencius seemed even more flexible on general principles. He said, "All that is to be expected of a morally superior person is *Ren*. Why must he act exactly the same as others?" (6B.6). For Mencius, "A morally superior person need not keep his word nor does he necessarily see his action through to the end. He aims only at what is right (appropriate)" (4B.11).[28] This remark seems to suggest that a person of *Ren* may not always live up to one's words as long as what one does is right or appropriate. Here the doctrine of living up to one's words, which would appear as a general principle, does not always determine what is appropriate. Unlike Kant, who believed that a person should never tell a lie, Mencius suggested that sometimes telling a lie is acceptable. In his story about Zeng Zi and his father Zheng Xi, Mencius told that after his meal Zeng Xi would ask Zeng Zi whether there was any food left for the family, and Zeng Zi always replied in the affirmative even when actually no food was left. In this way, Zeng Zi was able to give his father more gratification (4A.19). Though being honest is a virtue, whether we should tell the truth or a lie depends on individual circumstances. A person of *Ren* is one with good judgment who knows what to do and when.[29]

Noddings notes that even though not following general rules, a caring person is not capricious. Like Mencius, Noddings believes that moral life based on caring is coherent and one can be content if there has been no violation of caring.[30] No ethics can be entirely devoid of rules, general rules or rules of thumb. One difference between Confucian ethics and feminist care ethics on the one hand, and Kantian ethics and utilitarian ethics on the other, is that the former are not as rule- or principle-oriented.[31] A person of *Ren* or a caring person knows where and when not to depend on rules.

REN AND CARING WITH GRADATIONS

As a person of *Ren*, a person of caring, should I care for everyone equally? On this question feminist philosophers are divided. But with some feminist care philosophers the Confucian shares an important common ground.

Confucius distinguished between a person of *Ren* and a sage. Once his disciple Zi Gong asked him, "If a person confers benefits on the people universally and is able to assist all, what would you say of him? Would you call him a person of *Ren*? Confucius said, "Why only a person of *Ren*? He is without doubt a sage. Even [sage-emperors] Yao and Shun fell short of it" (6.28; my translation). Only sages are able to practice universal love. It is noble and admirable but far beyond ordinary people's moral horizon.[32] For ordinary people, the highest moral ideal is *Ren*, not sagehood.[33]

On the issue whether a person should care for everyone equally, Confucius and Mo Zi, the founder of Mohism, are diametrically opposed. Mo Zi, the major rival of Confucians of the time, also believed in *ai* or love. But he believed in universal love (兼愛 "*jian ai*") and urged everyone to "regard other people's countries as one's own. Regard other people's families as one's own. Regard other people's person as one's own."[34] Mencius condemned Mo Zi's universalism as an ethics with "no father" (3B.9). The difference here, however, is not whether one should love or care for other people. Mencius himself said, "A person of *Ren* embraces all in his love" (7A.46). And Confucius also said that one should "love all people comprehensively" (1.6). But Confucius and Mencius believed that a person practicing *Ren* should start from one's parents and siblings and then extend to other people. This is called "*ai you cha deng* 愛有差等" or "love with gradations." In other words, although one should love both his father and a stranger, he should love his father first and more than he does the stranger. Confucius believed that "the greatest application of *Ren* is in being affectionate toward relatives,"[35] and "filial piety and brotherly respect are the root of *Ren*" (1.2). A person of *Ren* must love first his father and elder brothers and then, by extension, other people. Mencius said, "Treat with respect the elders in my family, and then by extension, also the elders in other families. Treat with tenderness the young in my own family, and then by extension, also the young of other families" (1A.7). He believed that a person of *Ren* should be *Ren* to all people but attached affectionately only to his parents (7A.45). This means that one's parents exert a greater pull on him or her. Thus, when both one's father and a stranger are in need, the doctrine of love with gradations justifies one's helping one's father before helping the stranger.

In this regard Confucius and Mo Zi had different perspectives. Mo Zi had a utilitarian approach. For him moral life is desirable because of the benefits it brings with it. He said, "What the man of humanity devotes himself to surely lies in the promotion of benefits for the world and the removal of harm from the world. This is what he devotes himself to."[36] Mo Zi argued that only by universal love is it possible to generate the most desirable outcome of utilities. For Confucius, moral life is desirable for its own sake. *Ren* demands that one love one's parents first and other people second. This is the ideal moral life one should devote oneself to. If a man treats his father as he treats a stranger and vice versa, then he is neglecting the affectionate tie between him and his father and hence fails to be *Ren*.

In her book *Caring*, Noddings follows a similar line of thinking. She believes that morality requires two sentiments. The first sentiment is that of natural caring. Caring starts with a person's natural impulse to care. We naturally care for our own family and relatives and people close to us. The second sentiment "arises from our evaluation of the caring relation as good, as better than, superior to, other forms of relatedness."[37] This is the genuine moral sentiment. Because the most intimate situations of caring are natural, proximity is powerful in caring.[38] Noddings notes that "my caring is always characterized by a move away from self, . . . I care deeply for those in my inner circles and more lightly for those farther removed from my personal life. . . . The acts performed out of caring vary with both situational conditions and type of relationship."[39] In concurrence with the Confucian, Noddings concludes, "I shall reject the notion of universal love, finding it unattainable in any but the most abstract sense and thus a source of distraction."[40] For Noddings, this gradation of caring is justified by the fact that "my very individuality is defined in a set of relations."[41] This set of relations is my basic reality. What is right for me to do is defined in this reality. Thus, "an ethics of caring implies a limit on our obligation."[42] For people too far away, even if we would like to care, we simply cannot. While neither Confucius nor Mencius put a limit on the scope of one's practicing *Ren*, given their emphasis on one's filial duty and the extension to other family members and relatives, it is not possible for one to practice universal love directly to all the people in the world. If care as a natural sentiment arises from our daily life, it is only natural for us to start caring for people around us and then by extension for other people away from us; and if this kind of caring is the basis for the highest moral ideal, then it is only reasonable to have gradations among those we care about.

In this regard philosophers of the care perspective, such as Noddings and the Confucian, again jointly stand in opposition to Kantian and utilitarian ethics. Kantians and utilitarians subscribe to the concept of impartiality. For them all moral patients exert an equal pull on all moral agents. However, for the Confucian and the *one-caring,* parents and others who are closely related certainly have a stronger pull. Accordingly, although we should care for everyone in the world if possible, we do need to start with those closest to us. This is not to say that we should care only for people close to us. It means that starting with those close to us is the only reasonable way to practice *Ren* and care. It would be perfect if a mother could care, in addition to her own baby and her neighbor's, for every little baby in the world who needs care. Unfortunately that is not possible. So she should be content with giving her care to her own baby and, perhaps, her neighbor's. This is as far as she can normally go, and this is our way of life as people of *Ren* and care. Giving priority to people near us is not merely justified by the fact that the closer the needy are to us physically the more efficient our aid is. Even if it were equally efficient, we would still feel more obliged to help the nearby. This feeling can be justified by the notion of care with gradations.[43]

Is Confucian Ethics a Care Ethics That has Oppressed Women?

We have identified three major areas in which there are similarities between Confucianism and feminist care ethics.[44] Confucianism has been notorious for its oppression of women for a long period of time. Feminism is primarily a fighter for women's liberation. Is it possible for them to share philosophically significant common grounds? My answer is affirmative. I think the similarities between the two are not in the ways they treat women but in the way of their philosophical thinking, in the way they view the nature and foundation of morality, and in the way they believe morality should be practiced. These similarities are significant in comparison with influential Western ethics such as Kantian ethics and utilitarian ethics. Based on these similarities, we can conclude that Confucian ethics is a particular form of care ethics.[45]

If Confucian ethics is a care ethics, a question that naturally arises here is, How can it be possible for a care ethics to have been so uncaring for women and to have oppressed women? Apparently there is a discrepancy. To shed some light on the problem and to dissolve the apparent discrepancy, in this section I will show first, through a historical examination of the development of Confucianism, that to a large extent Confucius and Mencius, the founders of Confucianism, are not responsible for its history of oppression of women. Then I will show why it is not contradictory, and hence not impossible, for a philosophy that is essentially caring to have oppressed women. If either of the two accounts succeeds, the discrepancy is dissolved.

Confucianism was founded by Confucius. The major doctrines of this philosophy are in his *Analects*. Mencius contributed a great deal to Confucianism by providing substantial arguments for ideas propounded by Confucius. It is safe to say that by the time when Mencius died, Confucianism as a philosophy was already well established. It is not odd that in China Confucianism is called the "Philosophy of Confucius-Mencius" ("*Kong Meng zhi dao* 孔孟之道"). Confucian scholars of later stages only developed or modified and hence more or less altered the philosophy. These later versions usually have a specific name attached in addition to the generic term "Confucianism," example, "Yin-Yang Confucianism" or "Neo-Confucianism." Since Confucianism was established by Confucius and Mencius, Confucianism without later modifications certainly deserves the name of Confucianism.

It is a fact that under the name of Confucianism there has been oppression of women. But since when has it been so? If it can be shown that Confucianism became oppressive to women only at a later stage, that Confucianism had existed before it became so, one can say that oppressing women is not an essential characteristic of Confucianism, and hence Confucianism as propounded by Confucius and Mencius can be a care ethics.

The most notorious women-oppressive doctrine under the name of Confucianism is that the husband is the wife's bond. According to the *Bai Hu Tong* 《白虎通》, the encyclopedia of the Yin-Yang Confucianism, a bond (*gang* 綱) gives orderliness. It serves to order the relations between the superior and the inferior, and to arrange and adjust the way of humankind.[46] Then why should the husband be the wife's bond? Why is not the other way around? The principal justification of this is the yin-yang doctrine.

In Chinese philosophy, yin and yang are two mutually complementary principles or forces. The words originally referred to two natural physical phenomena, that is, clouds shading the sun and the sun shining respectively. Later their meanings were expanded broadly to cover two general kinds of phenomena. Yang represents light, warmth, dryness, hardness, masculinity, activity, and so on, while yin represents darkness, cold, moisture, softness, passivity, and so on. Between yin and yang, yang is the superior and dominant principle, and yin is the inferior and subservient or subordinate principle.[47] Accordingly, all phenomena in the world are results of the interplay of these two principles. Between male and female, male is the yang and female the yin. From this it follows that, prior to marriage, a woman must listen and yield to her father, after marriage, to her husband, and after her husband dies, to her son.[48] In reality, domination has translated into oppression. Under this philosophy, the wife is judged almost entirely on the basis of her relationship to her husband. She must remain obedient to her husband. For her, "to die of starvation is a small matter, but to lose her chastity is a large matter."[49] To serve and please her husband is her destined duty. When there is absolute power/domination there is abuse of the power/domination. Women's fate was thus doomed.[50]

But when was this yin-yang doctrine incorporated into Confucianism? Confucius himself did not talk about yin-yang. Like most of his contemporaries, Confucius believed in the Mandate of Heaven, but he never went so far as to attempt to work out a cosmological system, let alone a systematic theoretical justification of the oppression of women. The Chinese word for person or people is gender neutral (人 "ren"). In order to specify its gender one must use a gender indicator, for example, "female ren" or "male ren." The Analects only specifically mentions women a few times. It never suggests that men should dominate or oppress women. In one place it is recorded that Confucius went to visit Nan Zi, the wife of the duke of Wei (6.26).[51] But there Confucius did not make a statement in regard to relationships between men and women. In another place, Confucius did make a statement about women. He said, "Only young girls and petty people are hard to rear. If you are close to them, they behave inappropriately; if you keep a distance from them, they become resentful" (17.25, my translation).[52] Here Confucius offered an observation of young women rather than a theory about women in general. It probably reflects a social prejudice that already existed in his time. Given Confucius's later illustrious status in China, this short comment on (young) women may have considerably influenced people's view on women in general and reinforced prejudice against women. However, there is no reason for one to think that this view is an inherent or essential part of Confucius's thought or an inevitable consequence of his general philosophy.

Like Confucius, Mencius did not talk about yin-yang either. He, however, mentioned women in his book. For example, Mencius believed that, although men and women outside of marital relationships should avoid physical contact with each other, a man definitely should pull his sister-in-law out of a pond, by whatever means possible, including bare hands, if she is drowning. Although Mencius suggested that obedience was a virtue for women (for instance, *Mencius* 3B.2), his general attitude toward women was not negative. This is so perhaps partly due to his relationship with his mother, who brought him up single-handedly after his father died young. One can hardly imagine that a person from such a family would advocate a philosophy of the husband's being the wife's bond. According to Fung Yulan, the yin-yang doctrine probably did not enter the Confucian school until after Mencius died, and it was during the Qin and Han dynasties that the yin-yang doctrine came to be almost completely amalgamated with Confucianism.[53]

The philosopher most responsible for blending the yin-yang doctrine into Confucianism is Dong Zhongshu (董仲舒, 179–04 B.C.E.). Dong's prominent position in the state and his great scholarship in Confucianism and the classics facilitated his effort in combining Confucianism with the yin-yang doctrine. A substantial portion of his major philosophical work, *Luxuriant Gems of the Spring and Autumn Annals* (《春秋繁露》 *Chun Qiu Fan Lu*), deals with yin-yang. Dong believed that yin and yang are two opposing forces that follow the constant course of Heaven. There is an intimate relationship between Heaven and humans. Dong said, "The relationships between ruler and subject, father and son, husband and wife, are all derived from the principles of the yin and yang. The ruler is yang, the subject yin; the father is yang, the son yin; the husband is yang, the wife yin. . . . The yang acts as the husband, who procreates (the son). The yin acts as the wife, who gives assistance (to the husband). The 'three bonds,' comprising the Way of the King (*wang dao* 王道), may be sought for in Heaven."[54] Thus among the human relationships discussed by Confucius and Mencius, Dong singled out three. He believed that in the human world, the relationships between the ruler and the subject, the father and the son, and the husband and the wife, are the same as that between Heaven and Earth. Corresponding to the yang, the ruler, the father, and the husband dominate the subject, the son, and the wife respectively, who correspond to the yin, in the same way as Heaven dominates Earth.

Now, we can see who is responsible for the oppression of women in Confucianism. There is no evidence in the works by Confucius or Mencius explicitly indicating that they had such a view. If it is true that neither Confucius nor Mencius specifically spoke highly of women, it was so probably because women's social status was low at the time. While they did not oppose patriarchy out the time, there is no essential connection between their doctrine of *Ren* on the one hand and their views of women on the other. It is Dong Zhongshu who was most responsible for incorporating the yin-yang doctrine into Confucianism, which led to a women-oppressive version of Confucianism later on.

In the following I will answer the question of how it is possible for a care ethics to have taken part in the oppression of women. My point is that people may hold the same principle while they disagree on the application of it. Confucians may have excluded women from the domain of the practice of *Ren* because they did not believe that women were as fully persons as men were. The apparent discrepancy between the oppressive view toward women and the concept of *Ren* may be explained away by the account that many Confucians had a limited application domain of the concept of *Ren*.

Historically, it is not rare for people to hold a certain principle while practicing something that would appear contrary to that very principle. Ancient Athenians believed in democracy. Yet their democracy was limited to "citizens." Slaves and women were excluded from participation in democracy because they were not citizens. Imagine that a political change took place in the city-state and consequently all slaves and women were allowed to participate in democracy along with the "citizens." Now, should we think that the Athenians have changed their philosophy of democracy or that they continue to hold the same philosophy but have expanded the domain of its participants? I think the latter is the appropriate answer. A Christian may hold a strong belief in the brotherhood/sisterhood among her fellows, and yet at the same time may have taken black slaves. For her there was no contradiction simply because she sincerely believed that blacks were not among her fellow people to whom brotherhood/sisterhood would apply. Suppose later this person changed her view on blacks and realized that, after all, blacks were also her fellow people. Would one say that this person changed her principle of brotherhood/sisterhood or that she changed the application domain of the principle? I think the right answer is the latter.

The same logic holds true for our case on Confucianism. Even though Confucius and Mencius held restrictive views of women, it would not cause any contradiction for them to hold a care ethics. A care ethics may extend or reduce its application domain. For Confucius and Mencius, *Ren* is a human relation. It does not apply to animals.[55] Today a Confucian who is firmly convinced by Peter Singer's argument for animal equality may hold that *Ren* should be practiced on animals too.[56] In the same way, if a Confucian was convinced that women were not fully persons, he might well have thought that *Ren* did not fully apply to women. If it is the case, changing the view to include women into the domain of the application of *Ren* will only alter the application domain of the concept, not the concept itself.

So, is Confucianism a care ethics that has oppressed women? If by Confucianism one means Confucianism after Dong Zhongshu's yin-yang philosophy, the answer to this question is definitely affirmative. If one wants to say that the authentic Confucianism is the one before Dong, then there is no evidence that the Confucianism by Confucius and Mencius themselves was really oppressive to women. I have also shown that it is possible for a person to hold a philosophy that is caring in nature and at the same time exclude women from its application. If this possibility is real, then it is possible for Confucianism as a care ethics to have oppressed women. And furthermore, if this in turn is accurate, then it is possible for us to fully restore the concept of care of Confucianism by eliminating the women-oppressive doctrine from it.

Observations and Discussions

Now we can make a few interrelated observations. First, our investigation supports the claim that care orientation is not a characteristic peculiar to one sex or gender. Care is usually regarded as a feminine characteristic in Western culture, and care ethics as a "feminine" ethics. Confucian ethics has been one of a male-dominated society. For many, *Ren* is primarily a male or manly characteristic. If by "male" we mean the patriarchal characteristic, Confucianism has surely been a male ethics. Yet its ethics is a care-perspective ethics, not a rights-perspective ethics. Whereas for feminist ethics men in Western culture are generally not so ready to think along the line of the care perspective, for many Confucians, women probably have to overcome more difficulties than men before they can be *Ren*. If my "care" interpretation of the Confucian *Ren* is correct, it will confirm a view shared by many that different perspectives in ethics are result of cultural nurturing rather than a natural difference based on sex.

Second and more important, my study shows that care orientation is not a characteristic peculiar to a particular social group or culture either. Some feminists believe that the care orientation in morality is somehow related to social subordination. This belief is unwarranted. For example, by focusing on the similarities between feminist moralities and African moralities, Sandra Harding suggests that this kind of morality is a result of social subjugation. She writes, "We are different, not primarily by nature's design, but as a result of the social subjugations we have lived through and continue to experience."[57] Accordingly, we should expect similar cognitive styles and worldviews from peoples engaged in similar kinds of social activities. She seems to suggest that, just as the female moralities have a lot to do with male dominance, the African moralities have a lot to do with Western imperialist dominance. But given the results of our investigation of Confucian ethics, even Harding's account is too narrow. Confucianism took its form more than two thousand years before China became dominated by Western imperialism, and has continued to maintain its influence over the Chinese people, with the exception of a few periods. Thus it would seem as incorrect to say that the care perspective is essentially a morality of the dominated as it would be to say that it is essentially one of the female sex.

Third, as feminism spreads vigorously, it will increasingly confront Confucianism. Then, what is likely to happen? One may think that feminism will conquer and thereby replace Confucianism, or one may think that thousands-year-old Confucianism in its homeland will defeat feminism, as it has withstood so many other Western philosophies. It seems to me that neither is likely to happen. Since Confucianism is so deeply rooted in China and some of its neighboring countries that it has become an essential way of life, it is unlikely to be replaced by a new Western philosophy. But Confucianism will not defeat feminism either. As a philosophy, feminism represents a world trend of women's liberation. This trend is not likely to be defeated. Thus, given that Confucianism and feminism are not essentially opposed, we have reason to think that feminism may encounter no more, or perhaps even less, resistance in the Confucian world than in the West. Since, as has been shown, Confucianism and feminism share important common grounds, it is possible for them to work together in pursuing their causes.

Finally, based on this comparative study, How should we understand Confucian political philosophy today? First, Confucians can readily accept sexual equality between men and women in contemporary society. While Confucianism maintains that men and women are different ("*nannü you bie*" 男女有别), the superiority-inferiority thesis of men and women was only historically Confucian, not logically Confucian. Therefore contemporary Confucians have no problem welcoming sexual equality. The Confucian position on the issue of men and women can be described as "politically equal and socially equitable." Politically, women have the same rights and same opportunities as men. Socially, however, Confucians would not press for "blind" or indiscriminative social equality between men and women. From a care perspective, Confucians recognize that men and women may have different psychological and biological needs and capacities, and there should be different opportunities for them; socially Confucians emphasize equity rather than equality between men and women. Second, because the family is the origin and archetype of human care, Confucians place the family at the center, not the periphery, of their political philosophy. Like some feminist care philosophers, Confucians take the interest of the family as a primary consideration of political philosophy, and promote the kind of care from within the family to society at large. Third, Confucian political philosophers emphasize that governmental policies should be made from considerations of concrete social circumstances, not from abstract political principles. In the Confucian view, good society should be measured by how its people are being taken care of, and social policies should be caring and humane. These goals cannot be reached unless the government takes a practical approach to policymaking and is willing to adjust policies according to concrete circumstances. Furthermore, while recognizing the importance of the role of law and individual rights in contemporary society, Confucian political philosophy emphasizes the role of moral virtue in society and advocates a "thick" notion of good society. A good society does not only prosper economically, but also virtuously. A good society is to be led by virtuous leaders supported by virtuous people, for from the Confucian view only virtuous persons can adequately care for others and only virtuous lives are worth living. A good society is a caring society.

NOTES

1. This article was originally published in *Hypatia: A Feminist Journal of Philosophy*, 9:1, 1994. Thanks to the journal for permission to reprint it here. I have made some revisions, mostly stylistic, except the addition of a few notes and a section on political philosophy toward the end. Many thanks to Daniel Bell, editor of this volume, for his encouragement and suggestions for revision.

2. By "care ethics" I mean the feminist ethics with an emphasis on care instead of rights or justice, represented by feminist philosophers such as Nel Noddings and Carol Gilligan. I do not regard care ethics as the only feminist ethics. Just like feminism itself, feminist care ethics is not a uniform theory. The views of feminist care ethics used in this paper are held by some influential feminist philosophers although other feminist philosophers do not consider them to be authoritative. Confucianism as a philosophy centers on morality and hence is essentially ethic in characteristic. In the essay I refer to Confucianism both as an ethics and a philosophy.

3. Since the original publication of this essay, some scholars have conducted careful and informative examinations of the differences between Confucian ethics and care ethics. See Julia Tao, "Two Perspectives of Care: Confucian Ren and Feminist Care," *Journal of Chinese Philosophy* 27.2 (2000) Joel J. Kupperman, "Feminism as Radical Confucianism: Self and Tradition," in *The Sage and the Second Sex: Confucianism, Ethics, and Gender,* ed. Chenyang Li (Chicago and La Salle, Illinois: Open Court, 2000); and Daniel Star, "Do Confucians Really Care? A Defense of the Distinctiveness of Care Ethics: A Reply to Chenyang Li," *Hypatia: A Feminist Journal of Philosophy* 17.1 (2002), among others.

4. Virginia Held, "Non-contractual society: A feminist view," in *Science, morality, and feminist theory*, eds. by Marsha Hanen and Kai Nielson (Calgary, Alberta: University of Calgary Press 1987), 114–15. Some feminist philosophers, however, have criticized this mother-child model of human relationship. See Sarah Lucia Hoagland, "Some thoughts about 'caring,'" in

Feminist ethics, ed. Claudia Card (Lawrence, KS: University Press of Kansas, 1991).

5. Carol Gilligan, *In a different voice: Psychological theory and women's development*, (Cambridge: Harvard University Press, 1982), 21.

6. Ibid.

7. See Wing-Tsit Chan, "The evolution of the Confucian concept of Ren," *Philosophy East and West* 4.4 (1955): 295–319.

8. See Takeuchi Teruo, "A study of the meaning of Jen advocated by Confucius," *Acta Asiatica* 9 (1965): 57–77.

9. See Tu Wei-ming, "Jen as a living metaphor in the Confucian *Analects*," *Philosophy East and West* 31.1 (1981): 45–54.

10. In this article translations of Confucius and Mencius are, unless otherwise indicated, from Arthur Waley, *Analects of Confucius*, (New York: Random House, 1989), and D. C. Lau, *Mencius*, (Harmondsworth: Penguin Books, 1970), respectively, occasionally with my own revisions where appropriate. Following conventional practice, the source is indicated, for Confucius, for example, as "12.22," which stands for Confucius's *Analects*, chapter 12, section 22, and for Mencius, as "2A.6," which stands for *Mencius*, chapter 2A, section 6.

11. Another version of the word, as found in the Guodian Chu Bamboo Strips, consists of a part standing for the body on top of a part standing for the heart.

12. Lik Kuen Tong, "Confucian Jen and Platonic eros: A comparative study," *Chinese Culture* 14.3 (1973): 1–8.

13. Gilligan, *In a different voice*, 125.

14. Nel Noddings, *Caring: A feminine approach to ethics and moral education*, (Berkeley: University of California Press, 1984), 5.

15. Gilligan, *In a different voice*, 139.

16. Ibid., 165.

17. Ibid., 62.

18. Noddings, *Caring*, 84.

19. Ibid., 7.

20. It may be argued that Confucian care and feminist care are two kinds of care; one refers to a nonrelational virtue and the other to a relationship. This is, however, untrue. While some Confucian virtues may appear non-relational (e. g., diligence or *min* 敏), the vast majority of Confucian virtues (e.g., respectfulness or *gong* 恭, trustworthiness or *xin* 信) are definitely relational and have to be performed in relationship. In his "A Defense" Daniel Star has presented a careful study of the difference between Confucian *Ren* and feminist care. Star argues that Confucian *Ren* ethics and feminist care ethics are two distinct forms of particularism. The former focuses on particular role-based relationships whereas the latter focuses on concrete relationships. He is right in this regard. However, we should not underestimate the significance of the fact that both are particularistic in comparison with the predominant Kantian ethics and utilitarian ethics. In addition, Star may have drawn too sharp a distinction between Confucian (weak) particularism and feminist care (strong) particularism. On the one hand, concrete care cannot ignore entirely the roles involved in

the relationship. A husband's care for his wife, no matter how concrete the relationship, may have to be different from a student's care for his teacher. On the other hand, role-based care has to adapt to the concrete situation in order to be effective. For my reply to Star's criticism, see my "Revisiting Confucian Jen Ethics and Feminist Care Ethics: A Reply," *Hypatia: A Journal of Feminist Philosophy* 17:1 (2002).

21. While the majority of Confucian scholars maintain that Confucianism is centered on *Ren,* some have held that it is centered on *Li.* According to the latter interpretation, Confucian ethics is rule-based. Some authors (e.g., Ranjoo Seodu Herr, "Is Confucianism Compatible with Care Ethics? A Critique," *Philosophy East & West* 53.4 (2003): 471–89) have argued that *Li* is more or at least equally central to Confucianism as *Ren.* Although it is a very important issue, it is beyond the scope of this essay to launch a full-fledged argument on it here. I simply follow the majority and interpret Confucian ethics as centered on *Ren.* For a discussion of the relation between *Ren* and *Li,* see my "*Li* as Cultural Grammar—The Relation between *Ren* and *Li* in the *Analects,*" in *Philosophy East & West* (July, 2007).

22. Noddings, *Caring,* 14, 61.

23. Ibid., 25.

24. Ibid., 55.

25. Ibid., 54.

26. Ibid., 109. Some feminists such as Virginia Held have been critical of Noddings in this regard. See Held, "Feminism and moral theory," in *Women and Moral Theory,* eds. Eva Feder Kittay and Diana T. Meyers (Totowa, NJ: Rowman & Littlefield Kittay and Meyers, 1987).

27. Joan C. Tronto, "Beyond gender difference to a theory of care," *Signs: Journal of Women in Culture and Society* 12.4 (1987): 644–63.

28. "Right" here is a translation/interpretation of "*yi* 宜" which can also be understood as "appropriate." In *The Doctrine of the Mean,* chapter 20 states, "*yi* means setting things right and proper."

29. Thus being *Ren* requires both knowledge and skills. For more discussion of this matter, see my "*Li* as Cultural Grammar."

30. Noddings, *Caring,* 56–57.

31. For a discussion of care- and principle-orientation, see Lawrence A. Blum, "Gilligan and Kohlberg: Implications for moral theory," *Ethics* 98.3 (1988): 472–91.

32. In the "*Wu Xing* 五行" section of the Guodian Chu Bamboo Strips, discovered subsequent to the first writing of this essay, the four virtues of *Ren* 仁, *Yi* 義, *Li* 禮, and *Zhi* 智 are identified as the way of Humanity while the five virtues of *Ren, Yi, Li, Zhi,* and *Sheng* 聖, namely sagehood, are identified as the way of Heaven. "Sagehood" is clearly a virtue higher than *Ren.*

33. For a discussion of the difference between *Ren* and sage, see Chang Tainien, *Studies of Chinese ethical theories* (中国伦理思想研究 *Zhongguo lun li si xiang yan jiu*), (Shanghai, China: Shanghai People's Publishing House, 1989), chap. 11. Later Confucians, such as Cheng Hao ("a person of *Ren* forms one body with all things without any differentiation") and Han Yu ("universal love

is called *Ren*"), elevated *Ren* to the level of sagehood, which is evidently not Confucius's own idea.

34. *Mo Zi*, chap.15.

35. *The Doctrine of the Mean*, chap. 20.

36. *Mo Zi*, chap. 15.

37. Noddings, *Caring*, 83.

38. Ibid., 54.

39. Ibid., 16.

40. Ibid., 29. For a different view see Seyla Benhabib, "The generalized and the concrete other: The Kohlberg-Gilligan controversy and moral theory, "in Kittay and Meyers, 154–77.

41. Noddings, *Caring*, 51.

42. Ibid., 86.

43. Many feminists, like many later Confucianists, believe in universal love without gradations. This is not the place, nor is the author's intention, to develop a full-fledged defense of graded love. If the argument for graded love presented here seems inadequate or unconvincing, at least I have shown that some feminists share the view with Confucians in this regard. For a recent defense of the Confucian graded love, see Whalen Lai, "In defence of graded love," *Asian Philosophy* 1.1 (1991): 51–60.

44. Their view of the relation between the individual and the society can be listed as a separate common ground. I chose not to do so mainly because this is a view they share with communitarians in general and involves a large number of ethicists.

45. Some critics have argued that the similarities between Confucian *Ren* ethics and feminist care ethics are insignificant (e.g., Star and Herr). They have failed to understand the crucial contextual relevance to similarity and difference. Any two things can be similar in some ways and different in other ways. It is the context that determines if the differences or similarities are relevant or significant. In the landscape of contemporary ethical discourse, the predominant players are Kantian ethics and utilitarian ethics. It is in this context that I claim the similarities between Confucian *Ren* ethics and feminist care ethics are relevant and significant. Similarities, however, do not preclude differences in other ways. Daniel Star has argued that Confucian ethics cannot be a care ethics because it is different from the kind of ethics developed by such authors as Carol Gilligan and Nel Noddings. I contend that "care ethics" is not a uniform theory; different ethical theories are grouped under this term because of their "family resemblance" rather than narrowly defined essential characteristics. If calling Confucian ethics "care" ethics can highlight some of its significant features, I am not reluctant to do so. For a more detailed response to this kind of criticism, see my "Revisiting Confucian Jen Ethics and Feminist Care Ethics."

46. *Bai Hu Tong*, chap. 29. Quoted from Fung Yulan, *A history of Chinese philosophy*, Vol. 2. (Princeton, N.J.: Princeton University Press, 1953), 44.

47. It should be noted that some interpretations of the yin and yang give them a more equal treatment.

48. It should be noted that the last doctrine, obeying one's son, was never actually practiced in reality. Under the doctrine of filial piety, the mother was able to keep her son obedient, at least at home.

49. This saying is attributed to Cheng Yi 程頤 (1033–1107).

50. But according to Chang, chap. 8, it was not developed to such an extreme until Southern Song Dynasty (1127–1279).

51. Nan Zi was a notorious woman. Confucius's willingness to risk his own reputation to visit her, which made his disciple unhappy (6.26), may be taken as an indication that Confucius took this woman seriously, if not highly.

52. I translate "*nü zi* 女子" as "young girls." This usage is abundant in classic texts. The *Za Ji* Chapter of the *Li Ji* states that "*nü zi* do not participate in rituals with others when living with their grandmother 女子附於王母則不配." In his classic commentary on the *Li Ji*, Kong Yingda writes, "*nü zi* means unmarried [daughters]女子謂未嫁者也." The *Si Gan* Section of the *Poetry* has the expression of "*nai sheng nü zi* 乃生女子," namely "giving birth to a girl." In other places of the *Analects*, "*fu* 婦," not "*nü zi*," is used in reference to women.

53. Fung, *A History,* 9.

54. Dong Zhongshu, *Luxuriant Gems of the Spring and Autumn Annals,* chap. 53, quoted in Fung, 42–43.

55. In the *Analects,* we are told a story that Confucius's stable was burned down when he was out. Upon his return Confucius asked, "Have any people been hurt?" He did not ask about the horse (10:12).

56. Singer, Peter, *Practical ethics* (Cambridge: Cambridge University Press, 1979).

57. Sandra Harding, "The curious coincidence of feminine and African moralities: Challenges for feminist theory," in Kitty and Meyers, 311–12.

PART FIVE

WAR AND PEACE

Chapter Ten

THE IMPLICATIONS OF ANCIENT CHINESE MILITARY CULTURE FOR WORLD PEACE*

~

NI LEXIONG

I

Military affairs refer to social activities that aim to secure or protect self-interest by means of organized armed force. Culture generally refers to two areas: the process of being civilized from a beastly state, and to the material and spiritual products of this process. Military culture can be understood as the material and spiritual products arising from military activities during the process of civilization. Chinese military culture thus refers to the material and spiritual products arising from military activities during the civilizing process of the Chinese nation, with the Han Chinese at its core.

The main characteristics of Chinese military culture are listed below. Particularity, the first characteristic, originates from the particular living and geographical conditions of Han Chinese. The main reason for the particularity of Chinese military culture is that Han Chinese have lived in vast irrigated farming regions sealed off by different geographical areas since ancient times. Second, Chinese military culture is stable. New cultural products are generated by new demands, and the long-lasting stability of Chinese agricultural conditions has led to the stability of early cultural products, including military culture. Third, military culture can be regarded as a valuable tradition. The early cultural products have satisfied demands by being continually tested in history and they have developed into a tradition embodying valuable experience. Fourth, Chinese military culture is chararacterized by a kind of universality that is linked in complicated ways with its particularity. It is particular

* The article has been translated from Chinese. Li Wanquan did the initial translation, and it was rewritten by the editor in consultation with Li Wanquan and Ni Lexiong. We have tried to provide a literal translation wherever possible so as to preserve the original style and substance of the article. Square brackets are used to indicate information supplied by the editor.

from one perspective and universal from another. Some aspects may be historical and symbols of particular periods, while other parts have universal and eternal implications for China as well as other societies. Moreover, aspects of Chinese military culture, that seemed irrelevant in the period of their genesis, may have great value in later periods. Some Confucian ideas about war, for example, were considered as dogmatic and unrealistic in Confucius's own period of "the collapse of ritual and the (moral) badness of music," but came to dominate Chinese thought after the unification of China during the Qin and Han dynasties.

Let us take the example of China's Great Wall as a phenomenon of military culture to further clarify the above points. First, the Great Wall is a product of military activities, in contrast to the waterwheel, the plough, the harrow, et cetera, that are products of agricultural cultivation. Second, it belongs to the material forms of military culture, in contrast to the spiritual forms such as "deception is justified in war" and "be prepared for danger in times of peace." Third, the Great Wall is also a special characteristic of Eastern culture, in contrast to the material forms of Western military culture such as the castle, the triumphal arch, and so on. The Great Wall had an important military function in the past that has been lost in modern times. But the defensive character of traditional Chinese military strategy that it reflects, and the underlying idea of treating war as a means of maintaining peaceful life, still exist and continue to be of long-lasting rationality and universality.

With the rapid development of modern science and technology, the material forms of ancient Chinese military culture have become obsolete. The resources that have value for modern society and world peace exist mainly in the spiritual forms of military culture (including some spiritual factors that are latent in the material forms of military culture). Of course, many spiritual forms of military culture have been eliminated by means of historical selection, such as military thought in early religious times and in the period of divination—that from a contemporary perspective seem full of superstition regarding the effects of Heaven on human beings and thus should be regarded as blind and absurd. What can contribute to modern society and future world peace are some ideas in the spiritual forms of ancient Chinese military culture that have long-lasting historical rationality and universal meaning. According to the author's many years of research, these military culture ideas not only have certain tacit and inarticulated connections with modern Western culture but they may also consciously become part of world culture in the future.

II

In order to point out which ancient Chinese military culture ideas have particularly important meaning for the world now and in the future—which ones have universal validity—it is necessary to compare the contemporary international system with our country's Spring and Autumn and Warring States period [c. 770–221 B.C.E.] when these ideas were produced. By means of this research, we will find striking similarities beween the international relations of the international systems in two different times and places.

1. There is no real social authority higher than the state
The first obvious and important common ground—of the contemporary international system and that of the Spring and Autumn and Warring States period—is that people are organized as group units within their own states for the purpose of survival and social activity, without being subject to absolute highest social authority beyond all states with the power to compel the obedience of all states. There are differences between the two times. Social anarchy is global now, whereas it was regional then; at present the productive forces are developed and science and technology change from day to day, whereas the development of science and technology then was too slow to be noticed. However, the basic desires that dominate human behavior have not changed, and the basic fact of "social anarchy" means that there are striking similarities between the essence and phenomena of international relations in contemporary international society and in the Spring and Autumn and Warring States period.

2. The higher social authorities exist only in form
That there is no real functioning highest authority does not mean that there is no formal highest authority. The Zhou Son of Heaven in the Spring and Autumn and Warring States period and the contemporary United Nations should be regarded as highest formal authorities in their respective international systems. Because they do not have real power, they are valuable for large states and great powers to use and manipulate. Also, because the formal authorities have recognized validity in their times, they can function well in conflicts that do not concern the great powers, but their instrumental value to the great powers is much greater than the value they are supposed to have.

3. State interest is supreme
This kind of formal authority, however, cannot make the intercourse between states function according to the principles of morality and justice. People take their own state as the unit that allows them to survive

and take part in social activity, and every state pursues the principle of intercourse that the state interest trumps other considerations. This leads to the birth of another principle, namely, the law of the jungle— that the weak are at the mercy of the strong. The histories of the East and the West all show that the law of the jungle will be pursued in a society without a highest authority. Neither the Spring and Autumn and the Warring States period nor the contemporary international system managed to extricate themselves from the domination of the law of the jungle.

4. *The dominant principle in international relations is the "law of the jungle"*

In theory, the Spring and Autumn and Warring States period, as well as the contemporary world, require states to engage with each other according to the universal principles of morality and justice and to solve problems according to those principles even when there are conflicts of interests. However, as mentioned above, the state's interest is supreme because the state is necessary for people's survival and social activity, and when every state pursues this principle, the universal principles of justice and morality will definitely be forsaken. The realization of any international principles of morality and justice require that the unit of the state should have the capacity for self-discipline, meaning that when there are conflicts between interests and the principles of morality and justice, the unit of the state should forsake unconditionally its interests and obey the principles of morality and justice. The main difference between legal principles and the principles of morality and justice is that when people or organizations follow social standards, the former are linked with the concrete means of punishment specified by the institutions of social coercion, and start from the fear of punishment; the latter have this kind of connection, which starts wholly from willed obedience. When a certain social standard is very important and cannot be maintained by means of willed obedience, the coercive law intervenes, meaning that a moral principle has been transformed into a legal principle. This kind of transformation can only be successful within the state, because the state is built on the basis of coercion that overrides individuals and organizations. But the international system does not have a power that can override the state and cannot make this power have the same degree of punishment toward the state as the state has towards its citizens and organizations, that is, enough to force the state to obey international laws. Thus, the substance of interaction between states is the same that Hobbes mentioned, namely, relations between wolves that obey the "law of the jungle." "Those who fall behind will be beaten," is not only a historical law but also the empirical and truthful account of the weak after they have experienced the "law of the jungle." Human beings from ancient times have been ashamed and angry because they have not been able to extricate themselves from beastly standards. They have designed many plans to get rid of such standards, with [idealistic] voices getting louder in modern times, but whether it is the Spring and Autumn and Warring States period or the contemporary high-tech era, the "law of the jungle" phenomenon has hardly changed.

5. Universal moral principles are invoked as tools for realizing state interests

Under the domination of the idea that "state interests trump all," the international system has become the real jungle society, and numerous disasters and fears have been brought to peoples and states. Even the big states and great powers that temporarily gain unfair advantage in the "jungle society" also live with fear. Perhaps people understood that the situation is a bottomless abyss of pain, so human thinkers have begun to plan ideal blueprints designed to extricate us from lives governed by the "law of the jungle." In both Eastern and Western cultures, such attempts are termed "international idealism." Obviously, international idealism contrasts with the idea that state interests are above all and that the latter is the origin of the former. Let us briefly compare these two ideas. International idealism is responsible for the well-being of the whole country and its people, and it aims at the long-term future, and thus has the meaning of ultimate concern. The historical experience is that when people pursue "international idealism," then "state interests above all" will be despised; when "states interests above all" is pursued, "international idealism" either becomes an unpractical goal to be mocked or it becomes the tool in war for the realization of state interests. Therefore we see that in the Spring and Autumn and Warring States period and in the contemporary international system, some big states and great powers pursue the war game rule and "only dispatch troops with a just cause." The reason is that when the idea that "state interests above all" has become the universally followed consciousness, the values, ideas, and behavioral standards of international idealism that are beyond the parochial state's interests and the value of ultimate care for all human beings have lost their import, and the universal principles of morality and justice that belong to the category of international idealism as well as other ideal principles are shelved or reduced to being tools for the realization of state interests. At such times, "international idealism" as the tool for large states has the fraudulence that its creators did not anticipate.[1]

III

Because the "international system" in the Spring and Autumn and War-ring States period has the similarities with the contemporary interna-tional system noted above, several ideas regarding military culture that came into being in the Spring and Autumn and Warring States period still have universal meaning for the present and the future. Since the unity of the Qin and Han dynasties, Confucian culture has had domi-nant status in Chinese history, and Confucius's ideas on war and vio-lence have become mainstream in Chinese military culture. Confucius's ideas on war and violence have two levels, the ideal and the real. In an ideal society, according to Confucius, there are no violent phenomena, including war. "If truly good people were put in charge of governing for a hundred years, they would be able to overcome violence and dispense with killing altogether."[2] Ji Kanzi asked Confucius about governing ef-fectively, saying, "What if I kill those that have abandoned the Way to attract those who are on it?" "If you govern effectively," Confucius re-plied, "what need is there for killing? If you want to be truly good, the people will also be good."[3] "The Master said, "Many times did Duke Huan assemble the various feudal lords, and it was always through Guanzhong's influence rather than a resort to arms. Such was his benev-olence, such was his benevolence!"[4]

The idea that Confucius bars war and violence from the moral and ideal society of "benevolence" has its foundation in the moral principle of "the benevolent love others." Although he respects and admires Zhou rites to the fullest extent, he shows discontent to Zhou Wu, who over-threw Shang Zhou by force. "The Master said of the Shao music that it is both superbly beautiful and superbly good. Of the Wu music he said that it superbly beautiful but not superbly good."[5] According to Men-cius, Confucius's view is that the phenomena of confrontation of war and violence would not exist in an ideal society full of "benevolence": "Against benevolence there can be no superiority in numbers. If the ruler of a state is drawn to benevolence, he will be matchless in the world."[6] Moreover, the highest aim of Chinese strategy is "breaking the enemy's resistance without fighting." Strategists and statesmen like Sunzi consider the problems more from the economic perspective, such as trying to reduce manpower, material resources, and financial ability. Although Confucius did not explicitly put forward the military principle of breaking the enemy's resistance without fighting, his moral evalua-tion of Guanzhong clearly reflects this idea of reaching the same goal by means of Sunzi's "breaking the enemy's resistance without fighting." But Confucius considers the problem purely from the standpoint of moral concern for the people, not from the economic perspective. So

Confucius's "benevolence" constitutes the main ethical foundation that sustains the highest aim of the Chinese strategic idea of "breaking the enemy's resistance without fighting." Thus, in terms of the relation between war and culture, the fact that thinking about war and violence is informed by the value of ultimate concern for the people shows that the Eastern classical civilization dominated by Confucianism is a relatively mature civilization.

Compared with the ideal society of Eastern classical times, the ideal society of Western classical times did not substantially extricate itself from the "law of the jungle" of beastly societies. According to Aristotle, there are races and tribes, the so-called barbarian and civilized peoples, that deserve to be slaves as a result of their birth. Barbarians must and should live and work in thrall to the civilized peoples in accordance with the natural law. The beasts in the natural world are meant to be for the enjoyment of human beings, and the uncivilized peoples are similar to beasts. If the barbarians are not willing to be enslaved by civilized peoples, it is against the natural law. That the civilized peoples conquer them by war and violence and make them into slaves accords with the natural law and thus accords with the principles of justice and goodness. Because justice and goodness for Plato and Aristotle are essentially a kind of harmonious order, the natural law and order best accord with the principles of justice and goodness.[7]

Although Aristotle counsels that violence should not be used to make civilized people as slaves, such an eventuality is nonetheless practical in the real world. In reality, the distinction between barbarism and civilization depends on the verdict of war and violence. "The art of acquiring slaves for ownership differs both from the art of being a master and from that of being a slave—that is to say, when it is justly practised; for in that case it is, in a way, part of the art of war, or of the art of hunting."[8] According to Aristotle's logic, those with advanced war technology must defeat those with less advanced war technology, and thus the winners must be civilized and the losers must be barbarians. The winners are the masters and the losers are the slaves and such a society accords with the natural law. Thus it can be observed that Confucius's ideal society totally excludes war and violence, an idea that accords with the ideal society of the future as conceived by contemporary people. Aristotle's ideal society, in contrast, is simply based on war and violence. This ideal society is fundamentally dominated by the "law of the jungle." It is against the ideals of contemporary people.

Although Confucius rejects all kinds of violence in the ideal world, he eagerly endorses the idea of "war to restore the ritual order" in the real world. He thinks that normal social life is dependent on a harmonious order that has to be maintained by "rituals." War and violence in real politics should be used as tools to restore the ritual order. Throughout Confucius's life, he either taught by personal example and verbal instruction of self and tradition or earnestly practiced what he advocated, such as when he hears of Chen Chengzi's assassination and goes to court and reports it to Due Ai only after having cleansed himself ceremonially,[9] and when he personally commanded a battle designed to destroy the ramparts of the three noble families.[10] These phenomena show that, as far as war and violence are concerned, Confucius as a mature and tactful statesman pays comparative attention to the reality, and on the other hand they reflect the contradiction and conflicts between Confucius's ideal and the reality. The rationality of "war to restore the ritual order" is that war and violence have been changed from tools for seeking interests to tools for maintaining the rational social order. Perhaps Confucius is the first person in human history to advocate changing war and violence from beastly tools to rational tools, which is a great contribution by Confucius to civilization. The idea as expressed in the past, present, and future has implications for ongoing globalization in both the East and the West.

Regarding war and violence in real politics, Confucius puts forward the important idea that "rituals, music, and punitive campaigns are initiated by the Son of Heaven."[11] Leaving aside certain surface phenomena, Confucius sees the key points of society has having the "Way" or not having the "Way," that is, whether the authority to use war and violence lies in the hands of the highest social authority or the nobles. The "Son of Heaven" is just the sign and symbol of the highest social authority. The important point is that Confucius thinks that to maintain the rational order of life in a society, the authority to use war and violence should be in the hands of the highest social authority, which is the fundamental guarantee of peaceful life. This point still has implications for the modern world, because the key to the lack of sense of safety in the contemporary international system is still that the power of war is not completely in the hands of the highest social authority—the United Nations. Fundamentally, in the modern world the power of war is distributed to all states, which is an important reason why there is no guarantee of safety in the world. The Western scholar Hobbes once said, "during the time men live without a common Power to keep them all in awe, they are in that condition which is called Warre."[12] So what is the way out? According to Hobbes, "The only way is to erect such a Common Power, as may be able to defend them from the invasion of Forraigners, and the injuries of one another, and thereby to secure them in such sort, as that by their owne industrie, and by the fruites of the Earth, they may nourish themselves and live contentedly; is, to conferre all their power and strength upon one Man, or upon one

Assembly of men, that may reduce all their Wills, by plurality of voices, upon one Will."[13] The German philosopher Kant pointed out "that of abandoning a lawless state of savagery and entering a federation of peoples in which every state . . . could expect to derive its security . . . from a united power and the law-governed decisions of a united will."[14] Although Western thinkers realized that a unified authority was the foundation of the peaceful status of society, Confucius in the East more than two thousand years ago not only realized it but also specified more concretely that only when this authority has the power to control war and violence is social peace possible, which is also true today.

Mencius's ideas about war and violence are very different from those of Confucius. If Confucius rules out war and violence from the ideal moral and ethical realm, that is, from the world of "benevolence," Mencius's breakthrough lies in connecting the realm of war with the realm of morality and ethics. According to Mencius, "The people are of supreme importance; next comes the good of land and grains; and the ruler is the least important."[15] This idea of "people as the root" leads to the political view of "practicing benevolent government." At the same time, Mencius believes that the benevolent realm of ideal ethics is not impossible to achieve. "Benevolent government" is the representation of "benevolence" in real politics. When a tyrant cruelly kills the people and does not practice benevolent government, Mencius firmly insists that we should use the "army of benevolence and justice" to wage the war of "punishing/killing the tyrants." In this way, war is connected with the Confucian ethical ideal through real politics. War is not only a means of practicing "benevolent government," it is also a means of realizing the highest ethical ideal of "benevolence." So for Mencius the Confucian ideas of war changed from maintaining the social and political order to protecting people's right to life and thus practicing morality and ethics. War in Mencius's thought became the tool of morality and ethics, which is another contribution of ancient Chinese thought to world civilization.

Starting from the idea of "people as the root," Mencius opposes wars among states for power and profit:

Confucius rejected those who enriched rulers not given to the practice of benevolent government. How much more would he reject those who do their best to wage wars on their behalf. In wars to gain land, the dead fill the plains; in wars to gain cities, the dead fill the cities. This is known as showing the land the way to devour human flesh. Death is too light a punishment for such men. Hence those skilled in war should suffer the most severe punishments; those who secure alliances with other nobles come next, and then come those who open up waste land and increase the yield of the soil.[16]

Here, we see the rudiments of the classical humanitarian theory with Eastern characteristics. But Mencius is not satisfied with condemnation and therefore combines the idea of "people as the root" with ethics, for which war is made the tool. Hence the earliest idea of "humanitarian intervention" came into being in Mencius's theory. *The Book of History* says, "In his punitive expeditions Tang began with Ge. The whole world was in sympathy with his cause. When he marched on the east, the western tribes complained. When he marched to the south, the northern tribes complained. They said, 'why does he not come to us first?' The people longed for his coming as they longed for a rainbow in time of severe drought."[17] In Mencius's view, as long as the subjective motive accords with the objective consequence, with the people being saved from tribulation, the use of war and violence can be justified. In a world where cruel tyranny is commonplace, this kind of war is not only the necessary means to "realize benevolent government," it is also the realization of the highest Confucian ethical ideal of "benevolence," that is, "the punitive expedition waged by the most benevolent against the most cruel,"[18] which is not only an attempt to improve the rational social and political order in the real world, but also the pursuit of the ideal realm with the highest goodness and beauty. This kind of war is not restricted by other social standards, including Confucius's "ritual order" and "principles of non-interventionism." In this way Mencius's ideas about war certainly include and take for granted the principle that "human rights can override sovereignty." The contemporary international social system relies on universally recognized moral principles in the modern system of civilized values for conducting political and military intervention against tyrannous states that violate moral principles by coup d'état and autarchy by military men, for the appearance of UN peacekeeping troops, and for the idea that "human rights can override sovereignty." Such ideas about war were put forward more than two thousand years ago in China by Mencius and they are also expressed succinctly by the great Confucian strategist Sima Rangzu: "If you attack the state and love the people, you can be justified in doing so."[19] If in the future process of globalization the idea that human rights can override sovereignty prevails day after day and is not used by those with bad intentions, we will increasingly appreciate the great contributions by Mencius's ideas to the cause of human peace. Moreover, the above phenomena can be considered not only as Western civilization and Chinese classical Confucianism reaching the same goal regarding war by different routes, but also as the partial revival of traditional Confucian principles in the contemporary civilized world. Why exactly? Let us discuss in more detail below.

Mencius not only is the first thinker to call for "humanitarian intervention," he is also the first to strictly restrict the conditions for "humanitarian intervention." He is clearly aware that some states with bad intentions might try to use force to gain hegemony and profit under the banners of "an army of benevolence and justice" and "saving the people from extreme misery." Mencius points out that there are many tyrannies and that not every state can intervene: "Only a Heaven-ordained [state] can carry out war." Only when the subject and the object accord with each other regarding "benevolence" and "benevolent government" and truly realize the Way for Heaven can military intervention be carried out against tyrannies. It is not permissable "for a tyrant to punish another tyrant"; tyrant states cannot be qualified to carry out military intervention against other tyrant states. In modern language, those with bad human rights records cannot be qualified to carry out military intervention against other states with similar problems. When we observe that some large states with bad human rights records intervene in others' internal affairs, claiming that "human rights can override sovereignty,"[20] we have to admire Mencius's historical foresight.

Mencius says that "the Spring and Autumn Annals acknowledges no just war,"[21] because wars among nobles are not permissible according to the rituals. These wars must be contentions for hegemony. Mencius also goes right to the point when he says that the essence of a hegemon is one who "uses force under the pretext of benevolence will become a leader of the nobles, but to do so he must first be the ruler of a large state."[22] Its form is "the Five Leaders of the nobles intimidated nobles into joining them in their attacks on other nobles."[23] Mencius violently attacks international political conduct that aims at hegemony and is disguised under the name of morality and justice: "The Five Leaders of the nobles were offenders against the Three [Benevolent] Kings."[24] The essence of the (First) Gulf War and the Kosovo War that occurred in modern times is the same as "the Five Leaders of the nobles intimidated nobles into joining them in their attacks on other nobles." The situation analyzed by Mencius contains valuable lessons for us today. After Confucius completed the Spring and Autumn Annals, the future generations of unscrupulous ministers and bad officials were struck with terror. In the same way, Mencius's ideas against hegemony also made the future generations of hegemons unable to hide their (bad) deeds. Without question, Mencius's ideas about hegemony contained in his thoughts on war and violence still have important implications for now and the future.

Xunzi systematized and highlighted Confucianism in the pre-Qin period. He elaborated on Confucius's idea of "war to restore the ritual order" and Mencius's idea of "war for benevolence and justice," and tried to reconcile the contradictions between the two theories and supply the

Confucian ideas about war and violence with a basis in human nature. "Now, the nature of man is that he is born with a love of profit. Following this nature will cause its aggressiveness and greedy tendencies to grow and courtesy and deference to disappear. . . . [W]hen each person follows his inborn nature and indulges his natural inclinations, aggressiveness and greed are sure to develop. This is accompanied by violation of class distinctions and throws the natural order into chaos, resulting in cruel tyranny."[25] According to Xunzi, war should be a tool to eliminate the manifestation of people's evil dispositions. "The military principles of which I just spoke are just the means to prohibit violent and aggressive behavior and to prevent harm to others; they are not the means to contention and confiscation. Wherever the army of a benevolent man is, it has the effect like that of a spirit; wherever it travels, it produces transformation."[26] Xunzi follows Mencius's way of thinking in the sense of connecting the ideal with reality, and he summarizes Confucian ideas about "benevolence and justice" in war as: "Those with physical strength toil for those with moral power."[27] Xunzi thus completes the theoretical expression of war as a tool for morality and justice. He should be regarded as the thinker that systematized and highlighted Confucian ideas about war and violence. His ideas about war, such as "prohibiting violent behavior and preventing harm to others," will have greater and more important implications for contemporary and future world peace.

Other than Confucianism, the ideas and resources of other scholars in the pre-Qin period can be used in the cause of modern peace. Here we will emphasize the implications of Laozi's ideas of war and violence for the human pursuit of peace. Laozi's ideas of war originate from a naturalistic dialectical philosophy: "The Way gave birth to the One; the One gave birth successively to two things, three things, ten-thousand things. These ten thousand things cannot turn their backs to the shade without having the sun on their bellies."[28] These ten thousand things of course include the phenomena of war and violence. Although Laozi despises war—"Good weapons are nonetheless ill-omened things. People despise them, therefore, those in possession of the Way do not depend on them"[29]—this is just Laozi's subjective hope. In fact, according to his dialectical logic, the social phenomena of war and violence are ultimately natural phenomena. So we cannot help but have such indications and suggestions as "weapons are ill-omened things, which the exemplary person should not depend on. He should only use them when necessary."[30] Laozi contradicts himself here. According to the principle that "the Way gave birth to everything," those with Way have to recognize the presence of war and violence since they are products of the Way. Laozi's "exemplary people" are different from Confucian "exemplary people," as the latter are contrasted with "petty people" and judged by the standard of morality, whereas Laozi's "exemplary people" are not contrasted with "petty people" and moreover "among exemplary people, the left-hand side is the place of honor, but in war this is reversed and the right hand side is the place of honor." According to the principles that "those in possession of the Way do not depend on good weapons" and "good weapons are not tools for exemplary people," Laozi's "exemplary people" are synonymous with "people with the Way." In my view, although Laozi considers war to be an ill omen, he has to recognize that even "exemplary people" and "people with the Way" under certain circumstances need to resort to it. So Laozi's ideas about war reflect torturous logic and contradictions. On the one hand, from an objective standpoint, he realizes that war is part of the natural order and thus is inevitable, and moreover it is established in the starting assumptions of his philosophical system albeit not explicitly; it is concealed in his view that the exemplary person "should only use [weapons] when necessary." On the other hand, he opposes war from a subjective standpoint, but according to reasons that contradict his own philosophical system; and he has no way to justify his views.

Although Laozi's attitudes toward war are deeply contradictory, by comparing his views with those of others we can still find the desire for peace in Laozi's ideas about war. We know that Laozi's dialectical way of thinking by using the "Way" as the origin of everything is similar to Hegel, who uses "absolute spirit" to explain the origin of nature, society, and everything else. Hegel shows complete respect for war and violence, claiming that "through its agency . . . the ethical health of nations is preserved in their indifference towards the permanence of finite determinancies, just as the movement of the winds preserves the sea from that stagnation which a lasting calm would produce—a stagnation which a lasting, not to say perpetual, peace would also produce among nations."[31] Of course, in the Hegelian dialectic system war is a natural phenomenon, part of the expression of "absolute spirit," and a necessary tool and method for the realization of "absolute spirit." But on the level of the realization of objective reason, Hegel's view is that the state is not restricted by ordinary moral laws. "[T]he various peoples and the great historical personalities are the instruments by which the universal spirit realized its ends: every great people has a mission to perform in the divine evolution and can be understood only in light of the total development. When it has accomplished the purpose of its existence, it makes way for other stronger nations. The conquest of one nation by another is a confession of the Idea for which the one stand is subordinate to that of the victorious people: here might makes right, physical power and rational justice coincide."[32] According to Hegel, wars are wars about ideas, they are legitimate; so he openly supports war and violence. Although Laozi believes that war is part of nature, he does not go so far as to endorse the rationality of war and violence in history, rather he says that weapons should only be used "when necessary." The idea that exemplary people should only use weapons "when necessary" is the key to understanding Laozi's ideas about war and violence. On this basis, Laozi adds the requirements that "the Quietest, even when he conquers, does not regard weapons as lovely things, for to think them lovely means to delight in them, and to delight in them means to delight in the slaughter of men" and that "a host that has slain men is received with grief and mourning."[33] Moreover, with the precondition that the exemplary person should only use weapons "when necessary," Laozi tries his best to reduce to the minimum the harm created by war and violence and thus ends up defending the uncommon view that "he that has conquered in battle is received with rites of mourning." Such an idea is extremely rare in both Eastern and Western cultures; it encompasses both high wisdom and superior rationality, as well as an understanding of the sadness of the inevitability of war and the desire for peace.

Comparing Laozi's and Confucius's views on "just" war, there are obvious differences. Confucius actively advocates war in the real world if it is meant to "restore the ritual order," and Mencius and Xunzi also actively advocate "war for benevolence and justice." But Laozi does not actively advocate war whether or not the war is just. On the contrary, all wars are regarded as "ill omens" and regarded with the passive attitude that exemplary persons only use weapons "when necessary." So compared to Confucianism, Laozi adheres to passive pacifism. Subjectively, Laozi and Confucius both despise warfare. Confucius does not permit warfare in his ideal world, so it can be said that Confucius also regards war as something to be done only when there is no other choice in the real world. The difference is that Confucius is optimistic regarding the ideal future of human beings: "if truly efficacious people were put in charge of governing for a hundred years, they would be able to overcome violence and dispense with killing altogether." And the "ritual order" is the way to realize ideal "benevolence": "Through self-discipline and reviving ritual propriety one realizes benevolence. If for the space of one day one were able to accomplish this, the whole world would defer to this benevolence."[34] Thus when Confucius considers war and violence in the real world as "necessary" tools, he actively endorses them. Laozi observes more calmly and deeply than Confucius and he considers that war is part of nature and is inevitable. Laozi's system does not have any logically necessary connection between war and his ideal system of "a small country with few inhabitants" and "actionless activity and no contention among the people," so he believes that the only possibility is to regard war as carried out when there is no other choice and with an extremely passive and cautious attitude and to avoid anything that would stimulate people's zest for war. Laozi's ideas about war perhaps sadden those with idealistic martial spirits, but given the historical phenomena of slaughters used to gain power and profit under the banner of justice—and that justice under most circumstances is just an excuse for evil and leads in the real world to frequent warfare— Laozi's ideas about war for human beings are perhaps more important than those of Confucius's. Given this fact, it is better to fundamentally reject all wars, which would be more meaningful for people's real lives and more valuable for the creation of peace in the world. Laozi should be regarded as the wise man of Eastern culture and one of the deepest thinkers that has reflected on war in our traditional culture.

IV

Several years ago at the Shanghai Academy of Social Sciences, Xu Zhuoyun said that the many schools of philosophy in the pre-Qin period did not diverge much in terms of their "substance." He even went so far as to suggest that it is inaccurate to describe the pre-Qin period as one with many "different schools of philosophy," because judging by their cultural roots and substance there are no important differences between them but only diversity in a few respects. From a seemingly extreme standpoint Mr. Xu put forward a new perspective that will help us reflect on the ideas about war and violence among scholars in the pre-Qin period. In my view, the most basic and important attitude to war and violence in Chinese culture is not "love of warfare" or "pacifism" or "hatred of war" but rather "waging war with prudence." Although the thoughts of the various scholars of the pre-Qin period all have their own merits and demerits, the idea of "waging war with prudence" is commonly held. Confucius's approach to prudence includes "fasting, warfare, and illness."[35] Mencius calls for "the punitive expedition waged by the most benevolent against the most cruel," but he strictly specifies that "only the Heaven-ordained can punish those without the Way." Xunzi's view is that war should be used only "to prohibit violence and to prevent harm to others." Laozi's prudence regarding war can be seen in such sentences as "the weapon that is too hard will be broken, the tree that has the hardest wood will be cut down"[36]; "He who helps rulers by means of the Way will oppose all conquest by force of arms; such things are wont to rebound. Where armies are, thorn and brambles grow. A large military [victory] is followed by a year of dearth"[37]; and "the Lieutenant general stands on the left, while the supreme general stands on the right, the words are used for the place of the rites of mourning."[38] Guanzi's view is that "armies are used to punish/kill tyrants . . . armies are used to punish/kill tyrants outside and to prevent badness inside,"[39] but ultimately he insists that "the people with the highest goodness will not wage war."[40] Mozi's view is that war is meant to prevent robbery and theft inside and invasion outside: "Why should they make all those weapons? To protect themselves from invaders and robbers and thieves."[41] He cautiously divides wars into two kinds: the war of punishment/killing that aims to eliminate tyrants and to replace chaos with peace, and the war of aggression that aims to take cities and land. In his work "Against Aggression," Mozi severely attacks wars of aggression and concludes that "now if we want to practice benevolence and justice, to become people with the highest capabilities, to follow the Way of the sage, and to benefit the country and the people, we have to take seriously the theory of 'against aggression' and to avoid not considering it."[42] The successful military strategists do not suggest that we should use all our armed might to indulge in wars of aggression: "military action is of vital importance to the state. It is a matter of life and death, a road either to safety or ruin. Hence it is a subject of inquiry which can on no account be neglected"[43]; "even big states will be destroyed if they thirst for war."[44] So we can conclude that "waging war with prudence" is the commonly held foundation for various theorists's ideas about war in the pre-Qin period. This special characteristic differentiates Chinese strategists and Chinese military culture from other civilizations.

Next we will discuss briefly the Legalists that in our cultural tradition give the impression that they thirst for war. My view is that the representative of Legalism, Shang Yang, put forward the idea of "emphasizing agriculture and preparing for war" as the best way of dealing with a particular and short period in Chinese history. More concretely, with the Zhou dynasty in decline, and "the collapse of ritual and the (moral) badness of music," Chinese society at the time did not have a highest authority. In this condition, according to Hobbes's theory, the society is in a war of all against all and so are the states. The relations among states are neither legal nor moral relations. This kind of system is ruled by the "law of the jungle," with the weak at the mercy of the strong—the fittest survive and the weak are left to die. Under such circumstances, the Legalists regard the Confucian standards such as "ritual order," "benevolence and justice," et cetera, as being appropriate for a system governed by a highest authority but as inappropriate for an anarchical society. According to Shang Yang, "the people with benevolence can treat people with benevolence but cannot make others practice benevolence; the people with justice can love people but cannot make others love; thus we know that benevolence and justice are not sufficient to govern the world . . . the sage kings value laws rather than justice as it is sufficient to have the laws clear and the orders brought into practice."[45] As we are dealing with a period of extreme terror where the survival of the state is the key question, the issue is simplified and the main aim is to strengthen the state. Thus, Mr. Jiang Lihong says that "the way of Shang Yang is simply to emphasize agriculture and prepare for war." According to Jiang's teacher, Mr. Zhong, the Legalist's call for emphasizing agriculture and preparing for war is "the only way to survive and to realize one's will in a world where large states wage wars to gain territory and hegemony." He added, "people know that war is meant to provide security from outside but they do not know this it is also used to secure internal peace."[46]

I wholeheartedly agree with Jiang and Zhong's ideas. The Legalist idea of "emphasizing agriculture and preparing for war" originates from an anarchical system. In an environment characterized by "it's either you or me" and "hell is other people," the state must adopt the theory of "emphasizing agriculture and preparing for war"; it is not only necessary but also rational. So ancient Chinese Legalism's "thirst for war," seen from a macrohistorical perspective, is consistent with Laozi's view that exemplary persons use weapons only "when necessary" and should be regarded as merely a short-term response to an unusually harsh historical context. Since unity dominated in subsequent Chinese history, Legalist ideas about war and violence did not belong to mainstream thought and served only to supplement Confucianism in Chinese military culture. After the unification of the Qin and Han dynasties, it is only because of outside threats that Legalist ideas about war were not entirely relegated to the dustbin of history.

As mentioned above, "Waging war with prudence" is the foundation of Chinese military culture and one of the most important characteristics that separate it from other civilizations regarding ideas about war. This characteristic includes elements of pacifism, which leads to the idea of "breaking the enemy's resistance without fighting." These features of military culture originate from our particular living conditions—an irrigating agricultural society in great river valleys that are sealed off from other areas.[47] In this context, the highest aim of war is the maintenance of normal agricultural life, a standard that also determines whether the war is regarded as just and legimate; on the other hand any war, including just wars, objectively considered, will directly affect the normal course of agricultural life. Both factors are the ultimate explanations for pre-Qin scholars' special ideas about war and violence as well as the idea of "waging war with prudence." Moreover, the context naturally leads to the idea that when we are forced to resort to war and violence to maintain the social order, we want to reduce the harm done to society to the greatest possible extent. "Breaking the enemy's resistance without fighting" is the highest achievement of Eastern strategic thinking—the highest achivment of the Chinese Way of war—and it originates from these special living conditions and the social psychological background.[48]

Although it was put forward most explicitly by Sunzi, many other scholars in the pre-Qin period had similar ideas. Confucius's praise for Guanzhong—"Duke Huan often assembled the various feudal lords, and it was always through Guanzhong's influence rather than by resorting to arms. Such was his benevolence, such was his benevolence!"—obviously includes the idea of breaking the enemy's resistance without fighting. Xunzi said: "To triumph without having to wage war, to gain the objectives without resorting to force, and getting the whole world to submit to him without armies exerting themselves. Such is the one who knows the Way of a True King."[49] Laozi said: "The good victor defeats the enemy without rejoicing"; "It is the Way of Heaven for the good victor to win without contending"; and "to win the adherence of the whole world without interfering." And according to the ideas that "the greatest music has the faintest notes" and "the Great Form is shapeless," the natural inference is that "the great victor need not fight wars." Moreover, Guanzi held that "those with the greatest goodness do not fight wars." These thinkers of the pre-Qin period seem to share the same feelings regarding "breaking the enemy's resistance without fighting," meaning that this highest achievement of the Way of war is not merely the product of an exceptionally talented individual but rather should be seen as the logical expression of military affairs for an irrigating agricultural civilization sealed off by great river valleys. Sunzi is simply the most explicit spokesman for this view.

In comparison with the early Western ancient Greek civilization, the pacifist tendency in ancient Chinese military ideas has value that cannot be denied. Prior to Alexander's expedition in the Mediterranean sea and the Greek peninsula, there was no highest authority and Greek society had long been in a state of anarchy and dominated by the idea that the strong eat the weak in the "law of the jungle." Ancient Greek culture valorized violence and conquest, as represented by Heraclitus: "polemos pater panton" [warfare is the father of all things].[50] "We must know that war is common to all and strife is justice, and that all things come into being and pass away through strife."[51] Such is one of the mainstream views in the history of Western civilization. The American scholar Richard A. Gabriel points out that c. seventh-century B.C.E., such views have roots in Homer's idea that war is connected with the moral aspects of the human spirit, developing into the idea that war can cause people to have a noble spirit: "The emergence of this idea marks a very important turning point in the evolution of war. . . . Perhaps most important in terms of longevity was the Greek attitudinal perspective that war ennobled the human spirit. This concept became the foundation upon which a new civil religion was erected that saw war as a vital aspect of modern civilization."[52] Later, the idea in German culture that "shedding your sweat to obtain something that can be taken by shedding blood shows that you are too weak and useless,"[53] was added to it. Given its basis on this kind of civilization, Western military thought lacks the concern for human beings and the pacifist elements of Eastern thought. Notwithstanding the importance of Western humanitarianism in the Italian Renaissance, until the nineteenth-century such classical Western military works as Karl Von Clausewitz's *On War* and Mahan's *The Influence of Sea Power on History* lacked the humanitarian concern and pacifist tendencies of classical Eastern civilization. The Mediterranean sea's traditional culture of conquest and expansion had left the most profound marks on Western military culture.[54]

Lastly, let us note the possible implications of the universal acceptance by the modern Western world of Sunzi's idea of "breaking the enemy's resistance without fighting."[55] The Western support and respect of the idea of "victory without war" may show that the Western world is in the process of transforming itself from an anarchical world without highest authority—that has been mainstream for thousands of years—to genuine globalization.[56] The point of war is changing from the expansion of life-space to the maintenance of the existing global life order. Western civilization has realized that the relation between war and modern society takes the following form: all wars lead to the destruction of the rational life order, but at the same time war is the means to maintain the existing rational life order. This situation leads to the development of the concept of "victory without war" and it is also the cause of the acceptance by the Western world of the concept of "breaking the enemy's resistance without fighting." The emergence of the idea that "human rights overrides sovereignty" is similar; modern Western civilization and modern global civilization has drawn on the resources of classical Chinese civilization. From such developments we can observe the partial revival of Chinese classical military culture in the modern world.

NOTES

1. Marx did not anticipate that the Soviet Union in the Brezhnev period would invade and occupy Czechoslovakia under the banner of "socialist states

have limited sovereignty." Mencius did not anticipate the extent to which many ambitious individuals and groups in history would hit out at others under the banner of "an army with benevolence and justice."

2. *The Analects of Confucius*, 13.11 (modified). The translations of *The Analects of Confucius* are based on Roger T. Ames and Henry Rosemont, Jr.'s translation of *The Analects of Confucius: A Philosophical Translation* (New York: Ballantine Books, 1998). The translations have occasionally been modified by the editor, as indicated by "modified." In this case, "善" has been translated as "good" rather than "efficacious" (Confucius's concern here is not merely instrumental rationality).

3. Ibid., 12.19 (modified). "善" has been translated as "good" rather than "adept."

4. Ibid., 14.16 (modified). "仁" has been translated as "benevolence" rather than "authoritative conduct," but note that the Confucian idea of benevolence is graded love; love starts with close intimates and extends outwards with diminishing intensity.

5. Ibid., 3.25 (modified). "善" has been translated as "good" rather than "felicitous."

6. *Mencius*, IV.A.7 (modified). The translations of Mencius is based on *Mencius, Volumes One and Two*, D. C. Lau trans. (Hong Kong: The Chinese University Press, 1984). The translations have occasionally been modified by the editor, as indicated by "modified." In this case, "天下" has been translated as "the world" rather than "Empire."

7. "It is also clear that there are cases where such a distinction [between the natural slave and the natural freeman] exists, and that here it is beneficial and just that the former should actually be a slave and the latter a master—the one being ruled, and the other exercising the kind of rule for which he is naturally intended and therefore acting as a master" (Aristotle, *The Politics of Aristotle*, Ernest Barker trans. [Beijing: China Social Sciences Publishing House, 1999], 16).

"It also follows that the art of war is in some sense [that is to say, so far as it is directed to gaining the means of subsistence from animals] a natural mode of acquisition. Hunting is part of that art; and hunting ought to be practised—not only against wild animals, but also against human beings who are intended by nature to be ruled by others and refuse to obey that intention—because war of this order is naturally just" (Ibid., 21).

"Its objects should be these—first, to prevent men from ever becoming enslaved themselves; secondly, to put men in a position to exercise leadership—but a leadership directed to the interest of the led, and not to the establishment of a general system of slavery; and thirdly, to enable men to make themselves masters of those who naturally serve to be slaves" (Ibid., 319).

8. Ibid., 18.

9. "Chen Chengzi assassinated Duke Jian. Confucius having cleansed himself ceremonially went to court and reported to Duke Ai, saying, 'Chen Chengzi has assassinated his lord. I implore you to send an army to punish him'" (*The Analects of Confucius*, 14.21).

10. Confucius was the administrator of Ji and the ramparts of three feudal lords were going to be destroyed. Shusun's rampart was destroyed and it was Ji's turn. Gongshan Buniu and Shusun Ze led people to attack the Nu state. The Duke of Nu and three other lords retreated into Ji's house and ascended a platform. The attack failed and the arrows almost reached Duke of Nu. Confucius ordered Shen Juxu and Le Xin to fight against them and succeeded. The people of Nu chased and defeated them in Gumie. Gongshan Buniu and Shusun Ze fled to the Qin state. The rampart of Ji was destroyed (Du Yu, *Chun qiu jing zhuan ji jie* [*The Spring and Autumn Period: Critical Assessments*], II (Shanghai: Shanghai guji chubanshe, 1988), 1686); Sima Qian, *Shiji* [*The Book of History*], VI (Beijing: Zhonghua shuju, 1982), 1916.

11. "Confucius said, "When the Way prevails in the world, rituals, music, and punitive campaigns are initiated by the Son of Heaven. If the Way does not prevail in the world, then they are intitiated by the various nobles" (*The Analects of Confucius*, 16.2; modified). "天子" has been translated as "Son of Heaven" rather than "Emperor."

12. Thomas Hobbes, *Leviathan* (Beijing: China Social Sciences Publishing House, 1999), 96.

13. Ibid., 131.

14. Kant, *Kant's Political Writings*, trans. H. B. Nisbet (Beijing: China University of Political Science and Law, 2003), 47 (Original German source: *Kants Werke Akademie Textausgabe*, VIII [Berlin: Walter de Gruyter, 1968], 24).

15. *Mencius*, VII.B.14.

16. Ibid., IV.A. 14 (modified).

17. Ibid., I.B.11 (modified).

18. Ibid., VII.B.3 (modified).

19. Sima Rangyi, *Sima Fa* [*The Art of War*] (Beijing: Zhonghua shuju, 1991), 1.

20. There are three ways to enforce international social standards in both ancient and modern times: first, through the highest authority in the international system, such as the Zhou Son of Heaven in ancient China; second, through a force temporarily organized in the international system to play the role of policeman, such as Duke Huan and Guanzhong who punished the Chu state under the pretext that they did not pay tributes to the Zhou Son of Heaven and the United States together with the Western world who "kept the peace" in the Middle East and Kosovo; and third, through the self-awareness of states, that is, through the moral self-discipline of states. When people pursue "state interests above all," it is impossible to have a real highest authority in the international system and in the meantime it is easy for states, especially large states and great powers, to lose moral self-discipline. Thus the necessary international social standards can only depend on an international force temporarily organized. As for its content, this kind of international collective action must include both interstate conflicts of interest and the maintenance of justice. As for its quality, because of the pervasiveness of "state interests above all," when justice contradicts with this principle, justice will be forsaken. The ideal situation is when justice does not contradict this principle, but the real function of justice

is to function as the fig leaf of this principle. So in the "anarchical" international system, this kind of collective action functions essentially as the contention for power and profit among states.

21. Mencius, VII.B.2.

22. Ibid., II.A.9 (modified).

23. Ibid., VI.B.7 (modified).

24. Ibid. (modified).

25. Xunzi, 23.2 (modified). The translations of Xunzi are based on Xunzi, translated by John Knoblock (Beijing: Foreign Languages Press, 1999). The translations have occasionally been modified by the editor, as indicated by "modified." In this case, "乱" has been translated as "chaos" rather than "anarchy."

26. Ibid., 15.6 (modified). To be consistent, "仁" has been translated as "benevolent" rather than "humane."

27. Ibid., 10.7 (modified). "德" has been translated as "moral power" rather than "inner power."

28. Laozi, ch. 42 (modified). The translations of Laozi are based on *Laozi*, translated by Arthur Waley (Beijing: Foreign Languages Press, 1999). The translations have occasionally been modified by the editor, as indicated by "modified."

29. Ibid., chap. 31 (modified). Laozi said: "[W]hen there is no Way in the world, war horses will be reared even on the sacred mounds below the city walls." Here "Way" means "the Way to govern," not "the Way of Heaven." Mr. Chen Guying has translated this passage as "the political life of the state is not on the right path." This understanding is correct.

30. Ibid. (modified).

31. Hegel, *Elements of the Philosophy of Right*, trans. H. B. Nisbet (Beijing: China University of Politics and Law Press, 2001), 341.

32. Frank Thilly, *A History of Philosophy* (New York: Henry Holt and Company, 1931), 475.

33. Laozi, chap. 31.

34. The Analects of Confucius, 12.1 (modified). ("仁" has been translated as "benevolence" rather than "authoritative conduct" and "复" has been translated as "revive" rather than "observing.")

35. Sima Qian, *Shiji* [*The Book of History*], VI (Beijing: Zhonghua shuju, 1982), 1938.

36. Laozi, chap. 76.

37. Ibid., chap. 30 (modified).

38. Ibid., chap. 31 (modified).

39. Liu Ke, Ki Kehe, eds., *Guanzi yizhu* [*Annotations to Guanzi*] (Harbin: Heilongjiang renmin chubanshe, 2002), 202.

40. Ibid., 121.

41. Xin Zhifeng, Jiang Yubin, eds. *Mozi yizhu* [*Annotations of Mozi*] (Harbin: Heilongjiang Renmin Chubanshe, 2003), 126.

42. Ibid., 124.

43. *Sunzi bingfa* [*Sunzi on the Art of War*], translated by Lionel Giles (Changsha: Hunan chubanshe, 1993), 1.1 and 1.2.

44. Sima Rangyi, *Sima Fa* [*The Art of War*], 1.

45. Jiang Lihong, ed., *Xin bian zhu zi ji cheng shangjun shu zhuizhi* [*New Collection of the Works of Pre-Qin Scholars; Studies on Shang Yang's Works*], vol. IV, no. 18 (Beijing: Zhonghua shuju, 1986), 113.

46. Ibid., 19.

47. An irrigating agricultural civilization in the great river valleys sealed off from other areas is different from one that is not sealed off, as can be seen from a comparison of Egyptian history and Chinese history. An agricultural society that is sealed off has the tendency to assimilate all tribes and ideas, whereas it is difficult to assimilate people in an open agricultural society. Even if they both have big river valleys, their historical evolution is very different. Wu Rusong's review of the three-fold reasons for the origin of Sunzi's *The Art of War* has incisively identified the "sealed off" nature of the geographic environment but he was not sufficiently clear regarding the relation between such an environment and the pacifist tendency in military thought (see Wu Rusong, "*Sunzi bingfa de junshi wenhua diyun*" [*The real meaning of military culture in Sunzi's The Art of War*], in Huang Pumin, Xue Dujin, and Liu Qing, eds., *Sunzi bingfa jiqi xiandai jiazhi* [*Sunzi's Art of War and Its Modern Value*] [Beijing: Junshi kexue chubanshe, 1999]).

48. For a detailed analysis of the idea of "breaking the enemy's resistance without fighting" as the highest aim of war in our culture, see my "The Cultural Perspective on War," *Du Shu*, 1993, no. 3.

49. Xunxi, 9.11 (modified).

50. Will and Ariel Durant, *The Lessons of History* (New York: Simon and Schuster, 1968), 81.

51. Heraclitus, frag. 80 (quoted in Doyne Dawson, *The Origins of Western Warfare: Militarism and Morality in the Ancient World* [Boulder: Westview Press, 1996], 11). Note that Heraclitus's ideas about war are connected with the historical background that war and violence decide everything, which leads him to search for the rationality of war in the universe and to take war as the natural law: "according to this standpoint, so-called war and conflict cause the world's changes; peace and harmony cause the flames of war and ultimately violent eruptions; "war is the father and king of all things. It causes people to become God(s), it causes people to become slaves, it causes people to be free people" (Zhou Fucheng, ed., *Xifang lunlixue mingzhu xuanji* [*Collection of Classics on Western Ethics*], vol. 1 [Beijing: Shangwu yinshuguan, 1964], 10, 12).

52. Richard A. Gabriel, *The Culture of War* (Westport, Conn.: Greenwood Press, 1990), 86, 100.

53. Tacitus, *Ni er man ni ya zhi* [*Agricola, Germania*], trans. Ma Yong and Fu Zhengyuan (Beijing: Shangwu Yinshuguan, 1959), 62. Tacitus, *Germania*, trans. M. Hutton, revised by M. Winterbotton, London: William Heinemann Ltd., 1970, 153.

54. Professor Johnson, the famous specialist on Chinese military topics at Harvard University's Fairbank Center for East Asian Research, told me in an interview that the Western idea of "deterrence" is essentially the same as the Chinese idea of "breaking the enemy's resistance without fighting" and has existed since

ancient times. Professor Shen Dingli of the Center of American Studies at Fudan University told me that his colleague Dr. Wu Chunsi's research shows that the Western idea of "deterrence" has long roots but that it only become formalized as a Western concept in Bernard Brodie's edited volume, *The Absolute Weapon* (New York: Harcourt Brace, 1946).

In my view, even if it's true that "deterrence" is equivalent to "breaking the enemy's resistance without fighting," there are still deep differences between China and the West. The main reason is that prior to the twentieth century the Western idea of "deterrence" was never taken as the highest aim of the Way of War that needed to be elaborated and acted upon. On the contrary, the idea of glorifying war and violence made its appearance from ancient Greece to Rome to the Teutons and was transmitted in one continous line in Western culture, and the idea of "deterrence" was always marginalized. The classical case of besiegement and annihilation in Hannibal's "Battle of Cannae" has been re-spected and regarded as the highest aim in Western military thought for thou-sands of years. This kind of view has been targeted by our so-called sayings "to fight and conquer in all your battles is not the highest good," and "to destroy an army is second best."

55. The sealed-off nature of Chinese agricultural geography is the main rea-son for the early maturation of Chinese military culture. From the general expe-rience of history, a culture with some limits on violence is far more mature than one without. Moreover, a culture produces the need for limits on violence only after normal life order has been created after violence. It seems that "sealed-off culture" can realize the historical mission of "establishing order by violence" earlier and less painfully than "open cultures," so humanitarian concern and pacifist elements in military culture occur earlier in the former than the latter. The Western commercial civilization with the market economy at its core has been formed with the aid of war and violence, and only in modern times is it close to completing a truly unified global economic order, thus changing the whole world into a "sealed-off civilization" and leading to the demand for lim-its on violence.

56. Although the highest authority in the international political arena—the United Nations—is at present primarily a formal authority and the subject of manipulation by large states, its tendency is that of developing into a real au-thority. Since politics, whether in form or content, will accord with economic foundations, and since economic unification is being completed throughout the world, the appearance of a global political authority will manifest itself sooner or later. The transformation of Western Europe from nineteenth-century large-scale military and political conflicts to the contemporary "European Union," is strong evidence of this trend. In the nineteenth century, Spengler noted insight-fully that the West was similar to China in the ancient "Warring States period." In my view, Western material culture is superior to that of China, but in some important spiritual and cultural aspects such as ideas about military culture, the West is only beginning to approach the standards of Chinese classical times. Because Confucian civilization is essentially designed to function in a unified society, Confucius's idea of "restoring ritual order" could not be implemented

in an anarchical world order. But after the unification of China under the Qin and Han dynasties and Emperor Wu's "proscription of competing schools and sole respect for Confucianism," Confucianism became a useful tool for unifying China. Thus I boldly forecast that the Chinese tradition's Confucian culture may revive during the process of globalization.

Chapter Eleven

JUST WAR AND CONFUCIANISM: IMPLICATIONS FOR THE CONTEMPORARY WORLD

~

Daniel A. Bell

> Mencius said, "A true king uses virtue and benevolence, a hegemon uses force under the pretext of benevolence." Let us first consider the idea of the hegemon. According to Mencius's saying, a hegemon uses force to attack others in the name of benevolent justice. This kind of war is an unjust war. . . . In ancient times as well as today, most rulers are very clear regarding political realities, they won't lightly abandon the cover of virtue to launch such wars. . . . The best contemporary example is President Bush's war of invasion against Iraq! He used the excuses of weapons of mass destruction and terrorism in order to obtain oil resources and to consolidate his strategic position in the Middle East. This is the best example of "using force under the pretext of benevolence." Bush is today's hegemonic king.
> —Ming Yongquan, "Are There Just Wars?"[1]

It might seem odd that the most modern of technologies—the Internet—should be filled with references to ancient Confucian thinkers. Yet that is exactly what happened in response to the Bush administration's wars in/against Afghanistan and Iraq.[2] The theories of Confucians from what subsequently became known as the Warring States era were downloaded from computer to computer in Chinese-speaking households for the purpose of evaluating U.S foreign policy. But what exactly did classical Confucians say regarding just and unjust warfare? And does it make sense to invoke their ideas in today's vastly different political world? Why not simply stick to the language of human rights? These questions will be explored below.

The Ideal World versus the Nonideal World

First, however, we need to confront an apparent problem.[3] Whatever the relevance of Confucian political values, they do not seem to bear on the question of war between sovereign states. War involves the use of force to maintain or increase the state's territory. Yet classical Confucianism seems to rule out the possibility that rulers could justifiably use force to exercise authority over a particular territory and establish boundaries between that territory and the rest of the world. Instead, Confucians defended the ideal of *tian xia* (天下 the world under Heaven), a harmonious political order without state boundaries and governed by a sage by means of virtue, without any coercive power at all.[4] Moreover, this harmonious order can and should be attained by means of benevolence and positive example, once again without any coercive power. It is a kind of communism attained by entirely peaceful means, without any revolutionary uprisings.[5] This would seem to rule out the possibility of justifiable use of force. In this view, all wars are bad, and pacifism would seem to be the only justifiable moral stance. But are Confucians really pacifists?[6]

Confucius himself does point to the possibility of a sage-king who could spread "his peace to all the people" (14.42, Leys; see also 17.6).[7] In this ideal world, the ruler need not resort to coercion or punitive laws:

> Lord Ji Kang asked Confucius about government, saying: "Suppose I were to kill those without the Way to help those with the Way: how about that?" Confucius replied: "You are here to govern; what need is there to kill? If you desire the good, the people will be good. The moral power of the exemplary person is the wind, the virtue of the common person is grass. Under the wind, the grass must bend." (12.19; Leys, modified)

Confucius suggests that the moral power (*de,* 德) of the ideal ruler will eventually attract those living in faraway lands, bringing peace to the whole world and presumably doing away with the need for territorial boundaries between states:

> I have always heard that what worries the head of a state or the chief of a clan is not poverty but the inequitable distribution of wealth, not the lack of population, but the lack of peace. For if wealth is equitably distributed, there will be no poverty, and where there is peace, there is no lack of population. And then, if people who live in far-off lands still resist your attraction, you must draw them to you by the moral power of your civilization; and then, having attracted them, make them enjoy your peace. (16.1; Leys, modified)

Mencius draws on these ideas to elaborate upon the ideal of a sage-king who rules the whole world by noncoercive means. This end can be achieved by gaining the sympathy of the people:

> There is a way to gain the whole world. It is to gain the people, and having gained them one gains the whole world. There is a way to gain the people. Gain their hearts, and then you gain them. (4A.10; Dobson, modified)[8]

Mencius argues that the ideal ruler would win people's hearts simply by his[9] benevolence (ren, 仁), without relying on the use of force (see 1A.6). Even if people do not seem immediately receptive to Confucian norms, the ruler should not worry. He should cultivate his own personal virtue, people will be inspired by his example, and eventually he will gain the allegiance of the whole world:

> Mencius said, "If others do not respond to your love with love, look into your own benevolence; if others do not respond to your attempts to govern them, look into your own wisdom; if others do not respond to your courtesy, look into your own respect. In other words, look into yourself whenever you fail to achieve your purpose. When you are correct in your person, the whole world will turn to you. (4A.4; Lau, modified)

Mencius even seems to provide a time frame for ultimate success:

> If any lord implements the policies [government] of King Wen [an ideal ruler of the past], he will be ruling over the whole world within seven years. (4A.13; Lau, modified)

From a contemporary perspective,[10] all this might seem like pie-in-the-sky theorizing, of little relevance to the real world. Fortunately, that is not the end of the story. In fact, it would be surprising if Confucius and Mencius had not attempted to provide some practical, morally informed guidance in a nonideal political world of sovereign states delimited by territorial boundaries. Consider the fact that *The Analects of Confucius* and *The Works of Mencius* were penned during the Spring and Autumn and Warring States periods (c. 800–221 B.C.E.), a time of ruthless competition for territorial advantage between small walled states. In such a context, it would seem odd, to say the least, for two political thinkers explicitly concerned with practical effect to limit their political advice to quasi-anarchistic principles.[11] This kind of political thinking might have resonated more in the days of imperial China, when rulers saw themselves as governing the largest and most powerful empire in the world surrounded by as-yet-uncivilized barbarians. But China had not yet been unified in the Warring States period.[12] True, Warring States thinkers never quite abandoned the background ideal of universal kinship,[13] but the idea that political thinkers should provide guidance for leaders of a self-conscious, culturally unified, and politically stable community with the potential to spread civilized norms (what later became known as *Zhongguo*, 中国: literally, "Middle Kingdom")[14] would have seem farfetched to thinkers of the time.

Moreover, Mencius suggests that successful sage-kings come in five-hundred-year cycles—or more, since "seven hundred years have now passed since Chou began. As a matter of simple calculation the time is overdue" (2B.13, Dobson; see also 7B.38). Mencius seems to suggest that sage rulers would not last for more than a generation or two,[15] which means that—according to his own theory—the nonideal world of competing states delimited by territorial boundaries is the reality for roughly 90 percent of the time. Given the predominance of the nonideal world, one might have expected Mencius to formulate principles of political guidance for this context as well.

Confucius is even more skeptical concerning the prospects of sage-kings ever taking power. For one thing, he did not—unlike Mencius[16]—consider himself to be in the top moral/intellectual category, which is presumably a requisite for sagehood:

> The Master asked Zigong: "Which is the better, you or Yan Hui?"—"How could I compare myself with Yan Hui? From one thing he learns, he deduces ten; from one thing I learn, I only deduce two." The Master said: "Indeed, you are not his match; and neither am I." (5.9; Leys, modified; see also 7.34)

But even Yan Hui (Confucius's favorite pupil), along with everybody else Confucius has met, is subject to human weaknesses: "I have yet to meet the person who is fonder of virtue than of physical beauty" (15.13; Ames and Rosemont, modified). Nor is Confucius overly confident about the ability to cultivate one's personal virtue in an honest and non-self-deceiving way: The Master said: "Alas, I have never seen a man capable of seeing his own faults and of exposing them in the tribunals of his heart" (5.27; Leys). Even Yao and Shun, the icons of sagehood, proved to be deficient:

> Zigong said: "What would you say of a man who showers the people with blessings and who could save the multitude? Could he be called benevolent? The Master said: What has this to do with benevolence? He would be a sage! Even Yao and Shun would be deficient in this respect. (6.30; Leys, modified; see also 7.26)

In short, both Confucius and Mencius seem to recognize the difficulty, if not impossibility, of implementing an ideal, nonterritorial political order governed by a wise and virtuous sage-king who inspires the whole world simply by means of his exemplary moral character. But is there any evidence that classical Confucians did in fact attempt to provide practical, morally informed guidance for a nonideal world? In my view, many, if not most, of the passages in *The Analects of Confucius* and *The Works of Mencius* seem to assume the context of a nonideal political world.[17] It is difficult to otherwise make sense of, for example, the statement in *The Analects* that "An exemplary person has a moral obligation to serve the state, even if he can foresee that the Way will not prevail" (18.7; Leys, modified). In the same vein, it would seem odd for Mencius—if his only concern was to lecture rulers on the requirements of sagehood—to make the argument that people can transgress traditional norms in hard-luck situations (4A.17), including breaking promises (4B.11) and killing tyrannical rulers (1B.8). More pertinently, the passages on warfare[18] provide direct evidence that Confucius and Mencius allowed for the possibility that the use of force can be justified in nonideal situations.[19] One quote will suffice to make this point:

> Duke Wen of Teng asked, "Teng is a small state, wedged between Qi and Chu. Should I be subservient to Qi or should I be subservient to Chu?"
>
> "This is a question that is beyond me," answered Mencius. "If you insist, there is only one course of action I can suggest. Dig deeper moats and build higher walls and defend them shoulder to shoulder with the people. If they would rather die than desert you, then all is not lost." (1B.13; Lau, modified)

In a nonideal context, the justifiable course of action may be to reinforce, rather than abolish, territorial boundaries between states.[20] If Mencius—who is considered to be the most "idealistic" of the Confucians[21]—had only been concerned with the ideal world, he would have urged Duke Wen to rely exclusively on moral power to deal with larger states, in the hope that virtue would attract the good will of people outside and eventually make territorial boundaries obsolete.[22]

My claim, in short, is that several prescriptions in *The Analects of Confucius*[23] and *The Works of Mencius* were meant to apply in a political context of walled states competing for territorial advantage, including the need for morally informed, practical guidance in military affairs.[24] In the next section, I will discuss general Confucian principles that underpin theorizing on just and unjust war. I limit myself to the values espoused by Confucius and Mencius. *The Analects of Confucius* is, of course, the central, founding text in the Confucian tradition, and Mencius, who elaborated and systematized Confucius's ideas, became its most famous exponent.[25] Mencius continues to be the most influential theorist of war and just war in the Confucian tradition, and the third section is devoted to presenting Mencius's views on the topic. The chapter ends by considering the contemporary implications of Confucianism for thinking about just and unjust war.

GENERAL CONFUCIAN PRINCIPLES OF GOOD GOVERNMENT

The topic of just and unjust war must be approached somewhat indirectly. To the extent that Confucius and Mencius evaluated the justice of warfare, it was by means of applying more general ideals regarding good government that have implications for evaluating the justice of warfare. Those ideals are meant to apply in the ideal world, but they are also relevant for the nonideal world. Even in the nonideal world of competing states marked by territorial boundaries, rulers should strive to meet those ideals, to the extent possible.

At a minimum, rulers should strive for peace (*an*, 安 or *ning* 寧). In an ideal world, Mencius suggests, the whole world (*tian xia*, 天下) would be unified and peaceful (1A.6; 2B12; see also *The Analects*, 14.42). One benevolent ruler would have obtained sovereignty over the whole world without having committed a single unjust deed (2A.2), and no one would be fighting for the sake of gaining territory. At that point, it makes sense to ask, "What need is there for war?" (7B.4, Lau).

In a world of competing states, however, it would be foolish for states to act on the assumption that wars are unnecessary. In the days of early Confucianism, several states were ruled by blood-thirsty tyrants ready and willing to use ruthless means to increase their territory, and this called for different prescriptions. In this nonideal world, Confucians held that smaller countries must prepare to defend themselves. This involves a well-trained army—as Confucius puts it, "To send to war a people that has not been properly taught is wasting them" (13.30, Leys; see also 13.29). Fortified boundaries are also essential—as noted above, Mencius urges the governor of a small state to "Dig deeper moats and build higher walls and defend them shoulder to shoulder with the people. If they would rather die than desert you, then all is not lost" (1B.13). Rulers of small states must get the people on their side, train them for self-defense, and fortify territorial boundaries. There is no other way to secure the peace.

Put negatively, boundaries between states would not be justified if they did not serve the value of peace. In his own day, Mencius lamented the fact that boundaries resulted from ruthless wars of conquest:

Mencius said, "The setting up of border posts in antiquity was to prevent violence. Today they are set up for the purpose of engaging in violence."[26] (7B.8, Dobson; see also 6B.9)

Peace, however, does not simply mean the absence of violence.[27] It also refers to a united world that is governed by benevolence (*ren*, 仁). In an ideal Confucian world, to repeat, one sage-king would rule peacefully over the whole world, without any coercion whatsoever. In a nonideal, multistate world, rulers should still strive to realize the ideal. Even small states can be governed by relatively benign rulers that display benevolence:[28]

> Mencius said, "A hegemon uses force under the pretext of violence. Such a one has no need of the rule of a major state. A True King is one who, practising benevolence, resorts only to virtue. Such a one has no need for a major state. Tang the Successful had a state of only seventy miles square, and King Wen a state of only a hundred miles square. (2A.3; Dobson, modified)

But the True King should not be satisfied with a small state. He should try to spread benevolence beyond his borders.[29] The appropriate means, to repeat, is moral power, not force:[30]

> Allegiance which is gained by the use of force is not allegiance of the heart— it is the allegiance which comes from imposing upon weakness. Allegiance which is gained by the exercise of moral power is true allegiance. It is the response of joy felt deeply in the heart. (2A.3, Dobson)

The aim is to attract as many people as possible, including those living in faraway lands:

> It is all a matter of practicing good government [putting benevolence into practice]. But if you were really to do so, then all within the four seas [the whole world] would raise their heads to watch for your coming, desiring you as their ruler. (3B.5, Lau, modified; see also *The Analects*, 13.16)

There are no restrictions—racial, ethnic, or other—to membership in the Confucian state, beyond adherence to benevolence. Everyone can, in principle, be "civilized" (see *The Analects*, 9.14, 15.10).[31]

The key to implementing these ideals of good government is a virtuous and capable ruler.[32] In an ideal world, once again, one virtuous ruler would govern the whole world. The ruler would achieve perfect virtue by observing the correct rites (*li*, 禮), his moral power would have a "civilizing" effect on the people, and there would be no need for coercive laws and regulations. As Confucius put it,

> The practice of benevolence comes down to this: tame the self and restore the rites. Tame the self and restore the rites for but one day, and the whole world will rally to your benevolence. (12.1; Leys, modified; see also Mencius, 2A.3)

In the real world, however, the people will not always be swayed by the personal virtue of the ruler. The ruler should do his best to rely on moral persuasion and exemplary virtue, but some people may not respond to virtue:

> The Master said: "The moral power of the Middle Way is supreme, and yet it is not commonly found in the people anymore." (6.29, Leys; see also 8.9)

Even perfect benevolence will not always be reciprocated: someone might well respond to the benevolence with bad treatment, at which point the exemplary person should conclude that his interlocutor is an "utter reprobate" (4B.28, Dobson). Not surprisingly, Confucius allowed for the use of legal punishments when other mechanisms for promoting moral behavior (and preventing immoral behavior) fail to do their work (12.13, 4.11).[33] Mencius concurred,[34] going so far as to justify the use of the death penalty for those who neglect elderly parents (6B.7; see also 1B.7 and 7A.12).[35]

More worrisome, some rulers in the nonideal, multistate world are positively wicked.[36] In fact, Mencius could not find a single virtuous ruler in his own day, though he seemed to recognize that some were better than others (see, e.g., 6B.7), and some rulers openly claimed to be open to positive influence (see, e.g., 1A.4). This helps to explain why Mencius, like Confucius himself, moved from state to state, hoping to find rulers receptive to his advice. Unfortunately, perhaps, this was not to happen in his lifetime.[37]

Other than manifesting virtue, the ideal ruler should also implement the right *policies*. In practice, this means securing the conditions for people's basic means of subsistence and intellectual/moral development. In the nonideal world, however, there may be conflicting obligations that need to be prioritized. According to the *Analects*, the obligation to secure the basic means of subsistence of the people should have priority:

> Ranyou drove the Master's carriage on a trip to Wei. The Master said: "What a huge population!" Ranyou said: "When the people are so numerous, what more can be done for them?" The Master said, "Make them prosperous." Ranyou asked, "When the people are prosperous, what more can be done for them?" The Master replied, "Educate them." (13.9; Ames and Rosemont, modified)

In the same vein, Mencius argued that there is no point promoting moral behavior if people are worried about their next meal: "The people will not have dependable feelings if they are without dependable means of support. Lacking dependable means of support, they will go astray and fall into excesses, stopping at nothing" (1A.7; Lau, modified).[38] Depriving the people of their means of support will lead to internal strife, and it will be impossible to secure the peace. At a minimum, then, the ruler striving for peace must ensure that the people are well fed.

MENCIUS ON JUST AND UNJUST WAR

Let us see how Mencius drew upon these ideals of good government to evaluate the justice of warfare. Mencius, to repeat, argued that rulers have an obligation to promote the peaceful unification the world. As a consequence, he was critical of rulers who launched bloody wars of conquest simply to increase their territory and engage in economic plunder—wars that were, unfortunately, all too common in his own day (see, e.g., 7B.8). He was also critical of "Machiavellian"[39] advisers who aimed to help rulers achieve their nefarious purposes:

> Mencius said, "Those who serve rulers today promise to enlarge their landholdings and enrich their treasuries and arsenals. They are called 'good ministers' but in antiquity they would have been called 'plunderers of the people.' To enrich a ruler who is neither attracted to the Way nor inclined towards benevolence is to enrich a Qie [an evil king]. Some promise to negotiate advantageous treaties for their ruler so that he will be successful in war. These, too, are called 'good ministers' but in antiquity they would have been called 'plunderers of the people.' To try to make a ruler strong in war who is neither attracted to the Way nor bent upon benevolence is to aid a Qie." (6B.9; Robson, modified)

This kind of advice cannot lead to the desirable consequence of a unified world: "No ruler today, pursuing the path they presently follow, without a change of practice, could rule the world for a single day, even supposing he were offered it" (ibid., modified).[40] Mencius suggests that wars of conquest cannot even lead to short-term victories, and that they are disastrous for all parties concerned, including the conqueror's loved ones:[41]

> Mencius said, "King Hui of Liang is the antithesis of benevolence. The man of benevolence brings upon the things he does not love the things he loves. But the man who is not benevolent brings upon the things he loves, the things he does not love." Gongsun Chou said, "What does that mean?" Mencius said, "King Hui of Liang ravished his own people for the sake of territory and went to war. When defeated, he tried again and fearing that he might not succeed he drove the son he loved to fight and his son was sacrificed. This is what I meant by 'bringing upon the things he loves, the things he does not love.'" (7B.1; Robson, modified; see also 1A.7)

An unjust war, in short, is a war that is launched for purposes other than peace and benevolence. In an ideal world—a unified world without any territorial boundaries ruled by a sage-king by means of moral power—all wars are unjust. In the nonideal world, however, some wars can be just. The first kind of just war approximates the modern idea of self-defense. If a small territory is ruled by a capable and virtuous ruler who seeks to promote peace and benevolence, and if that territory is attacked by an unjust would-be hegemon, then the ruler of that territory can justifiably mobilize the people for military action. As noted earlier, Mencius suggested that the leader of the small Teng state threatened by larger neighbors should "dig deeper moats and build higher walls and defend them shoulder to shoulder with the people. If they would rather die than desert you, then all is not lost" (Lau, 1B.13). This passage suggests that the people's support is crucial for successful warfare (see also 2B.1).[42] It also suggests the people can only be mobilized to fight if they are willing to fight, with the implication that conscription of a reluctant populace would not be effective. Even the ruler himself does not have an obligation to participate in wars of self-defense. In some situations, rulers, no matter how virtuous, will not be able to defend their state against the superior power of larger states, and Mencius does not counsel in favor of suicidal "last stands." Rather, he suggests that abdication is a perfectly legitimate choice:

> Duke Wen of Teng said to Mencius, "Teng is a small state. Though I make every effort to please the large states, I never manage to rid myself of the demands they make upon me. What should I do?" Mencius replied, "In antiquity, when King Tai lived in Pin, the Ti tribes invaded his territory. He offered them furs and silk but still could not get rid of them. He offered them horses and hounds but still could not get rid of them. He offered them pearls and jade but still could not get rid of them. Whereupon he gathered the elders of his people and told them, 'The Ti tribes want to take our land. I have heard it said, a True King does not allow the people to be harmed by interfering with the things upon which their livelihood depends. It will do you less harm to have no king [than to be deprived of your land]. I am going to leave this place.' He left Pin, crossed the Liang mountain, and built a city at the foot of Mount Qi and settled there. The people of Pin said, 'A man of benevolence indeed! We cannot do without him,' and they followed him, as if to a market." (1B.15; Dobson, modified)

The ruler of a small state can flee to a more hospitable environment and start anew, and if he is benevolent, at least some of the people will follow.[43]

The second kind of just war approximates the modern idea of humanitarian intervention—Mencius labels these wars "punitive expeditions" (*zheng*, 征). States can legitimately invade other states if the aim is to bring about global peace and benevolent government. Certain conditions, however, must be in place.[44] First, the "conquerors" must try to liberate people who are being oppressed by tyrants:

> Now the Prince of Yen cruelly mistreated his own people and Your Majesty set out on a punitive expedition. Yen's people thought you were saving them from "flood and fire" [i.e., from tyranny]. (1B.11; Lau, modified)[45]

In the nonideal world, the tyrants are not likely to go down without a fight, and moral power may not work with truly wicked oppressors. Mencius suggests that the liberation of people may require murdering the tyrant: "He killed the ruler and comforted the people, like the fall of timely rain, and the people greatly rejoiced" (1B.11; Lau, modified).[46] Just as people may justly kill their despotic rulers (1B.8), so leaders of punitive expeditions may justly kill tyrants in foreign lands, if need be.[47]

Second, the people must demonstrate, in concrete ways, the fact that they welcome their conquerors:

> When King Wu attacked Yin, he had over three hundred war chariots and three thousand warriors. He said, "Do not be afraid. I come to bring peace, I am not the enemy of the people." And the sound of the people knocking their heads on the ground was like the toppling of the mountain. (7B.4; Lau, modified; see also 1B.10, 1B.11, 3B.5)

However, the welcome must be long-lasting, not just immediate. The real challenge is to maintain support for the invading forces after the initial enthusiasm.[48] Even punitive expeditions that were initially justified can go bad, in which case the conquerors should pack up their bags (or, more precisely, their weapons) and leave:

> The people welcomed your army [which had just carried out a punitive expedition] with baskets of rice and bottles of drink. If you kill the old, bind the young, destroy the ancestral temples, and appropriate the ancestral vessels, how can you expect the people's approval? Even before this, the whole world was afraid of the power of Qi. Now you double your land without practicing benevolent government, this will provoke the whole world's armies. If you quickly release the captives, old and young, and stop taking their valuable vessels, set up a ruler in consultation with the people of Yen, and take your army out, all this talk of relief of Yen will then cease. (Lau; 1B.11, modified)

Third, punitive expeditions must be launched by rulers who are at least *potentially* virtuous. The ruler being addressed in the passage quoted above (1B.11) is obviously hypocritical. He was supposed to have liberated the people of Yen from tyranny, but instead he subjected them to more tyranny. However, one can assume that Mencius bothered to talk to such flawed rulers only because he believed that they contained the seeds of virtue within them, or at least that they had sufficient good sense to respond to practical, morally informed advice. In an earlier passage, the same ruler—King Xuan of Qi—is being scolded over and over again by Mencius, who exposes the gap between what he is doing and what he should be doing. King Xuan patiently listens, at one point saying,

"Instruct me clearly. Although I am not clever, please let me try to follow your advice" (1A.7; Lau, modified). Mencius may be encouraged by such comments, and he keeps on plugging away. He might not be expecting radical moral transformation on the scale of, say, Emperor Ashoka of India, who adopted and promulgated a tolerant and nonviolent form of Buddhism after several years of atrocious brutality, but Mencius does seem to hold out the hope of substantial moral progress.[49]

Fourth, the leader of justified punitive expeditions must have some moral claim to have the world's support. In his dialogue with the flawed King Xuan, Mencius points to the example (model) of a justified punitive expedition led by King Tang:

> The Book of History says, "In his punitive expeditions Tang began with Ge." The whole world was in sympathy with his cause. When he marched on the east, the western tribes complained. When he marched to the south, the northern tribes complained. They said, "Why does he not come to us first?" (1B.11; Lau, modified)

The ruler, in other words, must have the trust of the world. Without this trust, punitive expeditions should not be launched. With this trust, even rulers with bad track records may be regarded as potentially virtuous leaders who can bring peace to the world.

Of course, the claim to have the trust of the world should not be taken literally to mean that every single person supports the punitive expedition. If that were the case, the punitive expedition would be unnecessary, and the actually or potentially virtuous ruler could rely on moral power to spread good government. At least one person—the tyrant who needs to be punished or killed—will resist. In the nonideal world, there will be an element of uncertainty regarding the question of whether or not the virtuous ruler enjoys the world's support. It may only become clear in hindsight, when more facts are available and more balanced judgments can be made.[50]

For Mencius, in short, a defensive war is justified only if an actually or potentially virtuous and capable ruler (one who aims to provide peace and benevolent government), with the support of his people, must resort to violence to protect his territory against would-be conquering hegemons. An offensive war is justified only if it is led by an actually or potentially virtuous ruler who aims to punish oppressive rulers and bring about global peace. The "conquering" army must be welcomed by the "conquered" people, and if the welcome is not long-lasting, the conquering army should appoint a local leader in consultation with the conquered people and withdraw as soon as possible. The punitive expedition should only be launched if the conquering ruler can make a plausible claim to have the world's support.

IMPLICATIONS FOR CONTEMPORARY SOCIETIES

Needless to say, this ancient Confucian world is far removed from our own, and one has to be careful about drawing implications for contemporary states. But, as Benjamin Schwartz notes, this conglomeration of separate states and principalities "resembled the emerging multi-state system of fifteenth- and sixteenth-century Europe (more, in fact, than did the *polis* of ancient Greece). We even find the emergence of many of the concomitants of the multi-state system—including a rudimentary science of international politics and efforts to achieve collective security."[51] Arguably, the Warring States period also has more in common with the current global system than with imperial China, then held to be the empire (Middle Kingdom) at the center of the world. Ni Lexiong argues that the Spring and Autumn/Warring States period shares five common characteristics with the contemporary international state system: (1) there is no real social authority higher than the state; (2) the higher social authorities exist in form rather than substance (the Zhou Son of Heaven in the case of the pre-Qin system, the United Nations today); (3) national/state interest is the highest principle that trumps other considerations in cases of conflict; (4) the dominant principle in international relations is the "law of the jungle"; and (5) universal moral principles are invoked as pretexts for realizing state interests.[52] Thus, it should not be entirely surprising if at least some Confucian prescriptions on just and unjust war are held to be relevant for the contemporary world of sovereign states in an "anarchical" global system.[53]

This is not just a theoretical point. As mentioned, Mencius's views serve as a normative reference point for contemporary Chinese social critics opposed to wars of conquest.[54] They also serve to underpin judgments regarding just wars. For example, Gong Gang appeals to the distinction between wars of conquest and justified punitive expeditions to differentiate between recent wars in the Persian Gulf:

> Mencius said, "A hegemon uses force under the pretext of benevolence," "a true king uses virtue and benevolence," "The Spring and Autumn Annals acknowledged no just wars. There are only cases of some wars not being as bad as others. A punitive expedition refers to a higher authority attacking a lower one. Peers should not launch punitive expeditions against one another." It is very obvious. One can say that the First Gulf War is a just war authorized by the United Nations, similar to "a guilty duke corrected [punished] by the Son of Heaven." It is like a conflict with a "higher authority attacking a lower one." In this war [the 2003 invasion of Iraq], the United States says it is using force to exercise benevolence, that it is acting as both a true king and a hegemon. But the Second Gulf War is not the same, because

without the authorization of the United Nations, the United States and the United Kingdom are attacking an enemy state with vastly different [inferior] power and resources. In this war, the United States is using force under the pretext of benevolence, and it is also maintaining its geopolitical, national security, and economic interests in the name of promoting democracy in the Middle East; it is obviously acting as a global hegemon.[55]

The key difference between the two Gulf Wars is that the first had the stamp of approval from the "symbolic" global institution, the United Nations. While it was led by a "hegemon," the United Nations lent moral legitimacy to the war, just as Mencius suggests that punitive expeditions can be carried out by a ruler with the potential to be a "true king" who brings about global peace. In the messy and dangerous world of competing states, it may be difficult to determine who constitutes the "true king" until long after the fact (of war), but it may not be so difficult to rule out possibilities. The Bush administration's willful disregard of global legitimacy in the second Gulf War shows that it did not even make an effort to gain the trust of the world.[56] One condition—the need to liberate a country from an oppressive tyrant—may have been met,[57] but that is not sufficient, according to Mencian theory.

Still, one may ask, why not use the traditional Western (Christian or Jewish) theories of just and unjust war to make such judgments? These theories are also meant to be universal in scope and arguably continue to be relatively influential in the Western-dominated international system. A reply is that Mencius, and the ancient Chinese texts more generally, have been less willing to embrace what moderns would consider to be evil in the name of doing good. As Karen Turner explains,

[I]n the Chinese texts I have found no parallels with the Old Testament's justification for slaughtering wholesale the people of an enemy in a holy war. Nor are the Chinese texts as brutally pragmatic as Aquinas, who was willing to admit that women, children, and fruit trees should be spared from war, but that for crimes against God, an entire city or nation could be justly punished so as to deter other such crimes. The Chinese texts do not regard war as a remedy for the sins of ordinary people unlucky enough to serve an evil regime, but as a punishment for those particular leaders who lead their subjects astray with improper demands. Thus force should be directed only toward the rulers who made the decisions and not toward their subjects.[58]

In this sense, the Mencian theory of just and unjust war is more normatively appealing than the traditional Western just war theory.[59]

So why not use the modern, international language of human rights to make such judgments? Defenders of human rights, needless to say, would

not justify the massacre of civilians, no matter what the potential benefits. Michael Walzer, the most celebrated contemporary theorist of just
and unjust war, explicitly argues that human rights are at the foundation of wartime morality: "individual rights to (life and liberty) underlie
the most important judgments we make about war."[60] The obvious response is that the "we" does not typically include Chinese intellectuals
and policymakers. In the Chinese context, the language of human rights,
when it has been deployed to justify military intervention abroad, has
been tainted by its misuses in the international arena.[61] Given the history of colonial subjugation by Western powers, as well as the ongoing
conflicts over economic resources and geopolitical interests, the language of human rights is often seen as an ideology designed to rational-
ize policies of exploitation and regime change. Even where military
intervention in the name of human rights may have been justified—as,
arguably, in the case of NATO's war on behalf of the Kosovo Albanians—
it is difficult, if not impossible, to overcome Chinese skepticism regarding the "real" motives underlying intervention.[62]

This provides a practical reason for invoking Mencius's theory of just
and unjust war (in the Chinese context and other societies with a Confucian heritage, such as Korea). What ultimately matters is the *practice*
rather than the theory of human rights. So long as people are protected
from torture, genocide, starvation, and other such obvious harms, there
is no need to worry about the particular political and philosophical justifications.[63] That is to say that states and other collective agencies
should do their best to respect our basic humanity, but whether such
practices are backed by human rights morality is secondary. And if
Mencius's theory leads to the same judgments regarding the justice of
particular wars as theories of wartime morality founded on human
rights, then why not deploy his theory in the Chinese context?

Having said that, Mencius's theory will not always lead to the same
judgments as theories founded on human rights—but this may speak in
favor of Mencius's theory. One key difference between Walzer's view
and Mencius's view regards the value of membership in a particular political community. For Walzer, membership in a particular political
community is a fundamental human good and also helps to underpin
judgments regarding the justice of warfare. Part of the justification for
(moral) self-defense is that a common life exists among members of a political community, one founded on particular cultural ties (linguistic, religious, etc.). If a state is attacked and its members are challenged in
their lives and form of political association, then the state can justifiably
resort to force to defend its territory (so long as it does its best to secure
rights to life and liberty). Conversely, if there is no common life between
members of the state, there is no moral justification for self-defense.[64]

Those being attacked would be justified in fleeing abroad, and the state would not be justified in conscripting its citizens.

For Mencius, in contrast, there is no moral force attached to valuing one's particular culture or language or religion or distinctive form of political association,[65] and he would certainly reject the idea that valuing particular ties or exclusive forms of common life can justify the resort to armed force in the international arena. The moral justification for the use of armed force lies solely in its necessity to promote the values of peace and benevolence at home and abroad. These values are meant to have universal validity, and the ruler most likely to promote them has the most moral legitimacy and the right to engage in just warfare, if need be. That is why moral/political advisers should seek out such rulers and why common people will (and should) migrate to territories governed by them.[66]

From a contemporary normative standpoint, it could be argued that Mencius's view is more attractive. So many unjust wars have been fought in the name of preserving and promoting particular communities of character—ancestral homelands, ethnically pure states, linguistic communities—that any theory, such as Walzer's, allowing for the possibility of justified violence on behalf of this cause may be weakened beyond repair.[67] Imagine, say, a war of self-defense where a soldier must face the choice between surrender (with guaranteed migration to a peaceful and relatively wealthy country, but with the likely dilution of the family's cultural roots) and ferocious fighting (and the probable killing of civilians in the aggressor state). A modern-day Mencius would likely recommend the former, but for Walzer it would be a harder call.[68]

The problem may lie with Walzer's particular theory, rather than with Anglo-American theories of just war founded on human rights. Walzer himself recognizes that his defense of cultural membership as part of the justification of self-defense may be the outlying view: "most moral philosophers working in the Anglo-American tradition disagree with me precisely on the value of membership. Mine is the minority position, so if followers of Mencius also disagree, that doesn't distinguish them from Western philosophers."[69] Let me then point to one feature of the Mencian view that distinguishes it from most contemporary Western accounts of just warfare. For Mencius, as for Confucius, the government cannot secure the peace if its people are not well fed. Hence, the first obligation of government is to secure the basic means of subsistence of the people. By extension, the worst thing a government can do—the most serious violation of "human rights," so to speak—would be to deliberately deprive the people of the means of subsistence (by killing them, not feeding them, not dealing with a plague, etc.). A ruler who engages in such acts, for the Confucian, would noncontroversially be viewed as an oppressive tyrant, and punitive expeditions against such rulers would be justified (assuming that the other conditions for punitive expeditions have also been met). In contrast, the sorts of violations of civil and political rights that might be viewed as constituting tyranny by contemporary Western defenders of human rights, such as systematic denials of the right to free speech or the heavy-handed treatment of political dissenters in the name of social order, would not be viewed as human rights violations sufficiently serious as to justify humanitarian intervention by foreign powers.

Such differences in emphasis can influence judgments of just and unjust warfare in the contemporary world.[70] For Western defenders of human rights, Saddam Hussein was noncontroversially regarded as an oppressive tyrant because he engaged in the systematic violation of civil and political rights: liberal defenders of humanitarian intervention such as Michael Ignatieff and Thomas Friedman supported the invasion of Iraq largely on these grounds.[71] For Confucians, however, so long as the Iraqi people were not being deliberately deprived of the means of subsistence, the intervention could not be justified. The demand (in some liberal circles) that the United States should also consider "liberating" oppressed people in wealthy Saudi Arabia would be even less justified.

In other cases, however, Confucians may be more likely to support punitive expeditions compared to liberal defenders of humanitarian intervention. In cases of deliberately engineered famines, such as Afghanistan government's total road blockade on Kabul in 1996, the Confucian just war theorist would argue for foreign intervention (assuming, as always, that the other conditions for intervention have been met). In contrast, liberal human rights groups such as Amnesty International denounced the shooting and torture of a few victims as human rights violations and treated the manufactured starvation of thousands as background.[72] Similarly, if it is true that the North Korean government has been deliberately promoting policies that result in the starvation of millions of people, the Confucian would have emphasized the need for foreign intervention in North Korea rather than such countries as Iraq.[73]

It is worth asking how much of this matters in practice. Even if Confucian views inform the judgments of critical intellectuals in China, do these judgments really affect the political practices of the Chinese state? Confucian theorists of just war are likely to prove to be just as ineffective as moralizing theorists of human rights in the American context (perhaps even more so, if the society lacks a free press and other public forums for communicating criticisms). It is obvious, for example, that war against Taiwan if it declares formal independence would not meet the Confucian criteria for justifiable punitive expeditions:[74] so long as the Taiwanese government does not kill or starve its people, only moral power could be justifiably employed to bring Taiwan back into the Chinese orbit. But it seems just as obvious that Confucian objections are not likely to hold back the Chinese government in such an eventuality. So what exactly is the utility of Confucian theorizing on just warfare?

A historical perspective may provide some insight. One feature of imperial China was that it did not expand in ways comparable to Western imperial powers, even when it may have had the technical ability to do so. Instead, it established the tributary system, with the "Middle Kingdom" at the center and "peripheral" states on the outside. In this system, the tributary ruler or his representative had to go to China to pay homage in ritual acknowledgment of his vassal status. In return, China guaranteed security and provided economic benefits,[75] while using moral power to spread Confucian norms and allowing traditional ways of life and practices to flourish.[76] Needless to say, the practice often deviated from the ideal.[77] Still, the Confucian-Mencian discourse did help to stabilize the tributary system and curb the excesses of blood-thirsty warriors and greedy merchants.[78] There may be lessons for the future. As China once again establishes itself as an important global power, with the economic and military means to become a regional (or even global) hegemon, it will need to be constrained by more than realpolitik. More than any other discourse, Confucian theorizing on just and unjust warfare has the potential to play the role of constraining China's imperial ventures abroad, just as it did in the past. Put more positively, China would also have the power and the responsibility to carry out punitive expeditions in neighboring states (e.g., if an East Asian state began to carry out a Rwanda-style massacre of its population, China would face international pressure to intervene). The Confucian discourse could provide moral guidance in such cases.[79]

Deploying the Confucian views on just and unjust war as a critical tool to make judgments in history can also influence political actors. Consider, for example, the Great Leap Forward in the late 1950s, which was carried out under radical rural leadership with Mao's blessing. The ostensible goal was to increase rural productivity by means of organizing all of rural China into people's communes, but the actual "result was famine on a gigantic scale, a famine that claimed 20 million lives or more between 1959 and 1962."[80] The key point is the Mao Zedong can and should be held at least partly responsible for the famine. In July 1959 Army Marshal Peng Dehuai pointed out some of the Great Leap's problems at a conference for China's top leaders. Mao's response was to launch a personal denunciation of Peng, purge him from his post as minister of defense, and reassert disastrous policies that led to millions of deaths.[81] From a Confucian perspective, a punitive expedition would have been justified.[82] Of course, such intervention did not occur, but making these sorts of implications explicit can put tyrants on notice if they engage in policies that lead to famine.[83] It is hoped that rulers of the future will think twice before doing so.

Confucian theorizing can also have an impact below the highest levers of the state, particularly once the war is already under way. The torture of prisoners at Abu Ghraib in Iraq is a reminder that evil deeds in warfare are committed "unofficially," by soldiers acting without the explicit authority of the top commanders. Nonetheless, these soldiers took implicit cues from the top, which set the tone for a cavalier approach to the protection of prisoners' well-being. Here the Confucian emphasis on the moral quality of political and military leaders may be particularly relevant. In Imperial China, the idea that those carrying out the war should be benevolent informed the practice of appointing generals who were held to be exemplary persons with both moral character and military expertise.[84] One important reason for emphasizing the moral quality of commanders is that they set the moral example for other ordinary soldiers, and their moral power radiates down to lower levels: "under the wind, the grass must bend." If the aim is to sensitize soldiers to moral considerations, the leaders should not, as in Clausewitz's idea of the general, simply be concerned with the practical skills required for victory.

There are, in short, two main reasons for invoking Mencius's theory of just war. The first reason is psychological. If there is rough agreement on the aims of a theory of just war—that it should prohibit wars of conquest and justify certain kinds of wars of self-defense and humanitarian interventions—then one should invoke the theory that is most psychologically compelling to the people being addressed. In the Chinese context, and perhaps in other societies with a Confucian heritage, the theory of Mencius is most likely to have causal power. The comparison here is not just with theories of human rights, but with other Chinese thinkers such as Mozi and Xunzi who have also put forward theories functionally similar to modern theories of just war. Mencius is unambiguously viewed as a "good guy" by most contemporary Chinese, so there is no need to qualify or apologize for aspects of his theory.

The second reason is philosophical, and it speaks to the normative validity of Mencius's theory. Compared to alternative theories, Mencius's theory has several advantages, such as the focus on material well-being and the lack of emphasis on communal particularity as justifications for going to war. Mencius's theory can and should be taught in military academies, both in China and elsewhere. And critical intellectuals should draw upon Mencius's views to evaluate the justice of wars in the contemporary world. Of course, there is no reason to take Mencius's theory (or any other theory) of just war as the final word on the subject. One lacuna, for example, is the lack of detailed prescriptions for *jus in bello*. Besides arguing against the large-scale slaughter of civilians (7B.3), Mencius did not explicitly draw the implications of his views on just war for just conduct in war.[85] But it should be possible to do so within the broad confines of his theory.

NOTES

1. Ming Yongquan, "Youmeiyou zhengyi de zhanzheng? Yilun Rujia (wang ba zhi bian)" [Are There Just Wars? A Confucian Debate on True Kings and Hegemons] (http://www.arts.cuhk.hk/~hkshp, visited 11 October 2003).

2. As were Chinese language newspapers articles—see, e.g., Chen Zhe, "Cong xiang gin zhuzi de 'zhanzhengguan' jiedu jinri de Mei A zhi zhan" [Interpreting Today's American-Afghanistan War Using the War Concepts of Various Pre-Qin Thinkers], *Lianhe zaobao*, 11 October 2001.

3. This section draws on ideas initially expressed in my essay, "The Making and Unmaking of Boundaries," in *States, Nations, and Borders: The Ethics of Making Boundaries*, ed. Allen Buchanan and Margaret Moore (New York: Cambridge University Press, 2003), 58–62.

4. See chapter 4 of this book.

5. Communism here means a society where the coercive apparatus of the state would have "withered away" and social order is secured by noncoercive means. Beyond that, of course, there are many differences between the ideals of Marx and Confucius. For example, the Confucian ideal is supposed to have existed earlier so it is a matter of recovering the past, whereas communism is meant to lie in the future and can only be implemented once the productive forces provide the material basis for humans to be freed of the need to engage in drudge labor. Another key difference is that Confucian familism would place more informal constraints upon individual action compared to Marx's ideal.

6. I will argue that Confucians are not pacifists. Edmund Ryden argues that, more generally, "there is no basis in the Chinese tradition for pacifism." Ryden, *Just War and Pacifism: Chinese and Christian Perspectives in Dialogue* (Taipei: Taipei Ricci Institute, 2001), 46.

7. The translations of *The Analects of Confucius* are based on one of two translations (as indicated in the main text): Simon Leys's translation of *The Analects of Confucius* (New York: Norton, 1997), and Roger T. Ames and Henry Rosemont, Jr.'s translation of *The Analects of Confucius: A Philosophical Translation* (New York: Ballantine Books, 1998). Both these translations have been criticized for excessive extrapolations that seem to make Confucius into a proponent of modern liberalism, and I have occasionally modified the translations (as indicated in the main text with "modified").

8. The translations of Mencius are based on one of two translations (as indicated in the main text): W.A.C.H. Dobson's translation of *The Works of Mencius* (London: Oxford University Press, 1963), which is helpfully organized by themes; or D. C. Lau's complete translation of *Mencius* (Hong Kong: The

Chinese University Press, 1984), vols. 1 and 2, which includes the accompanying Chinese text. I have occasionally modified these translations (as indicated in the main text with "modified").

9. I use the male personal pronoun because Confucius and Mencius seemed to assume (without argument) that the ideal sage-king would be male. Having said that, Chan Sin Yee argues that Confucius and Mencius did not argue in favor of the biological inferiority of women (in contrast to Aristotle) and that the central values of Confucianism do allow in principle for the equal participation of women in education. See chapter 8 of this book as well as her essay "The Confucian Conception of Gender in the Twenty-First Century," *Confucianism for the Modern World*, ed. Daniel A. Bell and Hahm Chalbong (New York: Cambridge University Press, 2003).

10. This form of idealism also seemed absurdly utopian to Legalist critics of Confucianism in the Warring States era. As Han Fei Zi brilliantly put it, "Now if one says that we must wait for the worthiness of a Yao or a Shun [two sage-kings of the distant past] to bring order to the people of the current age, this is like saying that one should hold out for fine grain and meat in order to save oneself from starvation." Han Fei Zi, in *Readings in Classical Chinese Philosophy*, ed. Philip J. Ivanhoe and Bryan W. Van Norden (New York: Seven Bridges Press, 2001), 135. Sima Qian, China's Han dynasty grand historian, also heaped contempt upon Confucian idealists: "What then shall be said of those scholars of our time, blind to all great issues, and without any appreciation of relative values, who can only bark out their stale formulas about 'virtue' and 'civilization,' condemning the use of military weapons? They will surely bring our country to impotence and dishonor and the loss of her rightful heritage; or, at the very least, they will bring about invasion and rebellion, sacrifice of territory and general enfeeblement." Quoted in Yitzhak Shichor, "Military-Civilian Integration in China: Legacy and Policy," in *Civil-Military Relations, Nation-Building, and National Identity: Comparative Perspectives*, ed. Constantine P. Danopoulos, Dhirendra Vajpeyi, and Amir Bar-or (Westport, CT: Praeger, 2004), 85.

11. I say "quasi-anarchistic" because, unlike anarchists, Confucius and Mencius still saw the need for a political ruler to provide for order without coercion. It is worth noting that even Laozi is not, properly speaking, an anarchist because he allowed for the use of military weapons that, if necessary, must be used with "calm restraint" (*Daodejing*, 31 *zhang*).

12. The first Chinese dynasty was founded in 221 B.C.E. by the ruthless Emperor Qin, who relied on legalist principles that emphasized the use of harsh punishments and quasitotalitarian control of the whole population. Emperor Qin is notorious for ordering the live burial of Confucian scholars and their books. Imperial China only began to be "Confucianized" during the Han dynasty (206 B.C.E.–220 C.E.).

13. See Benjamin Schwartz, "The Chinese Perception of Order, Past and Present," in *The Chinese World Order: Traditional China's Foreign Relations*, ed. John K. Fairbank (Cambridge: Harvard University Press, 1968), 279.

14. The references to *zhongguo* (中国) in Mencius (e.g., 1A.7) refer to the geographical location of the central states in the Warring States era and not to their

moral status (i.e., these states were not viewed as the natural heirs of the Zhou dynasty, and there was no particular expectation that they would form the core of a unified empire).

15. Only one passage in *The Works of Mencius* deals with the question of the succession of sage-kings. Mencius notes that after sage-king Yao's death, his unsagelike son took over. But the people paid homage to Shun, and the sage-Shun assumed the "Mandate of Heaven," ruling for a further twenty-eight years (5A.5).

16. See 2B.13.

17. The third "founding father" of Confucianism—Xunzi (c. 310–219 B.C.E.)—more explicitly distinguishes between prescriptions for ideal regimes and those for nonideal ones (comparable to Aristotle's distinctions in the *Politics*)—see, e.g., Xunzi's distinctions between true kings (*wang*, 王), hegemons (*ba*, 霸), and pure opportunists (11.1a–11.2c), in decreasing order of goodness. Unlike Mencius, Xunzi does recognize that hegemons can be partly bad and partly good and he even suggests that power politics would be the right strategy to adopt by a ruler who is aware of his own incompetence and seeks out capable ministers (11.2c). In this essay, however, I focus primarily on Mencius and Confucius because Xunzi is a more controversial character who is "blamed" for being a major influence on Legalism. If it turns out that even the relatively "idealistic" Confucian thinkers seek to provide useful guidance for rulers in nonideal contexts, this would make the case for the practical relevance of Confucian theories of just and unjust war even more compelling.

18. For a more general presentation and analysis of Confucian military thought, see *Zhongguo Ruxue baike quanshu* [Encyclopedia of Confucianism in China] (Beijing: Zhongguo dabaike quanshu chubanshe, 1997), 185–93). It is interesting to note that the otherwise comprehensive English-language *RoutledgeCurzon Encyclopedia of Confucianism*, ed. Xinzhong Yao (London: RoutledgeCurzon, 2003), does not have an entry on Confucianism and War.

19. Once again, it would be easier to make the case by invoking Xunzi's military thought, with its greater willingness to embrace realpolitik (see, e.g., Book 15, "Debates on the Principles of Warfare"). My strategy, however, is to show that Confucius and Mencius also seem to allow for less-than-ideal solutions to dilemmas in nonideal contexts.

20. The same sort of reasoning leads contemporary anarchists such as Noam Chomsky to endorse the possibility that walls can have legitimate defensive purposes in the modern world (in the case of Israel, if it decided to build a security wall within its internationally recognized border, although he condemns Israel's current wall as an illegitimate attempt to isolate Palestinians and annex land on the West Bank). Chomsky, "A Wall as a Weapon," *The New York Times*, 23 February 2004, A25.

21. For example, Peter R. Moody, Jr., comments on Mencius's "strong—not to say obsessive—distinction between what is expedient (*li*) and what is right (*i*) [yi], and the conviction that when the right and the expedient conflict, the only valid standard of behavior is the right." Moody, "The Legalism of Han Fei-tzu and Its Affinities with Modern Political Thought," *International Philosophical*

Quarterly, vol. 19, no. 3 (September 1979), 321. In the nonideal world, however, Mencius does allow for less-than-ideal prescriptions.

22. Perhaps because they do not explicitly distinguish between Mencius's prescriptions for the ideal world and those appropriate for the nonideal world, even otherwise sympathetic scholars criticize Mencius for his "unrealistic" theories on warfare. See, e.g., Liang Wei Xian, *Mengzi yanjiu* [Research on Mencius] (Taipei: Wenjin chubanshe 1993), 71–72.

23. According to E. Bruce Brooks and Taeko A. Brooks, the real Confucius was in fact a warrior who had the misfortune to live at a time when his skills as a charioteer and bowman were becoming obsolete. Brooks and Brooks, *The Original Analects* (New York: Columbia University Press, 1998), 270–71. The myth of Confucius as a learned scholar only emerged after his death. This is a controversial interpretation, but if true it would lend even more support for the thesis that many of the prescriptions in the *Analects* were meant to apply in a nonideal context of competing states.

24. This Confucian idea that war should be considered nonideal, an unfortunate but occasionally necessary event stemming from difficult circumstances, may seem obvious today (if not always to politicians: Castro said that Khrushchev had "no cojones" [balls] for having averted war during the Cuban missile crisis William Taubman, *Khrushchev: The Man and His Era* [New York: W. W. Norton, 2003], 579); President George W. Bush praised Blair for having had the "cojones" to stand up to antiwar forces in the buildup to the invasion of Iraq; etc.) However, it contrasts with the historical glorification of warfare and the romantic model of the heroic soldier characterized in terms of boldness and masculinity that has been so prominent in Western societies. See, e.g., Kurtis Hagen, "A Chinese Critique on Western Ways of Warfare," *Asian Philosophy*, vol. 6, no. 3 (November 1996) (http://search.epnet.com/direct.asp?an =9702072810&db=aph, visited 12 January 2003), 3–7; see chapter 10 of this book for an account of the ancient Greek view that has contributed much to this view. The mainstream premodern Western view helps to explain why antiwar modernists like Benjamin Constant had to run through the list of prowar arguments in order to show that they had become obsolete. He summarizes his critique of the premodern view with the statement, "La guerre a perdu son charme, comme son utilité" [War has lost its charm as well as its utility]. Constant, *Ecrits Politiques*, ed. Marcel Gauchet (Paris: Gallimard, 1997). 132. There would be no need for a Chinese critic of warfare to argue against the view that war is "charming."

25. The philosophy of Mencius became the orthodoxy in imperial China from the Song onward, and still today he is "regarded as a fountainhead of inspiration by contemporary Neo-Confucian philosophers." Shu-hsien Liu, *Understanding Confucian Philosophy* (Westport, CT: Greenwood Press, 1988), 55.

26. This passage suggests that fixed territorial boundaries existed even in the Golden Days of Antiquity (for the purpose of preventing violence), which suggests once again that Mencius may not have been overly optimistic about the possibility of a borderless world governed by one ruler.

27. Li Ming Han, "Cong Ruxue de guandian kan heping wenti" [Looking at the Issue of Peace from a Confucian Perspective], in *Dangdai Ruxue fazhan zhi xin qiji* [Opportunities for the Development of Contemporary Confucianism], ed. Liu An Wu (Taipei: Wenjin chubanshe, 1997), 271.

28. What, one may ask, does *ren* (variously translated as benevolence, humanity, or love) mean? As one may expect, there have been volumes of debate on this question in the Confucian tradition. Confucius himself is (deliberately?) vague, though one passage does provide some insights:

> Zizhang asked Confucius about benevolence. The Master said: "Whoever could spread the five practices everywhere in the world would implement benevolence." "And what are these?" "Courtesy, tolerance, good faith, diligence, generosity. Courtesy wards off insults; tolerance wins over the many; good faith inspires the trust of others; diligence ensures success; generosity confers authority upon others." (17.6; Leys, modified)

29. Mencius, however, suggests that large states based on benevolence will find it easier to "spread the message" abroad: "Today, if a large state were to put into effect government based on benevolence, the rejoicing of the people would be that of a man saved from the gallows" (2A.1; Robson, modified).

30. If moral power fails, however, then armed force can be justified—see the discussion of punitive expeditions below.

31. See, e.g., Wu Junsheng, "Tianxia yijia guannian yu shijie heping" [The Concept of One Family under Heaven and World Peace], *Dongfang zazhi*, vol. 10, no. 8 (1977), 9.

32. In imperial China, of course, Confucian ideals of good government were made to depend on more than the quality of the ruler—such institutions as civil service examinations and censors were designed to help promote those ideals. Still, Confucians typically emphasized the moral quality of the ruler, and this concern continues to influence evaluation of rulers in East Asian societies with a Confucian heritage to a greater extent than would be the case in most Western societies. In Korea, for example, it is quite likely that a publicly exposed liar such as Bill Clinton would have lost the "Mandate of Heaven" (that is, the moral right to rule) and been forced to resign.

33. See the discussion in Joseph Chan, "A Confucian Perspective on Human Rights for Contemporary China," in *The East Asian Challenge for Human Rights*, ed. Joanne R. Bauer and Daniel A. Bell (New York: Cambridge University Press, 1999), 226–27.

34. Even in an ideal state, Mencius suggests, the True King will *lighten* (but not eliminate) the penal code (1A.5). In another passage, Mencius says that "when worthy men are in positions of authority . . . its policies and laws will be made clear to all (2A.4; Dobson). The aim seems to be transparency, not the abolition of punitive laws.

35. Confucius also seemed to endorse the death penalty, though not as a first resort: "To impose the death penalty without first attempting to reform is cruel" (20.2; Lau).

36. Later Confucian thinkers—most notably, Huang Zongxi—explicitly drew the implication that there is a need for institutional checks on the ruler's

power. See Wm. Theodore de Bary, *Asian Values and Human Rights: A Confucian Communitarian Perspective* (Cambridge: Harvard University Press, 1998), chap. 6.

37. Confucius himself did not find any rulers receptive to his ideas about good government, and while Mencius had slightly more success—he served briefly as minister in the state of Qi—he soon became disenchanted with political life and reluctantly settled for a teaching career.

38. Mencius also provided concrete guidance for implementation of the "right to food": see the discussion in my book *Beyond Liberal Democracy: Political Thinking for an East Asian Context* (Princeton: Princeton University Press, 2006), chapter 9.

39. I employ this term because it has come to refer to realpolitik in the English language, though it would be more precise to refer to proto-Legalist advisers, who outdid Machiavelli himself in their "Machiavellianism" (see chapter 8 of *Beyond Liberal Democracy*).

40. This prediction, arguably, was proven wrong when the ruthless Qin emperor unified "China" (what was then considered to be the world) using Legalist methods. Perhaps Mencius's claim that the world could not be held for a single day was not meant to be taken too literally, and the fact that this dynasty proved to be relatively short-lived (at least partly due to excessive brutality and consequent unpopularity, according to the standard account) could then be used to support Mencius's point.

41. Mencius's supposed ideological opponent, Mo Zi, also argued that wars of aggression are bad not just for the defeated state but also for the aggressor state that experiences enormous human wastage and economic loss (see R. James Ferguson, "Inclusive Strategies for Restraining Aggression—Lessons from Classical Chinese Culture," *Asian Philosophy,* vol. 8, no. 1 (March 1998) (http://search.epnet.com/direct.asp?an=2752805&db=aph), 4.).

42. An essay by two high-ranking members of the People's Liberation Army specifically invokes Mencius as part of the philosophical basis for the Chinese military tradition's emphasis on the human factor (in contrast to the Western emphasis on the "weapon factor"), as in Mao's dictum that "Human beings are the most precious in the world. So as long as we have human resource [*sic*], we can work out whatever miracles in the world." Zhang Junbo and Yao Yunzhu, "Differences between Traditional Chinese and Western Military Thinking and Their Philosophical Roots," *Journal of Contemporary China*, vol. 5, no. 1 (July 1996). (http://search.epnet.com/direct.asp?an=9608225143&db=aph, visited 1 December 2003), 10, 5.

43. Mencius's example points to the relative ease of migration between states in the preimperial era. As Zhao Tingyang notes, the "free immigration policy" may help to explain why the Spring and Autumn and Warring States periods were culturally active and creative times in what came to be known as Chinese history: states had to develop their cultural appeal so as to attract people. Zhao Tingyang, "A Philosophical Analysis of World/Empire in Terms of All-under-Heaven," ms. on file with author, 12.

44. Mencius probably had the Warring States context of his own day in mind, and his aim may not have been to present and defend these conditions as

universal principles (in contrast to the moral imperative to pursue peace and benevolence that is clearly meant to be universal; I thank Chan-Liang Wu for alerting me to this distinction). In the final section of this chapter, I will argue that the Warring States era shares important similarities with our own international context, so there may be something to learn from prescriptions meant for that era.

45. This passage implies that it would have been legitimate to punish a ruler who cruelly mistreats his own people, though in this case the ruler being addressed (criticized) by Mencius wear on to mistreat the people being "liberated."

46. Lau translates the character *zhu* (誅) as "punished," but it can (more controversially, perhaps) refer to justified killing. In any case, the tyrant would not likely be "punished" with velvet gloves, and since Mencius allows for regicide by common people it would be odd for him to rule out the possibility that leaders of justified punitive expeditions could kill tyrants in the lands being liberated, if need be.

47. As Julia Ching and Philip J. Ivanhoe argue, the imperative to liberate an oppressed people does impose certain constraints on what can be done in the name of liberation: most obviously, the conquering army cannot use weapons of mass destruction that would cause large-scale slaughter in the name of liberating an oppressed people. See Julia Ching, "Confucianism and Weapons of Mass Destruction," and Philip J. Ivanhoe, " 'Heaven's Mandate' and the Concept of War in Early Confucianism," both in *Ethics and Weapons of Mass Destruction: Religious and Secular Perspectives*, ed. Sohail H. Hashmi and Steven P. Lee (New York: Cambridge University Press, 2004). In between justified killing of an evil ruler and unjustified large-scale slaughter, however, there will likely be some contestable practices in any punitive expedition.

48. As Xunzi put it, "To annex lands and population is easily done; it is the consolidation of a firm hold on them that is difficult." *Xunzi: A Translation and Study of the Complete Works*, trans. John Knoblock (Stanford: Stanford University Press, 1990), vol. 2, 15.6b, 234.

49. Confucius, in contrast, seems less concerned with the potential virtue of the ruler. He reports that Guan Zhong became minister of a "murderer" and then succeeded in imposing "his authority over all the states and set the entire world in order; to this very day, the people still reap the benefits of his initiatives" (14.17; Leys). This passage leaves open the possibility that good ministers are sufficient to produce good results for the people, even if the ruler himself does not morally improve.

50. See Mary I. Bockover, "The *Ren-Dao* of Confucius: A Spiritual Account of Humanity," paper presented at the 2004 annual conference of the Society for Asian and Comparative Philosophy (Asilomar, California, 20–23 June 2004), 16–17.

51. Benjamin Schwartz, "The Chinese Perception of World Order, Past and Present," 278–79. See also Victoria Tin-Bor Hui, "The Emergence and Demise of Nascent Constitutional Rights: Comparing Ancient China and Early Modern Europe," *The Journal of Political Philosophy*, vol. 9, no. 4 (2001), 374, 401.

52. See chapter 10 of this book.

53. There is, however, one important disanalogy between the Warring States era and the current international system. As discussed in chapter 5 of my book *Beyond Liberal Democracy*, large states in the Warring States era did adhere to the long-term ideal of a world government. In contrast, the international system of sovereign states is now widely held to be a permanent condition (at least since the collapse of missionary communism).

54. It does not necessarily follow, however, that moral opposition to the global hegemon necessarily leads to opposition to particular wars of conquest. One well-connected Chinese friend of mine privately welcomed the U.S. invasion of Iraq (before it occurred) because he anticipated that it would stretch U.S. military capacities and would leave the country less able to pursue its hegemonic policies in East Asia (e.g., less willing to defend Taiwan in the event of a conflict with the mainland).

55. Gong Gang, "Shei shi quanqiu lunli de daidao shiwei" [Who is the armed Guard of Global Ethics?], *Nan feng chuang*, September 2003 (http://www.nfcmag.com/news/newsdisp.php3?NewsId=296&mod=, visited 10 November 2001).

56. Even the "coalition of the willing" was composed of several countries like Italy and Spain where the large majority of citizens opposed the invasion of Iraq without U.N. support.

57. As argued below, however, Confucians and Western defenders of human rights may disagree over what constitutes tyranny.

58. Karen Turner, "War, Punishment, and the Law of Nature in Early Chinese Concepts of the State," *Harvard Journal of Asiatic Studies*, vol. 53, no. 2 (December 1993), 304–5. See also John K. Fairbank, "Introduction: Varieties of the Chinese Military Experience," in *Chinese Ways in Warfare*, ed. Frank A. Kierman, Jr., and John K. Fairbank (Cambridge: Harvard University Press, 1974), 7.

59. Of course, Mencius's theory can be misused, like any other theory. It could be argued that the act of focusing on rulers rather than the people when thinking about just war can make people in the aggressor state think of war as some sort of police action against one bad man, not as a real war that hurts many real people. Arguably, that is part of what the Bush administration did in order to convince so many Americans that war in Iraq was justified: the administration talked about bringing Saddam Hussein to justice, but it down-played the fact that a military campaign would likely kill thousands of Iraqi soldiers and civilians. I thank Steve Geisz for this point.

60. Michael Walzer, *Just and Unjust Wars: A Moral Argument with Historical Illustrations*, 3rd ed. (New York: Basic Books, 2000), 54. Walzer does not, however, construct a philosophical argument in favor of human rights ("How these rights are themselves founded I cannot try to explain here"), so his only argument in favor of using the language of human rights is practical (and therefore it can be defeated by competing practical considerations, as in the case of what may be relatively effective Mencius-inspired arguments for just and unjust war in the Chinese context).

61. As a matter of domestic policy, however, the language of human rights is much better received in China, by critics of the regime as well as official government circles. See my review essay, "Human Rights and Social Criticism in Contemporary Chinese Political Theory," *Political Theory*, vol. 32, no. 3 (June 2004), 396–408.

62. Of course, the (accidental?) bombing of the Chinese embassy in Belgrade sealed the matter in the eyes of (most?) Chinese. I personally experienced the reaction in Hong Kong. The one time I was truly made to feel like an outsider among otherwise sympathetic mainland Chinese friends and family members was when I argued that the war against Serbia was still justified, even after the bombing. I rapidly learned to keep my views to myself, in the interest of maintaining harmony with loved ones!

63. For a similar view, see Charles Taylor, "Conditions of an Unforced Consensus on Human Rights," in *The East Asian Challenge for Human Rights*, ed. Joanne R. Bauer and Daniel A. Bell (New York: Cambridge University Press, 1999).

64. Walzer, *Just and Unjust Wars*, 54.

65. These possibilities are not explicitly mentioned in early Confucianism, though passages in Confucius and Mencius do seem to allow for some sort of pluralism. Confucius famously said: "The exemplary person seeks harmony rather than conformity, the petty person seeks conformity rather than harmony" (13.23). Regarding attachment to particular tracts of land, Mencius does suggest that land may have value and that people can justifiably fight back attempts to conquer their land (1B.15), but the context of the passage suggests that abdication is a better option. (Mencius discusses the option of abdication first and in more detail, and the fighting for land option is presented as somebody else's view, i.e., "people say that . . . ," suggesting some skepticism.) In any case, the value of land for Mencius lies primarily in its importance for people's livelihoods, not in its sentimental value. (Confucius is more straightforward in condemning sentimental attachment to land: "The master said, "Exemplary persons cherish their virtue; petty persons cherish their land"; 4.11; Ames and Rosemont, modified; see also 14.2.) If land elsewhere can yield better harvests and those harvests are more likely to be distributed fairly (e.g., the well-field system), then it would be better to go there in the event of an attack (assuming this is a realistic option). Fan Ruiping has noted that Confucian Chinese have manifested attachment to their homeland because they prefer to be buried near their ancestral tombs (e-mail communication, 11 March 2004), but one cannot draw the implication (from the works of Mencius or Confucius) that people can fight for their homeland in part because they want to be buried near their ancestors.

66. If the economic conditions are satisfactory and the benefits fairly distributed (i.e., the well-field system is in place), however, Mencius did seem to justify curbs on the freedom of movement (see 3A.3).

67. My own view is that cultural particularity matters from a moral point of view and can justify such particularistic policies as welfare benefits for fellow citizens (even if more "bang for the buck" can be achieved by, say, using those

funds to help the needy poor in distant lands), but I would draw the line at (before) allowing for violence on behalf of cultural particularity. This intuition may stem from my experience as a Canadian communitarian (an Israeli communitarian is more likely to be sympathetic to Walzer's view), and it would, admittedly, need to be developed.

68. Walzer has controversially defended Britain's policy of terror bombing of German cities in the early (but not later) days of World War II on the grounds that "no other decision seemed possible if there was to be any sort of military offensive against Nazi Germany." Walzer, *Just and Unjust Wars*, 258. In a later work, Walzer further spells out his doctrine of "supreme emergency," which tries to provide a justification for overriding the rights of innocent people if such immoral acts are necessary to save the community from communal death. Walzer, *Arguing about War* (New Haven: Yale University Press, 2004), chap. 3.

69. E-mail communication from Michael Walzer, 10 March 2004.

70. I do not mean to deny that there are also "easy cases" where Confucians and Western defenders of humanitarian intervention would converge on the same judgment. If the government carries out or facilitates the massacre of large sectors of its own population (e.g., the Nazi Holocaust, the Rwanda genocide), then both would justify intervention by foreign powers.

71. It is worth noting that Walzer himself opposed the invasion because he argued that the Iraqi threat was not imminent and the U.N. inspectors should have been given more time (see Walzer, *Arguing about War*, 143–51).

72. In response to such cases of apparently misguided priorities. Amnesty has expanded its mission to include economic and social rights: see chapter 4 of my book *Beyond Liberal Democracy*.

73. Given the likely civilian casualties, however, Confucian critics would likely emphasize other means of opposition, such as remonstrance or targeted killing of the North Korean leaders responsible for the famine.

74. The Confucian would also condemn Taiwan's ethnically motivated proindependence movement because of the Confucian presumption in favor of unity and the lack of value placed upon cultural particularity. But would Taiwan be justified in defending itself if attacked by the mainland? For the Confucian, the judgment would depend partly on the moral character of the Taiwanese ruler, the degree of popular support in Taiwan for that leader, and the likely consequences of other options such as surrender (not so bad if the Chinese Army withdraws soon after invasion and the Chinese government restores the *status quo ante*).

75. See John K. Fairbank and Ssu-Yu Teng, "On the Ch'ing Tributary System," in *Ch'ing Administration: Three Studies*, ed. John K. Fairbank and Ssu-Yu Teng (Cambridge: Harvard University Press, 1960), 112–13.

76. See Immanuel C. Y. Hsu, *China's Entrance into the Family of Nations* (Cambridge: Harvard University Press, 1960), 8–9.

77. See, e.g., Alasdair Ian Johnston, *Cultural Realism: Strategic Culture and Grand Strategy in Chinese History* (Princeton: Princeton University Press, 1995). Johnston focuses on the Ming dynasty's grand strategy against the Mongols, and he is struck by "the prevalence of assumptions and decision axioms

that in fact placed a high degree of value on the use of pure violence to resolve security conflicts" (xi). This example may not be typical, however.

78. See Cho-yun Hsu, "Applying Confucian Ethics in International Relations," *Ethics and International Affairs*, vol. 5 (1991).

79. It could also be argued that moral considerations will play a greater role than they did in the past. Given the growth of worldwide trade, it is possible that fewer wars will be fought for economic reasons (if it is easier to buy scarce resources, there may be less of a need to fight for them), and more wars fought for moral reasons. I thank Mao Yushi for this point.

80. Jonathan D. Spence, *The Search for Modern China* (London: Hutchinson, 1990), 583.

81. Mao could also have taken note of the criticism by Nikita Khrushchev (then Soviet leader) of the new Chinese communes. Instead, Mao attacked Peng Dehuai as a traitor allied with Khrushchev (Taubman, *Khrushchev*, 392).

82. Assuming, once again, that the other criteria for punitive expeditions have been met. Given the likely civilian casualties (and opposition to such intervention among ordinary Chinese), such criteria would not likely have been met during the Great Leap Forward. However, less extreme means of punishing rulers, such as "smart sanctions" against state leaders and prohibiting travel, could less controversially have been invoked.

83. Mao himself was well versed in the Confucian tradition and may have been aware of Mencian views on justified violence against rulers, which may help to explain why he turned against Confucianism and affirmed Legalism during the Cultural Revolution. Some rulers in imperial China obviously felt threatened by Mencian ideas regarding justified violence: for example, the founder of the Ming dynasty, Emperor Hong Wu (1368–98), commissioned a special board of scholars to excise passages from Mencius that implied a lack of devotion to the ruler, with the result that eighty-five passages were deleted (see Ivanhoe, "'Heaven's Mandate'"). In Tokugawa Japan, Mencian ideas inspired rebels to rebellion or martyrdom against the ruling regime, though they were also used to support the authorities on other occasions. John Tucker, "Two Mencian Political Notions in Tokugawa Japan," *Philosophy East and West*, vol. 47, no. 2 (August 1997).

84. See Hagen, "A Chinese Critique on Western Ways of Warfare," 2, 12.

85. Perhaps because Mencius felt that war is so distasteful, even when it is necessary, he was unwilling to think through in great detail the implications of going to war. In contrast, the more hardnosed Xunzi did go into detail, and he proposed moral guidelines meant to apply once "the drum is sounded" similar to those of contemporary theorists of just warfare, such as not executing prisoners or engaging in the massacre of defenders of a city (see *Xunzi*, trans. Knoblock, 15.1f, 226–27). The actual practice of dealing with the enemy during the Warring States period occasionally went beyond contemporary notions of justice in warfare, such as supplying meat to invaders and adversaries in hot pursuit. Frank A. Kierman, Jr., "Phases and Modes of Combat in Early China," in *Chinese Ways of Warfare*, ed. Frank A. Kierman, Jr., and John K. Fairbank (Cambridge: Harvard University Press, 1974), 37. Julia Ching notes that such

practices also made military sense: "a time honored practice was to extend extreme courtesy and generosity to the enemy—capturing and imprisoning them during the fight, but releasing them soon afterward, showered with gifts and kindnesses. The reason? To decrease their will to fight or their desire for vengeance." Ching, "Confucianism and Weapons of Mass Destruction," in *Ethics and Weapons of Mass Destruction: Religious and Secular Perspectives*, ed. Sohail H. Hashimi and Steven P. Lee (New York: Cambridge University Press, 2004), 11, 28.

CONTRIBUTORS

DANIEL A. BELL is professor of political philosophy and ethics in the department of philosophy at Tsinghua University, Beijing. He is the author of *Beyond Liberal Democracy: Political Thinking for an East Asian Context; East Meets West: Human Rights and Democracy in East Asia;* and *Communitarianism and Its Critics.* He is also the coeditor of six other books in political theory and Asian Studies.

JOSEPH CHAN is professor in the department of politics and public administration at the University of Hong Kong. His current research focuses on Confucian political philosophy, theory and practice of human rights, and liberalism and perfectionism. He has published articles on these topics in major journals, including *Ethics, Oxford Journal of Legal Studies, Journal of Democracy, Philosophy and Public Affairs,* and *Philosophy East and West.*

SIN YEE CHAN is associate professor of philosophy at the University of Vermont. She has published articles on Chinese philosophy, feminism, and ethics of the emotions, in several journals, including the *Journal of Chinese Philosophy, Social Theory and Practice, Philosophy: East and West,* and *Asian Philosophy.* She also contributed a chapter on Confucian-role Ethics in *Constructing China* (eds. Kenneth Lieberthal, Shuen-fu Lin, and Ernest Young).

CHENYANG LI is professor and chair of the department of philosophy at Central Washington University. He is the author of *The Tao Encounters the West* and numerous journal articles and book chapters. He is also the editor of *The Sage and the Second Sex: Confucianism, Ethics, and Gender.* His research interests include Chinese philosophy and comparative philosophy. Currently he is writing a book on the Confucian ideal of harmony.

RICHARD MADSEN is professor and chair of the department of sociology at the University of California, San Diego and a coauthor (with Robert Bellah et al.) of *Habits of the Heart,* which received the *Los Angeles Times* Book Award and was jury nominated for the Pulitzer Prize. He is the author of *Morality and Power in a Chinese Village,* for which he received the C. Wright Mills Award; *China's Catholics: Tragedy and Hope in an Emerging Civil Society;* and *China and the American Dream.* He also coedited (with Tracy B. Strong) *The Many and the One: Ethical Pluralism in the Modern World.*

NI LEXIONG is professor in the department of politics at the Shanghai University of Political Science and Law. His books include the Chinese language works *Seeking the Enemy: Reflections on War Culture and International Military Problems; War and Cultural Traditions: Further Reflections on History;* and *Devising Strategy within a Command Tent and Determining the Victory: A Commentary on the Decisive Battle of World War Two.*

PETER NOSCO is professor of Asian Studies and head of the department at the University of British Columbia. A specialist in the intellectual and social history of early modern Japan, he is the author of *Remembering Paradise: Nativism and Nostalgia in 18th Century Japan* and the editor of *Confucianism and Tokugawa Culture* and *Japanese Identity: Cultural Analyses.* He has also been a guest editor of the *Japanese Journal of Religious Studies* and *Philosophy: East and West.*

MICHAEL NYLAN is professor of history at the University of California, Berkeley. A specialist in the classical period in China (Warring States through Wei-Jin), she is the author of four books, including *The Shifting Center; The Canon of Supreme Mystery; Constructing the 'Confucian' Classics;* and *Recarving China's Past.* She has also published numerous articles on topics as disparate as Sichuan archeology, pleasure theory, gender, and rhetoric.

HENRY ROSEMONT, JR. has published ten books, including *A Chinese Mirror* and *Rationality and Religious Experience.* With Daniel J. Cook he has edited and translated *Leibniz: Writings on China,* and with Roger T. Ames, *The Analects of Confucius: A Philosophical Translation.* He is Distinguished Visiting Professor of East Asian and Religious Studies at Brown University and Senior Consulting Professor at Fudan University in Shanghai.

LEE H. YEARLEY is the Walter Y. Evans-Wentz Professor of Oriental Philosophies, Religion, and Ethics at Stanford University. A specialist in comparative ethics, he is the author of *Mencius and Aquinas: Theories of Virtue and Conceptions of Courage* and *The Ideas of Newman: Christianity and Religiosity,* as well as numerous journal articles and chapters in fourteen books. His special interests include the comparative study of both the religious dimensions of ethical perspectives and the different forms in which ethics is presented in China and the West.

INDEX

absolutism, 90–91, 114
Abu Ghraib, 244
academies, private, 22, 26–28, 32, 39
affection, and *ren*, 177, 183. *See also* love
Afghanistan, 226, 242
agriculture, 10, 36, 129, 201, 202, 216, 217, 224n55
Alexander the Great, 218
alienation, 95
altruism, 130, 177
Ames, Roger, 148, 172n37
Amnesty International, 242
amorality, 48
Analects of Confucius: authorship of, 170n7; and civil society, 21; community in, 253n65; conflict in, 40; education in, 139; elitism *vs.* egalitarianism in, 34; filial piety in, 31; as fundamental text, 63; gender in, 148, 149, 150, 154; government in, 37; ideal social order in, 74–75; love in, 184; loyalty to family *vs.* state in, 52; nonideal political world in, 230; obedience in, 25; political unity in, 72; questions undeveloped in, 113; reciprocity in, 181; rectification of names in, 29–30, 50; *ren* in, 64, 117–18, 177, 178, 179, 180, 184; sage as ruler in, 229; and Spring and Autumn period, 228; voluntary associations in, 49; and Warring States period, 228; women in, 128, 188. *See also* Confucius
anarchism, 3, 228, 247n20
ancestors, 22, 90, 100n9, 102n19
Aquinas, Thomas, 239
argumentation, 123, 142–43
Aristotle, 69–70, 114, 128, 166, 207, 246n9, 247n17
artisans, 36
Athens, ancient, 69, 190
authoritarianism, 4, 7–8, 21, 53, 115
authority, 30, 127–28, 203, 208, 238
autonomy: and body, 88, 90–91, 98; and coercion, 135n1; individual, 34, 47, 49, 51, 53, 54, 55; in Mencius, 143; modern concept of, 115; of self, 20; and suicide, 130–31; Western, 143. *See also* freedom

Bai Hu Tong, 187
barbarians, 67, 75–76, 77, 79, 80, 87–88, 99n6, 207
being *vs.* doing, 51
benefactor-beneficiary relationship, 29, 30, 52–53, 54
benevolence *(ren):* and barbarians, 76; and coercion, 124; and death and dying, 131; diverse ways of realizing, 79; and family, 64; in family and public sphere, 168; and harmonious political order, 227; Mencius on, 72–74; of rulers, 36–37, 72–73, 118, 228, 231, 232, 234, 235; and suicide, 130; and war, 206, 209, 210, 211, 212, 214, 216–17, 218, 231–32, 234, 235, 241, 244. *See also ren*
Bible, 239
Biographies of Virtuous Women, 155
Black, Alison, 148, 152, 155, 162
Blair, Tony, 248n24
blood, circulation of, 91, 95
Board of Censors, 38
body, physical, 88, 90–91, 93, 95
Book of Changes (Yi-Jing), 134, 147
Book of Documents, 95, 96
Book of History, 210
Book of Odes, 95, 127–28, 150, 154
Book of Rites, 95, 97, 116, 133, 134, 149, 150, 151, 172n42
Brill, Alida, 43n6
Brodie, Bernard, 223n54
Brooks, Bruce, 170n7, 248n23
Brooks, Taeko, 170n7, 248n23
brother-in-law, 150
brothers/brotherhood: and barbarians, 88; and deference, 159, 161; and elective relationships, 29; and morality, 35; and *ren,* 64, 184; and ritual, 116; social extension of, 65; and society, 64; stability from, 118. *See also* siblings

Buddhism, 4, 21, 23, 25, 42n3, 48, 86, 88, 100n8, 114
Bush, George W., 248n24
Bush administration, 239

Cai Renhou, 162
capital city, 96
capitalism, 98, 114
care: as core concept, 114; equal, 184; and family, 81, 185, 192; feminist, 175–93, 193n2; with gradations, 184–86; and morality, 185; and motivational displacement, 181; in parent-child relationship, 11; and *ren*, 117, 178–79; and responsibility, 179; and rules, 181–82; and space, 95; for strangers, 81; ways of expressing, 121. *See also* compassion; sympathy
Castro, Fidel, 248n24
censorship, 28, 39, 123
Chan Sin Yee, 128, 246n9
charisma, 89–94
chastity, 172n36
Chen Chengzi, 208
Cheng Hao, 195n33
children: and civil society, 14; and gender, 151–52; love for, 118; and marriage, 134–35; and mother, 176; and women, 162, 166. *See also* father-son relationship; filial piety; parent-child relationship; son
China: central regions of, 67, 71, 75, 79; as global power, 243; imperial, 243; and marriage, 134; modernization of, 114; Neo-Confucianism in, 21; petition for redress in, 37–38; and political unification, 78; politics in contemporary, 76–77; revival of Confucianism in, viii–ix; and Taiwan, 242–43; and territorial boundaries, 62; trust in government in, 41–42; unification of, 228
Chinese characters, 42n3
Chinese identity, 76, 99n6
Ching, Julia, 251n47, 255n85
Chomsky, Noam, 247n20
Christianity, 86, 88, 100n8, 190, 239
citizens, 14, 25, 36, 37–38, 50, 51, 69. *See also* people; subject(s)
citizenship, 29, 35–39, 127–29, 168
civil, terms for, 3

civility, 10, 14
civil service, 22, 91
civil service examinations, 22, 77, 129. *See also* education
civil society, 3–16, 20–42, 46–55; in Europe, 20, 26; and family, 6–7, 20; importance of, 9–12; and individual autonomy, 47; as liability, 29–33, 50–51; need for, 23–27, 49–50; in North America, 20; and private *vs.* public spheres, 5, 6, 12, 21, 25; risks of, 12–14; and social roles, 14, 15, 16; and state, 20, 23–27, 29–33, 49; terms for, 3
clan, 23, 49, 96. *See also* family
class, 26, 86, 129
classicists, 86
Classic of Filial Piety, 8
Classic of Filial Piety for Women, 8
Clausewitz, Karl Von, *On War,* 219
coercion: and autonomy, 135n1; avoidance of, 124–26, 227; and benevolent rule, 232; dislike of, 123; and law, 124, 204; and morality, 124, 125; and persuasion, 123; and sexuality, 133–34. *See also* punishment; war
commerce, 21
commiseration, 158. *See also* sympathy
commodification, 25
communications, 25, 27
communism, 77, 78, 80
community: co-membership in, 47; commitment to, 10; in Confucius, 253n65; and empire, 97–98; and morality, 15; political, 61, 62, 70–71, 74–75, 80, 240–41; power of unified, 93; rites as joining, 91; and self-development, 23; shared possessions of, 93; and spatial schemas, 95; as suspect, 53. *See also* political community
community organizations, 11
compassion, 74, 75, 79, 131, 132, 133, 177, 178. *See also* care; *ren*; sympathy
concern, 168. *See also* care
concubinage, 164
Confucian diviners, 21
Confucianism: canon of, 22, 114; characteristics of, 21–22; and civil society, 3–16, 47; classical texts of, 87; classics of, 85; as coherent belief system, 86; core ideas of, 114; early, 147; economy in, 21; and epistemology,

11; essentialist interpretation of, 63; ethical tradition of, 63–66; and Mao Zedong, 255n83; modern relevance of, ix–x; moral action *vs.* unitary creed in, 85; and oppression of women, 186–91; as orthopraxy *vs.* orthodoxy, 85; perfectionist structure of, 114–16; as precepts and practices, 86; as problems and themes, 87; as self-conscious movement, 86; sympathy in, 86; as term, 85–87; and war, 217, 226–45

Confucius: on barbarians, 75–76, 87–88; and brotherhood, 65; and coercion, 124; and Golden Rule, 181; and legal punishment, 233; and loyalty to states, 72; on peace, 227; on specialists *vs.* generalists, 168; *Spring and Autumn Annals,* 76, 96–97; and tradition, 63, 113, 114, 116–18; and virtue of ruler, 251n49; on war, 206–9, 214, 215, 218, 227, 230, 231–33; as warrior, 248n23; and women, 128–29, 189, 191; and world political order, 67; and world under Heaven ideal, 68. See also *Analects of Confucius*

consideration *(shu),* 90
Constant, Benjamin, 248n24
constitutionalism, 8–9, 20–21, 35, 69
consumerism, 13, 32
contentment, sense of, 38, 39, 48
cosmopolitanism, 67, 72, 76–77
cosmos/cosmology: and coherence of Confucianism, 86; and emperor, 93; and gender, 148, 155, 161; and human relationships, 189; and order, 88; and ruler, 34, 92; and spatial schemas, 95. *See also* nature

courtesy, 79, 178
crime, 95
culture: adaptation of other, 86; of barbarians, 88; and boundaries, 87; diversity of, 79–80, 88; and identity, 99n6; Japanese, 28, 32, 33; marketing of, 26; and morality, 79; and nation-state, 80; respect for, 80; superior, 67–68, 75, 77–78, 79; and war, 240, 241, 253n67

daimyō (feudal lords), 27
Danfu, King, 89–90, 96

Daoism. *See* Taoism
death and dying, 131. *See also* suicide
de Bary, William Theodore, 4, 8–9, 10–11
debt, moral, 90
de (charismatic virtue), 94. *See also* virtue
deference, 158, 159, 161
democracy, 14, 79, 81, 190
di li (Earth's patterns), 98–99
disobedience, 31
disputation, 125
dissidents, 49–50
distribution, 74–75, 81, 88, 91
diversity, 75
division of labor, 128, 149, 151, 162, 163, 166–67, 168
divorce, 153, 160, 172n40, 173n49
dogmatism, 15
domestic sphere, 127, 147, 149, 153, 159, 160, 162, 164, 165, 166, 168
domination, 117
Dong Zhongshu, 147, 189, 190–91
Dōshikai (Society of the Like-Minded), 44n26
Due Ai, 208
duty, 116, 117, 119–20, 127–28, 151

early modernity, 26
East Asia, 3, 114; authoritarianism in, 4, 21; education in, 11, 12; and Legalism, 13; liberal regimes of, 11; voluntary associations in contemporary, 40–42
economy, 3, 21, 32, 35, 49, 168, 206
education: and civil service, 9; and civil society, 8; and coercion, 125, 126; criticism in, 11; in East Asia, 11; and elitism, 13; and indoctrination, 11, 12; in Japan, 26–28, 43n10; and moral cultivation, 10–11, 15; and morality, 123; private, 22, 26–28, 32, 39, 43n10; and public opinion, 9; respect for, 114; self-examination in, 125; and social consensus, 11; and social mobility, 91; and space, 96; from state, 98; of women, 127, 128–29, 153–54, 161, 162, 164, 167. *See also* civil service examinations; schools
Eisenstadt, S. N., 41
elders. *See* old and young, relationship between

emperor(s): and cosmos, 93; female relatives of, 128; and homosexuality, 133; loyalty to, 118; and morality, 123; respect for, 118; as sages, 184; virtue of, 93. *See also* government; king(s); ruler(s)

empire, 8, 69, 77, 78, 86; and boundaries, 87; and communities, 97–98; and Legalism, 13; and people's admiration, 93

entrepreneurship, 16, 33

equality, 10, 34, 67, 169, 184, 192

ethics. *See* morality

ethnicity, 53, 75–76, 77, 87, 129

Europe: citizenship in, 35–36; civil society in, 20, 26; early modern, 72; and imperialism, 77; individual and state in, 36; and liberalism, 34; multistate system of, 238; private *vs.* public in, 25; and rule of law, 34; sovereign states in, 72; and territorial boundaries, 62; voluntary associations in, 40

European Union, 81, 224n56

exemplary person. *See junzi* (exemplary person)

faith, 120, 159, 161, 182

family: and agricultural economy, 129; and care, 81, 185, 192; centrality of, 51; and citizenship, 29, 168; and civil society, 6–7, 20; conflict in, 40; and death and dying, 131–32; disagreements in, 122; division of labor in, 162, 163, 166–67; as economic unit, 35; as elastic entity, 64–66; and freedom, 16; friends as part of, 66; and gender, 151–52; and goodness, 35; hierarchy in, 161, 167; interests of, 40; as involuntary association, 20; laws concerning, 11; love for, 114, 184–85; loyalty to, 52, 64; and marriage, 134–35; as model for social relationships, 65; and moral cultivation, 10, 150; moral example of, 89; and morality, 15, 35, 123; and *nei wai* (inner-outer) distinction, 150; and political order, 64, 71, 78; regulation of, 24; remonstration in, 37; and *ren*, 64, 71; rituals of, 10; and ruler-subject relationship, 64; and self-cultivation, 15; and self-development, 23, 49; shared posses-

sions of, 91; and social roles, 29; society as, 25, 50, 64, 176; and state, 24, 25, 35, 40, 52, 160; and suicide, 130, 133; as term, 64–65; training in, 29; as voluntary association, 16; Western *vs.* Asian, 5–6; and world under Heaven, 81. *See also* clan

Fan Ruiping, 132

father: as center, 113–14; denial of, 123; love of, 118; and morality, 30; and rectification of names, 29, 30; ruler as, 31, 34; son's concealment of misconduct of, 31, 40, 44n23, 52, 156, 183; state as, 36, 39; virtue of, 155. *See also* paternalism

father mother official (*fu mu guan*), 30, 50

father-son relationship, 25; and authoritarianism, 8; filial piety in, 156; and gender, 164–65; and Heaven and Earth, 189; and hierarchy, 155; love in, 120, 156; and morality, 35, 156; reciprocity in, 157; and society, 64. *See also* children; parent-child relationship; son

Fei Xiaotong, 4–5

feminism, 165, 168–69, 172n38, 175–93

feudal lords, 68, 116

feudal lords (daimyō), 27

filial piety, 36; as absolute, 183; and disobedience, 31; in father-son relationship, 156; and gender, 152; and hierarchy, 161; insistence on, 50–51; laws concerning, 11; and marriage, 134, 156; and Mohism, 120; and *ren*, 64, 118, 184; respect through, 114; and self-development, 52; and social relationships, 65; stability from, 118; traditional, 116; ways of expressing, 121; and women, 159. *See also* children

Fingarette, Herbert, 7, 51, 57n14

Five Classics, 148

Five Sacred Mountains, 96

flexibility *(wu gu)*, 121

Four Books, 21

Frankel, Charles, 27

freedom: of choice, 16; and civil society, 16; and coercion, 124; in contemporary philosophy, 79; of expression, 11; and feminism, 169; and human rights, 242; from intervention, 98; and social roles, 16. *See also* autonomy

Friedman, Thomas, 242
friends: care for, 81; and civil society, 7; and elective relationships, 29; faith in, 120, 161; and family, 64, 66; and freedom, 16; reciprocity in, 161; and self-development, 52; and society, 64
Fung Yulan, 189

Gabriel, Richard A., 218
gender, 147–69; complementarity *vs.* subordination in, 148; distinctions in, 7; and division of labor, 149, 151, 162, 163; and duty, 151; and equality, 192; as functional role, 151–52, 156, 165; as innate, 162; and *junzi*, 152–53, 154, 156, 158, 159–60, 167, 168, 169; and physical separation, 149–50; and public sphere, 168; and reciprocity, 165; and respect, 165; and sages, 155; and sex differences, 148; and social roles, 147, 155–63; and space, 94; traditional roles for, 116; and wisdom, 152. *See also* husband-wife relationship; men; women
generosity, 93, 159
gentleman. See *junzi* (exemplary person)
Gernet, Jacques, 100n8
gift exchange, 91
Gilligan, Carol, 176, 193n2, 196n45; *In a Different Voice*, 179
global capitalism, 114
globalization, 62–63, 81, 210, 219
global market, 3, 13
global order, 81
global system, 238
Golden Rule, 181
Gong Gang, 238
gongmin shehui (citizen's society), 5, 13, 16
Gongyang commentary, to *Spring and Autumn Annals*, 96–97
good life, 115
goodness, 22, 35
Gottmann, Jean, 62
government: absolutist, 90–91, 114; authoritarian, 4, 7–8, 21, 53, 115; authority of, 23; and benevolence, 153, 235; and citizens, 36–39; and disagreements, 122–26; humane and benevolent, 36–37; and *junzi*, 152–53, 154, 160, 163; just, 36; Maoist, 11; and merit, 129; national, 67; petition for

redress from, 37–38; principles of good, 231–33; regulation by, 126; and *ren*, 126, 178–79; and social circumstances, 192–93; and subsistence of people, x; supervision of associations by, 6, 7; and Tokugawa state, 31; trust in, 41; tyrannical, 209, 210, 211, 212, 216, 235–36, 239, 242, 251n46; for *vs.* by people, 31; women in, 127, 128, 152–54, 158, 159, 160, 167–68, 246n9. *See also* emperor(s); king; political order; ruler(s); state(s)
Grand Union, 74–75
Great Leap Forward, 243
Great Learning, 15, 21, 24
Great Peace, 92
Great Wall, 88, 202
Greeks, ancient, 47, 62, 69, 190, 218–19, 238
Guan Zhong, 206, 218, 251n49
guanxi, 6–7
Guanzi, 216
Guisso, Richard, 148–49, 162, 172nn34, 42
Gulf Wars, 211, 238–39
Guo Yu, 148

Hai Tang, 161
Hall, David, 148
Han Confucianism, 113–14
Han dynasty, 8, 21, 23, 49, 95, 189, 201, 202, 206, 217, 224n56, 246n12
Han Fei Zi, 246n10
Han Yu, 76, 86, 195n33
Hansen, Mogens H., 69–70
happiness, 36, 37, 38–39, 47–48, 51. *See also* contentment, sense of
Harding, Sandra, 191
harmony, 114, 118, 119, 120, 123, 227
Hayashi Nobuatsu, 28
Hayashi Shihei, 38
heart, of right and wrong, 178
heart/mind, 88, 89
Heaven, 22, 25, 161
Heaven and Earth, 120, 189
Hegel, G.W.F., 213–14
Heian society, 23
Held, Virginia, 176, 195n26
Heraclitus, 218
heresy, 123, 125, 126
Herr, Ranjoo Seodu, 195n21, 196n45

heterosexuality, 133, 134, 135, 173n55
hierarchy, 86, 90, 114, 117–18, 120, 141,
    155, 157, 161, 167
historicism, 26
history, 98
Hobbes, Thomas, 37, 47, 204, 208, 216
Homer, 218
homosexuality, 53, 133–35, 173n55
Hong Kong, 6, 78, 114, 134, 167
honor, 130
Housman, A. E., 55
Hua Zhou, 160
Huang Zongxi, 8–9, 10–11, 26, 37
Hucker, Charles O., 45n42
Hui, King of Liang, 36
human beings, 64, 80
humane deeds, 96
humanism, 10, 12, 13, 33, 90, 179
humanitarianism, 210–11, 219, 235–37,
    242
humanity, 31, 64, 73, 91, 117, 177, 185,
    195n32, 240, 249n28; development of,
    47, 49–50, 79, 80. See also *ren*
human nature, 22, 107n65, 113, 141–42,
    162, 212
human relationships: and care, 182–83;
    elastic nature of, 66; and Heaven and
    Earth, 189; and political community,
    70–71; and *ren*, 64, 177–78; un-
    bounded nature of, 66. See also social
    relationships; social roles
human rights, 49, 53, 54, 81, 210, 211,
    239–40, 241, 242, 244
humiliation, 130
husband-wife relationship: and authori-
    tarianism, 8; bond in, 187; and civil
    society, 7; distinction in, 120, 156; and
    elective relationships, 29; and freedom,
    16; and gender, 151; and Heaven and
    Earth, 189; and hierarchy, 167; and
    morality, 35; mutuality in, 151; and
    physical separation, 149, 150;
    reciprocity in, 157; and *ren*, 127; and
    society, 64. See also gender; men;
    women
Hussein, Saddam, 242

idealism, 12, 36–37, 40, 68, 69, 205. See
    also perfectionism
ideal society, 50, 74–75, 115, 118–22,
    207

ideal state, 91–92
ideal world, 227–30, 231, 234
Ignatieff, Michael, 242
immigration, 81, 95, 250n43
individual: as autonomous, 34, 47, 49, 51,
    53, 54, 55; and community, 24; and
    feminism, 169; human rights of, 49;
    integrity of, 24, 55; and morality, 34;
    place of in social roles, 30, 51; and
    political community, 70–71; and
    relations, 185; and state, 24, 26, 31,
    33–35, 36; and suicide, 130–31; and
    Tokugawa state, 32. See also self
indoctrination, 11, 12
inferiors, treatment of, 90, 118. See also
    hierarchy; social relationships;
    superiors
inner-outer distinction. See *nei wai*
    (inner-outer) distinction
institutions, 22, 72
intellectuals, 114
interiority, 25–26
intermarriage, 77
international idealism, 205
international system, 203, 206, 210,
    221n20, 238
investigation of things, 15, 22. See also
    knowledge
involuntary associations, 20
Iraq, 226, 242, 244
Italian Renaissance, 219
Itō Jinsai, 26–27, 44n26
Ivanhoe, Philip J., 251n47

Japan, 6, 12, 21, 26–28, 31–33, 38–39,
    41, 42, 43n10, 47, 88, 114, 127,
    255n83
Jefferson, Thomas, 39, 47–48
Jesuits, 85, 100n9
Jews, 77
Ji Liang, 160
jiang jie (territorial boundary), 61
Jiang Lihong, 217
jiang tu (territory), 61
jiang yu (territorial boundary), 61
ji jia ren (our family people), 65
Jing, 22
Jing, Duke, 29–30
Johnston, Alastair Iain, 223n54,
    254n77
journalism, sensationalistic, 11

Judaism, 239
judgment, 158
junzi (exemplary person), 50, 54;
   challenges and trials of, 153, 160; and
   civil society, 10; and gender, 152–53,
   154, 156, 158, 159–60, 163, 167, 168,
   169; as ultimate goal, 46
justice, 176, 182, 203–4; in government,
   36; and reciprocity, 181; and social
   mobility, 86; and war, 210, 211, 212,
   214, 216–17, 218, 221n20, 226–45. *See
   also* morality

Kabuki drama, 28
Kaibara Ekken, 38, 48
Kansei reforms, 38
Kant, Immanuel, 46, 48, 53, 180, 181,
   183, 184, 186, 194n20, 196n45, 209
Kazumasa Hoshino, 132
kei, 22
King, Ambrose, 64–65
kingdom, 69
king(s): as center, 92; Chinese character
   for, 92; as example, 229; female
   relatives of, 154; loyalty to, 93; and
   ownership, 71; sage as, 91, 92;
   universal, 72, 100n9. *See also*
   emperor(s); government; ruler(s)
kingship, universal, 69, 77
knowledge, 11, 15, 22, 24. *See also*
   investigation of things
Ko, Dorothy, 171n24
Kōbe earthquake, 41
Kogidō academy, 27, 44n26
Korea, 21, 88, 114
Kosovo War, 211, 240
Krushchev, Nikita, 248n24
Kung, 40, 44n23

language, 42n3, 87, 88, 240, 241
Laozi, 212–13, 214–16, 218
Lau, D. C., 64, 171n22
law: and citizenship, 35; and coercion,
   124, 204; family, 11; and guanxi, 7; of
   jungle, 204–5, 238; and limitations on
   ruler's power, 9; and morality, 204; and
   punishment, 227, 233; rule of, 34
leader, 72, 115. *See also* ruler(s)
Legalism, 3, 4, 8, 13, 49, 216, 217,
   246n10, 247n17, 255n83
li (cosmic principle), 14, 48

li (ritual), 76, 181, 195n21
Li Chenyang, 148
Liang Qichao, 66–67, 68, 77
liberal democracy, 81
liberalism, 4, 8, 10, 12, 15, 34, 47, 53,
   120, 126
life, sanctity of, 131
Lik Kuen Tong, 179
literacy, 25, 27
Lo Pingcheung, 130
Locke, John, 47, 90
logos, 79, 80
love: and family, 114, 184–85; in father-
   son relationship, 156; with gradations,
   184; in Mohism, 120; in parent-child
   relationship, 185; and *ren,* 64, 117, 118,
   177, 178; universal, 120, 123, 184, 185,
   196n43. *See also* affection, and *ren*
loyalty: to emperor, 118; to family, 52,
   64; to king, 93; to parents, 54; and
   reciprocity, 181; to rulers, 54, 183; to
   state, 52, 72; to superiors, 86
Lu, duke of, 116

Macau, 78
Machiavellianism, 234
Mahan, A. T., *The Influence of Sea
   Power on History,* 219
Manicheanism, 88
Mann, Susan, 170n15
Maoism, 11, 42
Mao Zedong, 13, 243, 250n42, 255n83
market, international, 55
market culture, 20, 25, 26, 33
market economy, 13
marriage, 77, 134–35, 149, 153, 156, 160,
   161, 164, 167, 172n40, 173n49, 188
Marx, Karl, 219n1, 245n5
mass media, 62
Matsudaira Sadanobu, 38; "Prohibition
   of Heterodox Studies," 33, 39
Mean, 21
medicine, 91, 132
meditation, 15
Meiji Restoration, 38
men: and morality, 128, 167; psychology
   of, 173n44; and public sphere, 147; as
   role models, 167; role of, 116, 127;
   virtue of, 155, 158; and yang, 147.
   See also gender; husband-wife
   relationship

Mencius: and All under Heaven, 83n26; and authorship, 82n1; autonomy in, 143; and benevolent rule, 72–74; and brotherhood, 65; and canon, 114; and Central States, 86; and civil society, 21; contribution of, 113; and disagreements, 123; elitism *vs.* egalitarianism in, 34–35; and epistemology, 11; friendship in, 161; and fundamental texts, 63; and gender, 148, 149, 150, 153, 154; on government, 36–37; human nature in, 162; and husband-wife relationship, 127–28; and legal punishment, 233; love in, 184; and Mohism, 125; mutuality in, 8; and Neo-Confucianism, 4; noncoercive rule in, 228; and nonideal political world, 230; as orthodox, 248n25; and ownership, 71; political unity in, 72; on relationships, 7; *ren* in, 74, 177, 178, 179; and revolution, 31; sage as ruler in, 75, 229; sexuality in, 133, 134; space in, 95; and Spring and Autumn period, 228; on subsistence, 233, 241; territory in, 61; and tradition, 116; on virtue, 97; on war, 206, 209–11, 212, 215, 230, 231, 232, 234–37, 238–39, 240, 241, 244–45; and Warring States period, 228; women in, 188–89, 191; and world political order, 67; and world under Heaven ideal, 68; and Xunzi, 140–42; and Yang Zhu, 125
merchants, 21, 28, 36
merit, 129, 155–57, 161
metaphysics, ix, 113, 141
Middle Kingdom, 103n25, 229, 243
Middle Way, 86
military, 76, 201–19
Mill, J. S., 123, 125
mind-and-heart: learning of, 14; rectification of, 15
mind(s): cultivation of, 114; four innate, 158; in Neo-Confucianism, 22; rectification of, 24; and Song-Ming Confucianism, 114
Ming dynasty, 45n42
minister(s): Machiavellian, 234; and morality, 123; and rectification of names, 29, 30. *See also* ruler-minister relationship
minjian (people-based associations), 16

minjian shuhui (people-based society), 3, 6
Mo Zi, 123, 184, 185, 244, 250n41; "Against Aggression," 216
modernity, 20, 53, 115, 166–69, 202
modernization, 42, 114
modesty, 79, 178
Mohism, 49, 104n34, 120, 125, 184
Moody, Peter R., Jr., 247n21
moral cultivation: and civil society, 9–10; and culture, 79; and education, 10–11, 15; environment for, 30; and family, 10, 150; and political order, 12–13; and power, 13. *See also* self-cultivation; self-development
morality: absolutization of, 69; basic instincts of, 79; and boundaries, 87; and care, 185; and Chinese identity, 76; and civil society, 8, 9–10; and coercion, 124, 125, 126; and community, 15; and consequences, 126; and culture, 79; and death and dying, 131; debt in, 90; diversity of, 88; and education, 123; examples of, 50, 52, 54, 55, 89; and family, 15, 35, 89, 123; and father, 30; and father-son relationship, 156; and feminist care, 176–80; and general principles, 180–84; Gilligan on, 179–80; and Huang Zongxi, 11; and impartiality, 186; and individual, 34; influence of, 94; and *junzi*, 167; Kant on, 46, 48; and law, 204; and liberalism, 126; and men, 128, 167; Mo Zi on, 185; and names, 119–20; and nature, 48; and Neo-Confucianism, 21–22; and people, 126, 233; and perfection, 22, 115; and pluralism, 12, 113–35, 142; and political community, 70; and political order, 4, 12, 71, 72; and political ritual, 15; and politics, 123; and power, 15, 89; private *vs.* public, 120, 126; reflective attitude in, 122; and *ren*, 64, 117, 176–80; and rights, 176; and rites, 117, 121; rule-based, 180–84, 195n21; and ruler, 30, 31, 33, 54–55, 92, 126, 150, 227; and social relationships, 8, 70–71, 123; and social roles, 176; and society, 123, 176; and space, 94, 95, 96–97; and state, 36, 203–4, 238; and suicide, 130; transformation of individual, 123; as

unbounded, 92; uniformity in, 118–22; universal, 47, 205, 238; and war, 209, 210, 212, 232, 237; and women, 128, 129, 158–59, 165, 166, 167; and world under Heaven ideal, 68, 69. *See also* justice
mother, 172nn34, 35, 176
Mou Zongsan (Mou Tsung-san), 78–81
Mount Tai, 96
music, 152, 202
mutuality, 8, 15, 151. *See also* reciprocity

Nagel, Thomas, 122
names, rectification of, 29–30, 31, 50, 119–20
Nan Zi, 188
nationalism, 77, 78, 87
nations/nation-states: in contemporary philosophy, 79; and cosmopolitanism, 77; and culture, 80; equality between, 67; as given, 53; harmony among, 81; life in, 54; and multistates system, 72; and territorial boundaries, 62; and unificationism, 78. *See also* political community; state(s)
NATO, 240
naturalist ontology, 26
natural law tradition, 14, 15
natural principles, 21–22
nature: and human beings, 64; and morality, 48; and sexuality, 134; and virtue, 97; and war, 213, 214; and women, 161; and yin and yang, 134, 187. *See also* cosmos/cosmology
nei wai (inner-outer) distinction, 148, 149–50, 163, 166, 168
Neo-Confucianism, 4; and civil society, 47; development of, 21; discovery model in, 141–42; Hayashi school of, 28; and three bonds doctrine, 8; and yin and yang, 147
Ni Lexiong, 238
Noddings, Nel, 179, 180, 181, 182, 183–84, 185, 186, 193n2, 196n45
non-coercive groups, 20
North America: citizenship in, 35–36; civil society in, 20; individual and state in, 36; private *vs.* public in, 25; and rule of law, 34; voluntary associations in, 40

North Korea, 242
Nylan, Michael, 56n10

obedience, 25
Ogyū Sorai, 32, 38–39, 41, 47, 48
Okin, Susan, 168, 172n38
old and young, relationship between, 35, 120, 184–85
Ooms, Herman, 31
others, establishment and enlargement of, 65, 66, 117, 181. *See also* strangers
ownership, 71–74, 88, 92, 93, 98. *See also* property

pacifism, 214, 215, 217, 219
parent-child relationship: care in, 11; and civil society, 7; and elective relationships, 29; and filial piety, 116; and freedom, 16; love in, 185; as model for ruler, 31; reciprocity in, 157; remonstration in, 183; and *ren*, 64; and ruler-subject relationship, 31. *See also* children; father-son relationship
parent(s): and civil society, 14; love for, 118; loyalty to, 54; remonstration of, 37; ruler as, 25, 31
paternalism, 31, 115. *See also* father
patriarchy, 147, 175, 191
peace, 24, 77, 227, 231–32, 234, 235, 239, 241
Peng Dehuai, 243
people: confidence of in ruler, 30; and empire, 93; government for *vs.* by, 31; as grass in wind, 34, 124, 227; liberation of, 235–37, 239, 251n45; moral development of, 233; and morality, 126; plunder of, 234; priority of, 233; protection of, 209; as root, 209–10; ruler's responsibility for, 31; subsistence of, x, 233, 241–42; voluntary submission of, 73; and war, 234, 235. *See also* citizens; subject(s)
People's Liberation Army, 250n42
perfectionism, 114–16, 123, 126, 141, 142, 177. *See also* idealism
persuasion, 76, 123, 142–43
Petitions and Appeals Office, 38
Ping, Duke of Chin, 161
Plato, 114, 142, 163, 166, 207
pluralism, 113–35, 141, 142
polis, 69–70, 238

political community: distribution in, 74–75; Greek *vs.* Confucian, 70; and human relationships, 70–71; membership in, 240–41; and morality, 70; and respect for culture, 80; and territorial boundaries, 61, 62. *See also* community; nations/nation-states; state(s)
political dissent, 242
political leadership, 10
political order: centralized, 3; and ethnicity, 75; and family, 64, 71, 78; and morality, 12, 71, 72; stable, 4; and territory, 66–71, 73, 75; unity of, 71, 78; universal, 68; use of force for, 67–68; and virtue, 15; and voluntary submission, 73; world, 67. *See also* government
politics: benevolent, 118; in contemporary China, 76–77; disorder in, 116; Greek *vs.* Confucian, 70; and intellectuals, 114; and merit, 129; and morality, 123; and perfectionism, 115, 123; and self-cultivation, 15; and social roles, 120; and territory, 61; and women, 128; and world under Heaven ideal, 68
polygamy, 164
populism, 13
pornography, 11
poverty, 91
power: and civil society, 8; criticism of, 11; and moral cultivation, 10, 13; and morality, 15, 72, 89; naïveté about, 13; and political order, 4; and rites, 117; of unified community, 93
pre-Qin age, 68, 215, 217, 238
Principle of Heaven and Earth, 120
privacy: as honored by others, 43n6; and selfishness, 23, 29
private sphere: and Tokugawa state, 32; and voluntary associations, 29
private *vs.* public: and civil society, 5, 6, 6, 12, 21, 25; and gender, 149; and morality, 120, 126; in West, 176
profit, 21, 212. *See also* wealth
property, 47, 93, 98. *See also* ownership
prostitution, 133
public office, 86
public sphere: and gender, 152–54, 168; and men, 147; religious associations in, 20
punishment, 3, 124, 179, 227, 233. *See also* coercion

qi, 91, 95
Qian Mu, 65
Qin, Emperor, 246n12
Qin dynasty, 68, 189, 202, 206, 217, 224n56
Qing dynasty, 9

Raphals, Lisa, 148, 170n15, 171n21, 172n41
Rawls, John, 47, 115, 168
realpolitik, 12, 90, 250n39
reason, 14, 124, 162
reciprocity, 8, 117; in benefactor-beneficiary relationship, 30; and friends, 161; and gender, 157, 165; and general rules, 181; in ruler-subject relationship, 30; in social relationships, 120. *See also* mutuality
religion(s): and boundaries, 87; and Confucianism, 48, 51, 86; diversity of, 88; and humanism, 90; and public associations, 20; and ritual, 116; and *Rujia,* 63; and self-development, 46; and space, 96; and Tokugawa state, 32; and war, 240, 241
remonstration: by citizens, 36, 37–38, 50; and civil society, 8; duty of, 86; in family, 37; by minister, 54, 156; as obligatory, 50; opportunities for, 22; in parent-child relationship, 183; of ruler, 156
ren: and affection, 177, 183; and barbarians, 76; and care, 117, 178–79; and coercion, 125; cultivation of, 118; and death and dying, 131; definitions of, 177–78; and ethical disagreements, 121; and feminist care, 175–93; and filial piety, 64, 118, 184; and gender, 152; and government, 126, 178–79; and human relationships, 177–78; and husband-wife relationship, 127; and love, 64, 117, 118, 177, 178; and morality, 64, 117–18; and perfectionism, 177; and political community, 70–71; practice of, 119; and respect, 184; and rulers, 178–79; and sages, 184; and self-enlargement, 65; and social roles, 120; and suicide, 130, 132; and uniformity, 122; as unlimited, 66, 74, 81; and virtue, 117, 177, 180. *See also* benevolence *(ren);* compassion; humanity
respect: for elders, 64, 184–85; for emperor, 118; in family and public

sphere, 168; and gender, 165; and *ren*, 117, 184; and ritual, 158, 159; ways of expressing, 121
responsibility, 14–16, 179
revolution, right of, 31
rhetoric, 142, 143
Ricci, Matteo, 56n3
rightness, 156
rights, 176, 181
rites/ritual: as basis for human life, 116–18; and boundaries, 89; and changing ways of expression, 121; and death and dying, 131; diverse ways of realizing, 79; of family, 10; and government regulation, 126; importance of, 53; as joining communities, 91; in Mencius *vs.* Xunzi, 141; and morality, 121; and organization of space, 94; and respect, 158, 159; and *Rujia*, 63; selective use of, 121–22; self-cultivation through, 114; and social roles, 120; and space, 96; stability from, 118; traditional, 22, 116; and virtue, 121; and war, 207–8, 210, 211, 214; and world under Heaven ideal, 69
Rosemont, Henry, Jr., 30, 43n15, 148
Ru, 85, 86, 100n9
Rujia, 63, 113
ruler-minister relationship: and authoritarianism, 8; and civil society, 7; and freedom, 16; and gender, 164; and hierarchy, 155; reciprocity in, 157; remonstration in, 54, 156; and service to evil ruler, 54–55. *See also* minister(s)
ruler(s): ancestors of, 90; benevolent, 36–37, 72–73, 118, 228, 231, 232, 234, 235; as center, 88, 89, 90, 92–93, 113–14; and civil society, 14, 27; as compass and as carpenter's square, 94; confidence of people in, 30; and cosmos, 34, 92; evil, 54–55, 233; example of, 36, 150, 228, 229; as father, 31, 34; humane, 36–37; ideal, 92; as least important, 209; limitations on power of, 9; loyalty to, 54, 183; and morality, 30, 31, 33, 54–55, 92, 126, 150, 227; noncoercive, 227, 228; as parent, 25, 31; and rectification of names, 29, 30; and *ren*, 178–79; responsibility of for people, 31; sage as, 68, 69, 75, 159, 227, 229, 231–32, 234; and space, 94; state as possession of,

90–91; virtue of, 155, 232, 236–37, 251n49; voluntary submission to, 119; and war, 234, 236–37; as wind, 34; as wise and ethical, 67, 68; and women, 246n9. *See also* emperor(s); government; king; tyranny
ruler-subject relationship: duty in, 120; and elective relationships, 29; and family, 64; and Heaven and Earth, 189; and parent-child relationship, 31; reciprocity in, 30; rightness in, 156; trust in, 41. *See also* subject(s)
ruling elite, 36

sage(s): as center, 88, 89, 96; emperors as, 184; example of, 93, 155, 227, 229; and gender, 155; as king, 91, 92; in Mencius *vs.* Xunzi, 141; moral example of, 89; and *ren*, 184; as ruler, 68, 69, 75, 159, 227, 229, 231–32, 234; and space, 95; as ultimate goal, 46
samurai, 28
Saudi Arabia, 242
scholar-officials, 26
scholars, 3, 27
schools, 10–11, 22, 26–28, 32, 39, 43n10, 49, 89. *See also* education
Schwartz, Benjamin, 69, 76–77, 238
science, 202
secularism, 26, 54
self: autonomy of, 20; establishment and enlargement of, 65, 66, 117, 181. *See also* individual
self-cultivation: approach to, 24; by barbarians, 88; and gender, 158–59; and maturity, 98; and political order, 12–13; practice of, 22; as priority, 25–26; through rituals, 114; in world, 14–15. *See also* moral cultivation
self-defense, 231, 234–35, 240–41
self-development: and civil society, 9–10; and community, 23; and family, 23, 49; of humanity, 50; as religious quest, 46; and social relationships, 49, 51, 52; and social roles, 52, 53; as ultimate goal, 46, 49–50. *See also* moral cultivation
self-discipline, 204, 232
self-examination, 117, 125
selfishness, 23, 29, 37, 117
self-reform, 124
self-rule, 86

self-worth, 34
sexism, 53
sex/sexuality, 133–35, 148, 151, 161, 173n55. *See also* gender
shame, 79, 158, 178
Shang dynasty, 54, 99n6, 103n25
Shang Yang, 216–17
Shang Zhou, 206
Shanghai, 6
sharing, 93, 98
She, Duke of, 44n23
Shen Dingli, 223n54
shimin (city-people), 16
shimin shehui (city-people's society), 3, 6
Shōheikō academy, 27–28, 33
shu, 65, 117
Shun, Emperor, 35, 75, 101, 128, 150, 156, 164, 184, 229
siblings: and civil society, 7; and freedom, 16; and *ren*, 64. *See also* brothers/brotherhood
Sima Qian, 246n10
Sima Rangzu, 210
Singapore, 4, 12, 21, 114, 167
Singer, Peter, 190
Sinocentrism, 77
sister-in-law, 150
slavery, 207
social cohesion, 21
social consensus, 11, 12, 15, 119
social contract, 181
social mobility, 13, 91
social order, 12, 21, 218
social relationships: and civil society, 7, 9; and dissidents, 50; as elastic, 71; family as model for, 65; and gender, 147, 151; harmony in, 119; hierarchy in, 117–18, 120; and morality, 70–71, 123; and self-development, 49, 51, 52. *See also* brothers/brotherhood; father-son relationship; human relationships; husband-wife relationship; parent-child relationship; ruler-minister relationship; ruler-subject relationship
social roles: and civil society, 14, 15, 16; and family, 29; and freedom, 16; and gender, 147, 155–63; individual place in, 30, 51; and morality, 176; naming of, 119; in organic society, 28–29; orientation toward, 47; and politics, 120; responsibilities of, 119–20; and

rites, 120; self-development through, 52, 53; traditional, 116
society: Asian, 10; Confucian *vs.* Western, 4–5; destablized, 21; disagreements of with state, 115; disorder in, 116; as family, 25, 50, 64, 176; ideal, 50, 74–75, 115, 118–22, 207; mass, 13, 14; and morality, 123, 176; as organic whole, 28; orientation toward, 46–47; and perfectionism, 115, 123; promotion of, 114; stable, 10; subversion of, 125; terms for, 3; and Tokugawa state, 32; traditional, 116; and voluntary associations, 50; and war, 208; well-ordered, 119
son: father's misconduct concealed by, 31, 40, 44n23, 52, 156, 183; and rectification of names, 29, 30; remonstration by, 37; and self-development, 52. *See also* children; father-son relationship
Song Confucianism, 158
Song dynasty, 4, 21, 47, 48, 248n25
Song-Ming Confucianism, 113, 114
Son of Heaven, 68, 71, 72, 73, 208
South Korea, 6, 12, 127, 167
sovereignty, 62, 63, 72, 78, 79, 211, 227
space, 94–97
specialists *vs.* generalists, 168
Spengler, Oswald, 224n56
Spring and Autumn Annals, 76, 96–97
Spring and Autumn period, 68, 72, 203–5, 206, 228, 238
Star, Daniel, 194n20, 196n45
state(s): absolutist, 31, 32; associations independent of, 6, 7, 9; and citizen, 25; and civil society, 20, 23–27, 29–33, 49; commitment to, 10; competing, 231, 239; conflict in, 40; and disagreements, 115, 122–26; distribution in, 74–75; education from, 98; European, 72; and family, 24, 25, 35, 40, 52, 160; as father, 36, 39; and happiness, 36, 37, 38–39; as held in trust for all, 91; as highest social authority, 203, 238; ideal, 91–92; imperial, 8; and individual, 24, 26, 31, 33–35, 36; interests of as supreme, 203–4, 205, 238; as involuntary association, 20; jurisdiction of, 73; and Legalism, 13; loyalty to, 52, 72; and military, 203; and morality, 36, 203–4, 205, 238;

need for, 23–27, 49–50; order in, 24; organization of, 113; and perfectionism, 115; and political order, 66, 67, 68; as possession of ruler, 90–91; remonstration of, 36, 37–38, 50; and *ren*, 71; ruler as center of, 92–93; secure livelihood from, 98; and self-cultivation, 15; and self-development, 49; as shared possession, 90; as socially constructive and nurturing, 33; sovereign, 78; and territorial boundaries, 230; territory of, 61; as transient, 72; trust in, 41; and voluntary associations, 29; walled, 230; and war, 208–9, 221n20, 227, 238; wise leaders of, 115; and women, 127. *See also* government; nations/nation-states; political community

strangers, 81. *See also* others

subject(s): and civil society, 14; duties and opportunities of, 127. *See also* citizens; people; ruler-subject relationship

subsidiarity, principle of, 30

suicide, 129–33

Sunzi, 206, 218, 219; *The Art of War*, 223n47

superiors, 86, 114. *See also* hierarchy; inferiors, treatment of; social relationships

sympathy, 86, 117, 124–25, 177. *See also* care; compassion

syncretism, 77

Taiwan, 6, 7, 11, 12, 21, 78, 167, 242–43

Tang, King, 237

Tang dynasty, 38

Tang Junyi, 79

Tang society, 23

Taoism, 3, 4, 49, 88, 94

taxation, 179

technology, 81, 202

Teng state, 230, 235

territorial boundaries, 61–81, 85–99, 230, 234; as expandable, 88, 92; as inconsequential, 90; as permeable, 88, 92; and war, 231

theater, in Japan, 28

three bonds, doctrine of, 7–8

tian (Heaven), 22

tian xia. *See* world under Heaven (*tian xia*)

Tokugawa Tsunayoshi, 27–28

Tokyo subway system, sarin attack on, 41

tolerance, 15, 77, 124–25

trade, 62

tradition, 63, 113, 114, 116–18, 139–40, 201

transportation infrastructure, 25, 27

travel, 25

tributary system, 77, 78, 243

Tronto, Joan C., 182–83

Tu Wei-ming, 4, 5, 9–10, 12–13, 14

Turner, Karen, 239

tyranny, 209, 210, 211, 212, 216, 235–36, 239, 242, 251n46. *See also* ruler(s)

understanding, 125–26. *See also* knowledge; self-development

unification, 68, 72, 228, 234

United Kingdom, 239

United Nations, 81, 203, 208, 210, 224n56, 238, 239

United States, 11, 54, 238, 239

unity, 71

universalism, 109n80; and civil society, 10; compensatory, 87; and human nature, 162; Kant on, 48; lack of principles for, 48, 52, 54; and love, 120, 123, 184, 185, 196n43; and military, 201–2, 203; in Mohism, 120; and morality, 47, 205, 238; and political order, 68; of *Ru* thought, 100n9; and utilitarianism, 181; and Way, 26, 32

urbanization, 3, 10, 25, 26, 27

utilitarianism, 180, 181, 184, 185, 186, 194n20, 196n45

Vietnam, 21, 88

village, 23, 25, 49

violence, 76

virtue: charismatic, 94; cultivation of, 114; and cultural superiority, 79; of emperor, 93; of fathers, 155; Greek *vs.* Confucian, 70; Kant on, 46; of men *vs.* women, 155, 158; and nature, 97; and physical beauty, 229; and political order, 15; as relational, 194n20; and *ren*, 117, 177, 180; and rites, 121; of rulers, 155, 232, 236–37, 251n49; and semblance of virtue, 143; and world under Heaven ideal, 69 voluntary association(s): and civil society, 20; to combat alienation, 25; conflicting demands of, 39; in contemporary East Asia, 40–42; as destabilizing, 27; existence of, 21; family as, 16; and ideal society, 50; and individual autonomy, 47; intermediate between family and state, 6, 7, 10; and involuntary associations, 5–6; as not envisioned, 23; personal development in, 26; and private academies, 28; and private sphere, 29; schools as, 49; and state, 29; in Taiwan, 11; and Tokugawa state, 31, 32

Walzer, Michael, 42n1, 240, 241, 254n71
Wang Gungwu, 78
war: and agriculture, 216, 217, 223n55; in Aristotle, 207; and benevolence, 206, 209, 210, 211, 212, 214, 216–17, 218, 231–32, 234, 235, 241, 244; breaking resistance without fighting in, 206, 207, 217, 218, 219; Confucius on, 206–9, 214, 215, 218, 227, 230, 231–33; of conquest, 231, 234, 238; and culture, 240, 241, 253n67; defensive, 231, 237, 240–41; and justice, 210, 211, 212, 214, 216–17, 218, 221n20, 226–45; in Laozi, 212–13, 214–16, 218; and Legalism, 216, 217; Mencius on, 206, 209–11, 212, 215, 230, 231, 232, 234–37, 238–39, 240, 241, 244–45; and military, 202; and morality, 209, 210, 212, 232, 237; as nonideal, 248n24; as punitive expeditions, 235–37, 238, 239, 242; and rites, 207–8, 210, 211, 214; and rulers, 234, 236–37; of self-defense, 234–35; and states, 208–9, 221n20, 227, 238; trust in, 237, 239; and West, 207, 209, 218–19; Xunzi on, 211–12, 218, 244. See also coercion
Warring States period, 68, 72, 90, 99n6, 203–5, 206, 224n56, 226, 228, 238, 250n44, 255n85
Way: adherence to, 15; and ethical disagreements, 121; and rights of states, 73; and social roles, 52; as unchanging, 120; as universal principles vs. socially conditioned practices, 26, 32; and war, 215

Way of Antiquity, 85
Way of Heaven, 79
Way of the Ancients, 89, 90, 96
wealth, 25, 26, 27, 91. See also profit
Wen, King, 54, 55, 75
wenming shehui (civilized societies), 3, 10, 16
West: and autonomy, 143; and colonialism, 240; and constitutionalism, 9; and Enlightenment, 4; family as private in, 11; and imperialism, 243; interference by, 78, 87; invasion by, 77; liberalism in, 8, 12, 47, 53; natural law tradition in, 14; and political order, 4; private vs. public in, 176; society in, 4–5; universal moral principles in, 47; and war, 207, 209, 218–19
Westernization, 18
will, 24
wisdom, 79, 152, 159
women: and children, 162, 166; and deference, 159; and division of labor, 128; as docile, 155–57; and domestic sphere, 127, 147, 149, 153, 159, 160, 162, 164, 165, 166, 168; education of, 127, 128–29, 153–54, 161, 162, 164, 167; and filial piety, 159; in government, 127, 128, 152–54, 158, 159, 160, 167–68, 246n9; as inferior, 165–66; liberation of, 186, 192; and marriage, 153, 160, 164, 172n40, 173n49, 188; merit of, 161; and morality, 128, 129, 158–59, 165, 166, 167; and nature, 161; neglect of in texts, 164; objectification of, 164, 165; oppression of, 186–91; political influence of, 160; and politics, 128; as professionals, 168; psychology of, 173n44; and reason, 162; as relatives of ruler, 128, 154; as role models, 160, 167; role of, 127, 128, 129; and state, 127; status of, 127–29; subordination of, 53, 147, 152, 155, 161, 164, 165, 188; traditional roles of, 116; virtue of, 155, 158; and yin, 147. See also gender; husband-wife relationship
world order, 79
world under Heaven (tian xia), 65, 66–71, 72, 77, 79, 80–81, 227
World War II, 78

Wu, Emperor, 54, 55, 154, 224n56
Wu Chunsi, 223n54
Wu Rusong, 223n47

Xu Fuguan, 79
Xu Zhuoyun, 215
Xuan, King of Qi, 31, 236–37
Xunzi: and benevolent rule, 72–73; on consequences, 126; contribution of, 113; and fundamental texts, 63; on ideal regime, 247n17; and Mencius, 140–42; and ownership, 71; political unity in, 72; and tradition, 116; on war, 211–12, 218, 244; and world under Heaven ideal, 68

Yan Hui, 229

Yang Zhu, 90, 123, 125
Yao, emperor, 184, 229
Yasushi, Magoshi, 100n9
yin and yang, 86, 134, 147, 148–49, 187–88, 190
yi (righteousness), 130
Youzi, 40

Zhao Tingyang, 250n43
Zhou dynasty, 54, 68, 69, 72, 89, 99n6, 113, 116, 118, 121, 154, 216
Zhou Enlai, 13
Zhou Son of Heaven, 203, 238
Zhou Wu, 206
Zhu Xi, 3, 8, 48, 147
Zuo Chuan, 148